HOW TO BUILD A
Great
SCREENPLAY

HOW TO BUILD A
Great
SCREENPLAY

A Master Class in
Storytelling for Film

DAVID HOWARD

SOUVENIR PRESS

For Vicki & Jessa,
my beginning, middle, and end,
all my love always, David

CONTENTS

CONTENTS

CONTENTS

CONTENTS

CONTENTS

CONTENTS

ACKNOWLEDGMENTS

I would like to thank George Witte for his patience, insight, flexibility, and faith. Had he not been so generous with those fine attributes, this book would never have come to fruition. Many thanks go to Don Bohlinger and Tom Abrams for their timely advice, and to Alex Zamm and Lee Mayes for their helpful responses to the manuscript. I would especially like to extend my appreciation to all my former students around the world for asking why, how, what, when, and where so insistently to every aspect of what makes a story work. Their desire to know has given shape to all that follows here.

PREFACE

After the publication of *The Tools of Screenwriting*, a great many of my students and colleagues, filmmaking professionals with whom I consult and work, and readers of that book wished that there might be a companion book specifically about story structure. Here, I am happy to oblige that desire even while I insist that story structure is not the be-all and end-all of screenwriting. To say that everything in screenwriting boils down to how the story is structured is analogous to saying that architecture is simply about how I beams are assembled and welded into the frame of a skyscraper. Clearly that metal framework is important—a tall building will fall if there is a faulty structure. But to the end user of the building, this structure is usually invisible. Even if the structure is left visible, as in some modern deconstructionist architecture, it is turned into a design element. The same things are true for structure in a film. Most of the time it is invisible, and, when it *is* visible, it's made into a design element. And most important of all, the structure usually doesn't matter much to the end user, the audience, despite how much its absence would be felt.

What matters to the user of a building is the way it can be utilized, its purpose and content, its accessibility and ease of use, what he hopes to gain from it. Again, the same is true for the user of a story; the audience is usually much more concerned with the impact the story has on them, its content and accessibility and the purpose it fulfills—emotional connection, intellectual stimulation, spectacle, or some combination of these three basic uses of stories. The architect can't make his building fulfill its intended functions without a solid structure, and the screenwriter can't make a story fulfill its functions without the same. So in this sense, structure is utterly crucial to building an effective story. But it is only part of the building process. For this reason, I will weave together discussions of what a solid structure is and how to achieve it with extensive discussions of content, purpose, accessibility, and even ease of use. Story building cannot really be separated from what the story is about, what its intended purpose is, how the audience will have the story revealed to them, and how effectively they are made to connect to it.

What I strive to do in the following essays is break down all these individual elements of screenwriting so they can be discussed at length. I also point out not only the ways these elements can be used most effectively and "classically," but also ways they can be changed and manipulated—and what the expected results of those manipulations will be. The final goal here is not to see a story as a mechanical process—welding I beams together—but as the creation of an organism that takes on its own life, makes demands of its own, and may not even obey its creator. In some way, every screenwriter is a Dr. Frankenstein. We cobble together parts that we assemble from hither and yon—and we're not above skullduggery in the wee hours of the morning—and then hope for a spark that will bring it to life. We hope our creations don't come back to hurt us or others, but creating "life" is a dangerous business, one fraught with risks.

Story
and
Storytelling

We will start with an overview of the various typical elements of a story and their importance in the overall scheme. Then we'll separate story from storytelling for a more in-depth discussion of all the various elements at use in stories; how they interact, augment, or compromise each other; and how they are perceived by the audience.

THE STORY

Readers of *The Tools of Screenwriting* will remember there is one basic dramatic circumstance: *Somebody wants something badly and is having difficulty getting it.* This dramatic circumstance is at the heart of every well-written scene and is a significant element in every well-told story. But it isn't a definition of a story any more than this is a definition of a living human being: a heart pumping blood through veins and arteries to and from the lungs and brain for the replenishment of oxygen and nutrients. To look for a definition of a story, we must wrestle with a chicken-and-egg controversy. Can a story exist without an audience? Does the story attract an audience, or does the presence of an audience enable the story to become complete? Which comes first?

Clearly the material out of which a story is woven can exist without an audience. The words on a page or in the mouth of a storyteller don't need a reader or listener in order to exist. And a filmed story could exist with characters and events depicted on film, but never be seen by an audience. But in order for even one person to know the story—read the story, hear the story, see the story—then a transfer must be made. An audience of at least one is necessary for the transfer of a story to take place. Without that transfer from storyteller to audience, the story can be nothing more than ink on paper or sound waves or shades of color on film. That is to say, a story may exist outside of its audience, but it gains no value until it reaches an audience of at least one. The difference between an audience of one and an audience of millions is negligible, at least in defining what a story is and is not.

So a story requires an audience in order to have value, but what is that value? The teller of a story intends to have some kind of impact on his audience. The intention could be to make a friend laugh, to make a traffic cop not write a speeding ticket, to make a whole group of people think or cry or gasp or shriek. The intention could be to explain to the doctor where the pain is or to convince Mommy that "I'll die before dinner if I don't get a cookie right now!" Stories are used by nearly every human being nearly every day. We could then say: Stories involve the transfer of some kind of information from the teller to at least one person with an intention to create some kind of impact upon that audience. But not all information can create such an impact. Just pure data—numbers or lists of nuts and bolts—is transferable information, but it won't have an impact on the audience unless it already means something to them. A mechanic might be ecstatic to discover exactly what he needs in a list of nuts and bolts, but an indifferent audience would receive no impact from the same transfer of information.

Does this limit us to telling stories only to an audience that is already interested in the material? Not at all. The creation of interest within the audience is a crucial part of storytelling, and the means to achieve it is through character and action. One or more characters—who want something—provide the audience with the opportunity to connect with the transfer of information. Rather than depend upon the audience to bring a desire with them, a story itself should be capable of generating in the audience a desire to connect. But in a way, this brings us back to the chicken and the egg. Does the story itself automatically make the audience care, or is it the storytelling that makes them involved? Here, at least, we have a simple answer. It's the storytelling, not the events in the lives of the characters, that is the means to audience involvement, as we'll discuss at length.

But in classic chicken-and-egg fashion, the story has to exist for the storytelling to be created, so we must inevitably start with story. This is the beginning of work for every screenwriter.

THE STORY

The Chronology of Events

At first glance, a story appears to be nothing more than the sequence of events in the lives of the characters on screen. What happens first, what's next, what happens then, and so on until it's over. Clearly events have to occur for there to be something happening in a story. Everything can't happen at the same instant or we couldn't follow the action, so the events need to be laid out for the audience in a specific order. In life, events necessarily happen in chronological order, but not all stories follow an exact chronology. Still, in the lives of the characters—whether they are fictional or real makes no difference—the events must happen to them in chronological order. Events, and how they play out, influence subsequent events; they can have a direct impact on later events, or the influence can be indirect, through a character's preparation or reaction to an event. So understanding the sequence of events in the lives of the characters is a necessity for any storyteller even if the final story will have those events in a different order.

Any journey starts with the first step, but the story of a journey actually starts before that. The story would logically depict, at the very least, the last moment before the journey, then the first step, then the second, and on through to the last step. And the story would continue for at least another moment to show the completed journey. This step-by-step sequence is crucial information to have in building the story and storytelling. The start, the momentum created by the journey, the impact of the individual steps, the end—each of these elements must be part of the basic knowledge of the storyteller.

A Crucial Paradox

When imagining the events in a story, there is a strange paradox to consider. On the one hand, to reach and affect a wide audience, we want to make our events universal. But on the other hand, we must make the events we imagine specific so that they can be seen as "real and true." This battle between "the more universal the better" and "the more specific the better" trips up a great many beginning writers. One camp tends to create events that could take place anywhere, involving anyone of any description who could be wearing anything and who eats "food." The other camp tends to create events that could only take place at the corner of this street and that avenue in this city on this one day in human history and involving a person who is utterly specific: his hair is combed a certain way, he has an ingrown toenail on the big toe of his left foot, has green eyes (not blue), is missing his right canine tooth, and sucks on a mango-flavored sucker that is only made by such-and-such candy company in Toledo. Clearly there must be a middle ground.

Are specific and universal really contradictory goals? If by specific we mean "exclusive" or "utterly unique," then it tends to exclude universality. If by universal we mean "vague" or "all encompassing," it nearly negates specificity. But this isn't the only way to look at the question. All human beings share certain wants and needs, basic human events such as birth and death or hunger and yearning, and even such banal daily events as stubbed toes, sleepiness, or the enjoyment of a scrumptious sweet treat. Even if someone hasn't personally experienced a certain event, he probably knows someone who has or can at least imagine what it is like. But to spur that imagination, specifics are needed. So in fact, proper specificity promotes universality; the specifics of an event resonate in the memory or imagination of a universal audience that grasps the moment. And lack of specificity impedes universality, because it neither provokes memory nor imagination—the event is too vaguely depicted to stimulate the audience's thoughts and feelings.

Let's take that scrumptious sweet treat as an example. Almost any audience one could imagine attracting would have some experience of eating something sweet. But for the sake of argument, imagine a long-lost tribe that has no natural sweets in its world. Where the tribesmen find a theater or television is another story. But for argument, say they can't tell a bowl of ice cream from a piece of cake. They might not even know those are foods. The specificity of making a distinction between chocolate and vanilla ice cream will surely be lost on them. And in fact the visual of the ice cream may not be appealing to them. But if they witness the experience of a character eating and loving the ice cream, they should be able to imagine the joyful sensations they are seeing. They must have some sensual pleasure in their deprived part of the world that enables them to connect with the reaction of the character on screen enjoying his ice cream. In fact, the more clearly drawn the character and the more the eating of the ice cream is conveyed by the specific reactions of the character, the more able our disadvantaged tribe would be to imagine the sensation. The specific actions of the moment create the universal understanding or reaction within the audience.

This is how specific events lead to universal reactions—they provoke the memories and imaginations of the audience of similar experiences of their own. Without the specifics in the moment, the audience is left only with generic events, which tend not to stimulate the memory or imagination. Arbitrary and unutilized specifics are of no use in this situation, but well-conceived specifics that play into the events in the lives of the characters are key elements to be discovered in the invention of a story. But when is a specific arbitrary and when is it well conceived? If a specific description or attribute reveals nothing of the inner life of a character or nothing of interest in the past life of the character and will take on no significant role in the future of the story or the character, it probably is arbitrary or at least not well conceived. If an event or specific action that takes place in a scene gives no further information than its own existence, it quite possibly is unutilized.

But even something as simple and mundane as an itch can be useful. In *Rear Window*, L. B. Jeffries is in a cast up to his waist, and this is a crucial element in the story. Early in the film he has an itch deep inside the cast that frustrates him until he finally finds a long stick to thread between the cast and his leg. His satisfaction and relief when he is finally able to scratch his itch and the universal experience we all have of a difficult-to-reach itch help us identify with the character. It unites the audience and the character. While it serves no function in the story and sheds no light on the inner life of the character, this specific moment in his life is well worth its screen time because it creates a bond between the character and the audience. And it even fits with the story thematically, because it gives us an experience of shared frustration and then satisfaction—which is the exact circumstance of the overall story.

Life Is What Happens

The events portrayed in the lives of the characters must have specificity and must have their function in helping us understand the characters and the story, but there is yet another question that is often overlooked. What would be happening in the lives of the characters if these events we see in the story weren't taking place?

Beginning screenwriters often forget that characters need to have apparent lives that extend beyond the world of this specific story. If the only elements in the lives of the characters are those shown in the story, then the audience senses that the characters are obedient to the storyteller; they only exist while they are on screen and do not have a "life." So in addition to envisioning the events in the lives of the characters, the writer must also know what other plans each character would be pursuing if the events of the story weren't happening. In fact, one of the most effective means of creating a sense of life in characters is to develop tension between what the story demands of the character and what the character would prefer to do. If the character only reluctantly does what the story requires, this dynamic expands our understanding of the character's life well beyond the limits of the story alone.

This dynamic is fairly obvious in stories where a character is thrust into a situation not of his or her own creation, such as *Ben-Hur* or *The Terminator* or *It's a Wonderful Life*. But what if the characters volunteer for the dilemmas they face in the story, as occurs in *The Talented Mr. Ripley* or *Rocky* or *Jaws* or *Some Like It Hot*? Even when the characters make a conscious and informed choice to pursue a line of action that leads to the events in the story, there are other desires still at work inside them, other things they might be doing. No choice is made in a void, and each of these characters faces a moment of decision to pursue the events in the story instead of other things.

A good example of this dynamic is *Schindler's List*. Schindler voluntarily enters into his dangerous mission of rescuing Jews from the Nazi machinery, but his decision comes when he is weighing the consequences of action versus the consequences of inaction. Throughout the story, he is plagued by "what ifs"—what if he hadn't started this, what if he'd done more. We are shown many examples of his nearly doing other things or being tempted in other directions and having to reaffirm his commitment to the line of action he's taken. In *Three Colors: Red*, Valentine voluntarily returns the injured dog to the judge and continues to visit him, yet it is clear that there are other elements in her life, some of which she continually tries to return to, only to find herself drawn back into the judge's world.

The World of the Story

The characters and the events in their lives are not the only parts of a story that need to be imagined prior to the beginning of the storytelling. The world the story takes place in must also be created and has the same requirements of specificity and universality as do characters and events. And again, writers starting out fall into two camps—too vague and too exclusive. Even in an historical drama based on a real person who lived on one specific block of one city in one brief time period, the writer must discover the aspects of that specific location and its time and ethos that provoke the memories and imagination of the audience. Time and place, setting and mood and atmosphere don't come from a void. Even if a story is set in a fictional world, a fantasy world, or "the final frontier," there are aspects of that world that reflect back on our world. It is these aspects—and the variations on them given in the specific world of the story—that help create the connection with the audience. How does the story world we are asked to enter compare to the world we live in? How does it reflect or challenge our feelings about our world?

Even "our world" or a supposedly naturalistic story setting

must be envisioned clearly, from the ground up. It may surprise many writers to realize that it is their own worldview that has perhaps the greatest impact on the world they invent for their story—even if it's "this one." Is this a naturalistic story where society is good and supportive, or where it's cruel and indifferent? Is the atmosphere dark and gloomy, or bright and sunny? Do most people lie and cheat whenever they can get away with it, or are they basically honest, if flawed? Can nature kill you, or will it provide you with sustenance? Are the police enemies or saviors? Is water life-giving or a killer? Nothing can be taken for granted in the creation of a story's world, right down to the food and water. While the world may *appear* exactly like the one outside our door—people wear the current fashions, eat "regular" food, drive normal cars, and obey all the laws of physics and the universe as we perceive it—there is another layer at work here.

This other layer, which is grounded in philosophy, is ultimately more important in storytelling than the outward trappings of the world. Clearly we need the visuals, we need to be able to see what it looks like, what the living spaces are, how the inhabitants fit into the landscape, whatever it is. But the world could look like Eden and be filled with cannibals. It could look like Hell and be populated with ragtag saints. Compare the futuristic worlds of *Alien, Star Wars, Mad Max 2: The Road Warrior,* and *Sleeper*. Or compare the "realistic" worlds of *American Beauty, When Harry Met Sally, Enemy of the State,* and *Out of Sight*. Each of these stories creates its own variation on what is real, how the world and its inhabitants coexist, the feel and look of the world, and the undercurrent of well-being or its utter absence. A penthouse and a ghetto both exist in the same universe and have a view of each other; which do we spend more of our time in, and which is "happier" or more supportive, which is subliminally being fostered by the writer and which is subliminally being criticized? The choice is always up to the writer.

This isn't a choice to be ignored or taken lightly. In a sense, the world of the story is a character, or at least a force that will ultimately be at play in the story. The choice of a malignant or dangerous world—on Earth or elsewhere, now or in the past or future—is an obvious element in a story. The characters must contend with a hostile world in some fashion. But even the use of a benign or indifferent world will affect the story and its telling. In the absence of any battle with the world itself, the conflicts that generate and shape the story must come from other characters or from within the central character. The character of the world is a crucial decision for the writer to make in the building of a story.

These decisions ultimately create the "rules" of this world. Again, it's easiest to see if the world is hostile or utterly unreal. The audience must be taught that water can kill you in this world or that cars can fly. And, once established, the rules should be obeyed. Cars can't suddenly start to fly in the big chase scene in the world of *The French Connection* or the audience will rebel and disbelieve the story and quit being involved in it. But even in a benign or more mundane world, there are rules under the surface. In this world, will neighbors get involved and help, or will they hide behind locked doors? Does every locked door hide a crime or criminal? Or is every door unlocked? Do stairways tend to have banana peels on the top step? Does a fall down the stairs in this world cause death or laughter? If someone is shot in this story, does he bleed, suffer pain, and perhaps die, or does he just fall down dead, doing all his bleeding and dying offscreen?

Collisions

Stories don't "just happen." Stories are created by some kind of collision between conflicting forces. There are three basic kinds of collisions at work in stories: a collision with the world of the story—the world is hostile to the characters; a collision with other opposing characters in the world; and a collision between one aspect of a character and another, adversarial aspect of the same character. It is possible for one story to include elements of all three kinds of collisions.

Imagine a story with no collisions. It takes place in a benign world; there is no opposing character and no doubt or inner conflict in the character. The basic dramatic circumstance of *somebody wants something badly and is having difficulty getting it* shows us the reason we need collisions. In a story with no collisions, there is no difficulty getting whatever it is that the character wants; there is nothing standing in her way. While this may be wonderful to experience in life, it is anathema to drama. "Somebody wants something badly and has *no* difficulty getting it": it sounds boring, and it also is over quickly.

What sustains an audience's interest in a story is the quest, the attempt to do something that is difficult. No matter how rich the world is, how appealing the characters are, how active and exciting the events, these alone will not keep an audience interested and participating emotionally and intellectually. Some kind of quest or attempt to do something that is not a foregone conclusion is required to keep an audience involved. Even action that seems on the surface to be exciting, like a car chase, will be boring unless there is an underlying reason for it. If we care about at least one participant and know that he stands to gain or lose something in his quest during the car chase, it can be riveting. Without those underlying concerns, it's just so much revving and squealing and visual pyrotechnics. Similarly, what on the surface looks utterly boring, like a walk in a park, can be tense and fascinating if we know that a character we care about is pursuing a quest that is about to be fulfilled—or not.

Each of the three basic kinds of collisions has variations that give the storyteller a spectrum of choices. One doesn't have to be a physicist to become a writer, but there is an effective analogy in the physics of vectors to be explored. Two cars of identical weight, traveling toward each other at identical speeds along the same line and hitting head on, should, in theory, stop at the exact point they hit. If one is heavier or traveling faster, it will push the other away from the point of impact, but along the same path they have both been traveling. If they are not traveling along the same line, the resulting collision will send them veering to a different location and at a new and somewhat unpredictable direction.

What the hell does this have to do with screenwriting? Imagine two characters of equal power and intellect with exactly opposite desires; when these two "collide" the story comes to a stop, just like the cars above. So long as their desires are exactly opposite and their strength and intellect are equal, the result will be predictable. But if their wants or desires are somewhat tangential—opposed but not precisely, exactly opposite—then the result of this collision isn't predictable and it isn't an impasse. The former situation will tend to produce scenes that boil down to "Yes, no, yes, no, yes, no . . ." The latter situation becomes much more complex and therefore unpredictable. Add that unpredictability to the power and intellect each character commands and you have a collision that potentially creates an interesting story.

When applied to story collisions, the analogy works in this way: if a character versus his world is a completely even match, then it results in a stalemate; if a character versus another character is an even match, it's a stalemate; and, in the easiest form to see it, if a character versus himself is an even match, it's a stalemate. Unless there is another element that upsets the balance, the story just stops there and loses our interest.

Mismatched and tangential collisions often result in the best stories. Man versus mountain in a blizzard, Rocky Balboa versus Apollo Creed, Eve White versus Eve Black (*The Three Faces of Eve*) all are based on mismatched collisions. *Gandhi* and *The Terminator* are based on this kind of collision. On the other hand, many stories are created by tangential vectors colliding. Most James Bond villains want to control the world, while Bond always wants to stop them. These are opposing, but not exactly opposite, vectors. In *To Kill a Mockingbird*, Atticus wants justice for his client while the world of the story wants to sustain the status quo—opposing but not exactly opposite. In *Sling Blade*, Karl Childers wants to be free and friendly with Doyle in his world, but another part of him wants to set things right in the only way he knows how.

These films have all been based on actively opposing wants, either from characters or from the world of the story. But there are stories where the opposition is indifferent. A huge desert, a large corporation or government, a rival who doesn't even realize he is being competed with—these too can create collisions. But all the velocity, all the momentum that creates the impact must come from the characters who are in motion in their quest for something. Scaling a mountain in the best of weather could still cause a valid collision, as could crossing a windless desert. There is plenty of potential difficulty in those quests. An indifferent society by its very indifference could foil a character's quest and therefore provide a collision. What begins as a passive or indifferent rival (mountain, man, or aspect of self) can also become actively opposed as the story progresses, heightening the tension and unpredictability.

Where's the Antagonist?

As we've learned, antagonists come from three potential places: the world, another character, or the protagonist herself. When the antagonist, the opposing force in the story, is another character, he's very easy to identify. The Terminator, Dr. No, Noah Cross, any one of a thousand psycho killers, terrorists, Nazis—the world of film is filled with them. But what if the "antagonist" is really the world of the story and it isn't a mountain, meteor, tidal wave, or hurricane? How do you depict it, show it, dramatize it? If it's a system—government, bureaucracy, local society, a whole country or political/social movement—then there must be some representatives. They are not truly the villains themselves; they are the explainers, sustainers, and proponents of the system. A Nazi general might be an antagonist in his own right, but he could just as easily be the dramatized representative of the whole Nazi war machine. In *Brazil* and *RoboCop*, the opposing force is a huge faceless system of life—the world of the story—yet it has representatives who reveal and expose its existence and organizing principles. These representatives never take on the grandeur of a James Bond villain, despite the fact that they head up just as evil an empire. The whole empire is the true antagonist. For all his presence and menace, Darth Vader is more a representative of a larger entity than he is the sole antagonist of *Star Wars*.

And when a character is at war with himself? When the

primary conflict in a story is an internal struggle within the protagonist, he functions as his own antagonist. He does not need to
be schizophrenic or have multiple personalities; he just needs to
be torn between two impulses. *Trainspotting* is a fine example of a
story about a character at war with himself. On the one hand,
Renton wants to stay with his friends, be one of the pack—and
that means taking drugs. On the other hand, he wants to get off
the drugs, not because he doesn't like them, but because they are
making life difficult for him. The two competing and opposing
impulses are dramatized as he shifts back and forth from one to
the other. And the dramatization of each side establishes a cast of
characters who help pull and push him in these two directions.
His parents and girlfriend help pull him away from drugs, while
all his "mates" draw him back to them. As we see him shift from
one group to the other and see his interaction with them—both
positive and negative—we are given insights into the ebb and flow
of his inner conflict just as surely as if there were an outside antagonist.

Characters' Baggage and Unfinished Business

There is more to fleshing out characters than figuring out what
their other plans would be if the story weren't happening to them.
Characters need pasts and personal histories in order to come
alive in the story, just as much as they need an intended but as yet
unfulfilled future. Where was the character yesterday, last month,
last year, at age ten? Who was she? What did she care about, and
why? What did she fear, and why? In short, what makes her tick?
Whether or not the character's past is dramatized on screen,
formative aspects of it need to be known to the writer. Each of us
is shaped in our lives by our past experiences—we are polished
and scarred by what happens to us, what we do and don't do,
when we become fascinated and bored, what we discover we are
good at and bad at, whom we love and hate, fear and dread.
Those remnants of our past—the scars and polished spots—shape

our daily lives, actions, relationships, work, everything about us.

The same is true of characters in stories. They didn't get to be whoever they are just by existing today; if they did, if the story gives the impression that they didn't exist yesterday, that they merely serve the story and author, they don't have "life." A character who has his own set of strengths, weaknesses, blind spots, obsessions, foibles, fears, hopes, loves, hates, deep dark secrets, and the like is much more likely to come alive in a story than one who is a blank slate. Of course, the story could be about that blank-slate person colliding with the world and gaining his own scars and polished spots. But generally, a character needs to have lived before to feel real inside the story—and that means the remnants must show somehow.

Part of the author's work in creating living characters—whether they are men, machines, mice, or mermaids—is delving into their past to discover their baggage. What have they carried forward from the past, packed neatly (or otherwise) in their baggage? It isn't as helpful to think in terms of states of being as it is to think in dynamic and changing terms. For instance, it's only moderately helpful to know that a character fears his father. It's much stronger to imagine their interaction—perhaps the daily beatings or tirades or intimidation—that created that fear. What created the baggage the character has? What was the first moment of realization or the last moment of locking away the knowledge of the state of being? We don't necessarily know what creates a talent in baseball for one person and violin for another, so pondering the causes in the past might not be productive. But it could be immensely helpful in creating a live character to envision the last fruitless baseball practice for a hapless player or the first moment of fingering a pure and resonant note on the violin for a player of a different sort. If we can see a fire lit or see it go out or, more accurately, know the moment when it changed—even if it won't be dramatized—then we have a solid handle on the character and what makes him tick.

Some of a character's baggage remains unresolved and is destined to stay that way. A character who desperately wanted/needed to make peace with her dying mother and missed the chance can't ever complete the act. This is unfinished business for the character. It might be actively tormenting her or deeply re-pressed and forgotten, but either way it remains formative mate-rial in the creation of the character as we will meet her in the story. Again, discovering this material in an active, dynamic setting in-stead of a static state of being is much more productive. How hard did the character try to connect with her mother before her death? What would she have said if she'd had a chance? Whom or what has she blamed for her failure? Does she make any effort today to make amends through some other kind of act or thought, since the real act is impossible? How aware is she that this unfinished business is a factor in her life today? How big a factor is it?

When the unfinished business could conceivably be finished, it is equally revealing of character. Why has it remained unfin-ished? What was the closest the person ever got to finishing it? What is stopping him from completing it, even now? Where does he assign blame or responsibility? Does he consciously contem-plate still trying to complete it? What would it take to set that in action?

When starting a character exploration—the discovery process of trying to find out who a character is, what makes him tick, where he came from, and where he thinks he's going—keep in mind that you're better off knowing more about a character than can possibly fit into the story you're telling. This "overflow" con-tributes to the sense of life that some characters achieve.

Lightning, Decisions, and Protagonists

A great deal more will be said about protagonists, but let's as-sume for now that we are exploring a story with a clearly defined protagonist—a central character. What happens to this character, what he chooses to do, how his choices affect him and the people in his world and perhaps even the world itself—this is the mate-rial we are exploring to discover our story. In a sense, we follow this person's life path; it might not be from birth to death, it might not even be a matter of years or months or even weeks. Conceivably, we could be following only as much time in his life as the story takes to elapse. Maybe even less.

If that life path we follow is straight—there isn't a twist or turn in sight, no hill to climb, no valley or river to cross—then the end can be seen from the beginning. The story is predictable; we already know the end before we start. Even a story with plenty of twists and turns can be predictable, but one with no variations is, by definition, predictable. Predictable translates into "boring," and, as we will see later on, being boring breaks the one inviolable rule of storytelling.

So you need twists and turns—and valleys, rivers, hills, storms, mishaps, misunderstandings, and accidents—along the path the character takes in order for the story to be unpredictable. But what alters the path of the character? In a nutshell, two different kinds of things can change the path of the character and his story: he gets hit by lightning or he decides to run for cover. Either way, the path he was on before has been altered. An outer force or an inner force takes the progress the character has made so far and changes it. This is a twist or turn in the character's journey through the story.

Most stories have changes created by outside forces, inner forces, *and* combined forces. An outside impediment prompts an internal decision, or a decision brings the character up against an outside force. Let's take a character's path that is literally a path— a road story. Let's say she wants to get from California to New York without flying; part of her baggage is a fear of airplanes. She makes a decision not to take the train, but to drive. So her path changes with that decision. She buys a brand-new car so she won't have to worry about its breaking down (another decision). The car works well (an outside force) or it breaks down (also an outside force). Either way, it influences the road she takes through the story. Then she decides she wants to see the Grand Canyon (a decision), and that detour leads her to have an accident, which she wouldn't have had if she hadn't made the detour (an outside force as the result of an inner decision). Now that her car is destroyed, the train looks more attractive, but there isn't one near the Grand Canyon (an outside force) so she accepts a ride from someone to the nearest train station (a decision). But the person isn't what he seems to be and he kidnaps her (an outside force), but she cleverly manages to escape (a decision prompted by an outside force). You get the idea.

When envisioning and exploring a story, it usually becomes obvious that not every moment of the trip from California to New York can be onscreen. There have been a few notable experiments in film storytelling, like *High Noon* and *Time Code*, where the time in the lives of the characters matches the time the film takes place in. But in most cases, time has to be cut out. This story problem will be dealt with later, but for our purposes here, it's important to note what should be left in and what should be left out. Most of the time you want to include both the lightning and the decision to run for shelter; show the outside forces and the inner decisions. These are the moments of twisting and turning along the path, and with each new change in direction, a new status quo is established. After either an outside or an inner force alters the path, you need to record the establishment of the new status quo, but not the full duration of it. So long as the status quo is unchanging, you don't need to elaborate on it.

Let's follow our traveler. When she drives across California and the new car works fine, there is no change going on. The same status quo exists from the west side of the state, where she starts the journey, to the east side. That's the time we cut out, because there is no change in her path. But when she decides to see the Grand Canyon it is a crucial moment in the path of her story. We would want to include the last minute or two before the decision—whatever leads up to the decision— the decision itself and the first minute or two on the new path, heading in the new direction. Once she's on a new road heading toward the Grand Canyon, we cut out the time again until the last minute or two before the accident—the next change on her path. We cut out the unchanging status quo and return to real time with our characters and story only when the status quo is about to change.

It seems simple and logical: just show the established status quo as it leads up to the moment of change, show the change itself and the beginning of the newly established status quo. But beginning screenwriters often spend more time on status quo than they do on dramatic change. There is a tendency to show the character driving all the way across California, then to jump ahead to her on the road toward the Grand Canyon and explain to the audience that she changed her mind and turned off the road she had been driving on. This isn't a major loss when it's a simple decision to change roads, but when the screenplay is not showing the car collision or the escape from the kidnapper, the problem is monumental. It's antidramatic. There are writers who will jump ahead to her driving away in the kidnapper's car and explain to us after the fact that she tricked him and escaped. This is denying us "the good stuff," and it's also denying us a close relationship with the character.

This point goes to the heart of the audience's way of experiencing a story: we envision ourselves together with the character while at the same time enjoying the safety and security of some aesthetic distance. In reality we know we're sitting in a theater, we're not really running away from the tiger—but in our minds, we're right there beside the protagonist who is running for his life. We want to have it both ways, and with stories, it's possible to have it both ways; that's what's so attractive and universal about stories. We get to experience danger, change, adventure, passion, heartbreak, and still stand safely just outside it. We want to be inside the car when it crashes, but we don't want to get a broken bone. We want to fly through space, but we want to go home and sit in the garden afterward—while we're still thinking about it. We even want to feel guilt, regret, grief, horror. If it's a strong human emotion, we want to experience it through stories. Often we'd prefer to experience it *only* through stories. No one wants to be stalked by a monster in real life, but horror stories remain one of the most resilient genres.

So from this perspective, it's clear why you want to include the "good stuff" in your stories. When an event provokes major emotions in the audience or provides visual or even auditory excitement, then it is fulfilling one of the basic reasons we enjoy stories. But there is a deeper and more important layer at work here. When we are connected to a character whom we know and care about—we know at least some of her strengths, weaknesses, passions, rationales, obsessions, humiliations—we want to participate with her in the pivotal moments of her journey, the twists and turns in her path. Each time we are with a character who faces a new obstacle—makes a decision to run for cover or stay and risk being hit by lightning—it strengthens our bond with the character. It makes us care more. It makes us more involved in her story, specifically, not just the story of "some woman" on the road from California to New York, but this specific person, with these specific human traits. She doesn't even have to be human—think of Woody in *Toy Story*.

How does being there facing the decisions with her make us care more? Why does it strengthen our bond with the character? When a character faces a hardship or enjoys a triumph, wrestles with a decision or cavalierly acts without a second thought, it opens a window into the character. We know what the character is up against and we are there when decisions are made about those obstacles; this is inherently revealing of the character and her inner life. We see the inner workings of the person (whether plant, animal, or human). We peek in the window into the soul or soullessness of the character, or into some truths about the character, hidden or otherwise.

When everything is fine and easy and unchanging, a character is mostly defined by what he chooses to present, which is often a combination of truth and lies—self-deceptions along with conscious deceptions. But when he is literally or figuratively hanging from the side of a cliff, the pretenses come down, the lies fall away, and the reality of the person comes through. It might not be admirable, but it's truthful and revealing. When we've peeked in these windows and discovered a character we still want to spend time with, flaws and all, we care. And, in fact, the flaws are a crucial element in our caring. A perfect character whose every response to every crisis is perfect quickly becomes insufferable. A flawed character, who in spite of her weaknesses and faults manages to rise to an occasion or even fail valiantly, is much more likely to gain our empathy.

If we aren't there when the character makes the decisions or gets hit by outside forces, we don't have a chance to look in those windows and see the realities inside the character. As a result, we are kept outside the character and left to witness only what he or she does, not how he or she does it. The "how" is much more telling than the "what." It's only at the time of change that the truth of a character is laid bare; by the time the dust has settled from the change, the character may have been able to regain composure—meaning reestablish the fictions and half-truths of her presentation of self, the shields and self-deceptions. So the opportunity to get closer to the character is already over. If we jump over the escape and only cut to our traveler in the kidnapper's car after she's escaped from him, we have no way of seeing inside her. Did he let his guard down, or did she outwit him? What part of herself was tested and stretched by the attempt to escape? What part of her was overwhelmed, and what part rose to the occasion? We can't know if we aren't there at the time it actually happens. If we're told about it later, not only is the telling flat and lifeless, we don't even know if it's true or how the truth is shaded, intentionally or unintentionally.

Character Arc

The need for the intimate bond between character and audience is crucial to the change the character undergoes in the story—the character arc. If we aren't close with a character—if we don't share some intimacy with him, enough to know what is difficult for him, what is easy, where he is irrational, and where he is in complete command of himself—then it becomes difficult to see any change coming about. And even worse, what change we can see has little meaning or resonance for us. If we have been kept utterly outside of a character—by not sharing with him the challenges of lightning strikes and momentous decisions—then his transformation from coward to hero seems phony or difficult to understand and accept. But if we've shivered in the trench with him *and* we've been there when he overcame his own fear and pushed forward—if we've participated with him in the crucial moments of the events in his journey—then we will feel his triumph at becoming the hero. We will believe it, precisely because we experienced it with him. And even if he fails and doesn't become a hero, we have participated with him, felt his pangs and yearnings and suffered through his defeat with him. Whatever change he owns, we also own.

Does a character really have to change? Do characters always have to improve? Certain kinds of characters, in fact, can't change. Comic characters and superhero characters can't change or they jeopardize the entire foundation of their stories. If Laurel and Hardy learn from falling down the stairs, then the tumbles are "real experiences." This knowledge means they won't fall down stairs anymore and, worse still, we won't be able to laugh because the reality of the experience diminishes the humor. It's because they can't and won't change that we are allowed to laugh at their foibles. If we start to feel the pain of falling down the stairs with them, it ceases to be funny.

The same is not true of a straight character in a comic situation—even an outlandish comic situation. In *Some Like It Hot,* Jerry changes from a cad with women to one trying to do the right thing for Sugar. It's not a change as huge as coward to hero, but it's a change, a fulfilling character arc. The story is a comedy and not meant to be taken seriously or realistically. But Jerry himself is not a comic character—he is not like Laurel and Hardy—he is a "straight" character, meant to be taken realistically within the world of that story. He is affected personally by the events of the story. So he changes as a result of the story—the path he has been on.

Superheroes have a similar circumstance. Superman and James Bond can't change significantly without diminishing or destroying the stories in which they live. If James Bond changed as a result of his experiences—with women or with villains—he would have to change his approach and, as a result, lose his ability to be a superhero. Just as there is a difference between a comic character and a straight character in a comic circumstance, there is a distinction to be drawn between a superhero and an "ordinary man" in a superhero's circumstances. The ordinary man must change as a result of his experiences.

Two Bruce Willis roles requiring similar superheroic actions illustrate this point nicely. The John McClane of the *Die Hard* series is a superhero. Sure, he bleeds, he can't bend steel with his bare hands or see through walls, but he performs extraordinary deeds. His six bullets kill five villains, while their thousand bullets miss him or wound him just enough to make him bleed cinematically. But this isn't why he's a superhero. He can't learn from the impossible odds he faces or he would stop his pursuit and the story would end. Even if the motivation (his wife is always in the midst of the jeopardy) is enough to keep him trying, no rational "real" character would believe his various one-man solutions could succeed. He would take precautions and enlist help that would ultimately destroy the fun of the stories.

But Willis also plays Harry in *Armageddon* and performs feats that surpass anything McClane does in *Die Hard,* yet he is an "ordinary man" in superhero circumstances. Instead of his gun clips holding impossible numbers of shells, his machinery doesn't always work right, his plans don't always—somehow, miraculously—work. His attempts fail; he has to learn from them and try something else. He's a heroic character, no doubt about that, but one who has faults that play into the evolution of the story, irrational fears and blind spots that subjectively make his journey more difficult. McClane doesn't have fears that impact his decisions; Harry has fears that veer his story this way and that. McClane has weaknesses, but prevails nonetheless. Harry has weaknesses that jeopardize the mission, and, at times, he needs the help of others to succeed.

Comic and superhero characters therefore display a complete absence of doubt. A comic character or a superhero will blithely push ahead without serious consideration of the consequences. A straight character in either a comic or superheroic circumstance will experience a relatively normal amount of doubt. He may push ahead, he may do comic or heroic things, but his inner life has been exposed to us by the doubts. And those normal human hesitations and uncertainties about the future, the consequences of actions, the wisdom of this choice over that choice, all contribute not only to our bond with the character, but to the character's arc.

When a character faces doubts and works through them—no

matter what his choice—we are being given that window to the inside of him. At the same time, we are discovering the area where change must inevitably happen within this character, and we are participating in the process of that change. Imagine a character who goes through great trials, faces his own weakness, discovers his own strength, wrestles with his prejudices and false assumptions, unearths his hidden talents—and doesn't change! He doesn't have to improve, he doesn't have to triumph and succeed or even become admirable, but change of some kind is guaranteed if the journey has been difficult and felt inside the character.

This change is the arc of the character. It can be from bad to good, good to bad, somewhat bad to slightly less bad. Whatever the change, it is some kind of transformation in the character as a consequence of having experienced the events of the story. A character with an inner life who faces adversity that is strong enough to justify a story must change to some degree as a result.

When envisioning a story, it is often easier to see the end point than the beginning point. How the character comes out of the story sometimes leaps to mind more easily. In general, you strive to put the starting point on this arc as far removed from the end point as possible, within the realm of what this story can encompass. The arc doesn't always have to go from sinner to saint; a story can just as effectively cover the dissolution of a saint into a sinner. The choice is the author's, and this decision is a bedrock decision in the creation of a story.

What If This Story Were a Fairy Tale or Myth?

Carl Jung hypothesized that mankind shares a "collective unconscious." He spent much of his career exploring the similarities of myths, legends, and fairy tales from far-flung cultures around the world. Whether we believe this commonality of primal stories comes from God, genetics, aliens, or happenstance, it is amazing to note how cultures that could not possibly have interacted have similarities in their myths and religions, children's stories, and adventure tales. Human beings share the same basic needs of food, shelter, warmth and companionship, procreation and sex, and survival. We also share the common needs of trying to understand where we come from, where we are going, why we are here, and how we should behave while we are alive. These too are primal needs; they may be spiritual or psychological or emotional, but all cultures share these concerns.

Combined, physical needs and spiritual needs influence how we devise and experience stories. Some stories are made to help us fathom these needs to understand our origins or how we should live or what constitutes proper behavior within a given society; some stories are created for audiences to live out or learn from the fear of losing one of our physical needs. Because we share this same set of primal needs, no matter how sophisticated or primitive our society is, threats to these needs create similar reactions among all people—they generate visceral reactions. Visceral reactions are the core substance of stories.

At the heart of the story, is the threat to the planet by an alien invasion from space very different from the threat to a Stone Age tribe by missionaries bent on conversion? Aren't there striking similarities between the cavemen of *Quest for Fire* who go out into the terrifying unknown on a mission and the soldiers of *Saving Private Ryan* on an expedition into a similarly terrifying and unknown world? Isn't *Apocalypse Now* a similar quest? What fuels the story of *American Beauty*? Isn't it threats to the primal forces in the lives of the family, from within and from the outside? Isn't *The Godfather* at its core really a story about the transfer of power from one leader to another? It could be a tribal change in chief, a town's mayoral race, a bloody coup d'etat in a medieval kingdom, or the machinations behind the scenes of a modern impeachment.

Each of these is radically different in outward appearance because of the specifics of the world of the stories, the societies depicted, the individuals and their roles in those worlds. But on a human level—where audiences connect with stories—these are modern retellings of ancient stories. A great many beginning writers believe they will create utterly new and unique stories. They forget that human beings in their emotional core have not changed in thousands of years. What was felt by a caveman as he set out to hunt for food for his family is the same set of misgivings—hopes, fears, doubts, uncertainties—any soldier will feel when faced with galactic challengers in the future or any head-of-household in today's society. We're all human.

Anything we are capable of experiencing has been experienced before—and told in a story before. In fact, it's been told in a story in places and times that have never seen a movie, television, radio, or book. What the people in a story go through at its most basic is necessarily universal. The specific actions can and do change, but what is behind them and what they mean to the characters involved has already been retold thousands of times. There were no brand-new stories when films were invented, when Shakespeare wrote great plays, or when the ancient Greeks handed down their mythology, their plays, and their philosophy.

But a new retelling is possible and desirable. A new setting for an old story, a unique character in a familiar circumstance, a strange and inventive twist on events and goals we've all seen before—these are the substance of future stories. And they have been the raw material of future stories for thousands of years. Retelling worked for the Greeks, it worked during the Renaissance, it worked for Shakespeare, and it worked for every great screenwriter, whether he knew it or not. So let's embrace retelling and use it.

If your story has been told before, where? When? By whom? And how did that storyteller work with it? These are worthwhile questions to explore, and a good place to start is with the most enduring and classical of stories—myths, legends, and fairy tales. But this doesn't mean you take "The Little Mermaid" and set it in a suburban high school and call that your own story. Ask yourself what you can glean from past tellings, from other variations on this aspect of human life that have succeeded in the past.

The "hero's journey" is perhaps the most famous and accepted of the paradigms in myth—and in modern storytelling. Some believe it is the only form of story. And surely this paradigm accounts for a great many stories, from *Star Wars* to *North by Northwest* to *The Matrix* to *The African Queen*. The Hero's Journey: a flawed (read human) and doubt-stricken (read inner life) character reluctantly takes on a task that requires him to overcome his own fears and flaws (more inner life) in order to enter the dark and dangerous world of his adversary or rival (antagonist); through faith, perseverance, superior wit, or intelligence and, usually, with the power of a loved one, he somehow prevails. From *The Odyssey* to *Raiders of the Lost Ark* to *The Straight Story* to *Run Lola Run*, this paradigm covers a range of differing stories. And there are variations where the hero prevails not with success but with some kind of understanding, as in *Chinatown*, *Braveheart*, *The Unforgiven*, *Rocky*, and *Deliverance*.

But the hero's journey hardly covers all stories, whether mythological, legendary, or modern. There is also the paradigm of the antihero, the character who denies the quest, who strives to keep from taking heroic actions. The Antihero's Journey: a flawed and doubt-stricken character actively fights against taking on a task, but in the process nonetheless faces both his inner fears and flaws and an adversary and comes to some kind of resolution. This paradigm covers everything from *The Big Lebowski* to *The Usual Suspects* to *Casablanca* to *One Flew over the Cuckoo's Nest* to *The Terminator*. Again, success or failure isn't the real measure of the story; it's the nature of the struggle that provides the common ground.

There also are nonheroes whose life paths we will follow through intriguing and compelling stories. In this case, a nonhero could be seen as someone who actively tries to stay out of the way of personal or worldly heroic circumstances, neither accepting a task nor fighting against it, but simply avoiding it. Cinderella doesn't do battle with her stepmother so much as she circumvents her and in the end gets herself rescued. The same could be said of Jerry in *Some Like It Hot*. This sort of "nonheroic" story encompasses *Annie Hall*, *Bringing Up Baby*, even *Butch Cassidy and the Sundance Kid* and *Ed Wood*.

While the hero willingly rushes into battle and the antihero actively fights against the need for the battle (or his participation in it), the nonhero runs away from the battle. And it is the action of running away—which can still entail facing inner and outer conflicts—that provides the bulk of the story. There are even instances where the nonhero finally, by the end of the story, becomes either a hero or an antihero. *Trainspotting*, *The Fugitive*, and *Three Kings* fit into this paradigm. Heroic efforts can be put into avoiding difficult and demanding circumstances, yet still the protagonist could be seen as a nonhero. The intention of the character is the determining factor, not the quality of the actions he or she ends up taking.

There is still one more basic paradigm in fairy tales, legends, and stories of all kinds: the villain's journey. It is not uncommon for us to follow as a protagonist a character who is also the antagonist of the story. Whether it's following Jackal, the assassin, in *The Day of the Jackal* or Melvin Udall in *As Good as It Gets*, we are seeing the story through the lens of the person who is creating the conflicts for other, more "likable" or "admirable" characters. *Psycho*, *Taxi Driver*, *A Clockwork Orange*, *The Professional*, and *Raging Bull* all fit into this story pattern.

Villainous characters do not have to be evil, though Norman Bates can hardly be seen otherwise in *Psycho*. Their intentions are not admirable, nor do we hope they succeed at them, but that doesn't stop us from following their stories and caring as the events unfold. Here we could say the paradigm is: a character with evil or unworthy intentions struggles against outside and inner obstacles toward a goal we do not share with him. Very often, we are in a position to hope that the character fails at his goal and changes his approach to life. *Amadeus* and *All about Eve* follow characters we hope against most of the time. What about *Double Indemnity*? On the one hand, we follow Walter Neff through the creation of his nasty plot, but don't we keep hoping he'll stop before it's too late? Yet even that hope is denied us, because he is telling the story while already wounded. We don't share his goals, he is making bad choices, but they are choices we understand, so we are still able to care, even as we find ourselves aligned against him instead of for him.

The Audience's Fragile Involvement

If the audience's involvement in a film—its emotional connection, its caring about what happens in the story—is not dependent upon their liking or admiring the protagonist or upon the story being utterly new, then what is it dependent upon? More than any other factor, what keeps us emotionally involved in a story is understanding. We don't have to like or admire the character, but we must understand him and what prompts him to make his decisions. We don't have to know the world the story takes place in beforehand, but we need to understand it and comprehend its dynamics, how they relate to our own and how they differ. We don't have to like the events and the decisions made—we don't have to enjoy lightning strikes or want a character to run for cover—but we must understand these events as they unfold. We don't want to be able to predict the twists and turns along the path the character takes through the story, but we have to understand how each one comes about and see it as a natural outgrowth of what has happened before. These are complicated and not always complementary desires on the part of the audience, but the storyteller must satisfy them, make the audience care, and then maintain that connection to the finish.

If we have a prior attachment to a character—because of the actor playing him or the previous ten stories we've heard about this character—then we can have a certain level of interest in the progress of the story without a basic understanding of the events taking place and the decisions made by the characters. But familiarity is the most fragile of all connections an audience can have to a story and is the most likely to dissipate. In other words, a familiar character or a likable actor might get us into the theater seats and through the first minutes of a film, but they will not hold our attention unless we have been allowed to understand—and, as a result, emotionally participate—*during* the story.

A story in which we understand the characters, understand the decisions, see the lightning strikes as an inevitable part of the world the story takes place in; a story in which we cannot quite predict the twists and turns, yet when they come they feel like an organic part of the story we have been involved in so far; a story in which a passionate character desperately wants something that is very difficult to achieve or get—this kind of story will command our attention and generate our emotional involvement. If we are emotionally involved from beginning to end—whether our hopes or our fears for the characters are realized, or there is some kind of bittersweet ending—we will have had an experience that has truly touched us. That, ultimately, is what an audience wants from a story—an experience, one that is emotionally challenging and completes itself. But the story alone cannot do all these things; it is the telling of the story that is the key to audience involvement, on both an emotional plane and an intellectual plane.

THE TELLING OF THE STORY

Few film stories take place in real time, where the time in the lives of the characters matches the time the story takes place in. Many stories take place in something other than chronological order. Still other stories take place in several distant locations. In these sorts of stories, it's easy to see that the telling of the events in the lives of the characters cannot be an exact replication of those events as if they were real. But even in a film that is two hours long, which covers two hours in the lives of the characters and takes place in a close and finite set of locations, the story and the telling of the story will not be identical. The difference is the audience and its experience. Storytelling is creating and orchestrating the experience the audience has; the story itself is the events and decisions and the impact of those events and decisions on the lives of the characters.

In order for the audience to share in the experiences of the characters—or in some cases have a greater experience than the characters—what the audience knows, doesn't know, is made to care about, and sees as significant all become factors. A couple holding hands isn't going to have much impact on the audience, but if we knew one of them just returned from a long separation, that first touch could be very moving. Someone walking swiftly down the street isn't going to give us much to worry about, but what if we knew she just left a bomb somewhere or is on her way to a bank robbery? A child playing hide-and-seek won't be all that engrossing, but what if we knew that outside the house was

a kidnapper looking for an opportunity? The audience's experience is created by the storyteller; it isn't a given from the nature
of the characters we follow and the events in their lives. This
is the true heart of the art form of storytelling in any medium
and the crux of the problem faced by every screenwriter—how to
tell the story, not simply what is the story.

In this section we'll explore what is "value added" in storytelling over story alone. Throughout the rest of the book we will
be exploring the many ways in which the aspects of storytelling
correlate, bolster, or compete with each other, provide opportunities and create limitations, and the ways in which all these relationships can be altered—and to what effect on the story, the
characters, the audience, and the storyteller's intentions.

The Seamless Dream

Pick out your all-time favorite film. Remember the first time you
saw it? Didn't the experience go something like this: after you settled in and the film started, you read the opening credits (or these
days, perhaps there weren't any opening credits), you entered the
film's world, and it took hold of you and didn't let you go until it
was over. For an hour and a half or two hours or three hours, you
thought and felt a great deal, but all of it concerned the film and
its world and story and characters. You didn't think about your
own life and worries, you didn't think about outside events or issues at all. You were riveted.

What this kind of filmgoing experience most resembles is the
state of being we're in when we're dreaming. We are in the world
completely, we are with the characters and perhaps enjoying our
little bit of aesthetic distance as well. But the world we are caring
about for the duration of the film is *its* world, not our "regular"
world. Whether we're transported back in time, into outer space,
to the heights of mountains, to the depths of seas, or into the living
rooms of people who could be our neighbors, we are taken out of
our world completely. We are given an experience in someone
else's world, with someone else's concerns and goals, frustrations,

joys, defeats, and triumphs, and then our attachment is ended and we are released back into our own world. And when everything works this well, we have had a significant emotional and possibly thought-provoking experience.

This film experience is like a seamless dream. We haven't been "awakened" out of it during the dream, but have allowed ourselves to "go along for the ride." Often we're sorry it's over. Some of your favorite films might have broken that dream a few times, but still, the overall experience was much as described above. It is difficult, and rare, for a film to keep up the unerring magic of transporting the audience from start to finish.

The goal of a storyteller should be this kind of mesmerizing experience for the audience. You have your viewers willingly giving their attention, thoughts, and emotions to the experience you have created for them. If you use that opportunity masterfully, if you don't wake them from the dream you've created, if you don't force them out of your world back into their own, then you will have created a ferociously loyal audience. This is what is really meant by "giving the audience what they want." It isn't happy end versus sad end, admirable and likable characters versus villains; it isn't rockets and explosions or rollicking good laughs or crocodile tears—what an audience truly wants from a story and the telling of that story is this seamless dream experience. If the story can make the audience "one" with its world and characters, then the audience will be getting what it wants no matter what the ending, how likable the characters, how painful the tensions and frustrations along the path, how thoughtful or "merely entertaining" the film.

And this seamless connection between the audience and the storyteller's world holds true for a story that intends to be artistic, thought-provoking, entertaining, exciting, funny. Just go back to your favorite films and you'll see this to be true. Either they had that kind of impact on you or they aren't truly among your favorite films. Some films might be on your list of favorites because you think you *ought* to love them, because they fit some notion you have about what is acceptable and worthwhile. But ask yourself—no one is looking over your shoulder—what films did

I *truly* connect with? Which films got me excited about filmmaking, storytelling, screenwriting? What was the experience like for me? I suspect that nine times out of ten, the effect those films had on you was that of a seamless dream.

The Intended Impact

Every film is meant to be experienced from start to finish, but for the storyteller, the end may be the starting point. How do you want the audience to feel when the film ends? The answer can run the full spectrum from giddy to devastated, happy to stunned. Any final impact is possible; but having no idea is a bad idea. Just as it is true that "not deciding is deciding," not intending to have an impact is still having an impact. The experience you give is shaped partly by your decisions and partly by your skill—and the skill of all those who will contribute to the making of the film. But there is no choice in the matter of having an impact. Once the audience has been lured into the theater, what happens in the film and story will have an impact. They may storm out after ten minutes or fall asleep after thirty; they may become engrossed and hang on the edge of their seats for the duration or they may decide to reprogram their new electronic organizer. In large part the choice is up to the storyteller.

But the impact of a film is not simply its ending; it is a continuous process that is its most focused at the ending but has been in evidence from start to finish. One of the reasons that the end can be a starting point for the storyteller is that the ending's impact is often the clearest indication of his or her own intention. It's easy to think of the process of building a story as a conscious manipulation of the audience toward the writer's own ends. But in fact, most of the time, the writer has to discover what's truly on her mind, what her story is really about, not just seemingly about. One of the first and best clues is how you envision ending the story and, especially, how you want the audience to be feeling at the end. Once this clue is discovered (and it may take a draft to find it), then part of the process of building the story will be helping to make the experience point toward that impact all the way through.

But you should not find one note and then play it from beginning to end. For example, let's say that your intended ending is bittersweet and that you want your audience to be thoughtful about the gray areas of a controversial issue. In this instance, you will want to make your story have bitter areas as well as sweet areas. You must come down solidly in the black on the issue, then solidly in the white, and end with the gray. All along the way, you have been working to put the audience in a mood receptive to thinking about the issue in complex terms, so you need to rule out the simple solutions. The notes you play throughout the story aren't identical to the ending note, but they should be in the same key. They should be working toward and away from that final impact, not tangentially or parallel or at cross purposes. There is a need for the notes to be "harmonious" even if the intended impact is disharmony.

If you want laughter in a drama or seriousness in a comedy, if you want complexity in a love relationship at the heart of a simple good-versus-evil story, if you want a simple, pure love at the center of a complex and intellectually challenging battle over an issue, then you build the story throughout to have this kind of duality. You need to make sure that both parts are in the same key and from the same composition. When sentimentality is grafted onto the end of a mean-spirited antic comedy, it feels phony. When an overwhelmingly violent film tries to end with an anti-violence moment, it feels like hypocrisy. When a relentlessly dour and angst-filled film tries to "bring us up" at the end, it can't help but feel false. In each case, it's because the impact generated during the unfolding of the story does not support the impact of the ending.

It's far better—both for the storyteller and the audience—to have a clearly identified intention that is exemplified by the ending and that has an influence on the unfolding events along the way. Those events don't have to support the ending at every turn; it's better that they explore the full range of the ending's impact, but both sides must be represented at times during the film or an abrupt shift at the end will destroy the experience of all that came before it. The net result is one of a flawed and unsatisfying experience for the audience. It will seem as if the storyteller didn't know what his story was really about.

Camera as Storyteller

What can the camera see? Or, perhaps more accurately, what are you making the audience see? Another early and basic question the storyteller must answer is, where are the audience's eyes (and ears) as the story unfolds? Can we see only what the main character sees? Can we jump across town, across the country, or across the universe to see and know things that the main character doesn't? Can we see and learn things in the same space and time with the main character that he or she doesn't see or learn? There are three basic methods to choose from in deciding how the camera or its placement will be involved in the telling of the story: an omniscient camera, a subjective camera, and limited omniscience.

The omniscient camera "knows where the story is" and goes wherever is necessary to reveal the story to the audience. In *The Godfather: Part II, Star Wars, The Silence of the Lambs,* and *American Beauty*, the camera can go wherever it needs to in order to show us crucial elements of the story. In *The Godfather: Part II,* it can go back and forth through time; in *Star Wars* it can go across the galaxy and back; in *The Silence of the Lambs* it can go into the eyes of the killer; and in *American Beauty* it can follow the husband, wife, daughter, neighbor boy, and neighbor father as their paths intertwine. The most common way of telling a film story is with an omniscient camera, because it allows the greatest latitude to the storyteller in choosing what to show and what to hide.

The subjective camera is one that is essentially "on a leash" from the main character. We can only see what he or she sees and go where he or she goes. *Taxi Driver, Apocalypse Now,* and *Trainspotting* all have subjective cameras. Each also has a voice-over narration from the central character, so that we are not only seeing what he sees, but we are inside his head as well. This sort of camera as storyteller creates an incredibly close bond between audience and character by forcing us to see the story through his or her experience of it. In some cases, like *Trainspotting*, what we see isn't realistic at all, but instead the protagonist's perceptions, fantasies, and fever dreams—the story he is telling us. In *Apocalypse Now* and *Taxi Driver*, we have more realistic depictions of the main character's subjective experience, but still only know what he knows, nothing beyond that. *Brazil* is another film with a subjective camera, but with no voice-over. We see Sam Lowry's "reality," his dreams and nightmares, and can't always tell which is which, but our perception of the entire world and the whole story is through the eyes and ears—and mind—of the central character.

Limited omniscience is a combination of the two other modes of camera as storyteller. We have the close bond with the main character as in a subjective camera, but within a limited range, we can see and hear and know things beyond his or her experience of the story. *Life Is Beautiful*, *The Sixth Sense*, and *One Flew over the Cuckoo's Nest* all have limited omniscience. In *Life Is Beautiful*, we follow Guido's story closely—he is in virtually every scene. Yet we can see things within scenes that he doesn't, such as a reaction from the wife, or we can be inside a hiding space with Giosué as Guido is marched off to his death. In this sense, the camera is on a "leash" to the protagonist, but at times giving us a perspective somewhat different from the main character's. In *One Flew over the Cuckoo's Nest*, we go to a few, limited scenes that are beyond the reach of the "leash." But in this case, the subjectivity that has carried the story most of the way through seems to remain. We get brief shots of the hospital ward before McMurphy's arrival; we are given a scene where the nurse and doctor discuss his case and decide to keep him in the ward when his time is up; and, of course, we have Chief's escape after McMurphy's death at the end. Still, these few digressions from the main character are so minor in the overall telling of the story—and the subject of the scenes still returns to the main character—that this camera would fit the mold of limited omniscience.

In each style of camera use as part of the storytelling, the method should be established early in the film. It would not be a good idea to tell a subjectively filmed story for the first hour, then suddenly jump across the universe. That would wake the audience out of its seamless dream with a jolt and the question, How did we get here? Yet if we'd established the ability to go wherever we needed, the same jump would not disrupt the seamless dream because we had subliminally accepted the proven ability of the camera to follow the story, not just the character. Normally, the audience doesn't really consciously know that it has a limited or subjective or omniscient camera. But it will notice when the style of camera changes without warning.

When a story could be told subjectively except for one major event that comes late in the story, it's a far better idea to establish early that the camera can follow the story anywhere, even if it isn't absolutely necessary yet. This way, the audience becomes accustomed to having this ability and the story experience won't be destroyed by an abrupt change in the "rules" of how the story is being told. *Amadeus* is an interesting example of this at work. Salieri tells the story, and it is subjective to its core because he is giving his own version of events. So it could be that the story would be told solely through scenes in which Salieri participates and we could see only those things he sees. Yet for the full power of the ending composition scene, a clear distinction must be made between Mozart's mode of working and Salieri's, plus we need the ability to follow Mozart's wife's journey home to "rescue" him. We also find greater depth in the story by following Mozart's very troubled relationship with his father. So early in the story we are given a scene of Mozart at five performing—and Salieri is not in the scene, nor could he have been. Later we are shown brief scenes of Mozart composing, then an extended sequence of his playing with wigs and with "lower-class" musical theater. Salieri tells each of these asides, so they come off as utterly subjective (like Renton's stories in *Trainspotting*), but his accounts are trustworthy enough that they seem omniscient. So in the end, this could be categorized as limited omniscience—it is for the most part Salieri's subjectivity, plus his "unbiased" subjective view of outside events.

Genre, Style, and Tone

Just as what the camera sees is independent of the characters and the events in their lives, there are other aspects of the film that reside exclusively or almost so in the telling, not in the story itself. These elements function best when in service of the story and the intentions of the storyteller. Sometimes the same events—indeed, the same story—can be told for utterly different purposes, with different intentions. And a major means of changing our view of the story events to suit these alternative purposes is through alterations in genre, style, and tone. In each case, the question goes back to what target does the storyteller want to hit. What is the intention?

There are two basic ways of looking at genre, the fundamental and the paradigmatic. When stories were first being studied and theorized about, they were divided into comedy and tragedy. But this left a great void in the middle—stories that weren't intended to be humorous, but that didn't rise to the level of true tragedy, that dealt with the more normal ups and downs of everyday life. These were called drama, and eventually the word came to encompass all forms of storytelling. Thus, "drama" became a spectrum from laughter to tears—like the classic masks of drama—based on the intention of the work, on the intention of the author. So, fundamentally, all stories are dramatic somewhere on that spectrum. And a storyteller in control of his work aims for some particular point on that spectrum—a comedy with serious undertones, a tragedy with moments of lightness and frivolity, a pure drama leaning toward the comic or the tragic side. As with all other aspects of storytelling, it's better—or at least it creates a greater likelihood for success—if one picks a target and aims for it than if one leaves it to chance. A storyteller who leaves it to chance runs a risk of having his serious material laughed at or his hoped-for light moments taken seriously.

In the last hundred years or so, with the advent of cinema and targeted book publishing, genre has also come to mean a much more specific categorization of stories. At first genre meant just the larger categories like thrillers, road stories, epics, and slapstick comedies. But we have also seen the advent of tighter and tighter categories; initially it was romantic comedy or film noir or black comedy or docudrama, then tighter still to gross-out comedy, futuristic western, teen horror picture, and testoserone on wheels. With each successive tightening of the category comes ever greater specificity about the ingredients of the story and how they are assembled. In some ways, this kind of genre thinking leads to the rise of formula-based storytelling. Two teen gross-out horror comedies are necessarily going to include many of the same ingredients and bear distinct resemblance to each other. Two police procedurals will seem alike and include similar kinds of scenes. Two "major illness changed my life" stories will necessarily unfold in similar ways.

This sense of similarity based on genre can be both comforting and distressing to the storyteller *and* to the audience. On the one hand, both the storyteller and the audience know almost immediately what will be involved in the story. On the other hand, if the story is simply a rehashing of the exact same material in exactly the same way, why bother? Neither the writer nor the audience gets much from doing the same thing the same way another time. Chances are, the first time was better anyway, so why not just go to the original? This leaves the creator of a genre story three basic alternatives: follow the paradigm of the genre and hope the characters and the world of the story will provide sufficient newness to the story; fight the genre by turning it on its head or inside out or by trying to drop elements here and there; or tell the story outside the genre, defying the genre expectations, not by using them in different ways, but by surpassing, eclipsing, or tunneling under them. Each approach has its advantages and its drawbacks.

Following the genre gives both the writer and the audience a feeling there is a formula, a recipe, and all that can be changed is the damsel in distress or the murder weapon. Clearly these sorts of films get made and draw an audience that seeks the familiar, and this justifies the same thing being made again with a new damsel and a new weapon. The more specific the genre one chooses, the more of the recipe can be written out. Attractive teenagers are killed off, one by one, by some mysterious and playfully cruel killer who seems to have almost supernatural powers of intuition—which of ten or fifteen movies or movie series does this describe? The author knows going in—and so does the audience—what material there is to play with. Of course, the downside of this approach comes from the same source as the comfort—it all has been done before, in much the same way. This leaves the current version subject to comparison with all the previous versions, and it makes the events of the story and the ending fairly predictable.

To overcome these pitfalls, some storytellers fight against the genre while basically working within it. This choice in genre storytelling requires familiarity with the basic ingredients and the methods of mixing them and, thus, remains dependent on the genre and the audience's expectations. But it has the advantage of apparent familiarity laced with doses of the unexpected that add spice or unpredictability, a sense of newness, to the tried-and-true of the genre formula.

And then there is trying to write beyond the genre. Here the storyteller is striving to delve into new territory, to confound the audience's expectations. This genre choice includes everyone who believes he or she is not telling a genre story at all. Every story must, by definition, fit within a genre; it must reside somewhere on the spectrum from comedy to tragedy. But many authors resist the tighter categories—it's not a romantic comedy, it isn't a thriller, it isn't a teen slasher comedy horror sex romp! It's just a story, a good story, a drama with comic elements, or it's a comedy with real pathos. This approach has the obvious advantage of uniqueness, of an unfamiliar set of ingredients and perhaps a new mode of mixing them, of an expectation or hope of unpredictability. But it also has its downside, both for the writer and for the audience.

When telling a story outside of the familiar categories of genre—either the larger categories or the increasingly specific subcategories—the author has no other similarly told stories to draw on for guidance and possibly inspiration. This might be fine; in fact, the main purpose of this book is to find the inspiration for exploring new—or at least less familiar—roads in storytelling. But there is another side to this desire to "tell stories unlike any that have been told before." There is the problem of finding an audience. It's harder to attract an audience to a story or film that defies categorization, in part because we have all experienced so many stories in our lifetimes and have developed our own tastes and preferences. Before film and television, a person might have experienced a hundred or several hundred stories in his or her life. A voracious reader might have experienced a few thousand. But today, in most areas of the industrialized world, most people experience thousands, if not tens of thousands, of stories in their lives. And at any given time, we have two hundred channels of television, a wide variety of films in the theater, and ten thousand titles of films in the video store to choose from. We can experience any kind of story we want at practically a moment's notice. In this circumstance, trying to attract an audience to a film that defies all familiar description can be extremely difficult. It can also be rewarding. But either way, it's a risk, both for the storyteller and for the audience that chooses to indulge in the unfamiliar.

An adjunct of the genre choice made by the storyteller is the choice of style of storytelling. These two elements are intimately related, but not quite identical. Perhaps the simplest way to see the difference is to look at a couple of Mel Brooks films. Mel Brooks frequently has taken a genre and made a parody of it. *High Anxiety* and *Spaceballs* are good examples of his taking a popular genre and turning it into his brand of comedy. What he is changing is the style of approach to the material that is inherent in the genre. He uses the same exact material, but he changes our view of it or our attitude toward it by varying the style. A parody will always use the target genre's "rules" and conventions, most often in entirely conventional ways, but the difference is the intention; we are not meant to take those conventions seriously. We have been prepared by the style to laugh at the very rules and conventions that propel the genre story.

But style variations exist well beyond the realm of parody. Like the camera as narrator, the style exists outside of the story. But unlike the camera, which the characters are not aware of in most films, the style of a film does invade the world of the characters, though they do not perceive the style as unusual. If a film is animated, it makes a great deal of difference to what the audience sees. Animation obviously changes the "sets" the characters look at, but usually the characters aren't "aware" they are in animated locations. In live action films such as *Batman* and *The Matrix*, what we see is stylistically very different from our world, and this alters what the characters see and experience. Yet to them it is "normal." So we can think of style as an alteration in the presentation of the characters and their world, which changes the audience's perception of the story but seems within the normal realm to the characters.

Style doesn't have to be animated or futuristic or what is often referred to as "stylized." In one film, the style of a suburban neighborhood looks and feels like the world of *American Beauty;* in another, it's the world of *The Brady Bunch Movie*. The houses and trees and lawns aren't very different, but the whole style of what we see and the sense of atmosphere we absorb impact us in radically different ways. These are clear choices made by the storytellers and have an influence on everything from the script to the costume design, production design, even hair and makeup. A style is chosen in support of the intended impact of the story and then is created by the entire production team. And, of course, the style starts in the script.

Even two stories from the same era, about the same era, and made by the same director can have significant stylistic differences. *Schindler's List* and *Saving Private Ryan*—both Steven Spielberg films, both set in World War II, both with many of the same contributors in the production—have different styles. Despite its Holocaust setting and the utter horror of the concentration camps, the cattle cars on the trains, the murder and abuse suffered by so many in the film, there is a certain elegance to the world *Schindler* shows us. There's the obvious elegance of Schindler's suits, some Nazi-era architecture, scenes at parties. But beyond that, there is also something a bit refined about Schindler's factory, his office and his home; there's a perverse grandeur to Amon Goeth's home and the perch from which he shoots prisoners. Even the camp itself is given a richness of detail that makes the life there all the more real and, thus, all the more horrible. The camp isn't elegant in the traditional meaning of the word, but this richness of texture and detail make it seem quite different from the concentration camp in *Life Is Beautiful*, which had different storytelling goals. The style of *Saving Private Ryan* gives us nothing of elegance. It fills us with a sense of grit; it seems dirty and bloody, decrepit, ruined. Even in the incredible opening, the beach landing on D Day—even when we have a panorama of the scale of the invasion—we aren't made to see elegance or grandeur in it. We see dirt, blood, carnage. Later we see ruined buildings, rain and mud, we feel danger from every angle. In *Schindler* we know where the danger comes from; in *Ryan* it can come from any direction. Partly, of course, this difference originates in the story, but partly it is a result of changes in style meant to support different stories. It's storytelling. Choosing the style of presentation, the style of the visuals, even the style of the sound design should be in support of the intended impact.

Like style, tone also is an adjunct of genre, but even farther removed. Yet it is more than merely a variation. Let's go back to Laurel and Hardy falling down the stairs. Why is that funny in their films when the same event can be horrific in another film? It's not that the stairs are steeper or the fall any more potentially dangerous to one character than another. Part of telling a story is preparing the audience to receive the maximum impact from the story. Laurel and Hardy put us in the mood to laugh just by appearing on screen. But imagine we've never seen them before. What creates the conditions that allow us, even prompt us, to laugh? What is happening that the audience doesn't seem to see, but has such a profound impact on how it reacts to the events it is watching?

The tone of a story is most apparent with a sense of atmosphere or mood, but it extends far beyond that. Tone is often described in terms of light and dark. A light comedy, a dark comedy, a black comedy, film noir—these are tonal references that have become genre definitions. Certainly lighting, choice of time of day for scenes, and choice of locations will influence the tone that is set. The middle of the night in a cemetery will create a different tone—especially if there are strange noises, slight movements from the bushes, and so on—than the tone of a park setting on a sunny summer day. But put Laurel and Hardy in that cemetery and it will still be a comic scene. So the setting alone won't create the tone.

There is also the impact of the location and atmosphere on the characters. The audience can take some cues from the characters themselves, but only if it has been taught to trust its feelings as being accurate. We could have a sense of foreboding while a character has no feeling of danger at all. And even if Laurel and Hardy are scared out of their wits in the cemetery, it doesn't mean we will experience the scene as scary. We accumulate a subliminal feeling from our experience of the story as it unfolds about what this storyteller is willing to do to the characters. If a ghoul suddenly attacked and killed Laurel or Hardy, it would be so out of keeping with the tone of the story that there would be a massive defection of the audience. This doesn't mean you can't surprise the audience or even shift a tone to "darker" or "lighter." But the storyteller should establish the plane on which his story will take place and stay on that plane. Huge tonal shifts always bring the risk of a resulting precipitous drop in the audience's connection with the story—meaning a major loss of audience.

A significant part of setting the tone comes from the choice of what to show the audience. Part of what will help Laurel and Hardy stay tonally in a comedy—even if they are in a graveyard at night with lots of hoot owls and eerie noises—is what reactions you show and how you show them. Because you choose everything the audience sees and hears, you set the tone well beyond what the characters do. If you show Laurel quaking in his boots—literally—and it's that sound that agitates Hardy, because we have seen it and know the source of the sound and Hardy doesn't, then you have used the power of cinema to establish or accentuate the tone. If you focus the audience's attention on furtive moves in the bushes, the gleam of moonlight off a knife blade, or slathering drool from a lurking monster—even if we don't see the monster— it might dampen the comic tone the scene needs.

Conversely, if you are setting the tone for murder, intrigue, and fear, you might want to focus on the slathering drool or the sound of the quaking boots, without revealing the source of the sound. These tonal choices—what to show within what is happening and where it is happening, what we hear and how clearly we hear it and can identify it—will support a scary scene. So the tone of a film starts on the page, because the choices of images and sounds start on the page. You can't and shouldn't show absolutely everything and make the audience hear absolutely everything. That would be reneging on the role of the storyteller. Your job is to pick and choose from the thousands or millions of variations available to find the parts of the whole that tell the story most effectively for the impact you intend.

The graveyard could be made romantic if you chose images of the moon, lyrical light through gently waving trees, and bunches of flowers bathed in pastel light—and you downplayed the headstones, the dark ominous shadows, and had no unexpected or unexplainable sounds. Maybe there's even an orchestra playing in the distance. You have given the place a romantic tone by your choices. But you could use the same place, the same moon and night and orchestra, and, by making different choices, shift the tone entirely to fear or even comedy.

So genre, style, and tone are related means of preparing and sustaining the audience's relationship with the events and decisions in the story, the world of the story, and the lives of the characters. And each is a decision—actually a continuous series of decisions—for the storyteller to use in the telling of a story.

Separation of Experience and Knowledge

As you've seen, significant portions of the experience of the audience are independent of the experience of the characters. What we go through during a story is partly above and beyond the events and decisions of the characters in the story. One of the principal means of separating the audience's experience from the characters' is called dramatic irony. As readers of *The Tools of Screenwriting* will recall, dramatic irony is an incredibly effective method for creating both tension and audience involvement in the story. In brief, dramatic irony is the circumstance when we know something that at least one character on screen doesn't know. This separation of the audience's knowledge and awareness from the knowledge and awareness of the characters is a critical part of a larger issue in the telling of the story. Who knows what, and when do they know it? And there is a correlated question. Which parts of the characters' experiences do we share and which parts do we not share?

As you can see, what we the audience know or don't know in no way influences the lives and decisions of the characters, the events of the story, or the effect of those events upon the characters. Yet these differences of knowledge can have a profound impact on our experience of the same exact story. If a character knows there's a cobra in a shoe box he's carrying and we don't— we think there are shoes—his experience of carrying that box and ours will be very different. We won't understand his actions and reactions at all. Or imagine the reverse: we know there's a cobra and he thinks there are shoes in there. Our experience of his carrying it—or dropping it—is profoundly different from his experience. We've probably been on pins and needles while he's been whistling a tune, carefree and happy. Or he could know it and we also know it and we all have the same experience, we all share the same anxieties and fears. The choice of who knows what and which part we share in the characters' experiences is the backbone of storytelling.

When you are telling a story, you must keep track of who knows what among the characters and, especially, the audience. You can use this separation of knowledge to help orchestrate the impact of events on the audience. Let's imagine it's a couple with the shoe box. The man knows the cobra is there, the woman doesn't, and we know both that the man knows and that the woman doesn't know. The handing of the box back and forth, the handling of the box in general, their reactions when it's dropped—everything will be radically different between the man and the woman. And our reactions will have multiple layers because of what we know and what we know they know *and* don't know. This knowledge could be used to shift our loyalty or sympathy from the man to the woman or to reveal that there are lies at the basis of their relationship that we hadn't realized before. Or, if he is continually trying to warn her but she won't let him speak to her because she's angry over a spat, then it could be used to heighten our bond with them as a couple. The selective use of audience knowledge is a key element in creating different kinds of experiences from what are essentially the same events for the characters.

You can also choose to keep the audience away from events completely, either permanently or only for a period of the story. Again, this is a method of heightening the impact of the story and events on the audience. Let's say the couple with the cobra are in a comedy. One of them is going to get bitten and nearly die, but we don't want to experience those near-death throes with a character we have laughed at before and will again. You can cut to the hospital, saving the audience from an experience that would not fit with the tone and style of the story and would probably wake them from the seamless dream. You might cut to the character with his butt stuck in the air (because that's where he was bitten) while doctors save his life—and actually get a laugh out of his misery. He has had the entire experience, but we have only had that part that supported the story and the intentions of the storyteller.

From a storytelling standpoint, the weakest circumstance to create is one in which the characters know more than the audience. Let's return to the man with the cobra in the box when we thought he had shoes. Here we are put in a position of not understanding what is going on or why the man is acting the way he is. We are denied a chance to participate in his experience, even while seeing him have it. This lack of understanding, while it can be an effective setup in the short term, will grow tedious, irritating, boring, or downright anger-provoking if prolonged or repeated too often in one story. Watching a character whose actions and motivations are a complete mystery to us estranges us from the character. We are kept outside of his experience—diminishing our bond with him—and at the same time have been put in a position of experiencing things we don't understand.

In most instances it's a far better strategy to put the audience in at least an equal if not superior position. We should know what the characters know, at a minimum, and we should probably know some of what they don't know. If we know as much as the characters, then we will at least understand the events in their lives and the decisions they make and thus maintain or expand our bond with them. If we know a little bit more, then not only do we understand the events and decisions, but also we are in a position to add a layer of hope or fear of our own as those events unfold and those decisions are made. Because of our superior knowledge, we may want a character to say yes but understand completely while he vacillates between yes and no—because we are aware we know more than he does. He has the experience of making the decision—which we understand and participate in—but we also have another, perhaps even greater experience, of hoping fervently for him to say yes and fearing he'll say no because we know what it will do or mean in the future. So we can have an even more intense experience than the character because we know something he doesn't. We have sat on the edge of our seats the entire time our character has unknowingly carried the cobra in the shoe box; at the same time, he's had a pleasant walk in the park.

By choosing what the audience knows, what the characters know, which parts of the characters' experiences we participate in and which parts to truncate or drop altogether, the storyteller is in a position to orchestrate the experience the audience has for maximum intended impact. The impact can be different for the audience than it is for the characters it has followed in the story. This constant, and usually varied, ebb and flow of intimacy with the characters and their life events is a major source of the power of storytelling. It enables you to create a thought-provoking story about characters who lack introspection. It makes it possible to tell moving stories about characters who are stifled in their own emotional expression. You can make an audience care desperately about the future of a killer or even hope that someone fails in an attempt to do something admirable. By the effective use of this separation of experience and knowledge, you are able to give the audience an experience that equals or surpasses or even contradicts the experience the characters undergo.

Hope versus Fear: The Creation of Tension

As we've seen, what the audience hopes for and what the characters hope for need not be the same thing. The same is true of our fears versus their fears. But how do hope and fear fit into the scheme of storytelling? Hope and fear are about the future. They derive from uncertainty about future events in the story, future decisions the characters might make, future discoveries or revelations that might be unearthed, future outside forces and how they will influence the journey of the characters. When we discuss hope versus fear in dramaturgical terms, this uncertainty is a function solely of the audience and its experience. This is dramatic tension. We hope the man with the cobra in the shoe box won't open the box; we fear he might and get himself or someone else bitten. We don't know what *will* happen, but we know what *might h*appen and therefore feel tension about those possibilities.

Characters also experience uncertainty about their own futures, and this uncertainty can be dramatized in a story. At any given point, we might experience the same tension as the character, a different one or even the exact opposite tension. When our hero has to defuse a bomb as its counter clicks off toward zero, our tension and his tension will be the same. But if he hasn't found the bomb yet and he's looking for it in the wrong building, his tension about getting into that building is different from ours, which is about his finding the bomb in time. And if he is desperately trying to defuse the bomb, thinking that it will explode when that counter clicks to zero, but we know that the very act of defusing this bomb will trigger another bomb elsewhere, then our tension will be the opposite of his. We'll hope he fails to defuse this bomb in time even though we aren't against his final goal.

So dramatic tension is just as separable from the characters as the other aspects of storytelling we've discussed earlier. Clearly the storyteller needs to know exactly what the characters' hopes and fears are at any given time, but the real art involved in the telling side of storytelling is in the creating, sustaining, varying, elaborating upon, and completing of dramatic tension within the audience during the unfolding of the story. To put it simply, if we don't feel some dramatic tension about the future of the characters and the story events, then we are disconnected from the story. We don't care or aren't being allowed to care. If we don't care, the storyteller has failed to create a bond between us and at least one character, where we form hopes and fears about that person's future. If we aren't being allowed to care, then the storyteller has not informed us of what may or may not happen in the near future of the story. Both failures are deadly to drama.

If we don't care enough about at least one character to form hopes and fears, then we are indifferent. Indifference is boredom, being disconnected, uninvolved; it is far removed from the seamless dream. As discussed earlier, we do not have to like or admire a character, just understand her enough to care, to become engaged in her journey. Our hopes and fears can be at odds with the character's own hopes and fears, but you can't have an audience that couldn't care less, one way or the other.

So we must care. The road to caring, as discussed earlier, is through understanding, and also through being part of the decisions the character makes. It's knowing what the character knows and sometimes a little bit more. But there is another requirement to creating dramatic tension: we have to have some idea of what may or may not happen. If we know for certain what will happen, then the story is predictable. But a far worse circumstance is for us to have no idea about what might be around the next bend in the road. This is the circumstance when the cobra is in the shoe box and we don't know it. Maybe the character knows it or maybe he doesn't, but either way, we have no feeling of tension, because we have no reason to believe there is danger in that shoe box. Conversely, if we know the cobra is there, there is tension. If the character is a bad guy we wish would die, we hope the cobra will get out and kill him. If the character is someone we don't wish would die, then we fear it will get out and kill him. Either way, no matter whether we feel positively or negatively about the character, we have a circumstance that creates dramatic tension. And this is true if the man knows the cobra is there or not; in both circumstances we have dramatic tension for the very simple reason that *we know what might happen but we don't know what will happen.* Without this circumstance, we don't have dramatic tension.

So the creation of dramatic tension comes from having at least one character we understand enough to care about—positively or negatively, just so long as we aren't indifferent—and some small idea of what may or may not happen in the future. This isn't reserved just for snake bites and gunshots. The promise of a kiss, a pay raise, drawing a queen on an inside straight, a loose bolt in the airplane's wheels—anything that potentially causes either a positive or a negative future change in the life of at least one character will do.

If we know what the character wants, it is enough to create tension—even if what the character wants is impossible. The act of a character wanting something and trying to get it can create our tension. We could know that there are no queens left in the deck when a character bets on a hand that needs a queen for an inside straight. We know what he wants and we also know it is impossible to get. This is where our tension separates from the character's. He still hopes he'll get that queen, but we don't, because we know it's impossible. But we have fear about what will happen when he doesn't get it and hope that maybe he'll draw a king and at least get a pair or that he won't bet every chip he has on this hand. Just because we know what a character wants doesn't mean we know what will happen. But we know enough to worry, to feel uncertainty, to hope and fear. We are concerned about the future because of the knowledge we have. Knowing what a character wants at any given moment—not every single moment—creates the same circumstance. We have hope or fear about his wants or about the potential change his attempt to achieve his wants will bring about. But without knowledge, it doesn't matter how much we care about the character—we won't feel tension. And if we don't feel tension, we won't be connected, and, wonderful character though he may be, we will disengage from him and his story unless a new tension arises.

Dramatic tension is created by making the audience care about a character and making them suspect there is some potential change ahead, but it is not a static state of being. We don't just get tense about a character and his future and then stay that way until the story is over. Dramatic tension is in a state of flux throughout the course of a story. Some tensions last for only a minute—or even less—on screen, while others carry over many minutes of the story and still others span an entire act. Tensions come in all shapes and sizes; they don't all "belong" to a single character and they aren't all resolved in the same or similar ways in any given story. We can have a short-term tension about a secondary character and, for the moment, relatively little tension about the main character. But when that tension is resolved, our attention usually should be returned to the main character and his path.

A tension is resolved when the character strives to get what she wants and succeeds, fails, or changes her want. If the tension is from an outside source—a pothole on the path—then the character doesn't have to be actively wanting something. Passively, the character is probably not wanting to hit the pothole. But if the pothole is filled with gold, there is still tension because we hope in this case the character *will* hit it. Often when one tension is resolved—that is, it ceases being an active tension for the audience, at least for the moment—it can help create another tension. Our poker player fails to get the queen for the inside straight, but he does get the king and is now tempted to increase his bet. What will he do? We don't know, but we care, and therefore we feel tension, even if we don't know if any other player can beat his pair of kings. We know what he wants and feel tension about what might happen as a result of his pursuing it.

Often we are harboring two or three or more tensions at the same time, some shorter and some longer, some belonging to the main character and others belonging to other characters. We might know what a character wants and have tension based on his pursuit of that objective, and also feel tension about an upcoming pothole on his path. And at the same time, we can be worrying about the love interest, the antagonist and the pretty little girl next to him on the plane. Within the course of a single scene, each of these tensions could be triggered or tweaked for a short response from us—to promote our connectedness—then recede and allow another tension "center stage." But usually, each dramatic scene will have its own primary tension, while the others take a back, but not necessarily silent, seat.

There is a common fear among beginning screenwriters that letting the audience know what a character wants or revealing the potholes on the path of the story will lead to predictability. This is clearly not the case. As we've discussed, just because we know what *might* happen doesn't mean we know what *will* happen. If you hide what the characters want and the potholes on the path, then we continually will have no idea what might happen. As a result of "hiding the story," you have a fairly predictable outcome—boredom and disconnection from the audience. The key to foiling predictability is not in hiding the potential changes in the future, but in varying the ways in which the story deals with and resolves these tensions. If the hero wins every battle in the first hour, the next battle will be predictable: he'll win. If our poor victimized passive protagonist is dumped upon at every turn, then the next turn will be predictable: he'll be dumped on. But as long as we win some and lose some, as long as the outcome is unexpected because of variations in the way the tensions have been created and "cultivated," then the next tension won't have a predictable outcome.

The "Game" of Storytelling

Some readers are doubtless bristling at the suggestion that there is a game involved in storytelling. It's an art form; it's an intellectual enterprise; it deserves much more respect than a mere game! Storytelling *is* an art form, it *is* intellectual, and it most definitely deserves a lot more respect than it is usually accorded. But just like any other art form, it's also a game. Didn't Rembrandt and Renoir "play" with light? Didn't Mozart "play" with a musical theme—even other composers' themes—in a variety of ways? Is a Picasso painting meant to be an exact representation of reality, or is it meant to be subjective? Isn't that playing with us? In fact, a two-dimensional representation of a three-dimensional reality is, by definition, a lie. Our eyes are being toyed with, made to believe something that isn't true. Even a Henry Moore sculpture—in all three dimensions—is playing a game with our perceptions, our imagination and memories. What about M. C. Escher? What about the choreography of Twyla Tharp? The music of Louis Armstrong? The novels of Milan Kundera? The poetry of T. S. Eliot? Isn't each art form an elaborate game with its own set of rules and strengths and limitations? And don't the true artists use these rules, strengths, and limitations to their advantage and break through them using their knowledge and command over their medium? Isn't that, in fact, their art?

In this sense, storytelling is indeed a game—one that is far more complex than chess or bridge. And storytelling for film and television—screenwriting—uses elements of virtually all the other art forms: light, composition, setting, and "the moment" from painting and photography; movement and timing and interrelations with music from dance. It takes place over time and uses mood, changes in tempo and rhythm and recurring themes from music; it uses the intellectual challenge, the characters and relationships and inner worlds of fiction writing; and it uses language for emotional and intellectual impact from poetry. Perhaps a more varied and challenging game will someday be invented, but for the foreseeable future, screenwriting is unparalleled. No other game requires the use of so many art forms and tools; no other game has more complicated, unpredictable, and unique "raw material" from which to build; no other game takes place in time, in three-dimensional space but represented by two dimensions, using words, music, movement, visual images, sounds; no other game uses people, places, and objects with the same exactitude, or modulates the experience of its audience so thoroughly. No wonder there's no such thing as a perfect script or a perfect film. It's a marvel that there are screenplays and films that come close.

Reader-bristling point number two: storytelling, and, as a result, screenwriting, is the process of orchestrating the audience's experience. It is pure manipulation. I hate being manipulated! the bristlers cry. What they really mean is that they hate *feeling* manipulated. If they love films, if they love stories, then they love being manipulated. They just don't want to be aware of it. From the first FADE IN to the final FADE OUT, the audience of any film—feature, documentary, industrial, how to fix a faucet, even cinema verité—is being manipulated. Things are shown on screen and, as a result, other things are cut off; the image is small and distant or enlarged beyond real life. Either way, what we see is being manipulated. Time is cut out, which means it's being manipulated. Music comes from sources on screen and influences us, or it comes from the score—"out of nowhere"—and influences us. By editing two images next to each other the storyteller forces us into making connections of his or her devising—and thus we are manipulated.

When we go into a theater, sit down, and prepare to watch a film, what we are really doing is preparing ourselves to be manipulated for the duration. We hand ourselves over to the storytellers, with the hope and expectation that they are good at what they do, with the desire for them to give us an experience. In order to fulfill their side of the bargain, they must manipulate us: where we are and aren't allowed to look; what we are and aren't allowed to hear; what we care about and hope for and fear; what emotions we conjure up and what areas of thought we delve into. The real trick—and half of the art form of screenwriting—is in making all this nonstop manipulation *seem* not to be manipulation at all.

You want to hide the strings of the puppet show; you don't want to wake the audience from its seamless dream by making your manipulations obvious. But the audience is your ally, because they want what you want, they want to believe. It's just like the delight we take in a really good magic show—we want to be fooled; we don't want to see the springs, trapdoors, and scarves up the sleeve; we want to believe the impossible. And when the magician does his job well, we are thrilled, amazed; we laugh and cry out our disbelief at the believability of the falsehood. It's an amazing conundrum of the human psyche that we can believe and disbelieve all at the same time, be delighted by the experience and even feel genuine emotions while we know what is provoking them is not literally true. We are in a theater, after all, or at home with a video or watching a television program. We aren't out having an adventure or mourning a loved one or meeting with world leaders or kissing that movie star. Yet, because of this conundrum of believing and disbelieving, we are able to have those experiences complete with a full set of emotions.

Many of the key parts of the game of storytelling have already been discussed, primarily in the sections that deal with separating what the audience sees and hears and knows and cares about from what the characters see and hear, know and care about. But there are still other elements of the game that come into play, which also deal with orchestrating the audience's experience. Let's go back to that favorite film of yours, the one that came closest to putting you into a seamless dream all the way through. Wasn't there some moment during the film when you were just aching for something to happen or be revealed? Maybe you wanted two characters to admit they loved each other or for one to open the door and find out the secret before it was too late. It could have been for the climber finally to reach the top of the mountain or the scientist to find the formula or the composer to complete the symphony. It might even have been as simple as the recluse finally setting foot outside the door or a villain being caught red-handed. Whatever it was, chances are you were made to wait longer than you wanted. You were willing to continue waiting, hoping and fearing, aching to know or to be there. You were literally or figuratively on the edge of your seat. This process is called retardation.

At its core, retardation is simply making the audience want something and then making them wait to get it. The entire time between the first wanting of a future event and the final completion of it—win, lose, draw, or change—is the process of milking the audience's connection to the story and the characters. Obviously, this is a correlative of dramatic tension—establishing hope versus fear, elaborating on it and then resolving it. Retardation can't work without dramatic tension. How retardation takes off from that starting point is the game playing of storytelling in a nutshell.

How long can we make the audience wait? How long is too long? Can we make them think the dramatic tension is about to be resolved and then pull back from it? Will that be too frustrating? Or will it be deliciously frustrating? How many *years* did *X-Files* fans have to wait for Scully and Mulder to kiss? Did those fans quit watching out of frustration, or watch even more intently? How long do we have to wait for Rick to express his love for Ilsa in *Casablanca*? How long are we made to suffer with Agent Starling as she stalks the killer through the house at the end of *The Silence of the Lambs*?

And, of course, not wanting something is still wanting something. If we fear a potential future moment, retardation works just as effectively. In *The Godfather*, we fear Michael becoming fully enmeshed in the power and violence of his father's role of being the don. Even after he kills the men who set up the assassination attempt on Don Vito, Michael is swept away to the bucolic world of rural Italy and seems to have escaped permanent residence in the violent world of organized crime. So the question of his future role remains alive all this time—the answer is retarded—and our dramatic tension is prolonged, which extends and deepens our connection with the character and the story. But if the retardation were kept going too long, it would eventually weaken or sever our connection. Knowing how long is long enough and not too long is the finesse of the game.

Another correlative of dramatic tension is ellipsis. This simply means cutting out time. Ellipsis will be dealt with extensively later, but briefly, there are two forms of ellipsis: short term and long term. Short-term ellipsis could be cutting out the time it takes to draw a bath or boil water or unlock a lock or get dressed. It can also extend to driving across town or even flying to another location. But the dramatic tension being felt by the audience before the ellipsis continues over these short jumps in time—and so do the dramatic actions of the characters. These short ellipses are really a part of effective scene writing more than they are the game of storytelling. But longer-term ellipses become tools in playing the game. What constitutes longer term is relative; in a story that takes place over two hours in the lives of the characters, a long-term ellipsis might be a quarter of an hour; in a saga that takes place over a lifetime, a long-term ellipsis might be a decade or two.

If film is "life with the boring parts cut out," as Alfred Hitch-cock said, then ellipsis is the primary tool for that cutting. By longer ellipses we do not mean the cutting of little boring parts within larger actions that still carry dramatic tensions across the ellipsis. Longer ellipses cut out the time *between* dramatic tensions. When we have followed a dramatic tension and it finally is resolved, a new status quo is established by the resolution of that dramatic tension (not to be mistaken with *the* resolution of the story). This new status quo could remain unchanged for fifteen minutes or fifteen years. During that time, nothing of true interest to the story is taking place. If something of real interest does take place, then that would be starting a new status quo and should be dramatized. But so long as a status quo remains unchanging *as it impacts the story*, then this is the kind of time we ellipse in the game of telling the story.

For instance, a character completes a dramatic tension by getting a new job or moving to a new house or divorcing a spouse or starting an exercise routine; so long as that process or state of being continues without significant changes, we don't need to see that time in the life of the character. She might get a raise at the job, buy a new couch for that house, collect or pay alimony, or de-velop a great set of abs, but as far as the tensions and conflicts of the story are concerned, nothing of importance has happened. The status quo established by the resolution of the dramatic ten-sion remains intact. This is the time we want to cut out. By not re-turning to the character until something new is about to happen in the issues of the story, we have "cut out the boring parts" and intensified the experience the audience has of the life of the char-acter. We don't have to experience those ten years he spends sweeping floors as a janitor; we only have to return the last night, when he buys the lottery ticket that will change his life.

You don't want to carry an urgent and immediate dramatic tension concerning a particular character across a longer ellipsis. You might carry an overall tension about the character's life and goals across this chasm of time that we don't see or participate in. But the storyteller should not plant an immediate will-she-or-won't-she question in the audience's mind and then cut out ten years of her life. This will give us the feeling that she must have solved the problem when we weren't allowed to see. Just as retardation prolongs and intensifies our connection to a dramatic tension and the characters it involves, longer ellipses save us from long bouts without those connections.

Another orchestrating tool, which has partially been dealt with in the section "Separation of Experience and Knowledge," concerns the creating and revealing of secrets. As is now clear, you can keep secrets from some characters, share secrets with others; we can know what the characters know and don't know and who hopes for what, who fears what, and so on. How this fits into the game of storytelling is clear; the storyteller is picking and choosing what to let the audience in on and what to withhold from them, moment by moment, all with the aim of creating the maximum impact from the events, the wants, and the secrets. But secrets hold another tantalizing aspect for the audience that becomes an effective tool for the storyteller. Human beings naturally love secrets and conspiracy. Why are gossip and scandal so universal? They indulge the world's boundless enthusiasm for "being in on" secrets. Whatever someone else is trying to keep secret becomes the very thing we most want to know. This is a normal—albeit slightly perverse—human response. Look how effectively this notion was put to use in *Wag the Dog*. They only had to "try" to keep information secret and it was the most effective tool for disseminating lies and making them believable.

As storytellers we can use this natural affinity for wanting to be in on secrets to maneuver the audience where and when we want, placate them at times, tantalize them at times, make them part of a "conspiracy" or strengthen their bond with a character by allowing them to share a secret with the character. When we first meet Lester in *American Beauty*, he's masturbating in the shower and calling it the high point of his day. Isn't that letting us in on his secret, fostering a bond with him, putting us "in the know," and encouraging us to bond more with him than we do with his wife, who doesn't know his secret? Ultimately, the secret has nothing to do with the story, doesn't further the plot in any way, but it does reveal his character to us and makes us his "co-conspirators" in sustaining the secret. In *Shakespeare in Love* we're let in on the secret of the two lovers, fostering our bond with both of them far above all the other characters. In *The Apartment*, we're let in on Baxter's twin secrets, that he's falling in love with Fran Kubelik and that he allows his apartment to be used for other men's trysts. Of course the men who use his apartment know that secret, but they don't know about Fran. Fran Kubelik feels Baxter's interest, but she doesn't know about the apartment. Only we know both secrets. And the doctor next door, who thinks everything going on in the apartment is Baxter's doing, helps point out how "in the know" we are, because he is so wrong.

Secrets between two characters that we also share create bonds between the characters, which may or may not survive. In *The Godfather*, when Don Vito tells Michael that a friend will be the one to set him up to be killed, we share a secret with the father and son that they keep from all other characters in the story. We are insiders, and we harbor the secret along with them. And when Sal Tessio is the friend who betrays Michael, we feel an even stronger bond with Michael, because we shared the secret. Another example of bonding with a character—this one in an entirely negative way—is when Michael has his own brother Fredo killed in *The Godfather: Part II*. We share in his guilt and in the numbing prospect of having to sustain such a horrendous secret afterwards. In *Blade Runner*, Deckard is told the secret that has been kept from Rachael, that she is a replicant. So we are actually following two secrets—that Rachael is a replicant and that he knows. Participating in how he deals with the secret information strengthens our bond with him, while the secret itself increases our sympathy for her, because we know how devastating it will be if she finds out. While many of these secrets play into the stories, often a larger part of their impact on us comes from the increase in intimacy we feel with the characters whose secrets we share. Secrets make us feel like "friends" who have been confided in.

This is another aspect of secrets that becomes an effective tool—revealing them to other characters. Establishing a secret is just like setting up any other dramatic tension; we begin to hope and fear about its eventual discovery or revelation. We look for opportunities and danger signals. We anticipate what might force the secret out into the open or what might help keep it covered up. Combine this dramatic tension with retardation and the results can be doubled. In *Double Indemnity,* after Walter Neff has killed the husband and seems to have gotten away with it, he goes in to work and sees the man who had spoken to him at the back of the train, when he'd been pretending to be the husband on the crutches. We are Neff's coconspirators; even against our own will, we find ourselves hoping this killer will succeed in his plan. And this witness is a fly in the ointment. Our bond with Neff is milked and even deepened, while at the same time it seems to take forever for him to find out whether or not the man will be able to identify him.

But we don't necessarily have to reveal one character's secrets to other characters in the course of a story. We can end *The God-father: Part II* with Michael still maintaining his secret that he had Fredo killed. At the end of *Blade Runner,* Deckard still hasn't told Rachael she's a replicant. At the end of *Butch Cassidy and the Sundance Kid,* Butch still hasn't revealed to Sundance that he's always been in love with his wife. Unlike a dramatic tension that in some way requires a resolution (there will be much more on this later), a secret we share with a character can remain "unresolved" in the sense that it doesn't have to come out. Its true purpose is in making us closer to the character, not in fostering the story. And, of course, some secrets can do both.

Another element in the game of telling stories is variation. Variations in pace and intensity help keep the story from getting into a rut. And variations in duration, detail, and even distance from a scene serve to help keep the audience awake, alive, on its toes, and paying maximum attention. These kinds of variations aren't about fostering character identification, furthering the plot or themes of the story, or even directly heightening our tension. They are mostly ways of orchestrating the experience of the audience for the greatest intended impact by giving us a change in the nature of the experience. If every scene played out in exactly the same degree of detail and completeness, at the same pace and the same intensity, we would start to experience the film as a drone; we'd fall asleep. Even if every scene were at breakneck speed with rock video editing, it still would be the same and it would bore us to death. We need fast scenes, slow scenes, loud scenes, quiet scenes, light scenes, dark scenes, colorful scenes, intense and short and to-the-point scenes, long lyrical scenes. We need to be in the characters' faces and we need to see them from a distance. We need talky scenes and nondialogue scenes, crisply paced and edited scenes, and scenes that play out in one long shot. In a word, we need variety. This variety comes in the ways we experience the material of the story, not the material of the story itself.

Building
Stories

THE CREATION OF DRAMA

You've all seen bumper stickers or T-shirt slogans that declare: SHIT HAPPENS. Nowhere is that more true than in storytelling. For the storyteller, the backside of that T-shirt should read, BUT DRAMA IS CREATED! If left to chance, to some form of arbitrary selection, even the best potential collision between characters and a world will more often than not result in a boring story. A good storyteller makes thousands of decisions about what to reveal, what to hide, when to show things, when to accentuate, when to downplay, when to cut out, how to reveal essentially internal things, how to make sure the audience picks up the right clues but doesn't get ahead of the story. All of these decisions are the substance of storytelling with the goal of creating the seamless dream experience for the audience. Just as the notes in a symphony aren't just "any old notes in any old order," the moment-by-moment beats of a story are composed with care and precision.

Dramatic events happen in our own lives and in the lives of friends and relatives. These events can have a profound impact on our lives, and they "just happen." Why can't a story do the same thing? We are already involved in our lives and the lives of our friends and relatives; we care. For similar events to have the maximum impact on an audience, those strangers must be turned into friends, we must be made to care about them just as we do about our own lives. This occurs through the conscious efforts of the storyteller; there is no happenstance involved. Unlike real life, where we all strive for the easiest possible way through the thicket life presents us—the route that causes the least hardship, takes the smallest toll, and requires the least time facing difficult challenges—a story has the opposite goal. In a story the storyteller strives to create difficulties for his characters, tries to put them through the wringer for the express purpose of giving the audience a proxy version of that difficult and trying experience. In order to turn the substance of life's hardships and conflicts into the stuff of drama, the storyteller must make thousands of choices and find hundreds of interconnections among the people, events, themes, and travails that will amount to the story being told. In this sense, every story is a prototype, every story is built fresh, from the ground up.

Main Character or Ensemble Story?

Usually the first decision a storyteller must make is, Who is the story about? Who is my main character, my protagonist? Can it be two people's stories, in which they're both in the same boat, facing the same obstacles? What if I have a whole crew of people stuck in the wilderness as fire moves toward them from one side and cannibals move in from the other; isn't it all of their stories? Whose life we follow or whose want determines where the story goes or who makes the decisions that direct the audience's experience in the story or whom we are made to care about the most or whose eyes we will see the story through—not all of these questions will be satisfied in equal measure by every story, but these are variations on how to start the process of deciding whose story to tell.

Let's take the Battle of Waterloo as an example. You could tell it as Napoléon's story or as Wellington's. But you also could choose to tell it from the perspective of a foot soldier in the English army or a foot soldier in the French army, or a midlevel officer in either army, or an aide to either general. Or you could choose to tell it from the perspective of a boy who lived in Waterloo and upon whose family land the battle was waged. You might tell it from the viewpoint of a courier who desperately rode through hostile territory to get a do-or-die message to one leader or the other. Or you could tell it from the viewpoint of a deserter from either army or a spy for either side. There are many potential views of the same essential events available. So the events don't automatically determine whose story viewpoint will be taken.

A crucial element in deciding whose story to tell—whose viewpoint to take—comes back to theme. What part of the human experience do you wish your story to explore? Each potential central character, each viewpoint, comes with its limitations on how completely we can view the entire complexity of the battle and all that led up to it. And each comes with its own potential aspect of human life that you might explore. From world-conquering ego to cowardice to the collision of a romanticized view of war with the nasty reality of it, you have a wealth of themes you could explore.

As always, the question returns to, What do you want it to be? What is your intention? You could want to make an idealized version of the defeat of a tyrant or a gritty view of the "cannon fodder's" role in other men's ambitions. You could want to make a story about bravery and sacrifice or a story about futility or redemption. Because the carrier of the story—the protagonist—is also the carrier of the theme, it is not possible to separate the question of whose story it is from the question of what the story is ultimately about. Certainly it's possible to know going in that Napoléon will be the main character, but the question is, which Napoléon? Will it be the ego-driven madman out to conquer the world, or will it be a Napoléon following a fate he knows all too well is doomed and to which he is resigned?

The answer to the question—whose story is it, or who can carry the story's theme—isn't just in the body of the protagonist; it's in the nature of the character. Just saying that Abraham Lincoln or Adam or Madame Curie is the central character doesn't really nail down who the character is. It gives us a start. We can't make Abe Lincoln into a baseball player with a nervous condition or Madame Curie into a vaudeville comedienne who is a binge alcoholic, but the essential nature of the character is the real issue, not who the person was in historical context. And, of course, with a fictional story, we don't even have an historical starting point.

But a "real" person from history or a person solely from the mind of the author still requires the same wrestling to be done: What is the essential nature of the character? And this question returns us to, What is the theme?

So you're faced with a chicken-and-egg dilemma: How can you decide on the essential nature of your central character without knowing the theme in advance? How can you know the theme without knowing the nature of your character? The best answer—albeit a dissatisfying one to those of you who want a formula to work from—is to trust your instinct. Trust your unconscious mind. If you've been mulling over your story for some time, then chances are you've started to form, or half-form, ideas about your character and theme. Nail one thing down—your Napoléon deeply believes in fate—and then try it for a while as you explore what impact that first decision has on your theme and your approach to the story. Then take it a step farther and another step, working both to discover the essential nature of your protagonist and to discover and focus the theme.

Does this mean I can't tell a story about two characters facing the same dilemma? What about an ensemble story? Most of the time, as readers of *The Tools of Screenwriting* will recall, when there are two characters sharing center stage, one of them dominates; one of them makes the primary decisions for the pair. But multiple stories are possible. We can follow Colonel Nicholson, the builder of a bridge, and Shears, the man assigned to blow it up, as we do in *The Bridge on the River Kwai.* Here we have two stories interwoven, each with its own central character; each of them plays a secondary role in the other's story. The themes that the two protagonists embody are related to each other so that the entire film maintains a unity. But notice, this is not the story of two characters facing the same problem. Each man has his own dilemma—from opposite sides of the same issue. If they were both faced with blowing up the bridge, for instance, then one or the other would dominate. Two people don't share the same exact goal from the same set of strengths and weaknesses, obsessions and blind spots.

Two characters may be in the same exact dilemma—they are both hanging from the side of a cliff as a storm and night approach.

But if they are identical in their ability to climb, their fear of heights, their strength and fortitude and emotional reserves, then they are redundant. One of them should be cut. If one is a good climber and the other is a novice, but the good climber is injured and the novice has to take the lead in solving their shared problem, then maybe the better choice for protagonist is the novice climber. He could better embody the theme, which might be courage, for instance. He is facing for the first time a challenge that the expert climber has faced many times; experiencing the story through him could be more compelling and resonant for the audience than just another harrowing climb in a history of harrowing climbs for the expert.

Just as two characters don't face one dilemma in identical ways, a group can't possibly be the protagonist of a story. There are going to be as many variations on the approach to the dilemma—the goal and its obstacles—as there are people. If we try to make all of them protagonists, what results is a mishmash of conflicting perspectives that ultimately diminishes and probably destroys the story. So usually there will be one perspective that we take as "our own," and the other perspectives will become secondary. Some of those secondary perspectives could become subplots. We aren't limited to the leader of the group as the protagonist; we can certainly identify with the weakest person in the situation or the one with an outsider's view or the closest loved one of the leader. It depends on which part of the range of human problems—which theme—you want to explore. Then you choose the character that best carries that theme.

Does this mean that we can't have ensemble stories at all? No. We can tell ensemble stories, but what that really means is a group of interlocking stories, each with its own protagonist and each with a thematic link to the others. Here, instead of having a protagonist and several subplots, we are telling three or four or five different stories, each around its own single protagonist, and then weaving them all together into one "whole." None of the various stories dominates the others enough to be the main story, even if they don't all have the same amount of screen time. So an ensemble film is more analogous to a book of short stories than it is to a novel. There needs to be some thematic linkage among the stories so there is a sense of unity to the film, so that it feels as if these stories belong together. The various protagonists might play secondary roles in the other stories, but this isn't required by any means. There have been quite successful compilation films that follow widely different casts of characters in each story, where the linkage or unity is a prop or location or even a costume, as in *Tales of Manhattan,* where the story follows a tuxedo with tails.

So there can be multiple protagonists in a single film, but, except for an epic in which the film's length is often double that of a regular feature, one of the prices to be paid for multiple protagonists is the amount of story that can be told. There simply is less screen time per protagonist in which to develop characters, establish wants and goals, present obstacles, build effective dramatic scenes, and reach satisfying resolutions. Something has to give, and that something is often depth as well as length. We can't get as deeply into the life of a character in twenty or twenty-five minutes as we can in one hundred minutes. This reason alone is why most feature films are based around a single, clearly identifiable central character. Those hundred minutes might seem rather daunting when you're on page one of your first screenplay, but they really are a short amount of time to get the job done. Since our job as screenwriters is to get the audience involved in the lives of characters, elaborate and strengthen that involvement, and then bring it to an end, it's usually a lot easier and more effective to do that with one character than with two or more.

Protagonist and the Creation of Story

One of the most common complaints among beginning screenwriters is, "I know who my main character is, but I don't know what he wants." Or "She doesn't want anything." It might sound like a cheap paraphrase of an advertising slogan, but *nobody doesn't want something.* A person can want to be left alone; she can want to maintain the exact status quo of her life as it is today; he can want life to be easier or more exciting or less exciting or more serene; she can want her responses to be more under her control or less controlled; he could want a chance to make up for a past mistake or want the world finally to acknowledge a past triumph; he might want to avoid dealing with troubles that are eating away at his insides; she might just want to get home from work or to continue living or to end her life. All of these and thousands more are wants around which stories could be built.

For the purposes of building a story, let's assume our protagonist does indeed want something, even if we don't yet know what it is or it doesn't seem compelling enough to build a story around. As we discussed earlier, the creation of a story comes from a collision of a character who wants something with the world in which the story takes place. If the character's want is relatively inactive—she wants to maintain her status quo—then the world, or a person in it, must become the activator of the collision. Rising floodwaters are about to drive her off the farm or the local robber baron is taking over all the land in the county. Now there is a collision, because her desire to maintain her status quo is under assault from the outside.

If the protagonist's want is active—he wants to start his own business—then the world can be passive or indifferent. Or the world can be in active opposition, which makes it a collision between two moving objects—the protagonist against the antagonist or against an antagonistic world. Or an active want can be forced upon a character who was previously passive. He is given an assignment he must take, a goal chosen by outside forces; she discovers her child is in danger and instantly becomes active in attempting to do something about it. One way or another, the protagonist is ultimately responsible for his or her own dilemma—the collision between the want and the world. Even when an outsider comes in and "forces" the protagonist to take on a goal or to defend herself, in the end, the decision remains with the protagonist. The protagonist decides to accept the job rather than pay the consequences of not taking it or fights against being swept away in a flood rather than accept the loss of her life. If the consequences are dire enough—as in the loss of one's life in a flood—then the decision is a no-brainer, but it's still a decision.

So ultimately, in some fashion, the protagonist chooses his collision either by actively seeking something from a passive, indifferent or hostile world or by choosing to accept or resist an outside force from an antagonistic world or an antagonist. But what about a character who is hit by lightning or by a runaway train? Certainly these incidents can be part of a protagonist's story and might even be the single most important event in creating the story, but they can't be the actual collision that creates the story. It seems odd, so let's explore it. Our protagonist just wants to get home from work but is blindsided by a runaway train and badly injured. He made no decision involving that train, never knew it was coming. The story can't be just about that incident; it has to be about the consequences of that incident. The story will come from what decisions the protagonist makes as a result of having been hit by that train. Does he choose to fight for his life or does he choose to give up and die? If the story is only about "Will he be hit by the train or not?" then at no time can the protagonist have any impact on his own fate. He is merely a victim. Nothing he does or decides will make any difference in what happens to him.

This doesn't stop us from telling stories about people who are the victims of outside forces. It just means that the stories are really about what the people choose to do about having been victimized. It's not Sarah Connor's fault that the Terminator has come from the future to kill her. And it's a no-brainer that she doesn't want him to succeed, but she chooses to try to live rather than just wait for him to kill her. Without that decision, there would be no story. It isn't Captain Miller's idea to go through Nazi territory on a mission in *Saving Private Ryan*, but he chooses to obey the orders of his superior officers. Again, it might be a foregone conclusion that he will accept the assignment, but in a sense he is a victim of his superiors and their perception of him as someone up to the job.

A great many stories stem from characters who make a conscious and active choice to pursue something. It could be running for political office, running from the police, robbing a bank, trying to invent something, pursuing someone as a lover or as a target, or escaping a lover or a jailer. In this sort of story, it's easier to see how the protagonist is the creator of his or her own story. But it's best to keep in mind that all protagonists should be given the opportunity, however lopsided, of choosing the direction of the story. No matter how good a hand or bad a hand a character is dealt in a poker game, he still has the choice of making a bet, raising the stakes, folding the hand, or leaving the game altogether. Any of those decisions potentially creates that protagonist's story; the dealing of the hand is only the first part of instigating the decision.

Worthy Antagonist

In order for the protagonist's story to resonate for the audience, for us to find it compelling enough to warrant our time, attention, and emotional involvement, he or she needs to face significant obstacles to achieving the want. These obstacles are often, but far from always, personified in one person, the antagonist of the story. The history of cinema is filled with wonderful and detestable antagonists, from Nurse Ratched to Darth Vader to Colonel Kurtz to Al Capone. These antagonists directly oppose the goals of the protagonists and work not only for their own ends, but to foil the protagonists' hopes for success. The closer the match between the antagonist and the protagonist, the more uncertain the outcome of their collision course, the greater the tension and the unpredictability. We know what battle may be ahead of us but we certainly don't know what will happen. So a worthy protagonist deserves—and needs—a worthy antagonist. Weak opposition won't test the mettle of the main character; impossible opposition will make the ultimate failure predictable. Indiana Jones faces his rival, Beloche, who musters the support of a formidable array of Nazi soldiers and spies. Prince Hamlet faces the king, Claudius, and his minions. McMurphy faces Nurse Ratched and the power structure of the psychiatric ward. These are made into even matches so that the story won't be predictable and the battle between rivals will test everything the protagonist has and is.

How do we build a worthy and worthwhile antagonist? We start with the protagonist. Where is our central character weak, uncertain, frail, blind, ignorant? Whatever the weaknesses of our main character are, they are a good starting point for finding the strengths of the antagonist. And to make it a good match, the strengths of the hero should reflect the weaknesses of the villain as well. Where McMurphy finds humor in everything, Nurse

Ratched is humorless; where he fights against the system, she *is* the system; where he openly admits to his lifetime of mistakes and weaknesses, she sits in judgment of every one else's faults; where he pretends disdain for many of his fellow inmates while actually coming to care for them, she feigns great concern to mask her manipulative contempt for them. This is a good match, one that we can't predict a winner for—a worthy and complex antagonist for a worthy and complex protagonist.

But an outside antagonist isn't the only possible form of obstacle for a story to be well told. The world of the story can be antagonistic to the wants of the main character; even its indifference can create sufficient identifiable obstacles. Let's go back to our novice and expert climbers on the side of the mountain. The mountain is their chief obstacle and is indifferent to their efforts to scale its heights. If there were earthquakes, it would be actively antagonistic, but its very existence—its passive opposition to the goal of the protagonist—is enough obstacle to arouse our hopes and fears. But we could up the stakes by making the world more antagonistic, not merely passively resistant. If there are earthquakes, a blizzard and avalanches, the world of the story itself is antagonistic.

Ironically, we still look to the protagonist to help find the nature of an indifferent or antagonistic world. Her fears, weaknesses, blind obsessions, and ignorant areas are still the best raw material to mine for building a world hostile to the goals and wants of the protagonist. In *Brazil*, Sam Lowry rails against the world he lives in. That world is a sociopolitical construct, a system of government and way of life that is stifling to him. If he didn't find life in it unbearable, the world would remain indifferent to him and his plight. It is only because he chooses to take action against the world that the world bites back. There are identifiable "defenders" of that world who could be considered villains of the story, but in fact it is the system of life to which they are obedient that is the true antagonist. The world of the story is the antagonist.

The third potential location of the antagonist—besides another character or the world of the story—is inside the protagonist himself. Two aspects of the same character can be at war with each other; the protagonist is his own antagonist. We are put in the position of taking sides, of hoping one side prevails and fearing the other side will "win." This isn't limited to stories about people with multiple personalities or schizophrenia. The Michael Corleone character in *The Godfather: Part II* is at war more with himself than he is with the law enforcement establishment or other members of organized crime. One side of him wants to extract "the family" from the world he inherited and push the business toward "legitimacy." But the other side of him is mired in the long-established rules for behavior in crime families and his own specific family's traditions, which he wants to uphold.

So a story can be built around a protagonist who is ambivalent—who wants two competing and opposing things at the same time. Or it can be a battle between a character who wants something and is unable to force himself to do it or is too weak to do it. *The Lost Weekend i*s such a story. Don Birnam is a writer who is worthy of his brother's nearly endless patience and the love of his fiancée, but he is also an alcoholic who seems incapable of stopping himself. There is no outside villain, but there is a battle going on nonetheless, and we are encouraged to have hope and fear about which side will prevail.

When building our antagonist—whether it is the world, a character, or an aspect of the central character—we must decide the essential nature of the antagonist, just as we must with the protagonist. Is it evil, and, if so, does it know it's evil? Or is it just opposed to the character for its own understandable, and perhaps worthy, goals? Is it intractable, or is it capable of change? Let's compare two antagonists who are characters, Dr. No and Sergeant Foley in *An Officer and a Gentleman*. Dr. No is evil and knows it; he has his own goals but he makes no rationalization that they are for the good of mankind. He just wants dominance. Sergeant Foley is a good man. He is concerned about his job, about the men he trains, and is convinced Zack Mayo is not cut out to become an officer. He is the chief outside obstacle for Zack, but he warrants some of our sympathy and understanding. And, in the end, when Zack passes and Sergeant Foley salutes him, we don't hate him or even look down on him as a defeated villain. He's an antagonist, but that doesn't automatically make him evil.

When the world is the antagonist, it can present benign opposition; no matter how hostile it is to the characters there isn't evil intent behind it. Or it can be an evil world. Our climbers on the side of the mountain during earthquakes and storms face a hostile world, but not an evil one. In *Brazil* or *Logan's Run*, the world itself is evil, a malevolent design created either by evil designers or by misguided forces.

And when the antagonist is an aspect of the same character, we still have the same choices. In *The Lost Weekend*, when Don Birnam is at war with himself, the alcoholic is weak and self-destructive, but it isn't evil, it isn't out to do harm to the world and others. But in *Raging Bull*, when Jake La Motta is at war with himself, the antagonistic side is very dangerous. It might not be classically evil, but the lashing out is so violent and so harmful to others that it isn't far from evil in the essence of its character. And in *The Professional*, Léon is a hit man who befriends a troubled girl, Mathilda. The two sides of him are at war with each other even while there are also outside obstacles for him. The hit man side of him is a methodical and cold-blooded killer, a killer for hire—this side is definitely evil. The story becomes one of finding and accentuating the potential good person inside such a killer. And it certainly encourages our hope and fear about which side will win the battle.

Supportive and Reflective Characters

Now that we have the two sides picked for the primary conflict of the story, how do we find the rest of the cast? Are they just anybody we want to put in there? Or, conversely, is there a recipe or formula we can work from to choose whom else we need? Do we actually need anyone else, or can we tell the story with just the two sides since that creates the primary conflict, the main collision?

It's possible to tell a story well with just two characters, as has been shown in the highly acclaimed films *The African Queen* and *Hell in the Pacific*. In the first we have the protagonist, Rosie, facing an antagonistic world, the river and the jungle. And we have the love interest, Charlie, who is her partner in the quest. But she is the definite decision-maker in their partnership, so it is her story. There are other characters in the first and third acts, but the bulk of the story—and by far the most compelling part—features just the two characters. In the second film, we have only the American pilot and the Japanese naval officer and an indifferent world in which they fight out their battle, which is a microcosm of World War II.

But most stories have more than two cast members. There is no formula to help us choose the remainder of the significant cast, but there are guideposts to look for in the relationships of the other characters with the protagonist and antagonist. In essence, we look for ways in which these other characters work for or against one side or the other—both for the characters and for the audience. If the protagonist has a best friend, does he support the hero in his quest, or seek to undermine it either through designs of his own or failures of his own? Does the friend help pull the main character one direction or the other? Does the friend help us understand the journey of the protagonist more fully or to experience it more emotionally? And, of course, if there is an outside antagonist, he or she can also have a friend or assistant and we must ask the same questions of support, undermining, and the audience's experience.

There can also be indifferent characters who become enlisted on one side of the main conflict or the other, or even temporarily shift from one side to the other and back again. *Jaws* is a good example of the various potentials. Chief Brody is the protagonist and the shark is the antagonist. Matt Hooper is a friend who supports Chief Brody's goal of defeating the shark. Quint is a more complex character. At times, he is indifferent to the chief's quest and follows his own needs. At other times he is definitely in support of the chief. And when he destroys the radio in a fit of anger to make this a do-or-die battle with his lifelong enemy, he is abetting the shark by denying the chief the ability to "call in the cavalry."

There can also be characters whose primary dramaturgical role is to reflect on the plight of the protagonist. That is, by pursuing similar, related, or even identical goals but undergoing a significantly different sequence of events and a different resolution, this kind of character can help to flesh out our experience of what the protagonist is going through in the story. For instance, there could be two best friends who are both sprinters training for the Olympics in the same event. One is our protagonist, the other a reflective character. He might also function in other capacities, but for here, his primary job is to allow a broader exploration of the commitment to training, the dedication and sacrifice needed, the prices to be paid. The faster runner could be either the protagonist or his best friend; the one tempted into taking steroids could be either the protagonist or the best friend; the one with gigantic inner doubts could be either of them. It isn't automatic that the better or stronger or faster is going to be the protagonist. Here, the second, reflective character permits us is to broaden the exploration of the same issues the protagonist is going through beyond the limits of his singular experience of them.

Let's take a look at *An Officer and a Gentleman*. Zack Mayo is the protagonist, Sergeant Foley and the system he represents is antagonist, and Sid Worley is the reflective character, the best friend. Zack and Sid are both striving to survive the rigorous training exemplified by the sergeant, whom they consider the enemy. Both of them have girlfriends from the local community and both have military fathers about whom they have complicated feelings. Zack's ups and downs during the story and training are different from Sid's, as are their ultimate resolutions. Sid is very supportive of Zack while they go through the same training, but they exhibit different strengths and weaknesses, which is how Sid's character helps "reflect" back on Zack and his experience. Sid's story, which is a subplot of the film, helps point out what is difficult that Zack can do well, what he can't do well, plus what Zack is blind to, what he does and does not care about, how he changes. And particularly in the resolutions of their love relationships with the two women, Sid's story reflects back—and magnifies—Zack's story as it unfolds.

The "love interest" character can be an interesting amalgam of these various forces at work. Not every story has a love interest, but this kind of role is not by any means limited to romances, romantic comedies, and the like. The love interest could be a child, a grandparent, a pet, or a robot. The love interest is simply the character whose love, approval, acceptance, or attention is sought either by the protagonist or by the audience *for* the protagonist. In fact, the love interest can conceivably also function in another capacity, even as the antagonist. *October Sky* has such a circumstance, where Homer hopes and strives for his father's approval all the while he fights against him. His father isn't exactly the antagonist, but he is the chief spokesman for the antagonistic society against which Homer must fight. When Homer finally manages to achieve his father's acceptance in the end, it is immensely satisfying to him and to the audience. In *Schindler's List*, the love interest isn't Schindler's wife or one of his lovers, but Itzhak Stern, whose approval Schindler seeks and thrives on. He is the best friend and a supporter of Schindler's goals, but he also prods, disapproves, questions, and misunderstands. Ultimately, his belief in Schindler constitutes the love the story creates.

What we don't want for principal roles—the four or five other characters in addition to the protagonist—is characters who are utterly tangential to the main character and the main story line. This doesn't mean we just pick and choose characters in relation to the protagonist as if we're picking parts to build a bicycle. Rather, it's the other way around. First we want to people our story with the logical characters who would be in the life of the main character and, if necessary, the antagonist as well. But then we must discover how they can best lend a hand to the telling of the story. Could this character pull our protagonist toward or away from his goal? Could he be the love interest or a reflective character who helps us understand more of the protagonist's world or plight or worthiness? Could this character knowingly or unknowingly be abetting the antagonist or the antagonistic world?

In stories where the protagonist is also the antagonist, these questions become even more crucial. Here we probably want to find reflective characters on both sides of the issue—in essence a best friend for the protagonist side and a best friend for the antagonist side. As the story unfolds, how the protagonist deals with, relates to, fights with, or colludes with each of these "best friends" helps us to understand the push and pull that is going on inside the main character. *The Graduate* is a nice example of this dynamic at work. Benjamin is both the protagonist and antagonist. He is ambivalent in his relations with women—sex, love, honesty, commitment. On the one side is Mrs. Robinson, who pulls him in the direction of sex without love, without honesty, without communication. On the other side is Mrs. Robinson's daughter, Elaine, with whom he is truly falling in love, while he is wrestling with his inability to be honest and to communicate. So one relationship pulls him in one direction, and the other pulls in the opposite direction. As these two relationships evolve, become turbulent or passionate or dissolve, they help us to understand the inner push and pull on Benjamin.

Reflective and supportive characters also help with revealing both the past of a character and the change he or she may go through in the course of a story. If these characters have preexisting relationships with either the protagonist or the antagonist, the nature of that relationship can help reveal the past and present circumstances. And changes in the relationship can help us to gauge the changes inside the character. *Toy Story* provides a fine example of this dynamic. Before the Buzz Lightyear character is introduced, Woody has existing relationships with the other toys, which help to show us that he is king of the hill, "toy number one." When Buzz enters the story, the change his arrival causes in these relationships for Woody help us to see his dilemma and help to show us how the power structure in the toy world evolves.

What's important to keep in mind is the way in which these second-level characters need to be discovered. If we approach it from a checklist, recipe mentality, then we will get cardboard characters: the best friend, the love interest, the reflective character in the same boat, and the best friend of the bad guy. We've all seen them a million times, and there is nothing new in them. It's far better to find the people in the world of the characters and then, when exploring their inner lives—yes, secondary characters can have inner lives, too—discover how this character's life relates to the protagonist. You can get complexity this way; instead of the steadfast, loyal, never challenging, and unthinking best friend, you might find a best friend who also tries to woo the love interest or who pushes sometimes but pulls the wrong way at others. By giving the secondary characters some leeway, some chance to be more complex rather than merely types who fulfill a function, they have the possibility to take on a measure of life. This added complexity can only help flesh out the story, enhance the life of the protagonist, and keep the story from being predictable.

Tension from First to Last

We've already dealt with tension—the audience's simultaneous hope and fear about the future of the characters and the events in the story. But we haven't discussed how pervasive it is; nor have we covered just how small it can be. When we first begin to grasp the notion of tension, the idea that it is in our control to make the audience care and worry and fret, we tend to see this as solely being about the resolution of the story. Will James Bond be able to save the world from destruction? Will Rick help Ilsa get away from the Nazis in Casablanca? Will Captain Miller and his squad find and save Private Ryan? These tensions all exist and are felt by the audiences of those films, but they aren't the only tensions those films use.

Will Bond get "caught" by M flirting with Moneypenny? Will Rick foil Louis's plans with the young newlyweds? Will Miller tell his men what he did before the war? These tensions also exist and occupy our minds and emotions during those stories. Minute by minute we are made to anticipate—and therefore participate in— what may or may not happen. The potential consequences don't have to be dire or earth-shattering in order for us to take an interest and hope or fear. And the tensions don't all have to be about the protagonist and her quest or want. We can be made to hope and fear about all of the primary characters, including the antagonist, and can even be made to have short-term tensions about minor characters. Remember Yvonne, Rick's girlfriend, in *Casablanca*? She has a minor role because she is totally eclipsed by the arrival of Ilsa. But at the beginning, she is drunk and angry with Rick. Will she throw a fit? Will she do something against him? Will she allow the bartender to take her home? These tensions make no difference whatsoever in the eventual outcome of the story, they don't encourage us to wonder and worry about what will happen to Rick and Ilsa and Victor, but we feel them nonetheless.

It's important that we be made to feel tensions even this small, this far removed from the main story line. When we feel tension about the participants in the story, we become participants ourselves. If we don't feel tension, we don't feel connected; if we don't feel connected we start to feel left out and eventually we'll feel bored. We'll cease being an audience that cares one way or the other about the characters and the events in their lives. Remember the itch inside the leg cast that bothers L. B. Jeffries in *Rear Window*? We feel tension about this problem of his—which obviously has nothing to do with the story to come—and we feel his satisfaction when he solves the problem. We've shared his experience; we've been made his ally; we've been made to feel connected. In other words, we care.

So tension isn't simply a tool for connecting us to the plot of the story. Sure, there should be plenty of tension about the ultimate resolution of the story, but there had better have been tension about everything along the way or we probably have quit caring long before we've gotten to the resolution. If we are put in a position to care for many of the characters, to hope and fear about every step along the way, then we are fully enmeshed in the story. We are in the seamless dream because we are participating fully in the lives of the characters, to the exclusion of our own lives and worries. We are there with her picking the right dress for the ball and we're nervous when she dances for the first time in front of all those people and we're worrying with her when the prince doesn't seem to notice and we're exhilarated when he escorts her to the carriage. We've shared her entire experience, feeling tension at every stage, and are fully bonded with her. And at the same time, we've forgotten to worry about ourselves.

This means the audience needs to be let in on what the characters want from moment to moment and why it might be difficult to get. If we don't know the want or the potential difficulty, then we aren't being made to feel tension about the near future of the character. We need to be able to anticipate what might happen without being certain of what will happen. If we can't anticipate—because we don't know the want or potential difficulty—or if we can predict the outcome, then we won't feel tension. A minute of screen time without tension is usually a wasted minute. Unless we are given something else of equal value—spectacle, laughter, entertainment value of some kind—every minute of a story should be infused with tensions of all kinds. And even if we are given spectacle or comedy, we can still have tension at the same time and get even more from the same minute of screen time.

It's important to let us in on the tension early rather than late. From the moment a tension is established until it is resolved, we are participants with—or for—the character or characters. Our hearts and minds are hooked into the story. But before the tension is established for us, we are simply looking for clues to what the next tension is or what the character wants or what is about to come. This is fine for a short period of time, but we aren't getting the full impact of the events until we are allowed to participate in them. Nor are we experiencing the fullest possible bond with the characters when we see them in pursuit of goals that we don't know about. We are forced to be outside of the characters, rather than participating with them.

This multiplicity of tensions—from the small and momentary to the short-term to the overall tension of the story—allows us plenty of opportunity to vary the kinds of resolutions we deliver. And this variety supports our goal of making the story unpredictable. You have so many interim goals of different importance that you can have your protagonist win some, lose some, end at a draw or stalemate, and even abandon goals or change his mind. Whether it's Bond trying to save the world or Lester trying to find his freedom in *American Beauty*, we have seen him triumph a few times, bitterly lose a few times, be humiliated a few times, change tactics or change his mind a few times. This number of experiences shared with the character, and the full spectrum of resolutions it affords, means that the next tension won't be predictable and the final resolution won't be predictable.

But there is a potential problem with this multiplicity of tensions. The story could conceivably sputter ahead, getting up a head of steam when a tension is established, then coming to a dead stop when it is resolved, lying idle until the next tension is established, when it gets going again. This could be just as deadly as having no tensions, because we'd constantly be waking the audience from the seamless dream. There are two basic strategies involved in overcoming this potential problem: overlapping tensions and incomplete resolutions.

An audience that is fully engaged in a story is capable of sustaining worries about a great many issues concerning a significant number of characters, all at the same time. *American Beauty* is a great example. Aren't we simultaneously concerned about the futures of Lester, his wife, his daughter, the neighbor boy, and the boy's father? With Lester, aren't we hoping and fearing about his marriage, his job, his pursuit of the young girl, his drug use, his relationship with his daughter, even his rivalry with the neighbor, the boy's father? And with his wife, we're concerned about her potential for an affair, her ability to sell the house, her purchase of a gun, her understanding of the crisis her husband is going through. In fact, each of the primary cast members has several issues we concern ourselves with, feel tension about. These tensions ebb and flow, they heat up for periods of time and then recede, but they don't necessarily go away completely until we get deeper and deeper into the story.

The key to this working is that the resolutions for small tensions are incomplete in one way or another. Either the issue is kept alive by only a portion of the goal being achieved or failing, or the completion of a goal instantly creates a new and related tension. Let's track Lester's job woes in *American Beauty*. First he simply hates his job and doesn't seem to do it well. This establishes tension about how his career will go in the future. Then he is called into Brad's office and told he's on thin ice—more tension. And he's given a self-evaluation form. So the tension of the thin ice is prolonged. The tension about meeting with Brad is resolved in the sense that it's clear he's in trouble, but the decision is delayed. And we are made to feel tension about how he'll fill out the form. It's an incomplete resolution; part but not all of the issue is resolved. Then when he fills out the form in such a way as to get himself fired, it seems as if it will be a complete resolution, but he plays a trump card and blackmails Brad for a severance package. So again, it seems as if the issue is about to end completely, because he no longer has a job. But he does have some future income, which immediately creates at least two new tensions: what will he do and how will he tell his wife about being fired? So there have been interim resolutions. Some are partial and some simply create new tensions by the very nature of their resolution.

This ability to sustain a tension over a period of time and to turn it into a new tension, coupled with the many characters and issues about which the audience can be made to worry, creates the ability to keep the audience in nearly continuous tension without the story seeming monotonous or sputtering along, hiccuping through starts and stops. Imagine a detective who believes there is a clue to his case inside a building. We can be made to hope and fear about his getting into the building, whom he might meet once he gets inside, finding the clue, the meaning of the clue and how it changes his approach to the case, his ability to hang on to the clue, his chances of getting back out of the building, then about the clue being believable or usable, and what does this clue prompt him to need next? We've been put thoroughly into his gumshoes. If he has a partner or client or enemy also with him or working in consort with him or against him or tailing him, then you can imagine the exponential increase in the variety and intensity of tensions you can use on the audience.

Tensions must also be modulated in their proportions. We don't want concern over the waiter's life to overshadow the protagonist's life, unless the waiter is going to become a significant character. But if he's only going to be the waiter in one scene, it's not a good idea to make us care about him and have him dying of cancer while his aging mother and dog may potentially starve to death; it will simply distract us from the main story. In general, the tensions about characters—in aggregate over the course of the story—should be proportional to their importance in the story. In other words, overall, we worry most about the protagonist, somewhat less about his love interest, his best friend, his mother, and so on down through the importance of the cast members in the story. This could mean that we have a very intense period of worry about his mother for a short part of the story, but she doesn't play too much of a role elsewhere. And we could worry more steadily about the best friend, never with the same intensity as we do about the mother, but more regularly throughout the story. And the intensity of tension needs to be varied. We might be in a cooler period for the protagonist while we heat up for the mother, then heat up for the protagonist and have only moderate tensions about the best friend.

Tensions can throw things out of balance in a story when they are all out of proportion to the rest of the story. If you are telling a story about a boy striving to make it on the soccer team and you put a gun into his hands, the soccer team will inevitably be thrown into the backseat. How can we possibly have as much concern about a boy's chances of making it on a team as we have about the gun? We can't and we won't. This will be fine if the real story is about the boy with the gun, but if the real center is meant to be athletic aspirations or a social position based on team membership, the gun will throw the whole story out of balance, will destroy the possibility of the main intended issue dominating our hopes and fears. A rival soccer player who might hit our hero in the nose won't destroy the centrality of the main story line, but a loaded gun will, no matter whose hands it is in. And it isn't only guns; any life-threatening obstacle—from disease to killer storms—will overshadow a less dire obstacle. Any life-altering conflict, from the loss of a family member or a divorce through a change of residence to legal problems to a severe change in economic or social status, could overwhelm what is the intended main focus of a story. So one must use "big" conflicts carefully, and in proportion, in "small" stories.

But is the reverse true? How do small conflicts find a place in stories with "big gun issues" in them? If we are being made to fear for the future of life on earth, how can we be made to hope or fear about smaller issues of love or ambition or faith or bonds between two people? All life might end—won't that make it impossible to be concerned about small aspects of daily life? Strangely, this isn't true. Because the audience lives in a world filled with small issues—and if they are lucky they rarely have to face the "end of life as we know it" in their daily lives—they are immediately prepared to care about small issues. In fact, we need the small issues to care about the participants in saving our world from destruction. A character with no personal foibles and no personal conflicts, uncertainties, or concerns will be so shallow that we will find it difficult to care about him, no matter how heroic he might be in fighting aliens or stopping meteors from hitting our planet. We have to take time out from the big issues to focus our attention on the smaller, more familiar issues of the characters' lives in order for us to care about them as human beings. Even if they are toys, pigs, or machines, we care about characters only in relationship to how we see them as human beings. If they show no human characteristics, we won't care.

So you need balanced tensions and you need "normal everyday" conflicts to humanize your characters. But what about similar tensions—balanced tensions—inside a story? Is there any limit to how many there can be? Is there more tension from adding more balanced conflicts? Will a hundred guns give us more tension than one gun? Clearly, one gun or life-threatening device, from baseball bat to vial of poison, will change the dynamics among the characters and therefore change our set of worries as well. But more "guns" won't necessarily increase the intensity of our worries. One gun is a huge change in the world of a story, in its sensibility; a second gun will potentially add a bit more tension or uncertainty, because then both sides of the issue could be armed. Poison and its antidote function as two guns. But there is barely a blip on the radar screen of tension after two "guns." A dozen, a hundred, or a million guns don't make that much difference; death by this means has been established as a potential within this story, in this story's world. This is why stories based around life-threatening conflicts continually need to come up with bigger guns, not just more of them. If our hero has a pistol and the villain has a cannon, that's added tension. If our hero gets a cannon and the villain gets a nuclear bomb, we still add tension. But our hero getting a second pistol adds next to nothing to the overall ability of weapons to create tension.

In fact, this dynamic is true whether we are talking about guns or other primary conflicts within a story. If we have a character in turmoil in his primary love relationship and we add another potential lover, there is added tension. The potential for upheaval in the aspect of his life grows considerably from the potential for a change in partners. But if there are a hundred potential other lovers, you get no more tension—and possibly less— than if there is just one other. If the boy wanting to make it on the soccer team had one hundred teams to try out for, it actually diminishes the potential tension of the story. So more is not necessarily better. Getting more out of limited options is stronger than increasing the number of options. More intense drama can usually be created from one gun, one lover, or one soccer team than out of many. You get much more specificity, more do-or-die immediacy, more depth of involvement, and more excitement from a single, unique conflict than from multiples of interchangeable conflicts.

Actions and Goals

By now it's clear that all characters—not just the protagonist and antagonist, but also the other principals in a story—need to want something. The actions the characters take toward achieving their goals provide a significant portion—if not all—of the events that will make up the story. But are busy characters necessarily the same as characters taking actions? Are activity and action the same? Must all actions and activities be aimed at goals, at what the characters want? How does dialogue fit into all this?

Action and activity are not identical. An action has a purpose behind it; an action is something that a character undertakes while in pursuit of a goal that has been made meaningful for the audience. An activity is something that a character does in a scene, but it is in pursuit of a goal that we don't care about, even if the character does. A character flossing his teeth is pursuing a goal of healthy gums, but most of the time we do not concern ourselves with goals like these. If flossing were obsessive for the character, then we could be made to care and we could come to see it as an action worthy of our concern.

It's important to keep characters busy with activities. How those activities are performed can help us understand the inner lives of the characters. Baxter using a calculator in the opening of

The Apartment is merely an activity, yet how he does it reveals something of his inner life. While it's generally better to put characters in motion rather than force them into stagnant situations, actions are by far a more compelling tool for connecting the audience with the story and the lives of the characters than activities.

The key to action is meaningful purpose. If we know what a character wants and we see what he does to try to make it come about, then we are hooked into the character by hoping or fearing about the outcome of that action. Let's imagine we see a man sitting perfectly still in a chair with his eyes closed. It doesn't seem like an action at all, not even an activity. But if we know he's a boxer about to go into the ring, trying to gather a calm center for himself, or a corporate raider about to try to take over a company, gathering his wits, then this sitting and collecting himself is an action. But it's only a connection for the audience if we know the goal, the ultimate purpose. If we are kept ignorant of the underlying purpose, then we see what is in fact an action for a character, but we give it no more importance than an activity. We miss the real moment, we don't participate, we don't feel tension, we don't bond with the character.

So for an action to be a crucial part of the building of a drama, the audience must know what the underlying purpose is and be made to care about the outcome. If we don't know the goal or don't care, or if we can predict the outcome immediately, we won't feel tension, we won't connect. We can feel tension within a story without action if the world is active against the character, but eventually we will need to experience actions as well. If a character is assaulted by the world—let's say a huge storm comes her way—we will have tension about her future whether she takes action or not. Even if she is incapable of action, we will have tension because of the outside threat to her presumed want of survival. But for a story to become satisfying, the character also must have initiated action. The moment she starts to build a shelter against the storm or find her way into a cave or build a fire or put on seven layers of clothes or fix a radio to call for help, she has begun to take action for purposes we know and can worry about. What a character chooses to do about achieving a goal and how she goes about doing what she chooses is the greatest opportunity to open that window into the character's inner life.

The simplest statement of how this dynamic works is: if we know what a character wants and we see what a character does to achieve that want, we connect to the character. It doesn't have to be a positive connection; a negative connection can be just as powerful and involving as a positive one. No connection is the opposite of involvement, the opposite of caring, just as indifference is the opposite of love. Love and hate are closely related, just as negative and positive connections between the audience and the characters are closely related. The audience that has no connection to the lives of the characters is indifferent, uncaring, uninvolved—and well on the road to being bored with the story.

Sometimes the problem of action and purpose has to do with proximity. The character and the conflict don't seem to be close enough together. We either have to bring the conflict to the character or the character to the conflict. In *High Noon*, we have a sympathetic sheriff who has an hour and a half to prepare for the arrival of a gang of killers intent on murdering him. The conflict is being brought to the character, and his actions are in striving to get the town to back him up and support him in this upcoming conflict. In *Casablanca*, Ilsa and involvement in the world's problems come to Rick. In *Life Is Beautiful*, Fascism and repression come to the hero; he doesn't pursue them himself. But in *Schindler's List*, the same repressive and assaultive world is taken on by Schindler. He personally could stay outside the conflict inherent in the Nazi holocaust, but he chooses to enter it. In *Star Wars*, Luke could stay out of the intergalactic war but chooses to go into it. In *The Godfather*, Michael could stay out of the family crime business and is encouraged to do so by his father, but chooses to avenge the attempted hit on his father and thus enters the family business. If the character and the conflict don't collide, there won't be an opportunity for purposeful actions and therefore no means of creating connections between the audience and the characters.

Sometimes the character carries the conflict inside himself, but it's difficult for us to externalize it, to show it to the audience. A character desperately wants to win a gold medal at the

Olympics, but he isn't on the team and the bulk of the story takes place in his remote village. Here we need to bring in a surrogate, a local version, of the outer-world goal. He might have to race another runner or against a friend on a bicycle or a neighbor on a horse in order for us to externalize the conflict in a way that enables actions to take place in the location of the story. In *Cool Runnings*, four Jamaicans decide they want to race the bobsled in the Winter Olympics. There is no such thing as a bobsled in Jamaica, nor is there snow. They must first create a local version of a bobsled—on wheels—and then conquer a local hill. Once the conflict is externalized and actions can be taken to overcome it, we can connect to the characters and get involved in their lives. Later, when the team and their coach actually go to the Winter Olympics, we can more directly connect them with their ultimate goal of being worthy of racing in the Winter Olympics. In *The Silence of the Lambs*, surrogacy is taken to such an extreme it seems to become the central story. Agent Starling wants to catch a serial killer; in order to understand him, she must question and get to know Hannibal Lecter. Since her interaction with the killer who provokes the story is quite limited, much of the story is played out in the surrogate situation with Hannibal. Starling gets to know herself and the perverse inner world of the sociopath through interactions with Lecter, which give us engaging and horrifying conflicts and considerable tension. Yet this remains the preparation for the main goal of her story, the pursuit and capture of the serial killer and the possible release of his latest victim.

Surrogacy is a way of bringing the conflict to the character when the true conflict is not yet possible. In *The Dirty Dozen*, and in practically any caper story, the training and rehearsal time in preparation for the main event is a means of bringing the conflict to the characters in the form of a surrogate. The training period in *The Right Stuff* or *Armageddon* is the same thing; we aren't at the main event, the primary goal, but we need the conflict to be present now. If we don't have the conflict present—either by bringing it to the character or the character to it, or by creating a surrogate—then it becomes impossible to create meaningful actions toward the characters' goals and we are denied the opportunity to get inside them and to participate with them. In one way or another, a character has to be brought face to face with some version of the obstacles to his or her goal in order for a story to be dramatically told. We cannot simply wait until the end for the conflict to arise; it has to have been playing out all along.

When it comes to dialogue, there seem to be two camps that beginning screenwriters tend to fall into: dialogue is everything, or it is meaningless. Dialogue can become effective action; it can be a means to pursue goals both in finding out information and in terms of getting the world to do what a character wants. But it can also be a way of filling up time. There needs to be a purpose behind dialogue for it to become true action instead of mere activity. The character can have purpose—a greeting is a purpose, as is filling up a void in a conversation—but unless that purpose resonates with the audience, hooks into some established goal, that purpose won't necessarily be our own.

When Woody in *Toy Story* or Henry in *Henry V* gives a speech to "stir up the troops" in preparation for leading them into battle, the dialogue is action. In both cases, what the character says is a large part of what he does in pursuit of his present goal—getting others to join him in his quest or to support his action. Dialogue can be action when it is used to try to get information or to hide information or to give information to one character while simultaneously hiding it from another. It is action when the purpose behind it is to provoke an action or to stop an action, to explain the past or present, to reveal or hide a present or future intention. If a character wants something and talks in an attempt to get it or make it come about, then dialogue is action. If the talking is not in furtherance of a goal that is of some importance to the audience, then it is just like any activity. It means nothing more than what shows on the surface; it doesn't encourage our participation or anticipation and it doesn't connect us more fully with any character. Dialogue with no goal isn't necessarily worthless, but it will never be as strong and involving as purposeful action that we understand and have hope and fear about.

Where the mistaking of dialogue for action becomes most tenuous for screenwriters is in the area of delivering story. There is a tendency to use the mouths of the characters as an efficient means of conveying story. It might seem that the story is really progressing when the characters are saying what it is about, what they want, why it might be difficult to get, who they are, and what they care about—everything that the story is meant to convey and explore. This is confusing the author's purpose with the characters' purpose. The author wants to make the audience understand his or her story and care about the characters, know what may or may not happen—all the things we've been talking about. Dialogue is probably the easiest way; in the end, it is the least effective means to the author's end.

Dialogue is action when the *character* has a purpose. It is effective dialogue if we know the purpose behind it. But dialogue that simply tells the story to the audience is not fulfilling the character's purpose at all. This kind of dialogue is there to help the writer, not because it fulfills some goal of the character's. We can—and sometimes must—tell a portion of the story directly to the audience, but mask it with a second purpose that we give to a character. In such cases, the dialogue takes on two purposes, that of the author's and that of the character's. For instance, let's say our audience has to know how a carburetor works or how many legs a millipede has. We could film an elaborate demonstration of the inner workings of a carburetor or laboriously count the millipede's legs, but the information isn't worth much screen time. So it might be better to have a conflict between two characters about a carburetor or a millipede and in the process convey the information.

But conveying expositional information through conflict won't help with the larger issue of telling the story in the mouths of the characters. If the only action a character takes to pursue his goal is to go from person to person talking, no amount of masking by means of conflict will cover up the fact that nothing is happening. If there is some kind of balance between action and dialogue-as-action, a story can unfold in a satisfying manner. If the only action is dialogue, then one whole side of storytelling will be missing—what we can learn through visuals, through what characters physically do and how they react to changes, conflicts, successes, and failures. Conversely, if there is no dialogue at all, then there might be an element of the experience not fully explored. Intellectual concepts can be very difficult to dramatize without some kind of verbal support or explanation.

So most of the time we use physical activities *and* physical actions along with dialogue as an activity *and* dialogue as an action. The actions—physical or dialogue-based purposeful activity—will always carry most of the load of building the drama of a story. Activity without purpose, or dialogue that tells us what the author wants us to know, won't give us enough to share with the characters. We won't have the conflicts, the hopes and fears, the doubts and worries that form our bonds with the characters and with the story itself. Actions we participate in with them are the key to that level of involvement.

Character Arc

We've discussed the notion that in most stories, the central character needs to change as a result of the events and the experiences of the story. But how is that change created as the story is built? What happens where? Can the change take place anywhere and still be effective? What part must we participate in, and what part can be ellipsed?

Stories can be an elaborate means of showing us how people change and what it takes to make that come about. Clearly, there are stories in which the protagonist doesn't change, or stories in which the protagonist's change is not the most crucial element. But in the majority of stories, where the protagonist undergoes some change as a result of his or her experiences, the trauma of making the change come about is a significant part of the character's and the audience's experience. Meaningful change is never easy in life, and it can't be made easy in a story. If the change comes about too easily, we find ourselves wondering what was so difficult for this person to accomplish; why should we care?

When we first meet Melvin Udall in *As Good as It Gets*, he is a man none of us wants to know or have living next door. We come to learn why he's obnoxious and what elaborate set of phobias and neuroses control his life, but he's still a jerk. His character arc isn't from jerk to everyone's best friend. It's from someone so self-involved that he is profoundly abusive and insensitive, to a man who is capable of compassion and understanding, capable of involvement in other people's lives. We still don't have to like him, but he has significantly changed in the course of the story. That change hasn't been easy for him or for us. The primary conflicts, the main uncertainties we experience as the audience, concern pushing and pulling him toward that change. He is both the protagonist and antagonist of his story. In this sort of internal conflict, the character arc is crucial; which side of the character will prevail? Either way, the change in the character is the central issue.

But the character's change can be a smaller portion of the story. Let's say our story is about climbing a mountain, with the goal of rescuing the main character's brother stranded at the peak. Our protagonist probably needs to go through some change during the ascent, but in the end, our concern is his success or failure at the mission. You will devote less screen time to establishing the area of change and the process he goes through, but his potential character arc will remain a crucial part of the story. If there is no change in the character and he is neither a comic character nor a superhero, it means either that we have missed a level of intimacy with him or that the events of the journey were not so intense that they affected his life. Either way, it diminishes the audience's feeling of involvement in the events of his life. Either the difficult task of ascending the mountain has been so great that he's had to face obstacles that make him dig deep inside himself, or you have made the climb too easy for him. If he's had to face those difficulties and dig up fresh reserves, how can he be unchanged? And if he changes and the audience hasn't experienced it with him, then it has been denied the intimacy it sought from the story.

So the character arc can be the essence of the story, as in *As Good as It Gets,* or it can be a secondary but crucial aspect of our involvement in other events in the life of the protagonist, as in *Romancing the Stone, Raiders of the Lost Ark, The Terminator,* or *Schindler's List.* In *The Godfather,* where we follow two stories, we have examples of each kind of arc. In Don Vito's story, his character arc is secondary to his quest to sustain and create a future for the empire he built. His principal goal is how he will run the family and find a worthy successor. In Michael's story, the change in the character from idealistic young soldier to cynical new godfather, in all its meanings, is the center of the story.

How you build character arc into the unfolding of a story depends in part on its centrality. If it's the essence of the story, when the protagonist is also the antagonist and we are watching this battle to see which side wins—meaning the character arc is completed—then the character arc must be protracted throughout the story. If the character arc is secondary—if the protagonist's main conflict is not with another aspect of himself, but there is an antagonist or antagonistic world to be fought—then the character arc still may take place throughout the story, but in more self-contained or finite moments within the larger action. And occasionally, the complete character arc can take place in a short period of time. In *Gandhi,* his character arc occurs within the first act of the film. For a period of time in South Africa, Gandhi wrestles with how he should approach life and conflict and trying to get the world to do what is right. By the time he returns to India, he has successfully found his own way—his character arc is complete—and the story involves his attempt to put his realization into action and to have it accepted by the world. He knows what to do and never wavers from that knowledge, but his ability to impact a world that does not easily accept this vision is called into question. This question is what we hope and fear about, not whether Gandhi will find the right path for himself. In *Three Kings,* we have a similar circumstance. Archie Gates starts out selfish and greedy, but in the course of a single scene, his character arc is completed. He witnesses a group of soldiers torturing and terrifying a village and finally murdering a woman right in front of him. While he doesn't fully relinquish his selfishness and greed, he suspends them long enough to intercede on behalf of the victims. The change in his character is mostly completed in that scene. The rest of the story, as exciting and adventurous as it is, tests that change and his resolve.

But more often, the character arc, even in a story with an outside antagonist, takes place over time. Usually that span of time is the second act. The most common way of building a story involves establishing the aspect of the character that will be tested in the first act, pushing and pulling on that aspect throughout the second act until the initial, tentative change takes place, and then testing the change in the third act. In this sense, the principal transformation in the character takes place in the second act, but we don't know if it will be permanent or not until the story is completed. This paradigm helps sustain the greatest suspense and tension in the character arc, and it makes the change seem sufficiently deep and difficult to the character to warrant our emotional commitment.

To find the point of change when building a story, it can be useful to start at the end and work backward. Where should the character be at the end? Or *who* should the character be, what version of himself has he transformed into as a result of this story? Once you know the end point—Michael as the cynical godfather with the simultaneous christening of his first godchild and the murder of his enemies—then you have an idea of how to start the character—Michael the "innocent" returning war hero with girlfriend and idealistic views of his place in the world. Within the realm of the story, you strive to make the character arc as wide as possible. If a story takes place over ten minutes in a character's life, you can't believably have him change from devil to saint; that is too great a change given the scope of the story. You want the arc to be wide and yet stay in proportion to the story and the level of difficulty the character endures. Think of Andy Dufresne at the beginning of *The Shawshank Redemption* and think of him at the end. Contrast Luke at the beginning and end of *Star Wars*, Rosie at the beginning and end of *The African Queen*, Hank Mitchell at the beginning and end of *A Simple Plan*.

If you have a clear idea of who your character will become when the story is over and you start her at a believable distance from that transformed final version, then you know the distance to be covered in between—usually the second act. In the first act, we meet and get to know the unchanged person, the starting character. In the second act this character faces obstacles, pursues goals, is put through some kind of trauma—even in a comedy or a light drama, stories aren't "easy" on the characters—and in the process something changes in the character. This is the second act. In the third act, this newly minted version of the original character is tested—was this change a temporary aberration or a true change in the nature of the human being?

As with everything else in storytelling, there are variations available to us. The first tentative change in the character could appear only in the third act, after all the forces have pushed and pulled the character throughout the second act. Or, as in *Three Kings*, the character's change could come about all at once and then be tested repeatedly afterward. It all depends on which question is more important to the author—can the character change, or can the character live up to the change he has made? In *Three Kings*, Archie impulsively "does the right thing" even though his three companions urge otherwise. The suffering of those villagers is too awful for him to ignore. But an impulse is not a complete change in a character. He's made the change by taking action, the one we want him to take, but we don't have much faith in that change taking root. Can he sustain this "good" new version of himself, or will he abandon it as soon as it's convenient?

Character arc can become problematic when too little screen time passes both before and after the change happens. You can slowly build toward a change and be done with it quickly afterward, or you can have an abrupt change and then explore it for some time after it happens. But an abrupt change that isn't adequately tested and explored afterward is the worst of both worlds. In the end, the change in the character plays false and feels tacked on. The character arc is, in a sense, a measure of the inner life of the character, and we have to spend time with that inner life to believe in it. Even in a story with an outside antagonist, some part of the main character should be in conflict with another part of him. If not, there isn't much of an inner life and he is either a comic character or a superhero. If the protagonist is a version of a "real" person, then he or she has some kind of doubt and, thus, some inner conflict. Either this inner conflict gets worked out as part of the buildup toward the change, or it gets explored as a result of an abrupt and unanticipated change. The devotion of some screen time at one end or the other is what helps give the inner conflict at the core of the character arc sufficient depth for us to believe it within the context of the story. If we don't get to spend time exploring that inner life either before or after the change, then the change will seem like an attribute, not a characteristic. It will be as changeable as the hero's shirt instead of as permanent as his eyes.

Pivotal Decisions

We've discussed at length how crucial to our understanding of the characters is our participation in their moments of decision. Determining pivotal moments of decision is a crucial part of the process of building a drama, creating a story. If we can determine where and when the crucial decisions are made by the protagonist, then we already have a half-formed outline of the story. Where decisions are made, the life path of the character takes a turn. If the life path in the story doesn't turn, then the decision wasn't crucial, it didn't change anything, it just created more of the same. If the life path changes and there was no decision by the character, we have the feeling that we missed something. Even if a character is struck by lightning, as we discussed, there is some kind of decision—will the character fight the fate or accept it? The worst situation of all is when the character makes a decision that changes his life path, yet it is all done offscreen, so we know that we missed something crucial.

Let's look at a simple story in which it would seem the life-changing decisions are not made by the protagonist. In *The Terminator,* Sarah is the protagonist, but she certainly doesn't make the decision to be stalked by a killing machine from the future. What stages does she go through? What decisions are hers to make? First she denies she could be stalked, then she believes it to be true after her friends are killed, and she calls the police for help. She decides to trust them and wait for their help, but she is rescued from the Terminator by Kyle, not the police. Then they are both taken in by the police and she continues to place her trust in them, not Kyle. When the killing machine decimates the Los Angeles police department and again she is saved by Kyle, this time she decides to believe him and go with him. When the

Terminator finds them again and severely wounds Kyle, Sarah decides to take over rather than accept defeat and death. And she has to take on the killing machine one on one and kill it herself, depending on no one else for help.

She decides to call and trust the police, she decides to shift her trust to Kyle, and she decides to take over the defense of herself—and the future of mankind. She doesn't decide to have this story happen to her—in that sense, she is hit by lightning. But she makes crucial decisions about how she will deal with this attack of fate, and these decisions determine her life path. Her decisions determine how the story plays out, how it is shaped. Once she knows what problem she has to face, she makes her first crucial decision—to get help from the police. That's the first act of the story. She trusts the police and lets them guard her, defend her until the frontal assault on the police station wipes out the police. Kyle wants to help her, guard her, but it is her decision to go with him and trust him; it is not his decision. This is the midpoint, the middle of the second act. Later, when Kyle is wounded and she takes over the front line of their defense, it's the end of the second act. Again, it's her decision. In the end, she uses herself as bait to lure the killing machine into another machine she will use to kill it. So her decision is crucial in helping create the resolution. At every stage, even when she is the victim of fate, her decisions are still critical aspects of the shaping of the material into a story. Without the decisions, we don't have a story. Or, if we can shape the material without the decisions of the protagonist, then she plays too small a role in her own story.

What prompts decisions can come from a variety of directions. In *Saving Private Ryan*, Miller is given an assignment—his mission is handed to him. In *The Silence of the Lambs*, Agent Starling is also handed her problem—by an ally. In *North by Northwest*, Roger Thornhill is handed his problem by an enemy. In *Star Wars*, Luke decides to take on a problem only to learn that he was fated to have it anyway. In *Casablanca*, Rick has his problem foisted on him by a combination of "friends." In *October Sky*, Homer decides all on his own to try to build a functioning rocket. The protagonist's problem can start just about anywhere. It can be initiated by the protagonist, the antagonist, a friend, God, fate, or Mother Nature.

What is important is not where the problem comes from, but what the protagonist chooses to do about the problem. This is the true "want" of the story. Captain Miller wants to save Private Ryan and keep himself and his men alive in the process. Agent Starling wants to catch the serial killer and keep herself alive and her sanity intact at the same time. Roger Thornhill wants to escape the mistaken identity that has led spies to try to kill him. Luke wants to have a fighting role in the battle against an intergalactic evil empire. Rick wants to stay out of the world's problems so he can wallow in his own. Homer wants to build a rocket despite the opposition of his father, the school principal, and eventually the police, plus the many difficulties in making a rocket work. Whether the protagonist has gone out of his way to attract a problem or was hit in the face by it, the story is shaped by the decisions he makes about the problem. This is the want that will help us figure out how to tell the story.

Decisions are therefore the crucial actions in shaping stories. If the character chooses to face a problem, it determines where the story goes. If the character chooses to run away from the problem, it determines where the story goes. If the character chooses to ignore the problem, it determines where the story goes. Decisions of the protagonist become the pivotal moments in the overall story—the end of the first act, the end of the second act. These are the moments the path of the character takes a new direction. The character could be driven onto the new path—it could be a no-brainer, "take this path or die"—but it is still a decision. So decision becomes action. In striving to make our stories most effective, we try to make decisions into physical, demonstrable actions. The most dramatic way to show that a character has made a decision is to show what he does as a result of that decision. In effective storytelling, the decision and the action are put as close together as possible, preferably at the same instant. We, and the character, learn the decision in the moment of action. When Archie decides in *Three Kings* to stop the killing and torture of the villagers, it is the same moment he takes his action to do that, by marching across the village square to stop the Iraqi soldiers. The action demonstrates the decision; it becomes synonymous with the decision.

In fact, this bond between decision and action is so strong we only trust the action to be true. In *The Lost Weekend*, Don Birnam says he has decided to give up drinking, but his actions of hiding bottles, stealing money to buy bottles, begging for drinks, and, eventually, stealing a bottle of liquor all tell us that he hasn't made that decision. The actions tell us the truth—even when the character fervently believes the words, his actions reveal the decisions. This disparity, even within the character, can often be a source of story material. *Trainspotting, One Flew over the Cuckoo's Nest, The Usual Suspects, The Treasure of the Sierra Madre*, and many more films involve characters lying to themselves or others about their decisions and the truth revealed by their actions, not the words.

Sometimes it isn't possible to make the decision in the mind of the character coincide with an action that helps demonstrate that decision. In this circumstance, we turn the decision into a kind of tension—we know what the character wants to decide, but we don't yet know if it will be true. In *The Godfather*, Michael decides that he will be the one to kill the men who set up his father to be assassinated. But the men aren't there when he makes the decision, and his hit on the men—including a high-ranking policeman—takes considerable preparation. So, out of story necessity, we are put into limbo and we feel tension about the decision. We know it might be true, but we don't know that it is. We can want to believe in the truth of the decision, but the proof of it has to wait—and until it is proven, there is doubt. Hamlet promises the ghost of his father that he will get revenge upon Claudius for the king's murder, and we believe he has made that decision—or at least that Hamlet believes he has made that decision. But as he equivocates and lets opportunities pass by without action, our doubt about his decision is strengthened. We only believe a character's decision when his action proves it to be true.

So in building a story with the protagonist, we have him make a decision, then take an action based on that decision to prove the decision is real. Then comes a third part: the result of the decision, the result of the action. The result of the decision can be clear before the decision is made, or the result could be unknown or unpredictable. A suicidal character who jumps off a fifty-story building will definitely die in the fall; this is known in advance of the jump. There is no question about the result of the decision, in which case there is no question for the audience about the earnestness of the character's decision to die once he actually jumps. But a suicidal character who takes a lot of pills might not want to die; he might want help, want to be rescued, want attention. Both characters make definitive decisions and take actions that demonstrate their truth, yet they still are not identical in what they reveal to us or in how they change the life path of the character we are following.

In *Rear Window,* L. B. Jeffries's decision to track what he believes is a murder across the courtyard from his apartment does not have a predictable result. We don't know in advance that the police won't really believe him, and we don't know that the killer eventually will stalk him. We can't fully anticipate the result of his decision. But Captain Miller's decision to accept the mission in *Saving Private Ryan* has a known result. We don't know the exact details of the dangers that lie ahead of him and his men, but they are going into enemy territory after we've just seen how dangerous that is. The result of the decision is predictable before the decision is made. Sometimes we can use the predictable result of a decision to make an unpredictable twist in a story. After Thornhill has agreed to a fake death to help "save" Eve Kendall in *North by Northwest,* it seems as if she will be free from the spies, but in fact the charade has only helped drive her deeper into their web.

It is useful to imagine an hourglass as a means of shaping story material, a way of building a story from within the main character. We start out wide, with the means of instigating a want within a character coming from a variety of sources—the character, other characters, or the world of the story. And we end up wide, with the results of decisions being anything from predictable to unpredictable; the results of decisions can take us deeper into the unknown or directly to a known result. But in the middle, where our hourglass narrows to one grain of sand at a time, are the protagonist and his decisions. These pivotal decisions should be made by the character, should be shown to us in actions that we believe more than words, and should be made one at a time.

Even if a character's life path is going to change dramatically more than once, life-altering decisions and changes shouldn't happen all at the same time. More than one catalyst can hit a character, but the resulting decision still remains a single decision. A character can go from husband and father to childless widower in one traffic accident—but what decision he makes as a result of this horrendous life change is only one turn on his path. Later on, he might also quit his job, or change his appearance or even his gender. These decisions might be the distant offshoots of the earlier assault from fate, but they aren't going to happen convincingly all at the same moment. There must be other influences, other attempts to cope with the first turn on the path before another turn will be believable and emotionally involving for the audience.

So the decisions of the character, like the sands in the hourglass, must fall one at a time, and each must be fully addressed before the next one falls. If we try to crowd major changes together, they start to steal power from each other. Each decision is diminished by being incompletely explored, by being given too little time for the results to sink in. While characters make hundreds of decisions in the course of a story—will she take a taxi or the bus, buy a new blouse, or cross the street against the light— and each of these decisions potentially impacts what happens next, only a few of these decisions are pivotal. Only a few decisions determine which path we will follow for a significant portion of the story. Smaller decisions might determine if we walk on the sidewalk, in the gutter, or in the middle of the road, if we race from shelter to shelter along the path or amble along, basking in the sun or singing in the rain. These smaller decisions don't alter the path, but show how we explore the one we're on.

The pivotal decisions, the ones that put the story onto an entirely new path, therefore must be given sufficient screen time and be of paramount importance to the audience. You must devote time and attention to establishing the problem or the need to make the decision; you must elaborate on the actual making of the decision, and it must be important to the character and the audience; and you must adequately explore the results of that decision, whether they are predictable or not.

By determining the most important decisions the character

makes in the story, you are identifying your "money moments," those moments in your story that require and deserve all of the resources you have available to you—screen time, dramatic emphasis, the fullest use of all the tools of storytelling at your disposal. Without the money moments, all you have is a sequence of events in the life of a character, not a story that connects with and resonates within the audience. Without pivotal decisions, you have no money moments. And conversely, once you know our money moments, you are halfway to an outline of the story. They show you the rough outline of the life path you will follow on the journey the audience will share with the protagonist.

Time Compression and Intensity

Dramatizing a character's life path must be balanced against the need for time compression. While you need to give plenty of screen time to building up pivotal decisions, exploring those decisions, and showing the results of the decisions, you also have precious little screen time in which to tell events that might take days, weeks, months, years, or a lifetime for the characters to complete. How do you reconcile the conflict between the need to elaborate on moments—even if they are money moments—and the need to cover time in the lives of the characters? Clearly you will use ellipsis as the means of jumping over time, but how much time will you have to cut out, and what kind of time should it be? Perhaps most importantly, how much of the character's life must you include in the telling of her story?

To the extent that there is a rule of thumb, it would be something like this: include as short a period of a character's life as possible to tell the story effectively. For one character and the events that make up his story, that could be two hours of his life; for another, from before birth to after death. Cover the time the story demands, but no more. All the time that goes beyond what is absolutely required by the story itself is wasteful. It wastes our energy to ellipse it, it wastes the emotional commitment you have extracted from the audience, and it wastes the tenuous hold you have on the audience's attention and concern. If the story takes place in the character's adulthood and no formative event in his childhood is crucial to our understanding of the character, then it would be abusing the audience's connection to include significant amounts of his childhood in the story. If it's not pertinent to the story at hand, it has to go.

At the same time, strive to force events—and of course decisions—into the shortest possible time frame. This necessity is not in conflict with the need to elaborate on the decisions the characters make. Build up to a decision, make the decision, put it into action, and show the result. Then you want to jump to the buildup to the next important decision; you don't want to waste a lot of time with an unchanging path. You want to explore each new path so long as it has new twists and turns, new secrets and ramifications, but you don't need to use up months in the life of the character. The trouble with using months instead of an afternoon is that many things could change in those months. If your protagonist gets the world's worst haircut the afternoon before the gala ball, there isn't time for alternative solutions. If he gets that haircut a month before the ball, then there are dozens of potential solutions for this new problem. You don't want the audience to have nagging suspicions that other things could have been done, that there were other paths the character could have taken because he had enough time to find them.

So strive to compress the time in a character's life that must be dramatized. There will be less to ellipse, fewer chances for alternative solutions, and the nature of the character and his connection to his life and to the audience can be explored as one state of being instead of multiples—such as the character as child, as teen, as young adult, as mature adult, as old person. If multiplicity within one character is the essence of the story, then of course that is what must be covered. But if we are following Madame Curie as she explores the mysteries of radiation, you don't have to cover the full length of her life. We could learn information about her childhood and have premonitions about her eventual fate, but the core of our story is her relentless pursuit to unfold the mysteries. That short period within the whole of her life is where you should concentrate your energies.

The question to ask when building a story is not, How long

would it normally take a person or these people to do these things? The question should be, How short a time could it believably take for these things to occur? If the event is a pregnancy, we can't compress the time in the life of the character; we have to ellipse, because the audience won't believe a human pregnancy that is a week long. In real life, a person might spend years wanting to quit his job and follow his dream, but in a story we would try to put the beginning of that dream in the morning and the quitting of the job in the afternoon of the same day. We don't want to lose the thread we are following; we want the cause and effect to be close to each other and believable.

Expediency is not the only reason to compress time in the life of the character. The intensity of the experience you are giving to the audience can be diminished by superfluous time. If it takes years for the character to quit his job and follow his dream, then it seems as if the dream isn't that important to him; his passion seems tempered. The audience takes its cues from the characters; if they are passionate, we join them, if they are indifferent, so are we. It's rare that we are passionate about a character or his life or his decisions when he is blasé about it. By compressing the time between the bad haircut and the gala ball, you are forcing an urgency onto the character that the audience joins; we feel the urgency, we participate more passionately because something has to be done right away. If you dramatize the cause in the morning and show the effect in the afternoon, you have intensified the audience's connection to the story.

This point goes right back to the issue of pivotal decisions in a story. If the cause of a pivotal decision is separated from its effect by years in the life of the character, we tend to lose the connection or to disbelieve that they are cause and effect. Maybe something else came up during the interim that is the real cause, but we don't know what it is. Since you don't have much screen time in which to tell your story, you don't want to promote doubts about cause and effect unless that very issue is the substance of your story. You don't want to waste screen time by showing a cause, then adding time in the life of the character, then proving that the added time didn't change the character or the cause, and then showing the effect. This approach would add two or three extra steps that don't push the story forward or increase our under-standing of the character. It wastes precious screen time on un-necessary issues and, in the end, creates less convincing drama.

The Possible and the Impossible

When building a screenplay, you must take into consideration what is possible and impossible within the world of the story. You can tell a story about a character going after an impossible goal, but that impossibility must be put into its proper place within the rest of the story. You can't put the audience in the position of hop-ing only for something impossible within the world of the story. If our only hope for our stranded mountain climbers is that they will learn to fly like birds, then we have no hope at all. We might hope that they figure out a way to sail off the side of the mountain and drift down to safety, but that isn't the same thing as flying like a bird. But if we already know that one of the mountain climbers can indeed fly—as in a supernatural story—then this hope will be warranted and justified within the story and its world.

What difference does it make if a goal is impossible? For there to be genuine tension for the audience, we must be in a position to believe our character might succeed or might fail; if we know absolutely one way or the other, if we can completely predict the outcome, then we can't have tension about that outcome. So if you are intending to create tension in the audience about the achievement of a goal, that goal has to be achievable. It can be *nearly* impossible, but not impossible. David versus Goliath is nearly but not utterly impossible; so is Sarah versus the Termina-tor. Rosie and Charlie getting the *African Queen* down the river and onto the lake to sink the *Louisa seems* impossible and nearly is, but that outcome isn't certifiably—predictably, in other words—impossible.

But when Butch and Sundance decide to take on the Mexican Army, they can't possibly defeat them; we are absolutely certain of the outcome. The same is true when Thelma and Louise drive their car off the cliff; the outcome of the action is totally predictable. So how can these impossible events—endings in both cases—exist in well-made films, in films we all like and care about? Our hope cannot be based on success in these actions. Butch and Sundance have reached the end of their run; their hope—which we share—is to go out in style, together. It's almost identical for Thelma and Louise. What has been made important to us is the relationship between the two characters, not their success at an impossible quest. In both cases, we have been encouraged to hope and fear about the possibility of the pair splitting up. When they choose the same fate, choose to go out in style together, they have successfully completed their bonding under incredibly adverse circumstances. We didn't fully know—we couldn't predict—that they would manage to stay together all the way to death, after there had been tremendous pressure to part along the way.

So you can build stories around characters who pursue impossible dreams or attempt impossible actions, but you can't effectively tell their stories by making the audience hope for their success in those dreams and actions. You have to use tangential hopes and fears. As we discussed earlier, it is fine to separate what the audience hopes and fears from what the protagonist hopes and fears. We can invest our emotions in a character who is striving to do an impossible feat only so long as our hopes and fears are focused elsewhere on the character's life and well-being, not on his predictable failure.

This sleight-of-hand with tension is especially important when you are telling stories where the ending is already known. Joan of Arc is burned at the stake; Eliot Ness manages to catch and jail Al Capone; Gandhi dies at an assassin's hand; Lindbergh successfully flies across the Atlantic. For the most part, these real-life endings are known by the audience of the stories. So you can't build a story that directly takes its tension from an ending that is already known; that is the essence of predictability. While incorporating and acknowledging the actual historical facts, you can, however, still build tension. Will Joan of Arc maintain her faith? Will Ness become a vicious killer just like his enemy? Will Gandhi succeed in making the world see the wisdom and rightness of his approach to violence and power? Will Lindbergh be able to land his plane where he is expected? Our hopes and fears in these stories are directed not toward the outcome we already know, but toward some aspect of the character that is not known. This allows us an unpredictable resolution, even when the "ending" is known.

You also want to avoid tensions that are so easily resolved that they are predictable. There is no tension if the challenge to a character is too easy within the world of the story. Again, the difference between *seeming* easy and *being* easy is significant. Let's give our poor lingering and still stranded mountain climbers a rope that is hanging in just the right place to help them reach safety. It's too easy; they don't have to summon up their courage, they don't have to struggle against adversity, each other, themselves. They just grab the rope and, *zip*, they are dragged up to safety. If that's true, it's the death of the story, the end of tension. If it only appears to be a convenient safety rope and leads them to new and ever more perilous adventures on the mountainside, then it continues to create tension as you want it—unpredictable.

A great many stories—probably half of all detective stories alone—start with a chore that seems easy to complete. The "easy chore" is part of the bait to lure the protagonist and the audience into involvement in the troubles of the story. But if we are lured in by something that looks easy and turns out to be easy, then we will feel cheated; we'll feel as if there is no real story. It's one thing for Sam Spade to take an easy gig guarding a man at a meeting, but when his partner is killed and he's implicated, then that easy gig leads to a good story. What would the story be if all he did was the easy chore, collected his pay, paid his bills, and went home? In a word, boring. No audience will willingly continue to give its time and emotional energy to a story in which there are easy solutions, where the character is never taxed or made to breathe hard or work up a sweat or struggle against an uncertain fate. We want easy in our own lives, but we want difficulty in the lives of the characters we follow.

So a story has to take place in the spectrum between "somewhat difficult" and "just short of impossible." Totally easy or totally impossible makes dramatic tension disappear. When the ending is known to the audience or the quest of the character is truly impossible, then the creation of tension has to involve other aspects of the life of the character. It's interesting to see how often the ending is given away in films based on real events—whether it's the *Hindenberg* crashing or Gandhi being assassinated or T. E. Lawrence dying in a motorcycle accident. We are being told straightaway that the ending is not where we should be investing our hopes and fears. We will have to look elsewhere to focus our worries, to find our emotional connection to the lives we will follow. And when a character takes on a seemingly impossible goal, then we are similarly urged to aim our hopes and fears not directly at the impossible, but on some possible impact of the quest itself. In *Schindler's List*, he doesn't set as his goal—and thus we aren't encouraged to hope—the stopping of the Nazis' extermination of all Jews. Our hopes and fears are centered on a relatively small group Schindler strives to protect. Will he be able to keep them safe, against all the odds, and what impact will the struggle have on him? In *Brazil*, Sam Lowry tries to take on the society, as does Logan in *Logan's Run*. In both cases, we don't hope the character can actually change the entire society in which he lives; our hopes and fears concern his being trapped in that society, or his escaping from or rising above it.

Life Is Beautiful is an example of a circumstance where it's clear the character can't win. Guido can't beat the concentration camp and he can't indefinitely sustain hopes based on lies. But within this world of hopelessness and horror, we are made to invest our hopes and fears in just one relationship. Will he be able to keep his son's spirits up in the face of all the death, deprivation, and adversity? He can't stop the realities of the concentration camp, and he eventually loses the belief of his neighbors and coworkers. But his son is our focal center, and it is Guido's ability to keep Giosué going that is our principal worry. Our hope versus fear ebbs and flows with the incredible difficulty involved in sustaining the fiction with his son while the horrors multiply all around him. We might know that this man can't act this way and survive the concentration camp, but we don't know what impact his actions will have on the boy or how long he'll be able to sustain his fiction. So we don't have predictability, even under such lopsided circumstances.

FOUNDATIONS

If we accept the idea that stories are built, that stories don't "just happen" and can be made either boring or scintillating by the quality of the storytelling, then where does that leave us? We aren't hanging around waiting for inspiration; we're having to draw a story out of ourselves and form it, mold it, build it into something worth presenting to an audience. "That sounds a lot more like work and a lot less like a get-rich-quick scheme than I thought it would. Isn't there an easier way?" Sure, pick six numbers between one and forty-eight, fill them in on a card, and pay a dollar for your lottery ticket. When that doesn't work, come back here with your shovel and hardhat. We're ready to dig the foundation upon which to build a story, and that digging is remarkably like work—fun work, potentially exciting work, sometimes frustrating and aggravating work. But shaping and carving out of human experience, captivating an audience and wringing them of every emotion they brought with them, playing God in a universe of your own creation, these are wonderful things to spend your time doing. You'll barely notice the sweat, the dirt, the hardness of the iron reinforcing bars, and the smell of the cement as you lay the foundation in place. At the same time as you are placing and securing the foundation, you will be gathering all the other materials from which to build your structure.

Building from the Ground Up

"I just want to start writing; I'll find my story as I go." Screenwriting students and beginners say this over and over, and some of them disregard the admonition that this approach will make the writing of a screenplay a longer more frustrating, and less successful enterprise. It *seems* logical that the sooner you start churning out script pages, the sooner you'll reach the end. But the truth is revealed by the "Page 70 Syndrome." If you start writing and figuring out where you're going on the fly, it might be fairly easy to establish the characters and the world of the story, to add more complications to the lives of the characters and to feel as if you're in motion. Then, somewhere close to page 70, you'll come to a dead stop. You won't know which way to go next, all you'll see are problems with the complications you've created, you won't see any solutions or viable directions to go, and your characters will be off doing things that don't make sense in your story, or they quit obeying you, or they quit doing anything at all. Other characters will have taken over and blown their own roles out of proportion, and you no longer have any idea at all what story you're trying to tell.

You will have hit the wall, and the only solution is to go back and regroup, rethink what you're doing. But rethinking is harder than thinking. You've already invested considerable time and energy in the story as it exists so far, and it's more difficult to throw out an entire direction the story took—and all the work you put into it—than it is to envision that same direction early on and reject it as unworkable. So rethinking starts turning into a salvaging effort where you continue to try to find solutions based on the story you developed on the fly. You might even restart and get another ten pages into the script before the patchwork of slightly new, salvaged story starts to unravel. By this time you will likely have grown tired of, or even come to hate, your story. This process can go on for years if you're tenacious enough and unwilling to build story foundations before picking the art to hang on the walls.

The smarter, faster, easier, more effective, and, ultimately, more-likely-to-be-successful approach is to build a foundation first, make a plan for where you are going, and *then* let fly. You'll get to page 70 more slowly, but you'll get to the end—a more satisfying end—a lot faster. You won't have to throw out handfuls of pages, at least in the first draft, and you will enjoy the wonderful rush of typing "FADE OUT" during a period of time when you still like the story.

The time one spends building foundations is filled with hope and the sense that "I'm really onto something here." Once the writing of pages begins and characters have to walk and talk and scenes start to take shape, reality starts to creep into your relationship with your story. The witty character isn't yet as witty as you'd hoped he'd be, the jokes aren't as funny as they should be, the danger isn't as palpable—yet—as you'd hoped. If you have a game plan—good foundations and an outline—then these little doubts hovering around the edges of your brain won't stifle you. "Maybe this scene isn't as good as I'd hoped it would be, but the next one is surefire." Hope and a positive outlook go a long way to keeping the seat of the pants to the seat of the chair. Without that state of existence, no writer gets much of anything done.

So you've decided to avoid the Page 70 Syndrome and build from the ground up; you have a hard hat and shovel, a good attitude, a world of hope, and plenty of energy. How do you start? The good news is, you've already started. You've decided on your protagonist and have a clue about what kinds of decisions she makes. You also know what collision creates the story—between the protagonist and another character, between her and the world of the story, or between her and another aspect of herself. You also have a thought about who the character is at the end of the story or what kind of change she goes through. The starting line on the road to the first draft is a long way behind you already.

The bad news is that you aren't even halfway there yet, much less able to see the final FADE OUT. It's as if you have the huge cornerstones of our magnificent creation now hauled to the building site, but you don't have them precisely placed or shaped for the real construction to begin. Worse still, you can't totally be sure you have them placed and shaped perfectly until after you've put up the first version of your building—the first draft. At that time, you'll have to go back and reassess each of the cornerstones and make adjustments. So how do you ever get started? Make your best guess about each of the cornerstones, then envision how your story will take shape above them, make some adjustments, and reenvision from the adjusted version. Once you are reasonably satisfied, it's time to go to the next stage.

So what are the cornerstones? We've already discussed them all but not fully explored the interplay among them. In one corner, of course, we have the protagonist, and diagonally across we have the antagonist—whether it's a character, the world, or the protagonist himself. The other two corners are trickier. In one we have the world of the story—whether it's actively opposed, passively opposed, actively supportive, passively supportive, or utterly indifferent—along with questions of where, when, and what version of the world this story takes place in. And in the fourth corner, we have you. What do you want the story to be, what's on your mind, what do you want from the story? Like a rock-paper-scissors game with a fourth element that ups the variables exponentially, each of these four cornerstones can have an impact on the other three. Understanding the dynamics that your chosen cornerstones have among themselves is akin to laying the groundwork for a major building. Figure it out now or risk the entire thing tumbling down around you.

What do you want from your story? If you want it to be funny or sad or moving or thought-provoking, that bedrock decision of yours will have an impact on the nature of the protagonist you mold. That decision also will skew the world in which you place the story. And the alteration of the protagonist—to come into accord with your desire to make a comedy or a tragedy—will also alter the antagonist. This is where the hard hat and shovel are most crucial—rooting around inside your own head for what you really want to make of your story. Even if you have been hired to write a script from someone else's idea, you still have to make it your own, take it inside of yourself and discover what version of that idea resonates for you. So again, as so often happens, the question comes back to what you want it to be. What's important for you in this story?

The answer to this question comes from trial and error. If I make my Napoleon into a preening fool, what does that do to my goal of a tragedy? What if I make him morose, somber, and introspective? How about if he's a hopeless romantic, painfully out of touch with the reality around him, and seeing only the idea of himself and his conquest of the world? No long days in your chair turning out sweat-stained, hard-fought pages are at stake for you yet. This is just mind-doodling. Try it this way, try it that; see what version of your protagonist best dovetails with what you want to make of your story. A good guess is the best you can hope for until you go around the circle of your cornerstones.

Once you have that version of your protagonist in mind, hold him up against the antagonist. Is the antagonist strong where the protagonist is weak, clear-sighted where the protagonist is blind; is the antagonist worthy of the protagonist; will their battle be hard-fought and unpredictable? Once they amount to a good match, you need to place them in a version of the world that supports where you are going with your story. Perhaps that world makes life difficult for your protagonist; perhaps it displays a version of reality in which the collision between your two opposites will best be seen and felt and fretted over.

This process circles back to you. Did going from protagonist to antagonist to the world of the story succeed in creating a dynamic that seems fruitful for the purpose you had in mind? The answer probably is no—not yet. So you need to tinker, perhaps going around the same direction or perhaps changing the order. What if my Napoléon isn't *the* Napoléon but a Napoléon-like figure set in the distant future or New York in the 1920s or in professional football? Or, no, it is *the* Napoléon, but the world of my story isn't a world of velvet robes and diamond tiaras but one of blood and mud and guts and sweat and hardship. Maybe you need to tinker with the antagonist and see what impact that has. What if it's Wellington as the preening fool who only accidentally stumbles into a crushing defeat of his enemy? How does that impact your goals? How does that impact your protagonist? The world of the story? Each adjustment affects the other cornerstones, sometimes subtly, sometimes sweepingly.

How much foundation building is enough? How good is good enough? When am I done and ready to start writing? Just as starting to write pages too soon is a fatal trap, getting mired in endless foundation building is counterproductive. It's a marvelous way of avoiding writing, of staving off having to face the reality of scenes falling short of the mark, of characters being less interesting or mysterious or witty or compelling than they seemed in the early envisioning stages. So when is enough? When you feel somewhat more certain and secure about your story than you did when you started, but you still harbor a few doubts. No amount of foundation building will dispel all doubts, so you can safely keep on adjusting and leveling forever—if you never want to face writing. Give yourself credit for continuing to have imagination and the insights into your story that helped lay the first foundation. You can still solve problems when you're farther along the road—as long as you know where you're headed.

Main Character's Passion

Once you're armed with some confidence that your foundation is sturdy, the four cornerstones are all on the same level—as near as you can tell—then it comes time to turn your attention to the shape of one of them: the protagonist. Not just the shape, but the strength and density, the very nature of the material. Everything still hinges on the protagonist. The world and the antagonist are created in support of the protagonist's story and the theme that he carries for you. If he or she is weak or weakly envisioned or fuzzily conceived, everything else suffers from a compounding of that weakness. Nowhere is this clearer or more important than in the passion of the character.

How passionately does your protagonist want or pursue or strive to accomplish a goal? An indifferent protagonist translates into an indifferent audience—which is the same thing as a bored audience. If your character doesn't want anything, she should not want it in a big way. If he's lazy, he should be passionately lazy, energetically lazy. If she has a weakness for gambling, she shouldn't be betting a portion of her savings at the racetrack, she should be deciding between a sandwich and a bet with her very last dollar—and make the bet. Just as our relationship to danger as human beings is different from what we put our characters through, their relationship to themselves and their wants and goals does not reflect how most of us choose to live in reality. In our daily lives, most of us strive for some balance, all things in moderation—including moderation—some yin and some yang. Sure, we like excitement and an impetuous romance or an impromptu trip to Rio, but we still manage to pay our bills, don't provoke wars with our unreasonable neighbors, call our parents regularly, guilt or no guilt. We tend to live our lives somewhere in the middle of the road. It's a wide road and at different times in our lives we veer this way or that, but we strive not to career into either ditch on a regular basis.

Living safely is not usually true of our characters. If it is, then the character should passionately and obsessively strive for the middle of the road; an inch over the center line either way drives this character crazy. That "safe" character becomes just another character heading perilously close to the ditch in what he or she thinks is the safest manner to live. Characters who play it very safe or who rate a 52 on a scale of 1 to 100—in anything—tend to be too uninteresting for an audience to commit its time and emotions. A character who rates a 3 or a 95 is likely to be more interesting. A character who pulls back from the brink just in the nick of time, only to career toward the opposite ditch, is one who attracts our attention.

This isn't to equate recklessness with passion. But characters who are slightly "bigger" or who veer in wider arcs along the road tend to display the passion needed to drive a story forward and engage an audience. A marvelous example of transformation in a character is in *Last Holiday*. George Bird is a bank clerk who steadfastly lives at the dead center of the road. This clerk is so dull and boring, this film is perilously close to losing its audience before it gets rolling. But he displays one unique characteristic that saves the early part of the film—he is obsessively boring. He goes beyond dull and verges on being almost an automaton. Then he visits the doctor and is diagnosed with an incurable disease and given about two weeks to live. He decides to give himself a grand holiday in which he will spend every penny of his life's savings during his few remaining days. From an obsessively middle-of-the-road man to one speeding hell-bent for the ditch, he transforms himself into someone worthy of our attention and emotional investment. The boring middle-of-the-roader was just the setup for the real character we follow through the bulk of the story, a man wagering his entire future on a two-week stint of fun and life and liveliness. What he undertakes is slightly "bigger" than life, slightly bolder or more starkly drawn than the shades of gray most of real life seems to present.

By throwing everything he has into one quest, George Bird becomes a passionate human being; he transforms into a clearly defined character. By not holding back, by not playing it safe, he elevates himself to a position worthy of a story. He shows passion. And passion, like laughter, is contagious. It's the passion of the character that creates the audience's most important connection to the story. That connection translates into our caring, hoping, and fearing—the emotions that ensure an audience's involvement in the lives depicted in the film.

We will follow a character who passionately chases a dream that we don't share more closely than one who halfheartedly goes after a dream we do share. Lester in *American Beauty* passionately quits his job, starts taking drugs, lusts after a teenage friend of his daughter's, insults his wife, and thumbs his nose at society in every way he can think of—and we follow him raptly all along the way. He's riveting. We don't necessarily share his vision of life, but we become wrapped up in his vision—because he wants it so badly. What about a Peeping Tom, how's that for a protagonist? Let's put him in a cast that immobilizes him so he can't even take any action. It doesn't sound very promising, but L. B. Jeffries in *Rear Window* draws us into his story because of his passion for invading the lives of his neighbors and, especially, for solving the mystery of one neighbor's supposedly private life. On the other hand, can you imagine getting deeply involved in the story of someone with a "worthy" ambition—say getting admission to a college, making it onto a team, playing a musical instrument extremely well, being elected class president—when that person only halfway pursues the goal? If she doesn't want it enough to work for it, why should we care? The truth is, we won't.

So it becomes necessary to find the passion within your main character. It doesn't have to be positive or admirable or beneficial to the world. It doesn't have to be a passion to accomplish something; it's just as useful to make the passion for avoiding or destroying. But that passion needs to veer the character toward one side of the road or the other—or, as we've discussed, obsessively along the middle of the road. So long as you have a protagonist who is passionate about some aspect of his life, you have a chance of engaging an audience. Once you engage them, you have a chance to elaborate on that engagement. And then you'll be off and running.

Can't we tell stories about normal people, or must we write only about freaks who live—and die—near the side of the road? Of course we can tell stories about normal people. You've probably heard that stories usually are about ordinary people in extraordinary circumstances or extraordinary people in ordinary circumstances. Truly passionate people are extraordinary people. Even Alec Guinness's bank clerk is extraordinary in his dullness, the routineness of his life. Or consider Roy Neary in *Close Encounters of the Third Kind:* he's completely ordinary until he's visited by the alien spaceship. That thrusts him into extraordinary circumstances. It's the collision of the ordinary with the extraordinary that creates these stories.

So if the protagonist isn't extraordinary to start with, then the world of the story or the antagonist must create an extraordinary circumstance, at least within the realm of the story. The protagonist must be prompted into becoming extraordinary. Luke Skywalker is a farm boy with big dreams and no prospects, but the world of the story delivers a droid into his life with information of intergalactic importance. Atticus Finch in *To Kill a Mockingbird* is a small-town lawyer and single father, but the world of the story throws a case in his lap that turns the world upside down. Sarah Connor is just a waitress with a roommate and a few friends, but the Terminator, the antagonist, comes to kill her, driving her into an extraordinary circumstance. Guido in *Life Is Beautiful* is a regular husband and father, but the world of the story throws him into an extraordinary circumstance—one shared by a distressingly large group of people. This circumstance, combined with the character's own qualities, transforms him into an extraordinary character as the circumstance starts to seem more and more ordinary, though no more acceptable.

So the collision between the character and the world of the story—including the antagonist—needs to generate heat in the form of something extraordinary. That heat can come from the protagonist, from the antagonist, or from the world. Without the heat, you have an ordinary person with ordinary passions in an ordinary world with ordinary obstacles of ordinary difficulty—and you are left with the question, Why tell this story? You can have a *seemingly* ordinary person in an ordinary world and discover there is a hidden or unknown passion lingering inside that person. You can have an ordinary person in a *seemingly* ordinary world and discover there is an extraordinary circumstance lurking below the surface or just around the corner. But without heat—hidden or overt—from one side of the collision or the other, the resulting impact will only be a fender bender, barely worthy of an anecdote over dinner and hardly worthy of marshaling the efforts of hundreds of people and millions of dollars to present to an audience.

Objective and Subjective Drama

One of the decisions you will need to make—one of a series of decisions that will be required throughout the writing of the screenplay—has to do with the proportions of objective and subjective drama in your story. This subject has already been dealt with in *The Tools of Screenwriting*, but in a nutshell, objective drama stems from moments that are dramatic whether or not we know anything about the participants. Fights and guns and explosions and car crashes are objectively dramatic. Subjectively dramatic moments get their power from our knowing something about the characters and caring about them. A moment that would not be dramatic without our knowledge and concern for at least one character can be subjectively dramatic. The touch of a hand or a meaningful look can be incredibly dramatic if we know what it means to characters we care about.

Part of this decision is already made when you choose what kind of story you want to tell. When you decide that you want to make a thriller or action adventure story, you are opting for a higher percentage of objective drama. When you decide to make a political or social or courtroom drama you are opting for a higher percentage of subjective drama. Both approaches are entirely valid, but each comes with its own requirements. What is usually not a valid choice—or at the very least, it's a dicey and dangerous choice—is to tell a story that is entirely objective or entirely subjective. This choice leaves your story open to major onslaughts of boredom in your audience. Either too little seems to be happening or a lot is happening that we don't care about. Either way, you're running a grave risk of losing your audience.

The overwhelming majority of films incorporate both objective and subjective drama. But this fact doesn't mean you have to envision a building exploding in the middle of your romantic comedy; smaller objectively dramatic moments are still objectively dramatic. It's surprising how closely these two different forms of drama can be woven to the point where it seems as if they are one. This seamlessness is a worthy goal, meshing objective circumstances with a subjective situation in which we care about the people in the car chase or the gunfight. Putting a character from a courtroom drama in a dark alley in a bad part of town to pick up a bit of evidence inserts objective drama into an otherwise subjectively dramatic story.

In *Mad Max 2: The Road Warrior*, which seems an objectively dramatic film, we have a nice melding of both forms of drama.

After the opening montage/history lesson, we jump into the middle of a car chase involving Max. We've been given a little history of Max in the opening, but this is his real introduction. This scene could be purely objective drama—a man in a hopped-up car is being chased by a wild-looking duo on a motorcycle and another dangerous-looking car—if it weren't for the dog. But the dog is cute and worried and, most importantly, he's wearing a neckerchief. He's Max's dog, and the dog can't have put that scarf on his own neck; therefore Max did it. This tells us that Max cares for his dog to the point of dressing him rather nattily. We conclude there is something of a bond between them, which makes Max likable—after all, he cares about dogs. So we have seen information about Max that makes us care about his well-being more than the well-being of the crazies on the cycle and in the car. We have formed a first bond with Max—minor, but still meaningful—which gives us a subjective relationship to the otherwise objective events throughout the chase. Not only is this bond kept alive during the chase, but danger to the dog and the interplay between him and Max heighten our caring about them.

This shows that the tiny details can make the difference. It's a misstep to consider objective and subjective drama solely in their larger arenas and miss the little opportunities to weave dramatic events with quieter moments that involve people we care about and about whom we have insider knowledge that makes the drama more intense. A fine example of melding from a different direction than *The Road Warrior* comes in *Annie Hall*. Alvy has gone to California to try to convince Annie to return to him, and he has failed. In the aftermath of their awkward meeting, Alvy tries to drive his car but hits one car, then another, and is finally stopped by a policeman. *Annie Hall* is primarily a subjectively dramatic story, as love stories necessarily are. But here we have a scene that is objectively dramatic—smashing up cars in front of a policeman will surely generate an impact in the audience without our knowing or caring about the characters. Add this to our knowing and caring about Alvy and we have the best of both worlds. It's both subjectively and objectively dramatic.

It's important to know and accept which form of drama will dominate in your story. There is nothing wrong with a film that is dominated by objective drama, so long as it contains enough subjective drama to sustain our interest and sympathy, to generate our hope versus fear. And there's nothing wrong with a subjectively dramatic story, so long as it contains enough objective drama to give us moments of demonstrable action that we can hope and fear about. Once you've embraced the dominant form, the trick is in identifying those moments in your story that will help you keep the other form alive. It can be easy to stay in the courtroom scene after scene without so much as a thumped table or a screamed "Objection!" and this can lull the audience into complacency, if not outright boredom. And it's equally easy to follow a car chase with a shoot-out that ends in a huge explosion and a daring escape with characters dangling from a helicopter flying over miles of snipers while the rope ladder unravels—and never get around to renewing our interest in the people who are narrowly escaping.

It's usually best to keep both forms of drama alive throughout the telling of a story rather than in large disconnected lumps. The latter will produce the obligatory love scene or the obligatory chase that seems either like an afterthought or tacked on or both. But you can have a small, subjective moment in the midst of a larger objectively dramatic sequence, or a small, objective moment in the midst of a protracted subjectively dramatic sequence. The lovers are about to kiss and everything has been subjectively dramatic leading up to it—so you throw a wrench into the works. One gets on the bus and the other misses it and has to chase after it, or a car drives through a mud puddle, splattering one or both of them. Your lone righteous man—who has a sweet tooth—is against a world of corrupt and evil killers who have him trapped. He savors with utter delight the last of a chocolate bar, and lets a cat lick his fingers while he pets it. You don't have to stop the flow of the dominant drama in order to get some spice from the other form.

At this point, in forming the foundations upon which to build your story, the crucial decisions you make are recognizing which is the dominant dramatic form and, most important, looking for every opportunity to weave the second form into the first. The drama of *Saving Private Ryan* is largely objective; the men are in the midst of the D Day invasion and then penetrating into enemy territory, where death is behind every bush. But the men all have their squabbles and fears, their curiosity about Captain Miller's peacetime job. The subjective drama—both the information that makes us care about the soldiers and the moments that are dramatic only because of the information we know about them—is woven continually throughout the story. *The Silence of the Lambs*, for all its gore and terrible events, is primarily a subjectively dramatic story. More of the story deals with Agent Starling interrogating Hannibal Lecter, or trying to, and then investigating, than it does creeping through a dark basement after the serial killer. But there are plenty of thrilling and chilling scenes—kidnapping and mayhem, severed heads and body parts—that are objectively dramatic, and these also are woven throughout the story. *The Graduate* is primarily subjectively dramatic, deriving its power from what we know of the characters; the sometimes small actions they take resound with meanings the uninformed would not receive. But there are times, such as the justifiably famous scene at the church at the end, that are objectively dramatic. *The Untouchables* is an objectively dramatic story, filled with mobsters, liquor barrel smashing, a charge and shoot-out on horseback, assassinations, fights, and death. But there are numerous objective moments woven in, particularly between Ness and his mentor, Jim Malone.

As you can see, you can have your cake and eat it too. Many of the opportunities for keeping both sides alive won't occur to you until you are envisioning your scenes in much more detail than you are now. But at this point, it's important to stake claim to the dominant and secondary forms and keep in mind what kind of proportions you hope to achieve in the end. If you aim for a fifty-fifty split, chances are one side or the other will prevail, and it's a better idea to know that going in. Too balanced could be nearly as dangerous as totally on one side or the other. There is a wide spectrum available that still incorporates elements of both sides. Within the realm of objectively dramatic stories, there's still quite a distance between *The Terminator, Alien,* and *Raiders of the Lost Ark,* which are near the end of the spectrum, and *The Untouchables, The Godfather,* and *North by Northwest,* which are closer to the middle. Within the realm of subjectively dramatic stories, *Annie Hall, Sunset Boulevard,* and *Philadelphia* are closer to the end of the spectrum, while *The Treasure of the Sierra Madre, The Third Man,* and *American Beauty* are closer to the center.

Theme

Theme was also dealt with in *The Tools of Screenwriting.* In brief, the theme of a story is the aspect of the "human dilemma" that it will explore. Betrayal, loyalty, self-worth, ambition, jealousy, hypocrisy, obsession, alienation—these are all valid themes that stories could explore. Note that there are no verbs involved, no value judgments inherent in potential themes. Something like "love conquers all" or "jealousy destroys from the inside" is a value-charged thesis rather than a theme. While love might conquer huge obstacles for a character within the course of a story, or jealousy may eat at a character's insides, these situations are just part of a larger exploration of the issue. Once a verb is added, once value judgments are hung onto a theme, then it becomes a thesis that the story is obliged to prove. This is a deadly, story-killing mistake. It skews the story away from art or entertainment and puts it squarely in the realm of propaganda. It might be heartfelt and earnest, but it's still propaganda. And perhaps worse still, it's terrible storytelling. A story saddled with the chore of proving a thesis relegates all its characters to "positions." Their words and actions are subordinate to the author's goal of proving his thesis to be true. Characters no longer act from within their own goals and wants and needs and weaknesses; instead they only say and do things based on the underlying thesis.

But a story needs to have a theme. Even a feel-good comedy or a shoot-'em-up has some kind of theme, if it is effectively done.

A story that is just a hodgepodge of skits meant to make us laugh or action sequences meant to make us cringe or thrill might have no underlying theme. And it also won't hold together as a story. The same comic or action moments woven into a real story that has some flow and a beginning, middle, and end will, inevitably, have some kind of theme. It might be a smaller subdivision of one of the themes listed above or the many other major issues a story could explore; it might be well masked, but it will be there. In a sense, theme is what actually holds the sequence of events together and makes it into one story.

What is explored in a story—the issue, the aspect of the human dilemma—and what is ultimately "said" about that issue are two different things. The resolution of a story is the strongest statement of the author's feelings about the issue at hand. This is the closest we have—or should have—to an outright statement of philosophy by a story writer. The statement should be buried in the action, in the moment of the resolution. It is there to be discovered, not handed to the audience or slapped in their faces. If you can effectively make your point in a simple thesis, then make that statement and forget the story. The experience of a story is a much more complex thing than a statement of values; it's an experience of values, of life's complexities and uncertainties and triumphs and defeats. No thesis can cover all that; all it can do is destroy the experience.

So how do I find my theme? How do I know what mortar is actually holding my story together? Don't throw out your hard hat and shovel. This is another major area of self-exploration; what is really on your mind? You can't fully know your theme until you have finished the first draft—or two or three drafts. But you can and should have a pretty good guess by the time you sit down to start writing pages. You need to start looking in two places more or less at the same time—the ending of your story, as you envision it now, and your protagonist. What kind of change does your protagonist go through? What part of his life or being is challenged or threatened or transformed? How have you thought of ending your story? How do you want us to feel at the end of the story? Will it have a happy ending, a sad or tragic

ending, or a bittersweet ending? Will your protagonist have tri-
umphed or seen the light in time or been too late or not strong
enough? As you wrestle with these questions and others that are
provoked by your mind-doodling, you will stumble across
some issues, some faults in the protagonist, or feelings you have
about some aspect of the human dilemma. Try to find a consen-
sus or some thread of similarity among the things you discover.
This could be your first glimpse, however fleeting, of your
theme.

Your most likely problem will be having too many choices.
Let's imagine our story is about Lindbergh and his famous flight.
The theme could be about courage or perseverance or foolhardi-
ness or ambition or obsession. At times Lindbergh demonstrated
all of these qualities and probably quite a few more. So which one
is your focus? This brings you back to that nagging question,
What do *you* want? How have you decided to end it? What is the
difference between the Lindbergh who lands his plane in France
and the one on the ground at the beginning? How has he changed
or grown or come to understand something about the world or
himself or life? Or has he diminished, turned into a glory hound
who is no longer capable of empathy and understanding? How
should we in the audience feel at the end—about the story, about
Lindbergh, about the change in him, about the enterprise of a
stunt flight across the Atlantic? At some point, if you keep at it,
one issue or one potential theme will rise slightly above the others. Maybe your Lindbergh has courage and perseverance and
plenty of obsessiveness, but more than anything he is a reckless
fool who got lucky and never learned how stupid his exploit was.
Or maybe your Lindbergh is clear-sighted, ambitious, and coura-
geous, able to see the trustworthiness of his plane and his flying
talents when the fools on the ground are all telling him he's crazy.
His landing of the plane is a triumph, proof that he was right, that
he and his plane had what it takes.

This combination of your protagonist's character, the change
she goes through, the kind of ending you want, and how you want
the audience to feel about it all point toward your theme.
Chances are, they are not yet all pointing at one theme unless

you're as lucky as Lindy. More likely, you'll have to make them point there; you'll have to adjust and focus so that everything comes together. You hadn't fully thought of Lindbergh as an ambitious fool, but you'd been leaning in that direction. Now you need to push him a little farther in that direction, focus his character, clarify his nature in alignment with your theme. In the end, the protagonist has to be the bearer of the theme; it needs to inhabit him and become part of his inner journey.

What does this do to everyone else in your story? Once you know your theme, or at least have a good first idea of it, this can help you sharpen all the other characters. As we discussed before, the antagonist and all the reflective and subordinate characters are defined in part by their relationship to the protagonist. Once you know this critical issue about your protagonist—his foolishness will be challenged or his foresight will be threatened—then you have added information to use in clarifying the other characters. The antagonist should be significantly different from the protagonist on this issue. There should be reflective characters who are farther in one direction or the other than the protagonist—even more foolish or totally sensible—to push and pull on this aspect of him that the story will be exploring. All of the characters can be further developed by clarifying their position on the theme you have in mind.

In fact, the other characters can often help you realize your theme. One of the best ways to discover your theme after a draft or two have been written is to analyze the subplots in relation to the main story line. The journeys of the antagonist and reflective characters—whether they are full subplots or part of the overall story—should be thematically linked to the main story. You can't know the full implications of theme for your story at this stage. These relationships between the secondary characters and the main character only start to take on shape and life when the scenes are written, when the characters are up and running. Then you'll discover what's really been on your mind, what your story "is really about." But right now, you can work from an educated guess that will sharpen the edges of your characters and influence the way in which events are experienced during the story by the characters and by the audience.

Backstory

You now know approximately where your story will be on the spectrum between totally objective and totally subjective drama, and you have a good first guess about our theme. You also have your cornerstones in place and somehow generating heat. But how much of those cornerstones should be above ground? How much do you leave showing? Just because you know your Napoleon is a preening fool doesn't yet tell you how you will reveal it in the story or how many—if any—of the formative events of his life you will actually dramatize. Do you start with the little corporal, do we first meet him as a mature leader, or do we only join him at the preparation for the Battle of Waterloo or in the aftermath, on his way to exile, ruminating about his defeat?

How a character—any character, not only the protagonist—became who he or she is before the story starts is called backstory. Obviously, the backstory of the protagonist is the most important, but we may get pieces of past history about other characters as well—informative bits that help us to understand or sympathize with or detest or pity or admire a character for what has already occurred. This personal historical information broadens our connection with the character, deepens our understanding of him, and can serve as a springboard for our hope and fear about him; past behavior can be a predictor—but not a guarantee—of future behavior. The backstory can be a means of establishing and strengthening the union of the protagonist with the theme that he or she embodies.

To a certain degree, the more we know, the closer our connection to a character. But familiarity can breed contempt. We can know too much about a character, to the point of nausea or boredom. Given the severe time constraints of films, generally audience more often suffer from insufficient information rather than an overabundance. How do you know how much and which backstory information to include in the story? And how do you include it? Do you have to dramatize the backstory, or will telling about it be sufficient? Or is there another way altogether?

First you have to decide what to include, and then determine how to include it. Human beings are complex creatures, and you can't possibly leave in every formative event in their lives and still have screen time available to tell the story at hand. In general you want to limit yourself to revealing backstory information that is directly pertinent to the main theme or goal or pursuit of the story. There might also be some backstory in support of a major subplot. If, for instance, there is a major love story subplot, you might need to include backstory information about past loves, even though this is a war story about submarines and the primary information you need to give the audience is the reason behind the hero's nearly pathological fear of water.

You don't want to include backstory information that can safely be assumed about the character. In *American Pie* and *Porky's* and a hundred other teen comedies, you don't have to include backstory about why the teenage boys so desperately want sex. It's a pretty safe assumption that a teenage boy wants sex. It would actually require backstory information if your teenage male character *didn't* want sex. The same goes for priests having faith, professional musicians loving music, presidential candidates having overblown egos, paraplegics wishing they had the use of their legs, and kindergarten teachers loving kids. You don't have to fill in the exact events in someone's past if their current behavior seems pretty logical, if it can be assumed. If their current behavior is contrary to what could be assumed, then we need the backstory information that clarifies why your paraplegic prefers not to be able to walk again or how someone with a normal ego decides to run for president.

Where you most need backstory information is in the areas of a character's past that can't safely be assumed. These are often, if not always, the areas that make the character interesting or unique. Why won't Rick stick his neck out for anyone in *Casablanca*, even his long-lost love? What happened in Agent Starling's past that made her susceptible to Hannibal Lecter in *The Silence of the Lambs*? How did a joyful and prankish but not destructive guy like McMurphy get thrown in prison and then a psychiatric ward in *One Flew over the Cuckoo's Nest*? How did Luke in *Cool Hand Luke* get himself taken to a prison farm filled with real criminals who are much harder than he is? What happened in Joe Buck's past that made him think he could make a killing in New York as a gigolo in *Midnight Cowboy*? What turned Stevens in *The Remains of the Day* into a man incapable of letting go of tradition and going to the woman he loves? What happened to Louise in Texas that was so horrible she will drive around the huge state, even when running from the police, in *Thelma and Louise*? Some parts of the lives of these characters are recognizable and assumable, and some parts have to be explained for the audience to participate in their stories. The part that needs explaining is the backstory you need to include, the part of the cornerstone that needs to be above ground, visible.

Once you identify what must be explained or given as backstory information, it prompts the question, how do you deliver it? There are four basic approaches to revealing backstory: dramatize it, tell it in dialogue, leave remnants of the backstory in the present, or hint at it without ever being explicit. In *Casablanca,* the backstory between Rick and Ilsa is dramatized for us in a single flashback. We go into Rick's memory and get an encapsulated version of their love affair in Paris and how he was left stranded in the rain at the train station. In *Midnight Cowboy,* we also see flashbacks dramatizing Joe Buck with his grandmother. But here it is broken up into tiny bits—along with other flashes of a past girlfriend and a flashback of his leaving his dishwasher job in Texas. In *The Silence of the Lambs,* Hannibal Lecter seduces Agent Starling into telling about her past, from which the story gets its title, so we get her backstory in dialogue. Similarly, in *One Flew over the Cuckoo's Nest,* McMurphy tells his psychiatrist about his statutory rape conviction and his goal of serving out his jail time in the psychiatric ward rather than the more difficult jail. In *Cool Hand Luke,* we have a pretitle sequence that dramatizes Luke getting revenge on what must be a longtime enemy, parking meters. He's very drunk and very deliberate and we learn all we need to know about his crime and past. And in *Thelma and Louise,* we never learn chapter and verse about what happened to Louise in Texas; we are only given hints. But when her reactions to being questioned about her past are put together with her action of shooting the would-be rapist and her reaction to the prospect of driving through Texas, we gather just enough information to know that something big, something rape-related or shooting-related or both, must have happened to her. We don't learn exactly what happened, but we learn exactly what impact this unknown event had upon her, and knowing the impact is enough. In *The Remains of the Day*, Stevens is continually caught between the traditional duties and positions he is committed to uphold and the crumbling of the caste system in an England that is rapidly changing. His every interaction with his "superiors" and his increasingly desperate attempts to maintain the long-established rules of a proper household give us peeks into what formed him into the rigid man he is, without requiring either a flashback or a direct statement of who he is and what he believes.

Each of these tactics for revealing backstory is viable. You will recall from earlier sections that dramatized material is stronger than unsupported dialogue, that reluctantly revealed information is stronger than volunteered information and that actions reveal the truth more reliably than simple statements. All of these caveats apply to backstory and its inclusion in the story. So clearly, dramatized backstory is more compelling and visceral for the audience than dialogue-delivered backstory. Given all that, why would anyone choose a method other than dramatizing the backstory, in flashback or as a pretitle sequence or simply as the beginning of the story? Of course, these tactics often are used, but there are plenty of reasons to choose other methods. Time is one. Proportion is another. Distraction is another. Let's take them one at a time.

The screen time it takes to dramatize the backstory might not be worth the information to be delivered. Time is our most precious commodity as storytellers, and it must be spent wisely. If a suitable dialogue situation or a present-tense vestige of the past would provide reliable backstory information, then it might suffice to use those opportunities rather than dramatizing backstory. If a character knows her backstory and can be trusted in revealing it, then perhaps dialogue or current reminders will do the job. If the character is delusional about his own past or in a state of denial, not only might it be necessary to dramatize the true events so the audience can form its own opinions, but it also might be necessary to dramatize *how* the character depicts his past, as a means of contrast with the truth. In this case it would be counterproductive to save the screen time. The point of the story might be to force the character to see and accept the truth about himself, and it is crucial to our involvement in the story for us to know the truth ourselves.

Another reason not to dramatize the backstory is when those events might become disproportionate to the current story. Let's say you have a romantic story involving a woman who was sexually assaulted years ago. If the story is about an assault victim learning to trust a man again, then you might need to dramatize the backstory. In this circumstance, the essence of the story stems from that assault and the repercussions it has had in her life. But let's say the story isn't about that aspect of her, yet that assault did indeed have a formative influence. This could be Louise in *Thelma and Louise*. A backstory event that is dramatized is more visceral and real to an audience than one that is merely spoken about. It might grow out of proportion to its importance within the realm of the story being told. Therefore telling it or alluding to it or showing the scar from it might be more proportional to the story.

And another reason to stay away from dramatizing the backstory is distraction. What if we dramatized McMurphy's backstory of being convicted of statutory rape? What was that actually like? How young was the girl? How sleazy was he, how abusive of her trust or innocence? By putting that material on screen, we would be distracting the audience from the real issue of the story, which is not about whether McMurphy is a nice guy, but the treatment of these men in this hospital. We could be shining the light on the wrong aspect of a person, giving the audience a wrong impression of where the story is going or what is important in it. So you have to pick the method of revealing the backstory based on what is important for the story and which method best supports the story, not just reveals the character and her past.

Another problem to address when dramatizing backstory is where, when, and how to stop. If you start to tell what happened yesterday, what about the day before and the day before that and the day he turned twelve and the day he was born and the day he was conceived or what about when his parents met? You can keep going backward and never get around to telling the story. All of that information might be valuable for the writer to know, but it doesn't need to be dramatized in the story. Maybe a photo from his birth and a broken knife from when he was twelve and an anecdote about the meeting of his parents will be a better use of screen time and much less distracting and in proportion with the story. Or maybe you need one bit of information on screen and the rest inhabits the character.

One of the most effective means of dealing with backstory is by creating modern remnants, vestiges of the past that the character carries with her. Scars, mementos, habits, rituals, phobias—each of these is a potential remnant of backstory and helps make it more believable. We're more likely to believe a man wrestled with a bear and survived if he has scars to prove it than if we have to take his unsupported word for it. He still might be lying, but the scars will lend credence until proven otherwise.

Rituals, habits, and phobias are extremely interesting means of revealing a character's past. Each of them implies the past, implies that this same ritual, habit, or phobia has existed since before the story began. A character employing a ritual in the present helps us to understand something of what happened to the person in the past, or at least shows what was important to her once and remains so now. With phobias, we have an implication of a bad past experience. Some people may be born afraid of heights or water, but it's just as likely there was a formative event in the backstory, and the present existence of the phobia gives us both an entrée into the backstory and present-tense proof of the strength of its impact on the character. We don't need to see a person's near-drowning incident if we have an occasion to experience his total phobia about water and a brief line of dialogue to explain it. This technique is just as compelling as dramatizing the backstory in flashback and is more smoothly integrated with the flow of the story in its present tense.

What's at Stake?

We've discussed at length the creation and management of the audience's hope versus fear and the use of tension as a primary tool of storytelling. These form a solid emotional connection with the story's characters. But the connection can be made even stronger if the hope and fear can be manifested in some way, made more palpable or physical. Sometimes doing this is easy: we hope James Bond gets to the bomb and defuses it before it destroys all life on earth. We can measure our hope versus fear by the distance and the obstacles between him and the bomb. This setup works well in everything from *Star Wars* to *The Silence of the Lambs* to *Dr. Strangelove*. But often, there isn't a bomb or a serial killer's next victim to engage our hope versus fear. Even in a comedy, a romance, or a nonlethal drama it still helps the audience to have something identifiable at stake. What's at stake could be something placed at risk or something to gain or both. It doesn't have to be an object or an explosion; it can be a state of being or a kiss or a look or a moment of forgiveness. If we can know what's at stake in advance and recognize it when we get near it, then you have a way of focusing and intensifying our tension. Like the childhood game, we know when we're getting warmer and when we're getting colder. The kiss we've been hoping for is about to happen—it's warmer. Then they are interrupted—getting colder. Then one character has to leave the room—stone cold.

One way to consider what's at stake is to envision the best-case scenario and the worst-case scenario for your characters—from your audience's vantage point. If everything we hope for happens perfectly, what will be the new status quo in this world? If everything goes wrong, what will be the status quo? If Captain Miller and his squad succeed, they will find Private Ryan and all get back alive and healthy. If everything goes wrong, they will all die in the trying. If everything works out for Lola in *Run Lola Run*, she'll get the money in time to save her boyfriend. If everything goes wrong, he'll die. If everything goes right, Will Shakespeare will write a hit play and manage to keep his true love in *Shakespeare in Love*. If everything goes wrong, he'll fail to get his play written and he'll lose his lover—and perhaps his life or freedom. If everything goes right, Dr. Richard Kimble will find the one-armed man who killed his wife and clear his name in *The Fugitive*. If everything goes wrong, he'll be killed while being considered a dangerous escaped prisoner. Having both sides of the equation known in advance by the audience allows us to play the warmer-colder game ourselves as the story unfolds.

If one side or the other of the best/worst-case scenario also has a demonstrable person, place, or thing for us to hang on to, then we have an easy barometer of how the quest is going for our protagonist. It's as if we have a yardstick for our hope versus fear. Dr. Kimble catches a glimpse of the one-armed man—he exists— so we can tell when he's getting closer to his quarry and when he's losing sight of him. In *Cuckoo's Nest* the window to the psychiatric ward is eventually unlocked; all McMurphy has to do is climb through it to gain his freedom. While the physical manifestation of his quest has not been there throughout the story, once it is introduced, our hope versus fear is focused and intensified; it's made specific. The package of money Lola manages to get is an object for focusing our hopes. It exists, she seems to have succeeded in the harder part of the quest, and now she simply has to get to her destination in time. In *The Sting*, Lonnegan's suitcase of money is a wonderful object for us to focus on; if they get it, they get their revenge; if they don't, they have failed at their quest. The Maltese Falcon itself has this same function; so does the computer file in *Mission: Impossible*; so too the small hole in the Death Star in *Star Wars*. As you can see, objectification of the goal—identifying the quest with a specific task or object or goal line—doesn't have to exist throughout the story; it can be created along the way as a means of adding even greater tension. Specificity has a strong impact on our hope versus fear; elimination of all but the essentials focuses, and therefore intensifies, our tension just as the water in a river speeds up when the channel narrows. This bonding of the stakes with a specific object or goal won't work in every story, but in those it does work for, it can boost the tension to a new level.

What's at stake can add another level beyond heightened tension. Often, what's at stake is invested with greater meaning than what it appears to be on the surface. In a sense, the bomb squad officer's happy marriage is a subjective version of what's at stake, while the bomb itself is an objective version. We might have a character who screwed up in the past and that failure has haunted him to this day, but now he has a second chance. This subjective knowledge of ours does two things. It increases the likelihood of his failing again, since we know he was once not up to the task, and, at the same time, it makes the successful completion of the goal a personal triumph in addition to a salvation for everyone who would have suffered for his failure. Let's look at *Schindler's List*. Clearly, what's at stake are the lives of about 1,200 Jews Schindler has managed to gather and protect. That alone is plenty, but isn't there a personal stake for Schindler that goes beyond the potential of his being caught and killed for his deception? While it isn't spelled out in explicit terms, Schindler's relationship with himself is a complex one. He cheats on his wife; he profits off the war and the Nazis. But it is Stern's approval that he craves. The ring made for him at the end is a manifestation of Stern's approval, but it is one-on-one that he seeks acceptance—almost as if it's an atonement. Even though he could not put it into such words and the film never spells it out precisely, the relationship between these two men is the crux of what's at stake for Schindler; the large number of other people are, in a sense, the physicalization of his pursuit of acceptance and approval from Stern. By wrapping these two elements together into one answer for what's at stake, this story creates a value-added situation. There is both the objective stake—the number of lives to be saved—and the subjective stake—approval from Stern.

What's at stake in *Chinatown*? Of course we have the lives and futures of Evelyn and the girl, especially the girl who has been sought throughout the story. But there is a personal stake for Jake as well—his ability to help them, to feel as if he has successfully done his job for someone he cares about. His relationship to himself, his sense of self-worth or pride in his work, has constantly been challenged throughout the story. By the end, that inner stake for him is inextricably tied to Evelyn and the girl; if they get away, he's validated; if they don't, his self-doubt is given greater fuel. What's at stake in *October Sky*? First there is the scholarship for the winner of the science fair, and, closer to home and more visceral, there is the redemption of Homer in the eyes of his community by the successful launch of his rocket. On top of all that, there is the acceptance by his father, as demonstrated by the father's appearance at the final launching. The outer stake is subjective—redemption in the eyes of the town—and the higher, more intimate, stake is even more subjective—the acceptance by his father. The rocket that culminates is the physical manifestation of the triumph we are made to feel when all of these elements come together at one time, at the final launch. It isn't just luck that weaves these elements together and makes them come to a head at the same time; this is the essence of the craft and art.

One more crucial aspect of what's at stake within a story is who pays the price of failure. With Bond it might be all of mankind, in *The Silence of the Lambs* it's the latest victim, in *Chinatown* it turns out to be Evelyn, in *Casablanca* it would be the world fighting the Nazis if Victor Laszlo couldn't lead the battle. Who pays the price doesn't have to be the protagonist, and the effect is often stronger if it isn't. When the protagonist is the one who pays—with his life or freedom or money or prestige or self-respect—then he is betting what he already has, his own stuff or being, in his battle. Doesn't it raise the ante a great deal if he has to bet someone else's life? It's one thing to decide to climb a cliff and risk your own neck; it's another, even more tense situation, to risk dropping someone else to his or her death. Clearly, it can't always be that someone else has to pay the price of the protagonist's potential failure. If his sense of self-respect is what's at stake in the course of the film, no one else can possibly pay that price. But if you put that self-respect into a situation where it also requires the approval of another person—as in *Schindler's List*—then you succeed in giving an outside manifestation for the inner loss the character could suffer if he fails.

If there is no price to pay for failure, only something to gain from success, it seems as if the stakes are too low in a story. If the worst-case scenario is that the protagonist has to go back to the life he was leading at the outset, then it will feel to the audience that he hasn't had to put enough at risk. He was alive and functioning when the story began, wasn't he? Interestingly, the reverse is not true. If the best-case scenario is that the character succeeds in reestablishing the status quo she had at the opening—and we feel that was a worthwhile status quo—then this is plenty to have at stake.

When struggling with what is at stake in your story, you must ask yourself about the best- and worst-case scenarios, what stands to be gained or lost and who is at risk of paying the highest price. If nothing would change in the lives of the characters with either success or failure, then there is a major problem with your setup. As we discussed earlier, stories are about change, and change is painful, change comes at a price. What is that price? What is put at risk of being lost during the process of that change? What stands to be gained from the striving involved in the story? It can be merely a physical thing or a state of being for a character, or, between two characters, it can be the absence of an undesirable element or the attainment of a new high—physical, emotional, spiritual.

Just as you have had to adjust your four cornerstones to focus your story, you may have to tinker with what's at stake. It's great to have something physical, visible—like a rocket or a packet of money or a prison your character might be put into—but it's even more important to have the meaning behind what's at stake and to know who pays the price, depending on which way the story turns out. Finding a way to tie the physical object or state of being to the meaning behind it can be a challenge. A great example of this bonding comes at the end of *The Godfather*. What has been at stake is Michael's future; the struggle has been to keep him out of the world of the Mob, to keep him from becoming the next godfather in all its meanings. First he's been kept outside by his father, then he's taken an active role by killing the men responsible for the attempt on his father's life, but he's just as quickly been sent away, to a different world, a bucolic, peaceful, Old Country world. Then he's drawn back in by the death of his new bride. All along the way, our hope versus fear has been ebbing and flowing with these fluctuations. At the very end, when he is literally becoming a godfather for the first time in church, he is also rising

to become the new godfather of the Mob family with the simultaneous assassinations he has ordered. These two sides are bound
together into one state of being for Michael; he becomes the new
godfather, literally and figuratively.

The successful melding of a demonstrable state of being with
a metaphorical one is not an easy task. It might not happen right
away in the creation of your story. What's most important in the
foundation-building stage is to know what is at stake in the overall story and to keep your eyes open for a linkage with something
the audience can see and anticipate. It might be built-in like a
ticking bomb, but it's just as likely that you'll have to create it, to
make the story create this connection. It may take you a draft or
two to have a successful union. If you have the physical state—
your story involves the potential loss of lives or the gaining of millions, the attainment of a gold medal or an election to some
office—then the challenge will be to find the meaning behind it,
the value-added portion that makes success or failure more
meaningful for the audience and for the characters.

Six Types of Characters

You've clarified your protagonist and, along with him, your antagonist. You've dealt with reflective characters and supportive
characters. But you have not fully wrestled with the other kinds
of characters in your story, at least in their relationship to the
protagonist and his goals. Reflective characters push and pull
your main character and help us to see the wavering that might
be going on inside of her. But the issue is more complex than simply surrounding the protagonist with a group of friends. What
kinds of roles do these people take on, and how can they shift or
change? Must they always be what they seem, or can there be layers of complexity in secondary characters just as there should be
in main characters?

It probably sounds odd—and perhaps limiting—to hear that
there are six basic types of character relationships to the protagonist. But once you understand that truth, you'll also realize that
it is not in the least limiting; rather this can be one of the more

liberating discoveries in the exploration leading to a screenplay. In their relationship to the protagonist there are friends, enemies, and indifferent characters. Friends, of course, support and help and abet in whatever quest or dilemma the protagonist is enmeshed. Enemies try to fight against, foil, or undermine the protagonist. Indifferent characters don't have a position; they neither actively support nor actively oppose the protagonist and his goals. But we have another whole series of character types as well. We have pretend friends, pretend enemies, and pretend indifferent characters. Could there be a seventh type that none of these categories covers? Dead or in a coma have to count as indifferent.

These states of being, these conditions of characters in their relationship to the protagonist, are changeable. An enemy can turn into a friend, an indifferent character can become an enemy, a pretend enemy could actually be indifferent but become a friend. There are a great many permutations and they can be mixed and matched, repeated and reversed.

Let's try one single relationship, the love interest in a romantic comedy. Often the protagonist and love interest start out as enemies, then they become friends, then one hurts the other, who turns back into an enemy but can't admit it yet so is a pretend friend who is really an enemy. Once the truth comes out, one of them pretends to be indifferent but can't sustain it and declares the friendship, but now the other feigns indifference or pretends to be an enemy to test the first until finally at long last they kiss, make up, and remain friends. Pick your favorite romantic comedy and you'll find that it more or less resembles this sequence—perhaps the order changes or the number of flipflops is different—but the shifting among relationship types is a normal, perhaps even prerequisite, feature of romantic comedies.

Shifting the types of character relationships is hardly limited to comedy. Michael in *The Godfather* is a pretend friend as he is about to kill his enemies at lunch; then he is warned to beware of a friend who will set him up to be murdered, in truth a pretend friend who is an enemy. Isn't the essence of Nurse Ratched that she is a pretend friend who is a vile enemy? Chief pretends indifference, but is truly a friend. Harding, who seems like an enemy, turns into a friend. The whole of *The Usual Suspects* is based on the shifting sands of friend and enemy and acting under false pretenses. The same with *L.A. Confidential, Goodfellas, Reservoir Dogs,* and a whole host of films spanning the gamut from high art to lowbrow comedy to action adventure and intrigue. Even a film such as *Star Wars* with its simple characters and relationships has plenty of changing among character relationship types. The relationship of Han Solo and Princess Leia alone has many enemy and pretend enemy and pretend indifference stages. An excellent courtroom drama like *The Verdict* has its share of shifts in character positions, while a raucous romp like *Animal House* also has shifting character types.

This changing from one type to another, and particularly the use of pretending, is so pervasive it's hard to imagine a well-told story without at least some evidence of it. Drama is difficult to create—verging on the impossible—if every single character tells the truth at all times and everyone believes the truth that the other characters present. Human beings by their very nature deceive— each other and themselves, intentionally and unintentionally. They also change, sometimes faster than the perceptions of others can absorb. This lag between a change and others knowing about it can be the most interesting and productive area in a story. And when the truth is being told but being disbelieved, it is just as interesting and intrigue-laden as a web of lies. Herein lies the "work" the audience loves to delve into—ferreting out the truth from the lies, the misperceptions and miscues, false starts and false impressions, the good reasons behind the lies and the bad reasons behind the truth, the shifts from one relationship type to another and what repercussions that has on the other characters, their goals and quests and lives. This is the "good stuff."

Once you recognize that all of your characters at any given time must fall into one of these relationship categories—including the protagonist toward the others—and that this by no means requires them to stay in that category, it gives you a powerful tool as you work toward unfolding your story. Instead of stumbling ahead with only vague ideas of what's going on under the surface, you gain a clear vision that the best friend is—for the moment—actually indifferent and that the avowed enemy will for a short time be a true and trustworthy friend but will just as surely revert to being an enemy before the story is over. This can clear away the surface smoke from your eyes as you strive to envision the story in its moment-to-moment unfolding.

CARPENTRY AND CRAFTSMANSHIP

The moment-to-moment telling of the story is what we are drawing steadily closer toward. You've clarified what the story is about, you've wrestled with the cornerstones and the other crucial aspects of the foundation, and you've assembled much of the building material. Now it's time to deal with how you will go about cobbling together your masterpiece. Some of the following discussions are echoes of what has been dealt with before in *The Tools of Screenwriting*, but this is by no means a reprise of that book. Here I will endeavor to give you a start in the building trade, in the use of the tools, as well as a timely "heads up" about the pitfalls and the hallmarks to look for when creating any story. This is the craft of story building.

There is no better place to start this discussion than to deal with the often-heard question, "Can screenwriting really be learned?" This might seem like an odd place to be asking this question; you've read this far, you must believe you can learn screenwriting. But what you've been doing has been rooting around in your own mind for your story and your own concerns and wrestling with big issues like your cornerstones. You've been conjuring up ideas about what you want to make. There's a big difference between that and writing the first scene and then the next scene and the one to follow that, all the way to the end of your story. That's the practice, the real test of your ability to make what it is you're currently envisioning. You've been doing a lot of preparing to write, and this section is *still* preparing to write, but at last you're starting to deal with the actual process—in the minute, in the moments of the scenes.

So, can screenwriting be learned? If the question weren't asked so often and negated by some heavyweights in and out of the film world, it would be tempting to dismiss it as ludicrous and unworthy of our time. For centuries people have argued whether writing can be taught, whether a writer has to be born that way, or whether writing can be learned. Can storytelling be learned? Was Michelle Kwan taught to figure-skate, or was she born knowing how to skate? Did anyone teach Tiger Woods to play golf? How about Vladimir Horowitz and the piano? Did anyone teach Frank O. Gehry architecture? What about Pablo Picasso—did anyone show him how to use a brush and what application of paint produced what effect? It's self-evident.

People can be taught; people can learn the fundamentals of any art form or any other complex human endeavor. And their education can continue from the fundamental through more sophisticated understandings of "what's really going on" in any of these art forms. Whether a person becomes an artist or a master or *the* master of the form will take a lifetime of effort to discover, but first every artist or master learned the craft. Someone showed Kwan how to leap and spin, someone showed Horowitz where middle C is on the piano, and someone showed Tiger Woods what an iron will do versus what a putter will do. In fact, those teachers no doubt spent many years with each of these artists before they started inventing their own special moves, their own magical version of an activity that millions of others have tried—usually with considerably less success. It might be hard to imagine, but there must have been a time when Horowitz played off key, when Woods drove a ball right into the pond, and when Kwan fell on the ice. If they never did, they never could have become great artists.

Yes, you can learn screenwriting, but whether you will become an artist, a master of the form, or *the* master of the form, we will have to wait and see. All you can do is fall in love with the game and keep playing it, keep perfecting your version of it, and start to invent—by default as often as not—your specialties of your craft. You have to learn enough to start inventing for yourself within the discipline. At some point Kwan and Woods and Horowitz and Picasso surpassed their learning and became the inventors of their own methodology. None of them could have done this without the initial learning; it was that hard work and study and overcoming of frustration that enabled them to reach the point where they discovered some kind of "wholeness" in their art form. When Horowitz was no longer worried about hitting the right key or the right timing of his notes, he started to be free enough for his emotions and ideas, his loves and his own shortcomings to infuse his music. This is the point at which artistry begins; art can only be built on the shoulders of a mastered craft. Inability to hit the keys—or hit the golf ball or make the leap—never helped any artist become an artist.

So what we are working on here is craft; it is the carpentry of building stories from the ground up; it is the trade of assembling parts that on their own might be less than inspired or inspiring, but with luck, perseverance, practice, and more practice, the resulting structure can take on a life and worth all its own. It might resemble your original idea or even surpass it. There could come a time when you step back from the house you've built and realize, "Hey, I made that!" and it seems like so much more than any of those things you crafted and put into it. But set that glorious moment on the back burner for a while. We have to learn to pound a few nails.

There's quite a distance between a good idea for a story and a good script from that idea. That distance is measured in scenes and in the organization of the scenes and in the organization of the experience those scenes give to the audience. It's also measured in the quality of the moments and their impact on the audience. First we will deal with how to make the moments work—what elements do we need to use to create screen moments that work? Then we will tackle the even more difficult task of organizing the scenes, of shaping the overall flow and direction of the story to create the maximum impact.

There may come a time when a great idea for a story can feel like a curse. Nothing you create after that inspired idea measures up; everything else seems pedestrian and mundane. The feeling is probably right, but the truth is that this is no reason to stop.

A carpenter has a variety of saws and chisels and layer upon layer of material to add to the building—each in its own time and its own way—because it's impossible that every part will fit perfectly on the first try and look great and function correctly. A house doesn't look worthy when only the studs are up on the walls and the doors and windows aren't in yet, much less the paint, the hardwood floors, and all the other parts we normally see in a finished house. If the carpenter stopped when the stud wall looked bad compared to a finished and trimmed wall, he'd never get the house built. And he'd never get around to finishing and trimming that wall. First he has to get it standing; then he can come back and fix and finish and adjust and make it much better. Remember this: it's much better to have an imperfect wall that stands than part of a perfect one on the floor.

Creating the Audience's Experience

All that we have struggled with so far is for you, not for the audience. The audience isn't going to see the cornerstones the way you do, isn't going to know that you've crafted your protagonist and antagonist with care so that their strengths and weaknesses correspond for maximum conflict and impact and unpredictability. The audience is only going to experience your story one moment at a time, minute after minute, from beginning to end, whatever beginning and end you choose. They are going to learn things as you show them and teach them, to care about the things you make them care about—if you manage to be in control of your own story and its telling. They have volunteered and paid money and made themselves available to you—and vulnerable to you—so that you can give them an experience. If they don't have the experience you want them to have, it isn't their fault; it's your fault. You failed or fell short or made a misstep that sent them careening off in a direction you hadn't intended. If those failings and shortcomings and missteps happen in the moments of the telling of the story, it doesn't matter how perfect your conception of everything behind the scenes was. It's what's in front of the audience that matters in the end. You can't create the parts the audience experiences without first wrestling with all the hidden and backstage parts, but your stagecraft, your ability to make the moments do what they need to do will be what the audience experiences, and it had better be up to the high standards you set in your envisioning and fleshing out of your story.

Immediacy and the Sense of Here and Now

What is a moment? It seems like a stupid question, but it's amazing to see how often real moments in scripts are omitted and replaced by the idea of a moment. "They make love." "A gunfight ensues." "She bakes an apple pie." Each of these is the idea of a moment—in reality, a series of moments—rather than a real moment in a story. Not only is this a mistake simply on a technical level, but it represents a whole series of missed opportunities to create and orchestrate the experience you are giving. Many directors will accept such a description because it allows them to create the scene from scratch, without the writer's input. But this means the writer has blown a huge opportunity to influence the final product—the film—and convince the director of his idea of how they make love, how the gunfight unfolds, and how the apple pie is created *during the scene*.

You might as well just write "The *Titanic* sinks" and turn in 120 blank pages after it. This is giving away the most crucial aspect of your role in the making of the film: the envisioning of the story in its entirety, from before the beginning until after the end, envisioning all the unseen support structures and all the seen embellishments. What those people downstream from you do with your ideas might or might not match what you intended. But what they do is more likely to match your ideas if you expressed them clearly, if you created the moments in their entirety. If you let others invent the entire gunfight or the sinking of the ship, then there is little chance of the final product resembling your initial envisioning of the event.

Think of a film you've recently seen and a scene in it that you find especially memorable. What happened? When telling your friends about the scene, you might say they made love or there was a gunfight or she baked an apple pie, but that's the idea of the scene, not the real scene. In reality the pie was made throughout a scene in which other events were going on at the same time. First she gathered ingredients, then washed apples, pared them, sliced them, mixed dough, rolled dough, greased a pie tin, put the dough in the tin, and stewed up the apples with cinnamon and sugar. How much of this will be done during the course of the scene is up to you to determine. She might be 90 percent of the way through preparing the pie and we come in only when she is putting the strips of dough on the top and putting it in the oven. Or we might only see her wash and pare and slice apples, but we're able to tell she's starting to bake a pie by the pie tin and flour and other ingredients already assembled. Chances are good that we won't see the entirety of any of these ideas of scenes; we will see the part that implies the whole action, not the whole action itself.

Whatever part we see, it should be moment by moment. It should be taking place in front of us; it should have a sense of here and now. There isn't "a gunfight." First one person shoots and we know how that shot comes about and what happens, then another shoots back. If there are ten thousand bullets flying, we will lose track of who is shooting and what impact all those bullets are having. Those ten thousand bullets will likely have less impact on the audience than a gunfight that involves seven bullets. In the latter, we can have a human being shoot at another human being who is either hit or not hit, with some kind of impact on that person and on the audience. Where is the first person? What is going on that prompts that first shot? With what kind of gun, aimed at whom, with what intent—lethal or warning, accurate or haphazard? If we are in the moment, we are participating. If we are only in the idea of the moment, then we are outside of the experience the characters themselves are having. It's second-hand, just as when you tell your friend about a great scene. It won't be as vivid for him as it was for you, because you participated in it moment by moment.

So this sense of here and now is really the playing out of the scene, shot by shot, image by image; it's picking the entry point into the scene and picking the exit point; it's envisioning—and writing—not just what the characters do and want and say, but exactly what the audience sees and doesn't see, hears and doesn't hear. These things might change—for the better or worse—in the hands of a director and the actors and the cinematographer and sound designer. But first you have actually seen and heard the film you have in mind and you've put that down on paper as the starting point for all the others. You can hope they will only diverge when they have better ideas; it isn't always the case, but the screenwriter isn't in control of that phase of the film's creation. The closest to control a screenwriter has—other than being the producer, director, and actor as well, and this circumstance brings its own problems and limitations—is persuasion. If you paint a persuasive enough portrait of your scenes—they are vivid, compelling, and infused with a sense of here and now—then the others who will follow you in the making of the film will, perhaps, be persuaded to your way of thinking. It isn't always your fault if they don't see it your way—they may have their own agendas or march to a different drummer—but if you've written vividly and persuasively, you've done all that can be done to convince them to make the film you see in your mind.

And just as important as seeing your idea of your story get on the screen is making certain that what you envision is supportive of all the background and superstructure work you have been doing already. It's one thing to decide that your protagonist is witty and funny and liked by one and all; it's a far different thing to write scenes that show he is witty and funny and liked by all. Your actor can't do this all by himself. If your idea of creating the moment is writing "Funny joke here," then there isn't much hope the scene will reflect your view of your characters—unless someone else comes in to write your script for you. But then it will resemble his or her idea of your funny protagonist, not yours. So, hard as it is, it's necessary to envision every second of a scene, every action and reaction, every bit of dialogue. And all of this is on top of having already created the overall circumstances, the characters and their wants and the cornerstones and character arcs. You shouldn't write absolutely every beat of a scene, every little tic of the character in reaction to every single thing that happens. That level of detail would be disastrous. But you must have envisioned it, known it, and found the portion that implies the whole. You can't find the one evocative image or action that implies all manner of other aspects of the scene if you haven't discovered all those aspects first. This is writing in the here and now.

Exposition

Exposition is a cousin of backstory, and it has been dealt with before in *The Tools of Screenwriting*. In brief, exposition is information the audience needs in order to participate in and understand the events and relationships in the story. Exposition is information the characters already know but we don't. For instance, we can see two young men having lunch. They both know they are brothers, but we don't. We could get a wrong impression of them and their discussion if we didn't know this simple fact of their lives. This misunderstanding might be something for you to play with—giving the audience a false lead for a short while. But if that isn't your intention, it could be a big misstep that sends the audience off in the wrong direction, because you failed to establish that the two young men are brothers.

Where exposition departs from backstory is that it tends to be factual information rather than formative experience in the life of the character. Basic relationships among the characters in a story, the basic life circumstances of the various characters, their petty likes and dislikes, even allergies—anything that the characters know about themselves and each other that we need to learn to get the full impact of the events is exposition. There are two basic problems with exposition: it isn't inherently dramatic, and there often is too much of it. Once we grasp the notion that the audience doesn't know just by looking that two people are brothers or mother and daughter or knew each other seventeen years ago, there's a tendency to go overboard with exposition. Suddenly you're stuffing the audience chock-full of expository material without regard for its relevance to the story or how it's delivered.

Because exposition is factual material the characters already know, there's no reason for them to talk about it—the brothers know they are brothers. So it comes off wrong to have them call each other "brother" or order a beer "for my brother" or something like that. It's weak, at best. It gets the information across, but it is pedestrian. But if one brother is trying to get the other to pay him the twenty dollars he owes him, there's a conflict, especially if one is cheap or is angry about something. As they argue, we discover it's for the Mother's Day gift they bought together, but the one who doesn't want to pay is the ne'er-do-well who was sleeping one off in jail on Mother's Day and never got credit for the gift anyway and now doesn't want to pay up. We learn they are brothers, that they have very different relationships in the family, that one's a drinker and feels shortchanged in life. In the course of the scene, it almost seems accidental that we learn they are brothers.

This is how we want exposition to come off—as if it's the by-product of a dramatic or comic scene. Originally the scene may have been invented to deliver the expository information, but in execution it has taken on a conflict that masks the fact that this is the scene's purpose. If it appears to the audience the sole purpose of the scene or the moment in the scene is to deliver exposition, then it is being weakly or flagrantly delivered. We will feel we are being spoon-fed information. But if the audience is made to work for the exposition—pick it out from the material of a conflict or from a comic moment—then we are more likely to hang on to the material and much less likely to know that we have, in fact, been given exposition.

First, we need to identify what exposition we need to deliver, and then we can look for opportunities to deliver it. Two things to keep in mind about exposition: use the least that you can get away with, and separate the exposition from the need for it as much as you can. Avoid the temptation to front-load your story with every bit of exposition you can imagine the audience needs to know about the story. This is just as dangerous as delving forever into the backstory and never getting around to starting the actual story. By starting with endless exposition, you run a grave risk of boring the audience to death before you get them hooked on your characters and your story.

We'll deal at length later with the first act, but you probably have some idea that there's a point at which the audience is hooked into anticipating and caring about the future of the characters, particularly the protagonist. Until this hooking moment— until your bait is bitten on and the hook is firmly in the cheek of your fish, the audience—they have a chance to walk away, to remain indifferent about the future of your characters and story. While they are not yet hooked, it's a bad idea to throw a lot of expositional material at them, no matter how well masked it is by conflict. So in the first act, try to deliver only as much exposition as it takes to get them through the first act and hooked. Once they're hooked, they'll tolerate a lot more exposition. And by delaying the bulk of the exposition, you'll usually discover that you need less than you thought. So overall, there will be less exposition, which leaves more room for story.

At the same time, you don't want to give the audience crucial exposition just as they need it; this will make it seem like an afterthought. If they learn a character has a lifeguard certificate and then, in the very next scene, someone who can't swim falls into a lake, it seems rather convenient. Worse still, it hasn't encouraged the audience to work, to participate by retaining information. If they learned earlier that she had her lifeguard certificate—in a scene that seemed to be about something else— then, when it comes time for the nonswimmer to fall in the lake, they'll be screaming—in their heads—for someone to find the lifeguard. They'll have been encouraged to participate by gathering useful knowledge and having an opportunity to use it; they'll feel connected with the story. They will have worked and liked it.

So there are competing pressures here—separate the exposition from its needed moment, yet delay all the exposition you can. This is a difficult task, but they aren't mutually exclusive conditions. At this point, before your scenes are up and running, you can't know how to merge these competing needs, but you can begin to sort through what exposition you think you will need and start to envision ways in which it might be included without spoon-feeding it to the audience. Look for ways to make them work for the exposition, and you just might find the core to a scene that will do a great deal more than provide basic exposition.

Rising Action

The principle of rising action helps us discover the best order for the obstacles in our story. Generally, the obstacles should be in ascending order of difficulty. If you start with the toughest barrier to overcome, then everything after it will seem disappointing or anticlimactic. But if you take on first the river, then the cliff, then the mountain, then the mountain with a broken leg and in the middle of a blizzard, each step will be fraught with tension. Each new obstacle will provide an escalation of the tension. This is as true in a romantic comedy as it is in an action story. And it's just as true whether the character has some choice about which obstacles to tackle first or they are thrust at him one at a time.

If a person is faced with a dilemma more or less of his own choosing, he is unlikely to choose the toughest way of solving it first. Most likely a person will ask someone else to fix the problem for him, then try to hire someone to do it, then try to do it himself, then finally do it himself in the midst of a hailstorm—but only as a last resort. If she has been assaulted by the obstacles of the story, she is still likely to take the easiest possible solution first and only escalate to the more difficult alternative solutions as the easier ones fail or prove inadequate. As the storyteller, you should throw the obstacles at the character in ascending order of difficulty. Don't ask her to kill someone as the first solution and sweet-talk someone else as the final solution.

If you think of the first major obstacle for a character as being in the frying pan that she is trying to escape, then an ideal series of obstacles would be: out of the frying pan and into the fire; out of the fire into the heat vent for the broiler; after a wild slide down the heat vent, the broiler is unbearable and she must climb up and out, only to find herself in the oven. Only when she is finally trapped in the oven does she quit trying to escape and turn around to face the source of the problem, the gas supply; she must go toward the source of the fire itself. There has been a logical flow from one obstacle to the next; one solution has helped create the next problem, and the hardest has been left for last. Each step has tested the mettle of the character and created ever-increasing tension in the audience. Each obstacle can take its toll on the characters, seemingly increasing the odds of defeat with each successive obstacle faced.

Another way to look at the obstacles in the rising action of the story is as potential solutions instead of barriers. Let's imagine a story about a father in search of his runaway son. The first potential solution is going to the police. If that succeeds, the story is over. So the police must fail in some way, though they may provide a clue the father takes to the second alternative solution to his problem—he hires a private investigator. His problem hasn't changed, but his potential solution to it has. This second possible solution can't succeed or the story ends and the father has not been fully tested by his dilemma and ordeal. Again, maybe he comes away armed with another clue, but nothing more. So at last, he must go after the boy himself and get his first difficult glimpses into the world into which his son has run or been dragged. He can search on the edges of that world and ask people going in or coming out if they have seen him. Finally, when that too fails and he has no other alternative solutions available to him, he has to dive headfirst into that world himself, facing his own demons and his own shortcomings with his son in order to have a chance to find him.

In this circumstance, the goal has remained more or less constant, while the solutions have continually failed. In the frying pan circumstance, each solution is successful, but helps to create the next—and new—dilemma, which is a variation on the previous ones. Both methods are perfectly valid ways of organizing material within the principle of rising action. You can also work from a combination of successful and unsuccessful solutions, so long as the obstacles and potential solutions escalate in difficulty for that particular character. Each obstacle could be objectively difficult or subjectively difficult. One obstacle might be objective and successfully overcome, helping create the next obstacle, which is subjective. At the second obstacle, the character fails and is left with the same goal or want, but with one possible solution now eliminated. This provides you with many combinations of obstacles and solutions to orchestrate in a continuing series of escalating difficulty.

How do you sort the material you've been gathering to build your story? The thin, short, and easily installed boards will probably be used first, and the big, long, and a-bear-to-install lumber will be left for last. You can start to see your story's shape, even if you don't have precise measurements or know exactly how this board will fit with that one. Maybe you have too many short and easy ones and not enough of the tough stuff. Or, more likely, not enough material at all yet. But now you know what you're looking for and approximately how it might fit into the overall scheme of your story.

Point of No Return

The moment when the audience is hooked on the story and anticipating the future is not necessarily the same as the moment when the protagonist is locked into the story. When we know what our protagonist wants and have some reason to believe it will be difficult to achieve, we are hooked. Our attachment isn't as strong as it will become as the story unfolds, but we have shifted into the anticipating mode relative to the protagonist and the main story line. We are hoping and fearing, we are participating emotionally, and we have enough foresight into the potential obstacles in his path. This doesn't mean the protagonist himself is as hooked as we are. He must surely be passionate to some degree about his want or goal, but he might still be in a position where he could walk away or escape. He doesn't have to have passed the point of no return in order for us to be hoping and fearing for and about him, for us to be hooked.

Imagine a character trying to save a dog from a burning house. It can be a fairly contained fire at the moment he runs into the house to get the dog, and he has every reason to believe he can easily run back out with it. But we know that the house contains a painting studio filled with oils and turpentine. Our hope and fear aren't exactly the same as his; our tension about him is more intense than his own even while he's still in a relatively safe part of the house, from which he could easily walk back outside before it's too late. He hasn't passed the point of no return yet, though we are fully into the anticipating and participating mode of heightened tension. But suddenly the fire surrounds him, he has no easy means of escape, he has to press forward whether he wants to or not. Now he's passed the point of no return and our tension rises—as does his. But ours is still greater than his because we know of the flammables in the house and he doesn't. If he'd known of the flammables, he probably never would have entered the house to save a dog. To save his child or wife, he may have done it anyway. But the tensions—and the entrapment of the story—have come up behind him, though not necessarily at the same time we have known about them.

In this way, we can have a protagonist enter into a conflict he might never have taken on had he known all the details. But by the time he discovers the full extent of the conflict, it's too late for him to change his mind. Just as you need to identify when the audience is hooked into anticipating and worrying and hoping and fearing, you need to identify the moment when the character can no longer change his mind. If the protagonist could stop participating in the story at any time, then it ultimately diminishes the tension of the story. And it means the story has to bolster the character's reason for continuing as the fire rages or the bullets fly or his heart is broken. If he could walk away with no loss when the bullets fly, wouldn't he? If we know he's trapped—either by something he cares about more than the potential of being shot or by there being no escape except through the gunfire—then our tension escalates.

Clearly the entrapment doesn't have to be physical; it can involve something that the character considers more important than the physical or emotional danger he faces by continuing the pursuit. That entrapment can come from behind or in front. His bridge might be burned behind him or a loved one might be in the hands of killers. Either way, he can no longer walk away. The danger doesn't have to be lethal; it needs to be proportional to the story, to the conflicts and worries we are provoking in the audience. In a love story, the danger will probably be emotional; in an action story it will probably be physical; in a courtroom or social drama it might be jail or humiliation or censure. Whatever the nature of the "danger," it must be strong enough that the character doesn't easily decide to risk it, otherwise the story is being too kind to him. If the danger is sufficiently onerous that the character would urgently want to avoid it, then you have to find ways to make him face it. It won't always be entrapment in the oven or broiler; it's just as likely for a character to be stuck on a bad blind date or to discover a business rival has his finger on her most vulnerable spot.

Let's look at Chief Brody in *Jaws*. When he first sets out on the boat with his two experienced shark hunters, he believes this is his operation, he's in charge. He is, after all, the local law. He doesn't like the idea of going in the boat, but he enters into the danger willingly enough. It's his job. He doesn't seem to be trapped yet. We have more direct experience of the shark's terrible abilities but the same level of ignorance about his two companions as he does. It soon becomes clear this is not his operation, that Quint is in charge—for now—and eventually, the shark will be in charge. It's Quint who closes the door to escape, who pushes Brody past the point of no return. First Quint refuses to obey Brody—once they see the size and strength of the shark—and then he destroys the radio, closing off the possibility of calling for help. Brody no longer has any choice about taking on dangers that he surely never would have sought out had he known in advance.

Now let's look at Joe Bradley in *Roman Holiday*. When he first meets the runaway, Princess Ann, he has no idea who she is, but soon he realizes his good fortune. He's a bit down on his luck as a journalist and this is the scoop of the century because she doesn't realize he is a journalist; she thinks he's being friendly and helpful. He makes a deal for the inside story and then starts shepherding her around on a grand lark. He could still walk away; even though our tension is set, we are hooked. But then he starts to fall in love with her and he's past the point of no return. The emotional danger he faces by confessing to her is too strong for him to stop the escapade honestly, but his desire to be with her and love her is too strong for him to abandon her. In a sense, his bridge is burned behind him *and* someone he loves is in the hands of bad guys—himself in this case. In order to resolve his dilemma, he has to face his danger.

Willing Suspension of Disbelief

All of our work in storytelling revolves around creating an experience for the audience, engaging and then working their minds and emotions and wringing from them the reactions we have set as our goal. No amount of hard work and clever, even inspired, invention will succeed in creating that impact if the audience is unwilling to buy into the story. But they voluntarily came to the film, they paid their money, they sought this story out; aren't they already sold? They are ready and willing to be convinced, but they still need convincing. Haven't you sought out a film, paid for it, sat down to watch it, and somewhere along the line thought to yourself, "Bogus!"? You were willing to buy into the story, but the storytellers failed you. The fault inevitably lies in the screenplay. Somehow the storytelling failed to make you willingly suspend your disbelief. You retained—or gained even greater—disbelief in what was being presented in the story.

Audience disbelief will be a greater problem to overcome in a futuristic or supernatural story or an animated one or one set in a fantasy world. But even a story set in a recognizable part of our world, with regular human beings doing more or less regular things, will require some moment in time when the audience is encouraged to buy into the view of the world the story presents and the story itself.

Simply by presenting everyday parts of the lives of the characters, recognizable circumstances, and recognizable reactions from the characters, we lure the audience into the world—there is nothing yet to provoke disbelief. But they have, probably unconsciously, still reserved their full and total belief in the story. As we discussed earlier, there is usually going to be something extraordinary in the creation of the story—the intensity of a character's passion or the difficulty of his circumstance or a twist of fate. Something bigger than everyday life must intrude in this world to help provoke the story into existence. It can be distressingly common (being hit by a car) or bizarre (being hit by lightning) or an unusual choice (consciously getting oneself fired and going to work in a fast-food drive-through). This intrusion of the extraordinary into the world of the story, often the collision that creates the story or something that leads to the collision, is what puts the storyteller in jeopardy of losing his audience. The key to clearing this crucial hurdle in building and sustaining the relationship with the audience is in making certain the intrusion of the extraordinary is believable within this story.

In many stories this is a relatively easy enterprise. Soon after presenting the undisturbed ordinary world, you reveal something special, some precursor to the extraordinary event. This first teaser may not have the same degree of the extraordinary as the full-fledged collision; it could have just some of the spice of what's to come. It isn't out of proportion to the world of the story and the characters as we know them so far, so we buy into it. Once we buy in, we are prepared for the crucial moment, the arrival of the extraordinary. Oskar Schindler will eventually make an extraordinary decision: he will try to keep a sizable number of Jews alive in the heart of Nazi Germany. If the story simply jumped straight to that decision, the audience might not believe it. But at the beginning of the story, we are introduced to Schindler in a public bar dominated by Nazi officers. Schindler does something most people would not dare to do; he approaches and befriends the officers, with what we know are lies, in order to make business contacts. The moment isn't truly extraordinary, but it gives us an idea of the man, his audacity and self-confidence. By the time the scene is over, we have willingly suspended our disbelief and are prepared to buy into his later, bigger, decision.

In *Three Kings*, Archie will eventually make the extraordinary decision to try to steal Saddam Hussein's gold under the eyes of his own and enemy soldiers. This too would be unbelievable if it were the first presentation of the story. But there is a similar introduction of audacious behavior, nearly extraordinary and clearly foolish: he has sex with his media advisee while his men and officers are nearby. Again, there is a moment that we can buy into—in proportion to the story and world we are being introduced to—that enables us to willingly suspend our disbelief in preparation for the big unbelievable moment. And again, our willingness to suspend disbelief was set up by the earlier, more easily accepted incident.

But in some films, from the very first image we know we are

not in the world we live in; the film is animated, or it's a fantasy world or outer space. Just as with the recognizable world, we are lured into the world of the story and begin to accept it. But have we fully suspended our disbelief? Are we ready to buy into what the story needs us to accept for the full participation it asks of us? Probably not. We believe the world itself because we see it. But just because we accept Woody and the other toys walking and talking—and playing dead when people are around—doesn't mean we will make the leap to complete belief in the extraordinary. Before Woody can lead the quest to save Buzz Lightyear, he has to prove himself as a leader, be willing to take on challenges within the world of the story. He marshals all the forces of the toys who follow him to send a mission downstairs during the birthday party. Here we come to accept him as the leader; we suspend our disbelief in the floppy cowboy as the hero.

But sometimes it isn't extraordinary decisions characters make but the introduction of extraordinary circumstances that creates a story. Here the need for a willing suspension of disbelief is more obvious. When Roy Neary is visited by an alien ship in *Close Encounters,* we have not been prepared for it in advance. Instead, the reaction of the protagonist himself is used to dispel disbelief. He disbelieves and then comes to believe it really happened. He voices our doubts, and when he overcomes the doubts, we are presented with a fork in the road: either we overcome our disbelief as well and participate in the rest of the story or we retain our disbelief and remain outside of the world and characters of the story. When Phil Connors wakes up to the same song at the same time and discovers he is repeating the same day in *Groundhog Day,* this is an extraordinary event. He doesn't believe it at first, but by the time he steps in the slush the second time, he believes it and so do we, or at least we're faced with that same fork in the road. What we decide to accept and believe in will impact our experience of the story.

As you are assembling and sorting through the material you have and the things you still need to create, this is another crucial moment to identify. What is the nature of the extraordinary your story will deliver? Is it in the circumstances or a person? How extraordinary is it? It doesn't have to be supernatural or earth shattering; it only needs to be extraordinary within the context of the world of the story and the characters. But there must be something a little bit bigger, a little more than ordinary life. Either before or after that extraordinary intrusion into the world and the lives of the characters, you need to find a way to help the audience agree to stay with you for the duration. When the disbelief must be dispelled after an event or decision, it will usually be a character who voices the audience's disbelief. When that person is convinced, it creates the moment for the audience to join in. When the audience will need to accept an extraordinary event or decision or person, then we often stage a miniversion ahead of time that can prepare the audience and make that extraordinary decision, event, or person more believable. We still may need a confirmation moment after the introduction of the truly extraordinary, but most of the work was done with the earlier moment and the belief it created.

First you have to figure out what might be difficult to believe in your story. What would be your "Bogus!" moment if you were in the audience? Then work on who can help guide the audience through the process of suspending disbelief. It's a far better tactic to face the unbelievable head on than to try to pretend it isn't there. Avoiding the problem will only leave the question open for the audience. You could be far into the story, when the tensions should be at their highest, and your audience suddenly quits believing. The experience you were intending to give has just evaporated and cannot be regained. The audience might start laughing at the story instead of cringing in fear; it might quit laughing when it's supposed to laugh; it most surely will quit participating emotionally to the degree it was before. This is a disaster.

Another disastrous tactic is trying to change the rules after the suspension of disbelief has been accomplished. Once we've accepted that Schindler is audacious and full of enough self-confidence to play a deadly game with the Nazis, we'll accept where the story is going as long as what he does remains within that realm. If he picks up a gun and starts mowing down the Nazi guards in the middle of a concentration camp in front of the SS, then we will shout "Bogus!" and probably not just in our heads. This will not be within the realm of what we have accepted believing within this story. Once we've accepted that the Terminator is a killing machine from the future intent on murdering an innocent ordinary woman in the present, it would be a disastrous misstep to make her be an angel from heaven. That is not the story we signed on for.

You can probably get the audience to suspend its disbelief of nearly any kind of story and story event, but once they have made that decision, don't try to change the rules. You've set the ground rules for playing the game of enjoying the experience you intend; so long as you stick to those rules, you'll have a faithful and engrossed audience. You break your own rules and they will desert you. What this means is that you have to identify your most difficult-to-accept event or decision and prepare the audience to accept it. This is laying out the boundaries of the playing field for the game of your story. We can be made to accept nearly any boundaries and any shape of playing field, but once we've accepted them, you have to play the game on that field. So right now, as you're exploring your story, you have to figure out what needs to be on the field so you can be sure to set boundaries that encompass everything you'll need for the game.

There can be an element of salesmanship in making the audience willingly suspend their disbelief. You might have to demonstrate and test the circumstance or conditions or give a spiel to convince them to come to your way of thinking. You can take a likable character, give him the doubts the audience shares, and then win him over. The "shill" will then bring the audience with him. This is a common tactic in science fiction and fantasy stories. Or you might try the reverse. You can create a really disagreeable character who voices all the rational and logical problems the audience has, while the likable characters believe what the story requires. The audience will tar the rational side with their dislike of the character and go with the likable characters. This is a common tactic in horror films. When a character makes an extraordinary and perhaps unwise choice—to slay the dragon or woo the king's daughter, for instance—you might put the doubts of the audience into the mouth of a character who is demonstrably wrong about other things that we know to be true. Because he was wrong about those other things, maybe he's wrong about this too, and our hearts and minds go with the extraordinary decision and its maker.

Demonstration versus Explanation

You've no doubt heard the axiom "Show, don't tell." But what does that mean and how does it affect us here? Telling is akin to failing to have a sense of here and now. It's one thing to say they make love; it's another thing to show us *how* they make love, in the moments, as it unfolds. A great example of demonstration comes in the opening of *The Godfather*. We are shown the estate and the preparations for the wedding, the huge, dangerous-looking man nervously practicing a little speech, and then we meet Don Corleone in his den, surrounded by his advisors and meeting a series of guests. The estate demonstrates his wealth, the den and his men demonstrate the respect he commands, the nervous guests and their requests reveal the power they believe he has, the nervousness of his henchman shows the level of fear-based respect he generates, even in someone so formidable. We are shown how powerful Don Corleone is, we are shown how he wields his power; and those around him point our attention to just how commanding he is. Compare this opening with what could have been done, having one character say, "Don Corleone? He's the most powerful Mafia don in New York." Technically they cover the same ground, but one is real, visceral, evocative, compelling, and memorable. The other, we're not even sure if we believe it.

That early scene in *Schindler's List* where Schindler approaches the Nazi officers is similar. It demonstrates just how audacious, daring, and confident Schindler is. This is far stronger than telling us in dialogue that he is all those things. Worse still—since it wouldn't even get conveyed to the audience—would be putting that information in scene description. The script could have read, "Oskar Schindler, a bold and audacious man swaggering with self-confidence . . ." This would have communicated that information—weakly—to a small group of people, those involved in the making of the film. The audience would only see a

man swaggering and not know why, what it means, or if it's justified. Nor would it have a clue how that confidence manifests itself
in daily interaction.

This need to demonstrate the inner workings and outer travails
of the characters is by no means limited to character introductions.
Later in *Schindler's List,* there's a scene in which the Jewish children are being separated from the adults at a train station.
Schindler feverishly confronts the guards and convinces them to
allow the children to stay with the families through quickly made-
up lies and a bravura performance of his audacity. This story material could easily have been dispensed with—delivered in much less
screen time—if he and Stern had discussed the incident after arrival in the new location. We could even see the children there as
proof of his success. But what a loss this would be. Instead of sharing in the experience and the tension of "can he save these children?" we would instead be given a dialogue scene after the fact
when the events are explained to us.

Because stories are about experience and the goal is the trans-
ference of experience to the audience, showing is inevitably the
stronger method of delivering story material. It conveys the experience, it puts the audience in the here and now, it gives them the
chance to see the characters in action instead of hear about the
actions they have taken. This seems redundant of the section on
immediacy, but there's another element at work here. It isn't just
in the scenes and how they play out that we need to create the immediacy of here and now; it's also in what scenes we choose to
dramatize. All the parts of story building you've wrestled with so
far—the nature of your characters, the protagonist and the antagonist, the nature of the world of the story, the type of conflicts and
obstacles and potential solutions, the wants and actions taken to
achieve them—all these things must be shown, must be delivered
to the audience in a way that creates the experience you intend. It
isn't just a question of showing in the moment how they make
love or how she bakes an apple pie; the question is, will showing
them making love or her baking an apple pie help create the experience you intend, will it help reveal the nature of your character or his conflict or her view of upcoming obstacles or his
ignorance of his own weaknesses? What kind of material must

you demonstrate—at the cost of considerable screen time? And what material can you simply tell—saving screen time, but at the price of immediacy and power? And perhaps the toughest question of all, what things that you can demonstrate will convince the audience of the nature of your characters?

Let's go back to Oskar Schindler. If you were striving to build this story, you'd have concluded that he is a bold, audacious man, perhaps a bit smitten with himself, but possessed of an amazing self-confidence and an ability to change the minds of disbelievers, even cruel Nazis who could at any minute turn on him. Great, you've done your homework; you have a clear idea of the man. How are you going to show all that? Can't you just tell it? Certainly it's a lot easier to tell it. Get someone to stand up and spout off everything you've concluded about our character. Done. But the most this telling could possibly accomplish—no matter how well written and acted—would be to convince us that the speaking character believes this to be true about Schindler. We would not know if any of it is actually true, nor to what degree it is true, nor how it translates into action. We'd still need it demonstrated to us.

So you have to find actions that reveal the attributes you have ascribed to our characters. And to find those actions, you have to create conflicts and obstacles that challenge those attributes so you can see the characters in motion, doing whatever it is that makes them who you have decided they are. If it's Rocky, we need to see him box and spar. If it's Jerry/Geraldine/Junior in *Some Like It Hot*, we have to see him in all three guises. If it's Butch Cassidy, we have to see him rob trains. If it's Luke Skywalker, we have to see him learn to use his Jedi powers. If it's Agent Starling, we have to see her interrogate and investigate and deduce. If it's Julian Kaye in *American Gigolo*, we have to see him seduce. In all these cases, there needs to be some kind of challenge, some conflict inherent in the activity or in assuming the role the character demonstrates to the audience. The addition of conflict, or a test, gives depth to the attribute or decision or lifestyle or whatever it is you are showing. It's one thing to dress up like a woman; it's another to pass as Geraldine and be believed by the doubtful Sweet Sue and Beinstock. It's one thing to be given a light saber and told you come from Jedi stock; it's another thing to use it blindfolded against a toy that stings when you miss.

The same is true for secondary characters and for the world of the story. You've decided that the world of your story is a hostile one, tough, hard, ungiving, and unforgiving. You could have the wise old coot on the corner say, "It's a tough world out there." But what will that really do for you? Not much. You need to show us, to pick scenes and moments that show us this hostile world as it will be manifested in your story. Is it the hard world of people stealing other people's taxis in New York, or the tough world of on-the-make wise guys in New York, or the nasty world of corporate raiders and hostile takeovers?

You have to return to the decisions you've made about the world of your story and find actions, scenes, and conflicts that will demonstrate the world you have envisioned. If that weren't tough enough by itself, it's compounded by the difficulty that a staged demonstration of an attribute of the world or of a character comes off as just that, staged. When it's demonstrated that Schindler is audacious or Don Corleone is feared, respected, and immensely powerful, these demonstrations don't play as if they are there simply to demonstrate how each man lives his life. In reality, that might be the main purpose of the wedding scene or the bar scene, but its primary purpose to the storyteller has been ingeniously masked and we have been made to believe we are getting the scene for other reasons. Don't expect to be able to do this on your first try.

First, it's enough to invent or discover what kind of scene or moment, what demonstration, would actually reveal what it is you want to show us about your story's world. The opening of *Alien* is interesting to explore. We quickly learn we are in outer space, but there is a familiar toy, the computers are familiar, the grousing of the crew as they come out of hypersleep is familiar. We are having it demonstrated that this might be the future, but not that much has changed from our world. But when their smaller ship descends to the planet, we have it demonstrated that this is a very hostile environment, one of danger and death. We get the lure of the familiar, even in an unfamiliar location, and the entering into a hostile new world placed side by side. By choosing to show two worlds side by side, the writers have found ways of demonstrating that these are ordinary people—in a future time period—who are entering into an extraordinary and dangerous circumstance. They didn't choose to tell us these things; we concluded for ourselves, from what we saw and experienced.

We conclude for ourselves how powerful and feared is Don Corleone and how audacious Oskar Schindler. We are given the material that leads us to these conclusions, but we don't have the conclusions made for us by the storytellers. This is the crucial distinction between telling and demonstrating. If we see and hear for ourselves, we'll make our own conclusions; we'll trust those conclusions and remember them, hang on to them. If someone else tells us the conclusion, but doesn't show us the means of arriving at it, we'll be doubtful at best, we won't "own" the conclusion, and we'll be less likely to hang on to it.

If the material you need to convey about a character or the world of the story is basic, bedrock, crucial, and essential for the audience to believe and hang on to, then you'll have to demonstrate it for us. Less crucial information, especially that which doesn't have to be retained for a long time or isn't necessarily believed, can be delivered by telling. There's a kind of cost-benefit analysis one needs to go through here; the cost of dramatizing information is screen time, which has to be weighed against the overall benefit of that information in the story. How much screen time is this information worth? How crucial is it? If you're dealing with core material about the main character, the stuff that makes him who he is, it's worth a lot of screen time. If you're dealing with the traffic ticket a secondary character got last week, it probably isn't worth the screen time; it's probably enough to tell that part.

Now you have yet another way to sort through the material you've been assembling for your story. What information warrants full-scale dramatization, and which can be simply told? Just like backstory, the most crucial information about your characters and the world of the story will be the stuff that pertains to the theme and conflicts and the major pursuit of the story. Considerable screen time will need to be devoted to important characters and what makes them tick, to the creation of the goal or the collision and what will make it a difficult challenge. If you find that the scenes you've been envisioning are dialogue intensive and not very active or visual, you might have to do some rethinking.

Demonstration, nearly by definition, requires action and visuals. We could have a character who speaks a mile a minute and is utterly charming, in which case the demonstration of this aspect of his persona would indeed be dialogue intensive. But it would also be a visual demonstration of the impact he has on his audience; who listens to and buys into all that he's saying? In most other circumstances, you need to look for ways of showing what it is that you want the audience to conclude. If your Napoleon is a preening fool, then you have to create a scene in which he is so absorbed with himself, his appearance and height and gold brocade, that he completely misses something that should be obvious. If your Lindbergh is a reckless glory hound, then you have to create a scene in which he takes chances for a news photographer or a crowd. There might be plenty of dialogue, but the essence of the scene, the real demonstration, will be in what we are shown that leads us to the conclusions the storyteller wants.

One more thought on the cost-benefit analysis: it's far better, stronger, and more efficient to spend the screen time to set out an idea or information well than it would be to save a little time and do it halfway. Chances are, if you scrimped the first time, you'll find you need to do the same information again later. In the end, you will have spent more of your precious commodity—time—and had less impact. Both the sequence at the beginning of *The Godfather* and the one at the beginning of *Schindler's List* are rather long, and it might be tempting to shorten them up, to "get on with the story." But, in fact, if those scenes weren't allowed to accomplish what they need to, the entire film would be slowed down.

Number of Clearly Definable Characters

How many times have you seen a film with a fairly large cast and had to ponder who this or that person was and what they had to do with everything again? The problem might not be with the quality of the scenes and the characterizations. The size and composition of the cast might be the problem. If we are asked to follow too many characters of mostly equal importance, there comes a point at which the characters start stealing time and attention from each other. It isn't that the audience is stupid or has a short attention span or that the storyteller failed to give effective introductions to the characters. You have to remember a film audience is catching everything on the fly. We are gathering information about all the conflicts and the characters, plus their expectations and hopes and fears; we are keeping track of our own hopes and fears and suspicions; we are making educated guesses trying to get ahead of the story and then feverishly striving to catch up when the story lurches ahead of us unexpectedly; we are trying to figure out the world, the places, and the things we see as well as the social interactions and mores being depicted; we are struggling with our own emotions and all the suspense and mystery and surprise that we are bombarded with throughout the story. There's a lot on our plate when we are an active, participatory audience. We can't page back and reread. We have to manage to do all this while the story is unfolding.

So it shouldn't be surprising that there is a saturation point, a point at which we can't keep up effectively. It isn't strange that there's a limit; what's strange is how high it is and how variable. In a normal-length feature film, we can expect the audience to keep track of everything necessary to have a complex relationship with about half a dozen characters, including the protagonist and antagonist. There are plenty of exceptions, but by and large an effective cast is about five or six fully fleshed-out characters. Try it—pick a film you like and know well. How many characters are there who really have some complexity to the life you see in them? The story might include everyone in the high school, and the whole football team and the whole cheerleading squad seem to be major parts of what is happening. But the reality will be that you'll focus on one or two characters from the team and one or two from the squad, and the rest will be followers or cohorts; they will be characterized more by a single aspect of their being than will the other, more complex characters.

If you try to push the limit and make ten characters of significance and depth, the audience will start to lose track or confuse characters or fail to pick up all the nuances and bits of information necessary to sustain the complex relationships you have tried to create. They will necessarily simplify one or several characters. Something you intended to be significant will be missed. And the audience may well start to feel lost in the story. But there is a way past this problem. We can have a short but in-depth relationship with a character. In the overall scope of the story, the character may not have more depth or meaning than one of the followers of the football team, but for a few minutes of screen time, this character can become a real presence, one with depth and complexity—at least in relationship to how much screen time is devoted to him.

Two nice examples of this sort of character relationship appear in *The Godfather*. The first is Captain McCluskey, the police officer partly responsible for the assassination attempt on Don Corleone. His character introduction and his death are only minutes apart, but during the time in between, he is a real presence. He is important, and though we don't learn chapter and verse about him and his life, we develop a fairly deep understanding of who he is and how he lives. What the character lacks in length of time he makes up for in intensity. The second character dealt with in this same fashion is Michael's Italian bride. Her role is all in one finite section of the story, but during that time, it is intense.

If we're stuck with only six meaningful characters for the bulk of the story, is that enough? Actually, plenty of wonderful films don't even use that many. *The African Queen* has only two characters of any depth. *Hell in the Pacific* has only two characters, period. *Jaws* has four—and that's if you include the shark. *The Terminator* has three. *One Flew over the Cuckoo's Nest* has four. In all of these films—except *Hell in the Pacific*—there are other characters of varying degrees of importance. But they are not characters we delve into deeply and broadly. We might get involved with the mayor in *Jaws* or Brother in *The African Queen* to a degree greater than other characters, but these characterizations are purposely made less than alluring; they don't make us curious about the characters the way we feel about Brody, Quint, and Hooper or about Rosie and Charlie.

How do these six "deeper" roles play out in a typical story?

Protagonist and antagonist, of course. Love interest, perhaps, or best friend, or one of each. A rival who is an enemy, or a pretend enemy who becomes a friend, or a friend who becomes an enemy. An assistant or henchman or front for the antagonist. There are many variations, of course, and in some stories there isn't an outside antagonist, so even that role might be missing. But it is then likely replaced by the chief supporter of the antagonistic side of the protagonist or the leader or spokesperson for the antagonistic world.

Let's take a look at *American Beauty*. We have Lester, our protagonist and antagonist. We have his wife, Carolyn, who is at various times enemy, friend, pretend enemy, pretend friend, and even indifferent. We have Ricky, who is a friend. We have Lester's daughter, who is an enemy. We have her friend, Angela, who is sometimes indifferent, sometimes an enemy and sometimes a supporter of the antagonistic side of Lester. And we have Colonel Fitts, Ricky's father, who is a pretend indifferent and true enemy. Six characters. There are other characters—the gay couple, the realtor Carolyn has an affair with, Lester's nemesis at his first job, his ally at the fast-food shop, and Ricky's mother. Each of these plays a worthy and, at times, evocative role in the story, but none of them creates a complex relationship with the audience as the primary six do.

What about an epic story, one that actually contains two complete stories, with two protagonists? *The Bridge on the River Kwai* has Colonel Nicholson as one protagonist and Shears as the other. And Colonel Saito is a significant player, as is the camp doctor, plus Major Warden, who drags Shears along to blow up the bridge. That's really it. Shears woos a nurse, there are other men in the squad intending to blow up the bridge, Nicholson commands many men, but none of the other roles amounts to a strong relationship of any depth with the audience. But at various times, every single significant character shifts among the six character types, playing a variety of kinds of roles and relationships in the two stories. So five characters—plus all the shifting roles they play in each of the two stories—are enough for a three-hour epic. Six characters ought to be enough for a regular hundred-minute feature, especially when you consider the multiplicity of roles these complex characters play in the unfolding drama.

There is another reason behind limiting ourselves to about half a dozen significant characters. Not only is there a limit on what the audience can absorb and care about and keep track of, there's a limit to the time you have available. Each character of depth and complexity requires screen time for those things to be created. If you add a few more complex characters, then you necessarily have to steal the time from somewhere. You could get it from the story and tell a smaller, simpler story. You could get it from the world of the story and create a thinner, more sparsely drawn world. You could get it by stealing from the time you put into creating, nurturing, and elaborating on the bond between the story and the audience.

But the truth is, you've already stolen from all of these sources to get to six characters. This represents a fairly nice balance among all the needs of storytelling, allowing adequate time for the complex characters, the story, the world, and the relationship it all has with the audience. Clearly it is possible to value these aspects differently and shift the balance for a particular story. Just be aware that it will come at a price. If you're willing to pay that price, then make the adjustments. You can also make the adjustments the other way, using fewer significant characters, leaving more time for other aspects of the story, the world, and the connection with the audience. Films like *The Terminator, Jaws,* and *My Fair Lady* have large set pieces—action or special effects or singing and dancing sequences—that take up screen time. Using fewer significant characters frees up time for large production numbers or special-effects extravaganzas.

Given that you can have a character shift from friend to enemy to indifferent and all the pretend variations, six characters can play a wide range of roles during the course of the story. This is a far better tactic for two reasons. The first is it easily keeps you within the manageable realm of complex characters. But the second and more important reason is that having a significant character shift about among the different kinds of relationships actually deepens the audience's relationship to those characters and broadens our understanding of the complexities of the human being. By using your primary cast for this sort of multiplicity of relationships, you draw stronger, more fully fleshed-out and realistic characters. So holding yourselves to fewer characters strengthens your story and, most especially, the characters in it.

Character Motivations

Your protagonist isn't the only character who wants something badly. In fact, your other characters don't know that they aren't the protagonist; only the audience knows who is the main character. As far as the other characters are concerned, this is their own story—it's their own life. So all your significant characters have to have wants that we can identify. Even the smallest parts can be peopled with characters who want something, have some kind of attitude or goal, hidden or overt. On top of all these confusing and conflicting wants to orchestrate, the character's wants don't even have to be based on reality as it exists in the story. A man who fervently believes the beautiful woman next door is secretly in love with him—and we know he is delusional—is just as strongly motivated by his belief as another man whom the woman actually loves would be. The motivation doesn't have to be true, factual, achievable, or based on an accurate understanding of the world. The basis of the motivation is the belief of the character, however baseless it might be. A half-believed truth is less of a motivation than a strongly held misperception.

Just look at Colonel Fitts in *American Beauty*. He believes Lester is a homosexual having an affair with his son. He couldn't be further from the truth, but that in no way stops him from taking action on what he believes is true. And it doesn't diminish our participation in the story just because we know he's wrong in his perception. The fact that we know both the truth and the falsehood he believes actually strengthens our bond with the story and the tension we feel about the future. Melvin in *As Good as It Gets* is a man consumed with phobias; among other fears, he passionately avoids stepping on cracks. Most of the rest of us grew out of this superstition in our childhood, but we see how desperately he will avoid cracks in the sidewalk and in hallways. His belief in something bad stemming from stepping on a crack is what drives him, whether we believe in it or not. Norman Bates believes his mother is alive in *Psycho* and takes action in part based on that belief. It doesn't matter—from a motivational standpoint—that this is patently untrue.

The audience must be put in a position of being able to fathom whatever is behind the actions of the characters. We don't need it laid out all nice and neat for us, spoon-fed to us; in fact, most of the time, we'd rather work at figuring out what makes people do what they do. We don't have to know every single detail of how Melvin came to believe in the power of cracks, but we do need to know that he believes it and this belief motivates his actions. When a belief is long term and deeply held by a character, it's usually enough that we know of its existence; we don't necessarily need to know the origin. If a misperception or misunderstanding is short term, it's usually best to show us how it comes about within the body of the story. So we are with Colonel Fitts when he misunderstands a secret meeting between Lester and Ricky and again when he sees the video of Lester working out naked. The same is true in *North by Northwest;* when Roger Thornhill is mistaken for George Kaplan, the misperception that creates the whole story, it is played out in front of us so we see how it comes about.

A long-term truth can preexist and we accept it as part of the person; a recently acquired bit of knowledge will usually be a stronger, more believable motivational force if we see the character gain it. In *The Godfather,* Michael's love for and belief in the goodness of his father doesn't need to be explained to us; it can simply exist as part of the basis of the character—so long as it's shown to us that it is part of him, not just lip service. But when Don Corleone is in the hospital and Michael discovers the police guard is missing and comes to believe there is another attempted hit on his father in progress, it's clearly much stronger if we are with him and participating in the moments when he learns the facts that lead him to that belief, because that new belief is the basis of a major action of his.

In *Thelma and Louise,* there's an interesting collision of old and new beliefs in a secondary character. Louise calls her boyfriend and asks him to send her all the money in her savings account. Up until this call, he has believed she loved him, that they were a steady couple. We see him have the misperception that Louise is running off with another man. He acts on the newer—untrue—belief, which brings him to her in Oklahoma. He delivers the money, but he also carries an engagement ring. He's now acting from his long-term belief, which is fighting against his newer and untrue one. This is the full essence of his character and role in the story; he battles between what he thought to be true and what he now inaccurately believes to be true. He acts based on both beliefs and his actions help provide clarity for the audience about what is actually going on with Louise and what she is giving up in her flight.

In *Life Is Beautiful*, the father, Guido, intentionally gives his son falsehoods to believe in, and the boy acts in accordance with what he believes to be true. We know all along that his father is lying. In *Chinatown*, Evelyn continually gives Jake different falsehoods that motivate him, and he often acts based on misperceptions of the complicated relationships among Evelyn, her father, her husband, and the girl. We aren't ahead of Jake; we learn the truth as he does. We don't lose interest in a character because he acts on believable information that turns out to be untrue. Whether we know the truth ahead of him or only at the same time he finds it out, it doesn't make us believe he is stupid or unworthy of our attention in the story. So long as we know how he came to believe the false information and it seems believable at the time, his actions based on that falsehood remain justifiable.

Many romantic comedies are based on this very situation. There is a case of mistaken identity or a petty lie that looms ever larger between the lovers or potential lovers. In *Some Like It Hot*, we can know that Geraldine and Daphne are really men, but so long as it's believable that the others really think they are women, the others can all take actions based on that belief and we will understand their motivations completely. In *Mr. Deeds Goes to Town*, Deeds believes Babe Bennett is his friend, while we know the truth, that she is a journalist who is the source of all the nasty articles about him. It actually builds our sympathy for and attachment to the character for us to know a dangerous truth that he doesn't, even while we wish he wouldn't take the actions he takes because we know they are based on untrue beliefs.

What a character believes completely influences what he wants at any given time. This is the cause-and-effect mechanism of motivation. Colonel Fitts believes Lester has seduced his son into a homosexual affair and takes two different actions based on that belief. Without the belief, his actions would be decidedly different. In some cases—such as the small wants and actions of minor characters—we might not need to spend the time figuring out the belief that lies behind the action. It might be enough to show the action; we take it at face value, in the absence of information to the contrary, and leave it at that. In some cases we learn the belief first, then see the action based on it, as with Colonel Fitts.

But we also can sometimes figure out the underlying belief based on the action taken as a result of it. There's a wonderful moment in *Erin Brockovich* in which she is trying to convince Donna Jensen of the pollution in her water supply. Donna's children are frolicking in a backyard pool while the two women talk, and Donna continues to deny the evidence being presented. Suddenly she races out the door and drags her children from the pool; her action has shown us quite dramatically that she has just changed her belief system. There are also times where we are left to ferret out the beliefs that underlie a character's actions. In the same film, Erin's next-door neighbor takes care of her kids and fixes her plumbing at a time when it seems unlikely she will enter into a relationship with him. On the one hand, it's easy to fathom what he might be hoping for with her, but on the other, he seems genuinely to enjoy the kids and is not overtly pursuing intimacy with her. While he eventually gets what we suspect he wanted all along, his underlying belief—that a relationship might be possible or that it's worth a try or that he isn't going to try and will simply enjoy the children and see what happens—is never made explicit to us. We see the actions, make some assumptions, and then test them against further actions. And all the while we are being lured into delving deeper into the character.

There are three levels of motivation that characters can have: they can want something in a scene; they can want something over a longer term, over the course of a significant part or even the whole story; and they can have a life dream. The more significant the character is in the story, the more likely we are to need to know all three levels. If the waitress who serves lunch in one scene and never appears again wants to flirt with our main character, we don't need to know any more about her than that. That's what she wants in the scene; what longer-term goal she might have or what her life dream is will not be important enough to us to spend the screen time on it. But if the love interest in the story wants to flirt with him, that can be a valid want within a scene, but we will eventually need to know what her longer-term want is and, quite possibly, her life dream as well.

What is a character's life dream? This is a deeply seated motivation, a goal or desire that doesn't even have to be achievable. Norman Bates's life dream is probably to have his mother remain with him. The fact that she's dead makes this impossible, but it doesn't stop him from wanting it, wishing it, even acting upon that bedrock desire of his. What's Salieri's life dream in *Amadeus*? To be as blessed by God with musical ability as Mozart has been. It isn't going to happen and he is painfully aware of that fact, but that doesn't stop him from wanting it and wishing for it. This desire is still a primal motivating factor in his life and in the decisions he makes. What is Kane's life dream in *Citizen Kane*? To regain the love, family, and simplicity he had that is wrapped up in the sled, Rosebud. This is still his life dream long after his parents are dead. Some life dreams are achievable but still remote. Luke Skywalker dreams of being a Jedi knight and fighting against the Empire. He manages to achieve his life dream. But George Bailey in *It's a Wonderful Life* has a life dream of leaving town, of getting out. It is an achievable dream, but not one that he achieves.

Most stories will only deal with the life dreams of a few characters: sometimes only the protagonist, sometimes both the protagonist and the antagonist, sometimes the love interest or the best friend. Even the cast of significant characters won't all have life dreams that are seriously dealt with. In *October Sky*, Homer's life dream is right out there in the open—to build rockets like his hero, Wernher von Braun. His father's life dream is equally out there—to run a great mine and have his son follow in his footsteps. But what about Homer's three friends? Do we have a clear idea of their bedrock secret aspirations or dreams? Aren't we even a bit surprised at the end when it's revealed that they went to college and all got out of the mining community? And what about the teacher? She has goals within the story, but a life dream isn't part of what we know about her.

This leads us to a kind of stratification of characters. There are those about whom we only know short-term wants and goals; we only get as close as learning the wants within individual scenes. Then there are characters about whom we also learn their longer-term wants and goals, for the course of the story or a significant portion of it. And finally we have the characters about whom we also know their deepest motivating factors, their dreams or wishes or desires, whether attainable or not.

When wrestling with the cast of your own story, it's a good idea to try to identify which characters fit into which strata. Clearly your cast of significant characters will all fit into the middle strata or the top strata; we should at least learn what they want within a larger segment of the story, even if we don't learn their life dreams. But there may be more than simply your protagonist in the highest strata. It could be the antagonist whose life dream we also learn. It could be the love interest or a friend. It isn't going to be determined by amount of screen time. Homer's father spends less time on screen than Homer's friends, but he is the antagonist of the story—however sympathetic he might be—and it is the collision of his life dream with his son's that is the center of the story. In *An Officer and a Gentleman*, we learn Zack Mayo's life dream—it's the film's title. We also learn his best friend's life dream. Sid Worley hopes to live up to the expectations of his father and brothers. And Paula, the love interest, has a known life dream—to escape the drudgery of her small-town life by marrying an officer, a dream of her mother's that failed. But we never learn the life dream of the antagonist, Sergeant Foley.

Keep in mind that it isn't necessary that the character actually pursue the life dream. Not all characters will be Norman Bates or Luke Skywalker or Zack Mayo. The life dream is more often an important bit of bedrock information about what makes the character tick. It can sometimes be the key to our understanding of the character. Salieri can't force God to bless him, but this desire is the key to our understanding the man and what he does. Or the life dream can be tangential to the conflicts in the story, but still basic in the makeup of the character. McClane in *Die Hard* desperately hopes to get back together with his estranged wife. While he does so by the end, this life dream is not what he pursues in the story. It's part of his emotional makeup, it's part of why he does what he does. But at the same time, nothing he does in trying to foil the bad guys is directed at trying to reignite his relationship with his wife. He can't; once the antagonist and his men take over the building, the two never have another scene together until the very end of the story.

Subtext

Human beings, by their very nature, often don't approach the things they want directly. We frequently find some roundabout way of going after the things we need or want. If what we want is simple and noncontroversial, we might directly ask, "Please pass the salt." But what if a couple are quarreling and haven't spoken in days, or they have just suffered a tragedy together. In one of those circumstances, "Please pass the salt," could actually be a request to start interacting again or a first tentative approach that really means, "Please acknowledge I'm alive." It could be one character trying to assert or reassert dominance over the other, or it could be a plaintive request for the other to see that, "Hey, I'm suffering here!" Depending on the context—the preexisting circumstances between the characters, what we know about them, and what they know about each other—there are many things a simple, fact-based statement could mean besides or in addition to what it means on the surface. All these other potential meanings come under the category of subtext. Subtext can therefore only be based on subjective drama. "Please pass the salt" can only mean exactly what it says on the surface if we don't have additional knowledge about the characters and circumstances.

Subtext not only depends on our subjective knowledge but is also a major means of exercising our special insider connection with characters, to add new layers of meaning to interactions and deepen our understanding. We can enjoy knowing the subtext at the same time we can know that another character on screen doesn't get it—he only knows the surface meaning. Putting the audience in this special position milks—and rewards—the intimate connection the audience has established with the characters in subjective circumstances. This sort of moment, when we know added layers of what's "really going on," makes us feel like real participants; we are in the know even more than some of the people in the story. We learn more about a character's inner life when we see how he pursues his goals; what form of subtext does he choose and how does he vary it with other characters?

Subtext helps make the interaction in a story more closely resemble real human interaction. If every character says everything on his mind and only speaks the truth and only the whole truth, then we will start to reject the story as unrealistic. Our life experience tells us people behave otherwise. Even if we grew up in a monastery, we'd have learned that silence can speak volumes, that the technical truth can be hiding a lie and that half a truth— while technically truthful—can in fact be a lie. This is how human beings interact, whether they admit it or not. In fact, a character who always and only tells the whole truth is such an anomaly it makes a superb character, like Chance in *Being There*. But he constitutes an extraordinary person in ordinary circumstances. Other characters—and human beings—tell the truth sometimes, lie sometimes, shade the truth or the lies into gray areas, use words to cover up real meanings, and even use actions to cover up words. When we see these shadings of gray among the characters in a story, it more closely resembles how we see life being lived around us. It seems more realistic. And when we understand the hidden meanings, the half-truths and the half-lies and all the gray areas, we feel truly connected to the characters and the story. This is what adds the depth to three-dimensional characters and stories.

Subtext is necessarily created in the moments of stories, in the scene work, rather than in the background research and digging work that you are now doing. But it's important to know that your characters need their own modes of getting what they want and of dealing with shades of the truth and with the unspoken. For instance, you can envision your characters as ones who strive to be frank and honest at all times or who hide behind lies even when it isn't necessary. Or you could have a character who punctures holes in other people's subtexts or is persistently a step behind everyone else in catching on. Or a character can be trying to discover subtext when there is none and missing it when it is there. How a character deals with, relates to, uses, and understands subtext can be a primary means of understanding or defining a character. Preston Sturges's *The Palm Beach Story* makes wonderful use of this in differentiating its characters. Tom Jeffers tries to use the truth, but shades it to his advantage. His wife, Gerry, uses lies that she shades to her favor with smatterings of truth. John D. Hackensacker III is an "aw, shucks" millionaire who blurts out what he thinks and feels without a thought to shading it one way or another. And Princess Centimillia sees hidden meanings and subterfuge everywhere—and not necessarily where it really is. All of this is played for comedy, but the same ingredients, using the characters' own relationship to the use and creation of subtext, can be an effective means of defining the character or a significant side of a character.

A character needn't be consciously aware of his shadings of the truth or the hidden meanings in his words or actions for there to be subtext or for us to become aware of it. A character can believe that he simply wants the salt passed, but we know better—we are not quite as wrapped up in his distractions as he is. In fact, in this instance, there will be an element of dramatic irony in our knowing that a character is meaning more—or revealing more than he thinks he is—by the subtext of his words and actions. We will be anticipating when he will discover what we already know about his hidden messages.

As part of the discovery period you're in right now, it would be a good idea to experiment with your characters. If your protagonist is with his best friend and together they meet a woman they both find attractive, how would they deal with each other? How would they deal with her in front of each other? And when the other isn't there? What about your antagonist when he meets the protagonist's mother? What about the rival, who may turn into a friend later, when he is interviewing the protagonist for a job? Even if these exact interactions won't be part of the story, imagining potentially charged circumstances between characters and exploring your thoughts about how each of them would deal with the surface and subtext levels of communication can be valuable in helping to define the characters clearly in your mind. Chances are, you will have formed the basis of some scene that will be in the story, even if it isn't between the same two characters in the same circumstances you've envisioned. You will have discovered how a character says what he means without saying it or says more than he means without knowing it. This experience of realistic complexity with your characters will help you find the key to the character and perhaps some of the scenes you will end up writing.

Recapitulations

The continuous nature of telling a story in film is the source of much of its power. There are no distractions or diversions, there's no setting the book down or going to the other room for a snack or answering the phone. Once you have engaged the audience, they will, you hope, be yours from beginning to end. One of the key elements to sustaining that connection is to keep the action going; the characters must continue to face obstacles and keep heading into ever greater danger, whether it's physical, emotional, or even spiritual. But one of the biggest drawbacks to this relentless continuity is that a lot of information and twists and turns are thrust at the audience one after the other. This can lead to confusion. Some of the audience may have missed or forgotten a crucial bit of information or have confused the change in a relationship between two characters. The simpler the story, the less likely this is to happen. But with a complex story—one with a fairly large cast or many twists and turns or a complex mode of being told—the potential for a confused audience increases sharply.

A primary method of making certain that the whole audience is "on the same page" is including strategically placed recapitulations, or recaps. A recapitulation won't replace having delivered the information well in the first place—that remains the most crucial task of all. But when you have covered a lot of territory in the story and it's critical that the whole audience have the same information in mind, a well-placed recap can be the difference between a piffle and an explosion.

This doesn't mean you have to bring out a news anchor to recap the events so far, "with pictures at eleven." Because a recap of information and events we already know is a form of exposition, the same rules apply. Conflict and humor are the best ways to mask that a recapitulation is actually being delivered. In *Aliens*, Private Hudson has two modes as a Marine—he's intensely working or fighting until there's a letup, then he shifts into his other mode and starts to whine and complain about their dilemma. While he's screaming about the impossibility of their getting out of their trap alive, he is recapitulating all that they have been through and helping to focus the audience's attention on the exact nature of the remaining problems in their situation. In *Frenzy*, Chief Inspector Oxford's wife is taking cooking classes. While he suffers through—and tries to escape from—fish head soup, he recaps the events of the investigation so far and what his current thinking is.

Often, but by no means always, the recapitulations are embodied by a single character. Dr. Watson performs this function for Sherlock Holmes. Whether Watson is right or, much more often, wrong, his theories, questions, contributions, and miscues function as a means of clarifying for the audience where the case stands, what is left to be done or figured out or who must be questioned next. It can be the detective's client to whom he must give a report or the policeman who is hopelessly lost in the case while our hero is on the right track. It can be the mother or best friend who is constantly mired a step or two behind the story, who helps you to focus exactly where we are.

Recapitulations can be so important to a story that a specific type of character is created whose obsession in life is keeping track of events, changes in relationships, or even the evolving values of the characters and the story. This is a *raisonneur* character. Tom Hagen in *The Godfather* is just such a character, and the story would suffer greatly without him. This story has a large cast of secondary characters and a complex world of alliances, rivalries, family relationships, and positions. Whenever there is a need to clarify what it means when a rival family is moving in on some aspect of the Corleone family or what it means in the Mob dynamics when Don Corleone is shot, it's Tom who figures it out. His role goes beyond the realm of recapping into actually clarifying the dynamics as they evolve. This can be crucial in a large, difficult-to-follow story such as *The Godfather*. While twists and turns on the path of the story occur, he helps the other characters sort out what it means—abetting their decisions, which then lead to actions. At the same time, these moments help us understand the complex dynamics. Whenever those dynamics require clarifying, his obsession with this aspect of the lives in the story keeps him at the center of the recapitulations.

Recaps don't have to be separate scenes for no other purpose than reviewing what has happened so far. In fact, more often, a recapitulation is part of scene that is much more focused on the future. Part of the process of deciding what to do next or how to go about solving the next dilemma could be assessing the past to look for a clue to the future, or some variation on "I haven't come this far to stop now." Anytime a character says something like "I've been shot at, beaten up, stabbed, and choked. I'll be damned if I'm going to let a padlock stop me," as he shoots the padlock off a door and enters the next problem of the story, he's really giving a brief recap that helps lead into the next obstacle. Sometimes a recap can be embodied in an object. Our intrepid travelers started out in a pristine white sailboat that now has a broken mast, blood on the deck, and a hole in the side, and is towing a rubber raft filled with dynamite. A tour of the boat itself—in preparation for going into the final battle, perhaps—could be an effective recapitulation of all the story has taken us through so far and a reminder of just how long the odds are against our hero and his crew.

How does this need for recapitulations impact you in gathering the material and information you need to build our story? First, you have to venture a guess as to how complicated your story will be. Are you planning to tell it in simple, chronological order, or will there be some variation on time continuity? Will you necessarily have a lot of secondary characters, or is it going to be a cast of only two or three? Is the world of the story unfamiliar and/or extremely complex? Is the protagonist or antagonist such a complex or conflicted character that it would be possible to misconstrue some of his actions? These questions assess your need for recaps. Once you have a general idea of how crucial having recaps will be, the next question is, should there be a single character who embodies them or will they be simpler moments we can catch on the fly?

Generally, the greater the need for recapitulations, the more screen time must be devoted to them and the more likely a character will need to carry the weight. But even the simplest story with a limited cast and a familiar world will require a few recaps. Remember, the audience is picking up everything on the fly and caring about a great many things all at once. It's safe to assume they could need a nudge here and there in the right direction so they are perfectly primed for the major shake-ups you have ready to deliver to them.

Where should recaps go in the story? Clearly, recaps are more necessary later in the story than they are earlier. We need to have had enough experience in the world of the story to require reminding or reassessing. If there are only going to be two or three recapitulations, the most likely places to look for opportunities will be in the second half of the second act and then in the third act. But right now you don't know your acts, so the pertinent questions at the moment are who and how. Who will carry the recaps that you need, and how will you get them across without a news anchor reading them dryly?

The protagonist is not necessarily the best character to carry the load of recapping, though there are plenty of instances where he or she does it. A lot depends on how doubt-plagued the protagonist is. If you have an introspective and conscience-driven main character, then he might indulge in his own recaps. If you have an action-driven character who is always ready to jump into the fray, she's less likely to pause for a recap. But it can be helpful to have a character who has been in the story for the long haul, someone who has first-hand experience of the events, decisions, and people involved in the recap. So it might be necessary to discover a part of the nature of the best friend or the love interest or another of the significant second-level characters that prompts him to be retrospective or introspective or analytical of the evolving events and relationships in the story. Sometimes being doubtful is enough. Doubt can prompt even an action hero to stop long enough to justify his next leap into battle, and that justification becomes a recap.

There might be a client for the detective or the mother of the victim the police must answer to who hasn't been in every part of the story, but who sustains a vested interest in the events of the story. A report or justification—however reluctantly delivered by or coerced from the protagonist—may function perfectly as a recap. And the character who prompts a recap from another character doesn't necessarily have to be the sole character to perform that function. You have enough latitude, especially in stories with modest needs for recapitulation, to vary how and what prompts a recap.

If you have decided you don't need a single character to carry the load of recapping throughout the story, then the next question becomes, how do you go about threading your recaps into the story seamlessly and with conflict and humor? Much of that decision-making has to come in the actual writing of the scenes. But you can already be identifying the events that will need recapitulations to precede them. Maybe you don't know exactly how it will all come about, but you have an idea that near the end of your story, your protagonist will have to climb a mountain or rob a bank for a good cause or tell the woman who fervently hates him how much he loves her. You probably have an idea of what is going to be most difficult for your character to achieve or overcome or face. Shortly before that event is a likely place for a recapitulation. Remind the audience of why this is hard for the character, what it will mean if he succeeds or fails, what she hopes to gain or avoid losing, what weaknesses this obstacle will test in him, what past failures make success seem even more unlikely. Whatever will heighten our participation and suspense, whatever will increase the unpredictability of the outcome of the next crucial event—this is the material you will be looking for. And you will be looking for an unobtrusive place to put it before the big event.

Perhaps the last instant before the crucial event isn't the best place for the recap; it might feel obtrusive. Just as it's necessary to separate other exposition from the need for that information, here we want to separate the recapitulation from the event, while keeping it near enough to fulfill its function. If it's too far removed, a recap will become a reminder when we don't need it and it doesn't help. Strategically, then, look for a place in which there are other more pressing events or preparations for the characters to contemplate. Those pressing needs will distract the audience from the recap just enough that it doesn't seem conveniently located, but it will leave the information—and hope and fear it helps generate—still feeling fresh.

Again, *Aliens* and Private Hudson provide good examples. The dwindling team, trapped inside the building, has to locate the potential ways in which the creatures can get to them to kill them. Hudson whines about all their problems and all the ways in which it's impossible for them to survive. In the course of his rant and the other characters' responses, we're reminded that the little girl has survived, Ripley has survived, the creatures can be killed, the team is not without resources in the battle. We have a recap of their situation as well as an assessment of the near future. Then they prepare themselves and their space for that future. We are distracted from the recap just enough—but not too much. We are made to worry about the future, but not in the instant that that worry must be focused. We are given time to mull it over.

In *The African Queen*, a two-character story told in chronological order with a simple goal, we still need a recap for maximum impact. Rosie and Charlie have managed to get the boat down the river and onto the lake, where the original plan was that they would sink the German battleship that controls the lake. It's amazing that they have managed the impossible-seeming mission this far, and they recap what they have done in getting onto the lake. They also look forward to—and remind us of—the final mission. We are shown the battleship and the difficulty of their next and last task. Then they have to prepare their boat for that last step of the mission. Again, we have had a recap that has flowed into a preparation for the future important event and its difficulty. And again, we have had a distraction from the recap that, in its own way, actually supports the recap.

When Captain Miller and his men finally find Private Ryan, they have to explain to him and his commanding officer what they have been sent to do—a recap—and convince him to come with them—preparation for the future of their story. And then the town they are in comes under attack, distracting us from the recap, but also keeping alive what it has fostered in us. When the Rebellion in *Star Wars* analyzes the plans inside R2-D2 and sets up its plan for destroying the Death Star, we have a reversal of the order. Here, we have the discussion of the future and its difficulty for Luke and the others, and then Han Solo decides to leave, his part in the mission complete. In trying to convince him to stay, Luke recaps all they have been through and how crucial Han will be to the future goal. And again, we have the distraction in the form of the preparations for the upcoming battle plus Princess Leia's good-bye with Han.

So first, you have to decide on the extent of the need for recapitulations, start to identify the areas where they are likely to be inserted, find the character or characters who might prompt them, *and* find the distractions between the recaps and the big future events they are preparing the audience for. At this point, don't strive to have it all nailed down, but, rather, have a good idea of what will be needed and a general idea of how you might find ways of getting it across seamlessly. If a character will carry all or most of the load of recapitulation, then the nature of the character must incorporate traits that enable this function to come across as unforced.

Dealing with Coincidence

Coincidence is one of the nasty little secrets of storytelling. Whether a character is assaulted by the story or voluntarily chooses to take on the goals of the story, there is some element of coincidence in the formation of those circumstances. His superiors could have chosen someone other than Captain Miller to find Private Ryan. Oskar Schindler could have failed to get a contract to manufacture pots and pans for the Nazis. R2-D2 could have stumbled upon another farm boy instead of Luke Skywalker.

McMurphy could have landed in a psychiatric ward run by some-one other than Nurse Ratched. Every story has some kind of co-incidence without which the story simply would not come about. This kind of coincidence must be accepted and dealt with as one of the inevitable realities of storytelling.

Sometimes it can be explained away by drawing attention to it and complaining, "Of all the gin joints in all the world, she has to walk into mine." How many protagonists—with anything from cancer to a suicide mission—ask "Why me?" Sometimes you can show the circumstance first, solidly planting its existence, then drop the character into it with a sense of inevitability. McMurphy is brought into Ratched's world in handcuffs by the police after we've seen some of the life on the psychiatric ward. Sometimes there is a kind of predestination at work—Luke is the son of a Jedi knight and Princess Leia is in search of a Jedi master. Some-times you have an authority figure explain it. Captain Miller's superior officer says simply, he's the best man for the job. And sometimes you make a major conflict or accomplishment out of the coincidence and elaborate on the achievement of it. Schind-ler's efforts to get the contract that enables all the rest of the story is a serious effort and is fully dramatized.

All these are acceptable and workable methods of dealing with the unavoidable coincidences that lurk at the core of most stories. But whenever possible, strive to avoid coincidence, espe-cially if it isn't basic and formative, like the ones above. If your hero paints himself into a corner and only then discovers there's an unlocked door conveniently waiting for him there, we'll reject the coincidence as being too easy on the character. And too easy for the author. If your hero needs a hundred dollars to retrieve his gun from a pawnshop, and without the gun he won't be able to stop the villain from destroying life as we know it, it will feel like an awful coincidence if he just happens to find a hundred-dollar bill on the sidewalk.

Ironically, the reverse coincidence is not true. If he already has the hundred dollars and loses it or has it stolen on his way to get the gun, we won't rebel. If he paints himself into a corner in which he knows there is a door only to find it locked and un-breakable, we won't cry foul. If a coincidence works against the character or makes life more difficult for the storyteller, the audience tends to buy the coincidence. If it makes things easier for either one, we tend to reject the coincidence.

Unnecessary coincidences are the most aggravating of all. If our protagonist has to go to New York City to find her long-lost sister and the first person she meets in the city is married to that sister, it will play completely phony. We won't buy it for a second. If she goes to a village of fifty people and the first person she meets is married to the sister, it won't seem so far-fetched. But the real question for the storyteller is whether the coincidence is necessary at all. You have to accept unavoidable, story-creating coincidences, but do you have to create ones that could be avoided? Maybe the bulk of the story won't be about the finding of the sister, but rather about their interaction once she is found. In this case, you don't want to put a lot of screen time into the search. But you don't have to make it an unbelievable coincidence to shorten the time. Maybe she and the sister have an uncle who still lives at the same address in the city, and who leads our heroine to her sister. A linkage can be created that bridges the coincidence and turns it into an acceptable—and believable—story event.

So you have two kinds of coincidence to root out in your stories—the unavoidable but necessary ones, and the ones you can and should find ways to avoid. First, let's go back to the collision that creates your story. Is it between the protagonist and an antagonist, an antagonistic world, or an antagonistic aspect of himself? There is probably some bedrock coincidence involved in how the protagonist comes to be set against an outside antagonist or an antagonistic world. If the essential conflict is internal—the character is at war with himself—then there is probably some element of coincidence in why this preexisting condition is coming to a head now. Here you will start to be able to put our finger on the coincidence you have to learn to live with, the one you have to make the audience accept.

The coincidence likely will be something that makes life tougher for the character and/or the storyteller, so you'll have a good start on making it acceptable. But you might have to create the moment when it is explained—the authority figure, the preexisting circumstances the character stumbles into, the "why me" moment. This is akin to the willing suspension of disbelief. When Rick bemoans Ilsa's coincidental arrival in his gin joint out of all the gin joints in the world, he's giving us that moment when we either buy into the resulting story or we opt out. We already buy into Nurse Ratched's world before McMurphy is brought into it, and the revelation that this will be a disastrous collision comes after we've already bought into the two sides being placed together. When R2-D2 finds Luke, the robot's mission is something of an obstacle for Luke; then, when Luke falls for the hologram of Princess Leia and takes on the mission, it results in the deaths of his adoptive parents. This tragic turn of events from the coincidental—but ultimately predestined—meeting certainly helps in making it acceptable to the audience.

Coincidence often means leading the audience down the garden path. You know that at the end of the path is a coincidence—Nurse Ratched or Ilsa or a robot with secret plans that will lead the boy into chasing after his wildest dreams—but when the audience is asked to take that first step down the path, there is no sign yet of the coincidence. You establish the place or the person or circumstances first, when it looks to be easily acceptable. Then you add another element—a second place or person or circumstance—and this addition leads to the discovery that this whole setup is actually a coincidence. Now comes the most crucial moment, luring the audience into accepting the story after they discover, often unconsciously, that there is a coincidence at the center. But they have already accepted the first two parts—Nurse Ratched's world and McMurphy's entrance into it. The fact that these are the two worst people in the world for each other—the coincidence—already *seems* like a natural outgrowth of reasonable, noncoincidental things. The reality is, the audience has cleverly been led down the garden path to the coincidence and seduced into accepting it, often without even realizing it.

Clearly, this selling of coincidence must be done early in the story. As we've discussed with the willing suspension of disbelief, we can't change the rules once we've established them. But early in a story, the audience is usually prepared to buy into whatever it takes to make the story move forward. Because our unavoidable coincidence is usually formative of the story—the collision of

McMurphy and Ratched or Rick and Ilsa—it's natural that it will happen early in the story. But sometimes, as with Luke Skywalker or Sarah in *The Terminator,* the full realization of the coincidence can't possibly be right at the beginning. We have to find out information first—that Obi-Wan knew Luke's father, that Luke is the very Jedi knight needed to win the battle—and only then can we fully comprehend that it wasn't truly coincidence that led R2-D2 to Luke. Sarah wouldn't become the mother of the savior of mankind if the Terminator hadn't come to kill her, bringing Kyle to guard her and father the savior of mankind. In both these cases and in many others, there is a kind of predestination at work in the story. How do we make the audience accept predestination, when they might not believe in it in life? Isn't this changing the rules after we have established them?

This is where storytelling connects with an aspect of magic—sleight of hand. The predestined collision is sold to the audience as a coincidence, and only later do we find out that it wasn't a coincidence at all. This can, in fact, be the huge twist or surprise in a story such as *The Crying Game* or *The Sixth Sense.* So the method looks identical to the audience, but it has one extra wrinkle for the storyteller. First you must convince the audience to buy into what seems to be a coincidence. Easy enough; it's just like any other story. But *you* know that you have a moment coming up much later that will pull the rug out from under that coincidence and potentially make the audience reject all that has come before it—it seems to be changing the rules. It's a dangerous game, but when it works, it's a game well worth the risk.

The key is to give clues along the way that the coincidence we bought into isn't as real as we thought it was. But the clues can't be so strong that they undermine the moment that reveals the predestination, which should generate considerable wallop. In other words, you've made the audience believe in a coincidence, then slowly eroded that coincidence's foundations, but nearly secretly, while the audience was being made to look elsewhere. Once you reveal the shocker—Luke is the only Jedi knight capable of helping the Rebels, or Malcolm actually died and is in the process of being helped by Cole in *The Sixth Sense*—the audience might have an instant of feeling cheated, but then they begin to realize that the clues were there all along, we just didn't quite pick up on them. The rules weren't really changed; we just didn't fully understand them, didn't see the little signs that showed the real rules. If those clues weren't there all along, then the big twist would indeed feel like a cheat and probably make the audience reject the story rather than revel in being fooled, the way we do with a good magician.

While all this effort is necessary with coincidences—and predestination—which form the basis of stories, it should usually be avoided with other coincidences. It's almost inevitable that when devising your story you will come upon a situation in which you need to create a person or circumstance in order to enable something of serious value to your story to move forward. You've locked your hero in prison and now have to get him out. You've made her fall in love with a deceiver the audience hates and you have to open her eyes to the reality of who he is. You've made the boy deeply worship a professional athlete and now it's crucial to your story that he meet the jock. If your hero is put in a cell with a convict who is planning a perfect escape, it will be the same as painting himself into a corner and finding an unlocked door. If she just happens to come home early to find the jerk with another woman, it's at least hard on her, but it's also what we want for her, so it will still be too easy—on the storyteller. And the athlete just happens to come to the boy's school. Bogus!

But I need it to happen or my story will die on the vine, you cry. The problem isn't that it happens, it's how it happens. As so often is the case, one of the keys is conflict. The bigger problem isn't that a prisoner is planning an escape, it's that our hero was placed with him—by the storyteller. If a prisoner is planning an escape and our hero has to fight and overcome obstacles in order to go with him, it isn't a convenient coincidence. It's still a coincidence that someone is planning an escape, but by making the hero work for his chance at it, his escaping doesn't feel quite so coincidental and so phony. But it's usually better still to get rid of the coincidence altogether and have your hero invent his own mode of escape rather than hand him an escape on a silver platter. When the woman needs to see through her nasty lover, it will be stronger to put the onus of discovery on her rather than make it a fortuitous accident. Give her half a clue in one place, half a clue somewhere else, and make her put them together to build suspicion and then investigate for herself. Send the athlete not to the boy's school, but someplace across town, far outside the boy's realm of travel. Make a difficult but possible expedition out of his getting a chance to meet his hero.

This is fine if you have the screen time—and can justify it—to dramatize rather than make things easy for yourself or your character. But there are still going to be some coincidental moments that can't be avoided and for which you can't spend the screen time. Sometimes the coincidence absolutely has to work to the advantage of the character. If he hadn't gotten a flat tire, he never would have met the person who helped him realize he was actually leaving his soul mate and helped him decide to go back to her. Again, some sleight of hand can help. In the end, the coincidence is a good thing for the character—and therefore harder for us to buy into. But we will buy into coincidence when it seems like a disadvantage, and only later will we recognize that in the long run, it turned out to be an advantage.

Another tactic, and the most pertinent to this stage of developing your story, is to make the coincidence preexisting, long before you need it. In *Rear Window*, L. B. Jeffries will eventually need a telescope so he can see the goings-on in the killer's apartment more closely. He could have one in his apartment all along, but it would seem rather obvious, since there is no way he could use it to watch the stars from his inner-city apartment. But by making him a professional photographer and putting his equipment around the apartment from the outset, it doesn't seem like a coincidence that he has a huge telephoto lens when he needs one.

By separating the revelation of the coincidence from the time in which it is needed in the story, you allow the audience to see it as just a regular part of the world and the character's life. It doesn't seem like an afterthought that was just placed there to fill a story hole. It isn't a door just invented to be in the corner to allow the hero to escape; it was there all along. From the storyteller's point of view, the door was put there in the first place to enable the hero to escape, but it was planted much earlier to mask that fact from the audience. And sometimes, that very same door will find another use as the story evolves.

At this point, do everything you can to avoid coincidences by finding connections, such as the uncle of the long-lost sister. If you must have a coincidence to keep the story moving, at least try to make the character have to work to achieve it. Put a conflict into the mix. Or strive to make the coincidence be or seem detrimental to the character and your story. If all else fails, at least make the coincidental information preexist in your story so it doesn't just come in at the last minute to save the day for you and your characters. Start thinking now, and several things could happen. You may find a way to get rid of the coincidence altogether. Sometimes what starts as a coincidence or its solution becomes an integral part of a character or the world of the story you are venturing into. You may find a way to make a coincidence be or seem to be a disadvantage. Or you may find a way of making a coincidence exist in the character and the world long before it is called upon to solve a problem. If you start to think about it only when you've painted your character into the corner, then you'll be stuck with inventing that unlocked door behind him. And you'll have your audience crying foul.

Creating Living Characters

All the great twists and turns along the path of your story won't have much impact on your audience if your characters don't resonate for them. It's easy to assume that this is the actor's job. They get the big bucks, so why shouldn't it be their job to make the audience care about them? No matter how charismatic or good-looking or sympathetic an actor is, on screen or in real life, there still must be a platform for those traits, a means of showing off those advantages. Two-dimensional or stillborn characters will nearly negate those wonderful traits your actors may bring to the story.

What makes a character come alive? Is it enough that the character wants something badly and is having difficulty getting it? If you add backstory and enough exposition, will that make a character come alive? If we understand a character's motivations, then does he come alive? What about his weaknesses? His humiliations? If we can know a character's arc, her change, then don't we automatically have a living, breathing character? Even if she's an animated character or the title character in *Babe*?

As was touched on briefly in the section "The 'Game' of Storytelling," the basis of living characters is that they have an inner life and an attitude about themselves. The overriding impression of "life" that a character can generate stems from the sense that there is much more here, much more to this human being, than can fit into the story. This is true even if the character isn't technically a human being; in order for a pig, a robot, an insect, or a toy to become a character, it has to display complete humanlike characteristics—wants and needs and desires and doubts and fears, weaknesses and strengths, phobias and obsessions. Without this sort of anthropomorphism, the pig, robot, insect, or toy necessarily remains a prop or an object. The pig might still want to root about in the trash, but it won't truly become a character until more humanlike characteristics have been ascribed to it.

Inner Life and Character Attitude

One of the biggest reasons to resist turning out pages but instead spend time exploring your story before writing the scenes has to do with the inner lives of characters. Even if you could push through the Page 70 Syndrome and complete a draft on the fly, the characters would mostly be doing your bidding; they would be puppets with the strings visible. You know what you need your characters to do—run into burning buildings or break up with their lovers or rob banks or get drunk rather than face a challenge—and they'll do exactly those things for you. Nothing more: no attitude, no resistance, no inner life. They might have their reasons, wants that we know about; through the course of the story, they might go through an arc, some change. But that change will be perfunctory and rather difficult to believe. The reasons and wants will be attributes or even shallower, as changeable as their shirt or glasses.

If you can't answer the question "What would this character be doing right now if he weren't forced to be in this story?" then your character probably doesn't yet have enough inner life. If you can answer it part of the time, you still need to work to develop a fully rounded, living, breathing human character. What was this person doing the day before the story started? What does he do when the camera isn't recording his activities? Does he have goals and wants and needs and fears and hopes that go outside the realm of the story, or does everything about him dovetail perfectly with *your* design for the story? Real life is messy. Real life has things that don't easily fit. There are junk drawers in life filled with all the things that can't be filed neatly with the rest of the stuff. The impression of life that a story generates has to have this messiness, the things that don't fit, the things that burst out at the seams around the edges, things that have nothing to do with the events of the story and the needs of the author. But they have everything to do with the sense of life you can infuse into a character.

You need to know more about the life of your character than can possibly fit into the story. You need to be able to create the things that won't fit, that have to be stuffed into the junk drawer of this person's life. Maybe the tail end of something will be sticking out of that junk drawer in some scene, or maybe it will never get onto the screen. This information will still inhabit your thoughts about the character and, as a result, find its way into the *life* of the character. This is how you'll find the inner lives of your characters—by knowing what you can't use, what doesn't simply support the story, what they would be doing if this story weren't occurring in their lives or what they'll do next year or what they did last year or what they cared about then or will care about in the future. If you have a large pool of material about a character that can't actually seep into the story directly, then some of it will seep into the character himself—all in your head, of course, but it will get there.

The inner life you've generated will find an outlet. That outlet won't be the actual material you've invented and discovered about your character; it won't be discussing what he was doing last year or would be doing if he weren't here. That outlet will be the character's attitude, his relationship with himself, the way in which he creates and presents and imagines and sees himself. An attitude doesn't have to be accurate or on target to infuse a character with life. A hapless would-be Superman doesn't have to fly in order to achieve "life" through this attitude about himself. A character with no attitude about himself is subservient, an obedient character who will do what the story needs of him. But an obedient servant can have incredible attitude about himself, and this will foster a sense of life. Stevens in *The Remains of the Day* is a servant, obsessively obedient to his ideas of the rules of society and decorum. But these are *his* ideas, and they stem from his attitude. He knows his place and diligently strives to maintain it, even in a shifting world. So, in fact, this character does not fit neatly into the world of the story; his obedience isn't to the needs of the story or the storyteller, but to his own, inner defined needs and rules. All of which means he is a character with life, despite the fact that he is subservient and obedient.

A character with attitude is one who marches to his own drummer. The importance here is not whether the character's drummer is common in the world; it certainly could be. What's crucial is that the drummer not seem to be the storyteller's. If all the characters simply march to the drummer established by the story and the storyteller, they lose their sense of life, and so does the story. We might still go along with the story and its thrills and chills and explosions and twists and turns, but a critical element will have been lost. We won't ever fully engage our emotions with a story featuring puppet characters whose strings we see, who obey the story and the storyteller at every turn. We'll become more involved in the pursuits of a doll or a pig that generates life than we will in the pursuits of a character played by a flesh-and-blood actor who obeys the story and its teller at every juncture.

Don't take this to mean that a character's attitude is simply one of rebellion against you, the storyteller. It's much more important that the character simply be on her own road—seeing herself in this way, having these feelings about herself—which is entirely hers, not just a finite segment of someone else's road, namely yours. Having a character who is on her own road creates a feeling that if the story ever let loose, the character might just wander off—or run away—to do something that is defined by her own life. This tension between the character as a reluctant participant in the story and the needs of the story creates a feeling of life, a feeling that there is so much more than simply what we're seeing. It seems that we're *seeing* the tip of the iceberg, but we're *feeling* the impact of the whole iceberg being there. That is when characters start coming alive.

Protagonist and Antagonist

How do we reconcile the creation of the antagonist from the weaknesses and blind spots of the protagonist, as discussed earlier, with the need for important characters to march to their own drummers and have distinct attitudes generated by their inner lives? It's true that the starting point for discovering and fleshing out an antagonist should be the nature of the protagonist. And it's also true that, in part, the antagonist is defined by his opposition to—or being the opposite of—the protagonist. But the process can't end there; that would result in the very essence of the obedient characters you're striving to overcome. At some point the antagonist needs to take on a life of his own; he needs to have his own inner life that perhaps mirrors the complex inner life of the protagonist but isn't limited to just being a negative copy of it.

At the same time, the level of complexity in the characters needs to find a balance. If your protagonist has only a modest amount of inner life, then the antagonist would probably have about the same. But a complex protagonist deserves and needs a complex antagonist. In *An Officer and a Gentleman*, Zack and Sergeant Foley reach this level. In *The Godfather*, the two sides of Michael reach this level. If you have a nicely rounded protagonist, with a full, rich, and knowable inner life, and an antagonist who is merely a cardboard villain, the mismatch will undermine the battle between them. If you have a rich and complex villain and a cardboard hero, the same imbalance will destroy the effectiveness of the story. Clearly, the most compelling circumstance is when both the protagonist and antagonist have complex inner lives that we come to know and feel as we are engaged in the story. Othello and Iago are just such a pair. McMurphy and Nurse Ratched are a good match.

When you're fleshing out your protagonist and antagonist and striving to give them complete inner lives, backstories, and a full set of wants, you might start to notice moments of convergence—little aspects of their lives that almost seem to meld together. A common hallmark of stories is that the protagonist starts to resemble the antagonist over time, and vice versa. They don't switch roles, but they learn from each other, copy each other, take on each other's tactics. They meet each other halfway. The victimized protagonist turns aggressive and lethal against the killer-antagonist, while the antagonist starts to see himself as a victim. The timid, insecure hero thrust unwillingly into a dangerous game gains self-confidence and assertiveness, while the power structure supporting the villain erodes and takes his self-confidence with it.

This can simply be a common paradigm at work, but it can also be a sign of living characters, characters who are alive and learning from what the story puts them through and from the successes of their rivals. Don't get carried away and start making flow charts and forcing your characters to take on the traits of their opposites. That's just one more way to drive the life out of your characters, to deny them their free will. But the discovery of one or two aspects that shift from one side to the other can be liberating. When you discover the moment that McMurphy drops his usual self-deprecating honesty and takes on Ratched's kind of subterfuge—he pretends to do one thing while having radically different intentions—it could be the discovery of the pivotal moment in the character. When you discover that Sarah has to become a cold and ruthless killer in order to rid herself and the world of the Terminator, you are finding the ultimate test of her character arc.

Keep in mind that the protagonist isn't turning into the antagonist, or vice versa. They may take on aspects of each other, there might be areas of convergence that resonate through your story and make it feel woven together into a whole, but they must retain their differences. It comes back to intentions. When McMurphy adopts clever dishonesty, his intention is not to inflict harm but to escape the infliction of harm. An aspect of how he works comes from Ratched's arsenal, not his own, but he doesn't adopt her goals. When Rick kills Colonel Strasser in *Casablanca*, he takes an aggressive and warlike action in a neutral country; this is a huge change for the previously noninterventionist Rick. While Rick's battle has been largely with himself and with Ilsa, Strasser is a manifestation of the antagonistic side of Rick. Until now, Rick has never interfered when Strasser did evil things; Strasser has been in support of the antagonistic side of Rick. When Rick attacks him— acting as the protagonist—he uses the methods of the antagonist, but for the purposes of the protagonist's side. Rick's intentions remain true, but he has to adopt part of the means of the opposition.

Now, while you are fleshing out the two sides of the collision of your story, keep in mind that it will be helpful to discover a convergence, but it will be counterproductive either to force one to happen or to make it systematic. Keep an eye open for opportunities as you explore your characters and flesh out their wants and backstories and inner lives. But allow convergence to be a happy accident, a discovery you make while you are busily rounding out your two most important characters. If you don't find one at this stage, don't worry. It will find its way into the material. Be open to the moment when it arrives and be able to recognize it.

It's important to explore the negative side of your protagonist and the positive side of your antagonist. This holds true both for their perceptions of themselves—their attitudes that help reveal their inner lives—and for their actions. A villain who does only villainous things and has only evil motivations is a far more predictable character than one who harbors some level of ambivalence or has some smidgen of a positive trait. And a hero with no downside is not only predictable but, ultimately, boring. We always know long in advance what this character will do. So while you are exploring a full life for your characters, it's important to encourage some sign of the opposite of their role in the story—a flawed hero and a villain with at least some worthwhile traits or actions. Again, if this leads you to a convergence, it's a nice epiphany, but not one that can be forced into the material. Explore with eyes open to what will help create the best representation of life in your characters; the bits and pieces could come from a variety of directions.

BUILDING STORIES

Secondary Characters

Clearly your protagonist and antagonist should be the characters
who get your greatest attention and your best efforts at creating a
sense of life in them. But the second level of characters also can,
and should, have life. The love interest, the best friend, the supporter of the antagonistic side—these characters and their actions will be considerably more meaningful in your story if they
take on the complexities of life. There is a limit, as discussed earlier, not just to the number of characters who can have screen
time devoted to their lives but also to the depth you should strive
for with secondary characters. If you create such a well-rounded
and fully complex best friend that he starts to steal our attention
from your protagonist, you may be fighting against your own best
interests. You might need to create a huge junk drawer for your
protagonist to contain his odds and ends that don't readily fit
with your story. But just one or two things about a secondary
character might be the difference between his "coming alive" and
remaining dead on arrival, just a cardboard carrier of plot events.

Let your imagination take you where it will and take lots of
notes along the way. But given that work time is our second most
valuable commodity—after screen time—know when to stop and
put the time and energy into another character. With secondary
characters, you will probably be looking not only for the junk in
their junk drawer but also their modes of convergence with either
the protagonist or the antagonist. Again, don't obsess and force
convergences to happen, and don't panic if they don't seem to be
there. There will be plenty of time to find the way in which the best
friend is influenced by the antagonist or influences the protagonist. You still may stumble upon how the love interest actually
mouths the same opinions—from a very different angle—as the
antagonist.

What is most important—and the only way in which these
convergences can happen—is that the characters are marching
to their own drummers. They might support the protagonist
through 90 percent of his quest, but that support should stem
from the character's own need. That other 10 percent of action
taken solely on his own, following his own drumbeat, will usually

be the greatest demonstration of his inner life. Compare Harding and Billy Bibbit from *One Flew over the Cuckoo's Nest*. Harding is initially in opposition to McMurphy, but comes to be a supporter once the protagonist brings life and liveliness to the psychiatric ward. Billy quickly comes to idolize McMurphy. Harding immediately asserts his independence of thought and purpose and shows us tempting strands coming from his own junk drawer. Billy dives into a supportive and subservient role, though we are still continually given tantalizing tidbits of his inner life, his demons, and his junk drawer. But in the end, when Billy meets his tragic end, it is his own action, from his own inner life; it has nothing to do with his long-term support of McMurphy—though obviously it greatly affects McMurphy. And even when Harding falls in behind McMurphy after his initial resistance, it doesn't mean he ceases having an inner life of his own. He's still marching to his own drummer when McMurphy confronts him about being voluntarily on the ward, unable to take the step to free himself. Harding is acting for himself, not McMurphy or the story or the storyteller. The story and storyteller can use his actions and his drummer to their own ends—don't forget who is really in control here—but the source of Harding's actions and his sense of inner life is that private drummer.

Underlying Motives

So much of what we are dealing with in this section has to do with what characters want and what they do to achieve those wants. But are there wants that work better than others? Are there wants that don't work at all? How can I tell if the wants I'm ascribing to my characters are strong enough and compelling enough and deeply rooted enough? Is there such a thing as too many wants?

Given that "nobody doesn't want something," you have to figure out what all of your characters want, even if it's as simple as being left alone or seemingly as easy as sleeping. Wants that stem from simply being unreasonable tend to be much weaker than wants that grow out of something deeper inside the character. There are plenty of unreasonable people in the world and they also want things, so why can't you use them in your stories? You can use them, but you have to do so carefully. The problem with unreasonableness as the basis of a character's motivation, as his want, is that he can change to being reasonable at any time. The underlying want feels arbitrary. I don't like blue-eyed people today, so what I want to do is destroy anyone with blue eyes. This sort of unreasonableness feels as if it's based in nothing but convenience for the storyteller. The arbitrariness of it means that at any time the want can be shifted; now I don't like brown-eyed people and I love blue-eyed people. How can you build any tension or suspense when the basis is shifting sands that can change on the whim of the character—meaning the needs of the storyteller?

There are instances where this very flightiness is the core of the tension. The Red Queen in *Alice in Wonderland* is a perfect example. She changes what she wants and cares about from minute to minute. The exaggeration of this arbitrariness is what defines the character and is the source of her being a dangerous and tension-inspiring character. Most of the time, characters fall short of this degree of exaggeration, so you have to be careful that the motives and wants you assign to them won't blow away in a light breeze.

Yet you can take an unreasonable want and give it a solid underlying reason; even if we don't buy the character's conclusion, we can still buy into *his* believing it. If the character has only seen one blue-eyed person in his whole life and that blue-eyed person killed his brother, then we can see that the dislike of blue-eyed people isn't arbitrary. It isn't built on a solid, logical basis, but it isn't about to change in the next scene to hating brown-eyed people. What's at work here is the difference in motivational depth. In the arbitrary mode, the want of destroying blue-eyed people comes from nowhere and can therefore be changed at any time. The deeper mode has the same unreasonable prejudice or want, but it is rooted in something less likely to shift in the character. We can trust that the want is attached to the character and will only be changed through a strong—and dramatizable—process.

What's ironic is that a character's irrational fear or obsession, while unreasonable on the surface, is a perfectly effective motivational basis. A character with a pathological fear of heights or

spiders or enclosed spaces may not be reacting to the same realities the audience lives in. We may see the fear as unreasonable.
But at the same time, such a strongly held and primal fear feels
deeply attached to the character; it doesn't seem likely to change
on a moment's notice. So it's the capricious nature of an unreasonable want that you need to avoid, not the unreasonable conclusion of the character who holds that want.

The same is true for prejudices. We don't have to agree with a
prejudice in order to accept it as the basis of a character's motivation or the source of his want. But if the prejudice isn't deeply
held or primal—or at least difficult to uproot—then it will smack
of the same capriciousness we won't accept in unreasonableness.
In other words, you can use just about anything from the loftiest
to the basest of human desires, wants, and needs to shape a character's motivations, but whatever you use has to be firmly attached to the character, not just draped over him.

This lesson is clearest with humiliations and triumphs. These
can be incredibly effective sources of underlying wants and motives for characters of all capacities. A character who has suffered
a profound humiliation will be seriously touched by that experience. In most cases, it will be an extremely painful experience,
something the character will try almost anything to avoid repeating. So we can build a solid character motivation on a past humiliation and the fear of a future humiliation. It will be deeply
rooted in the life and psyche of the character and, if big enough,
seem primal and difficult to change or overcome. At the other end
of the spectrum, a past triumph can be just as affecting to a character and can become the source of a compulsion to repeat the
event. Just as a major humiliation saps a person's or character's
sense of self-worth, a triumph can fill it to overflowing. That experience of having brimmed over with self-worth could become
addictive to a character and serve as the basic motivation behind
actions in the story. In both instances, the linkage between either
the humiliation or the triumph and the character has been made
strong enough for it to continue to be a factor in his future motives. Petty humiliations and petty triumphs won't work; but the
pettiness is in the character, not in the audience's realization of it.
A character who blows a past humiliation or triumph way out of

proportion is just as motivated by his belief in it as one who has experienced a large humiliation or triumph. As long as he believes it and it affects him as if it were true, it *is* true as a motive.

Now that you have assembled your basic cast and have fairly clear ideas of what they are in pursuit of—or want to escape from—this is a good time to assess those wants for their underlying strength and usefulness. Is the primary want or goal unreasonable or capricious? Or is it deeply held—no matter how irrational or unreasonable it would be for other people, is it firmly attached to this character? A bit of effort, an hour of character exploration to find a deeply rooted bond between a character and the motivation, can be money in the bank right now. If you start building the story on the shoulders of characters whose primary wants can be changed as easily as their hair color, you will find your story teetering and on the verge of collapse. Chances are you'll have to go back to this point later, when it will be much more difficult to rewrite.

Is there a single overriding want, or is your view of a character muddled with a long list of "wishes"? This can be a problem that leaves a character out of focus. Let's say we have a character stranded on a desert island. He might dream of glasses of beer, big juicy hamburgers, and the waitress at the café he used to frequent. But as much as he would like those things—and might run out for them the minute he gets back to shore—these aren't serviceable wants for the story. Even if all the wants on a laundry list of things "it would be nice to have" could be achieved, this is a less effective means of clarifying a character and putting him in motion. There needs to be some prioritizing among the wants, because they will come into conflict with each other at some point. He can't drink the beer and bite into the hamburger at the same moment. And what happens if his favorite waitress stops by and flirts? If there is one clear want or goal, one simple and strong and firmly attached underlying motivation for the character, then there is no problem having the other, lesser wants. Our man on the desert island wants off the island. Or if the story is about his return and he has the chance to pursue beer, hamburgers, and the waitress, then which dominates? Which pursuit will make him drop the other two in an instant? He "would like" the other two, maybe one more than the other, but he truly and deeply wants only one above the others. Once you have this set of priorities for your characters, it's time to turn your thoughts to how to build them into a story.

TIME AND STORYTELLING

After establishing the characters, their wants and conflicts, and your own intentions for how you want to impact the audience, the next bedrock decisions to be made have to do with time. How much time will the story take? How much screen time? How much time in the lives of the characters? How will you deal with the time to be cut out or ellipsed? Will you follow chronological order, or will time be shifted around in any way? Will real time actually be lengthened or stopped? Many of these decisions have to do with how you, as a screenwriter, will "spend" your most precious commodity, your screen time, to get the most story and impact.

Screen Time and Drama

Like music and dance, storytelling is a time-based art form. In all three forms, what happens when is of paramount importance. What things happen at exactly the same moment? What happens one after the other? Which one first? Which lasts longer or shorter? Answering these questions is part of solving the problems inherent in any of these art forms. You need the melody or the steps, the variations and the different instruments or dancers, of course, but until you add the dimension of time into how the music or dance plays out, there is no art yet, just the means of creating the art. This is just as true of storytelling, but there are other layers of added complexity that music and dance don't have. A musical composition or a dance has only one direction for time to flow—from beginning to end. There are a great many variations and games to play with how it flows forward—with simultaneous and syncopated and contrasted events using time as their contrasting element. But still, the music starts, it goes forward, and ends. There's no such thing as playing the last note first. The first and the last note, or the first and the last step, might be identical; there might be some way in which one is made to be a reminder or an echo of the other. But you can't put the end stanzas of music at the beginning; if you put them there, they *are* the beginning.

In a story, you can put the ending at the very beginning of the telling, yet the events you show are still the end of the story in the lives of the characters. This is because a story is attached to a life or lives, unlike music or dance—unless, of course, either of these also incorporates a story, which then becomes storytelling through music and/or dance. *Sunset Boulevard* can start with Joe Gillis dead in the swimming pool and the telling of the story will lead us to know who he is and how he came to that fate. You can change the order of events in time in order to achieve a particular impact or to reveal a past event or motive when it is most useful to your intentions. You can jump out of chronology just once or continually throughout a story. You can even tell a story in reverse chronology. Or you can start very near the end, go back in time, follow chronology, catch up with the starting moments, and then stay in chronological time after that. This is all made possible because in a story, the basic raw material from which we build is not notes or steps, but something infinitely more complex—events in the lives of "actual" characters. The road to creating audience emotion is through the lives of people. It is less direct than musical notes or dance steps, which also create audience emotion but in a much more ephemeral way, one not so tied to the specifics of "real lives."

And because your raw material is "real lives," you can also cut out parts of those lives and imply parts and artificially prolong parts. This in no way is meant to diminish the intensely complex and delightful art forms of music and dance, but in music the next note is the next note and in dance the next step is the next step. They necessarily follow in sequence, no matter what variations and syncopations are involved. In a story, the next moment in time might be minutes, days, or even years after the previous moment in time. Or the next moment in time might be before the last moment in time in the lives of the characters. You have to sculpt your stories not only from the moments in time you include, but from the ones you leave out and how you leave them out. And you have to build the order of those moments not necessarily on a simple start-to-finish progression, but rather based on the impact you want to achieve. Choosing what to leave in and what to leave out and in what order to deliver those things you leave in and how to jump over what you won't deliver—all this is the art form. Time and its management is at the core of the process of storytelling.

Time is the essence of drama. Without time and the many ways in which we can manipulate and play with it, you wouldn't be able to create much impact in a story. At best you could have a string of well-envisioned and well-motivated events in the lives of characters the audience knows and cares about. This is not without value, but there isn't any art involved until the storyteller takes that set of circumstances and uses it for a purpose—the intended impact on the audience. At the core of using characters, their lives, and their events, is managing time—picking what we learn and don't learn in time, what happens at the same time and what comes first, giving what kind of impact to the next event. You aren't limited to simple chronology in your quest for that impact on the audience. If you have to change the order from the "reality" in the characters' lives for the maximum impact, you can. Laying out the information—characters, wants, events, conflicts, everything—in an order and time of your choosing is the very heart of drama. It's entirely based on time—both as it's experienced by the characters and, even more important, how it's experienced by the audience.

For instance, you can start with a woman giving birth and only reveal later who the father is or how she felt about getting pregnant. Or you could have the moment she discovers she's pregnant and jump ahead to the delivery. Or you could jump

ahead to her imagined delivery and then back to her in reality,
faced with telling the father he's the father. You don't have to put
one note after the other or one step after the other; if you have
a compelling reason to alter time for the audience, you have
many choices available. Every choice comes at a price. Any particular choice might be worth its cost or it might be "too expen-
sive" in screen time or confusion to justify being used.

You are continually in the situation of having to decide not
only what impact you hope to generate and how to get it, but
whether the expected impact is worth the price you will have to
pay to get it. This is a major element in the art form of storytelling, and you are now beginning to face the first of those decisions. As readers of *The Tools of Screenwriting* will recall, there
are three kinds of time in screenplays: real time (the time it actually takes for an event to occur), screen time (the time on screen
devoted to showing an event), and time frame (a limitation or
deadline known to the audience in advance so it can anticipate
and expend its emotions where they are most crucial). In addition
to these ways in which a storyteller must deal with time, there are
two other parameters: the order of time (do we follow chronology?) and the amount of screen time balanced against the
amount of story to be told. Before you can begin to deal with the
various ways time impacts the scenes—real time, screen time,
and time frame—you must make some basic decisions on how
you will use time in the organization of your story material. You
must balance amount of story with the amount of time to tell it.

Time and Complexity

Can you tell complex stories about complex characters in a complex manner? It sounds like the best of everything: you have deep
and well-rounded characters, you have lots of twists and turns
and pretend friends turning into die-hard enemies, and you have
an intricate and oh-so-clever way of weaving it all together that
wows the audience with your ingenuity and bravura command of
all things cinematic. If you had all the screen time in the world

and you peopled your story with *raisonneur* characters and had lots of recapitulations and you knew that the audience could only see your story on video so they could stop it and back it up and go over things they didn't catch the first time, then you probably could make it work. But in the real world of telling a story in a film, you don't have these conditions. You have to choose what's most important for yourself and find a way to make it work for the audience. If it doesn't work for an audience that is watching the film from beginning to end, without stopping and backing up, then it doesn't matter how clever all the characters, story events, and plotting elements are. The audience will get lost, confused, or bored, and all that effort will be for nothing.

In most instances, you can have two out of three areas of complexity. You can have complex characters in a complex story that is simply told. Or you can have complex characters in a simple story that is complexly told. Or you can have simple characters in a complex story that is complexly told. The reason for the limitation stems from time and the audience's attention. It takes considerable screen time to make characters who are complex. It takes screen time to keep the audience oriented and participating when the story itself is complex. It takes screen time to overcome the potential for confusion and disorientation when the telling of the story is complex. At some point, these things start to take away from each other, not only making life difficult for the storyteller but conceivably making full participation impossible for the audience.

It's also possible to have only one complex area out of three or none out of three, but these are choices best avoided unless there is some overriding consideration involved. If you have something else of more importance than the story and its telling involved in the film, then there might be a reason to tell a simple story about simple characters in a simple way, or a simple story about simple characters in a complex way. As long as storytelling is your principal interest, some level of complexity in the characters, story, and storytelling is desirable.

What do you get and what do you lose with our three primary choices? With complex characters and complex story but simple telling, you have a very strong circumstance for most stories and storytellers. You have sufficient time to create fully rounded characters with complex inner lives, and you have time for twists and turns and surprises and plenty of suspense along the way. What is missing is the ability to do many variations with time—from changes in chronology to flashbacks and dreams and flash forwards and many of the other tricks cinema allows. This sort of story is probably best told from beginning to end, which means some special advantages of film storytelling can't be used. If you need or want to use these cinematic devices as a major means of telling your story, the middle choice might be best. You can have complex characters and tell their story in a complex way, but the story itself should be fairly simple and straightforward. This choice allows room for visual, temporal, and cinematic razzma-tazz, and will be especially useful for stories that involve major set pieces—specials-effects extravaganzas, sports, war, dance, and musical films. The third choice, complex stories that are complexly told, should usually be about rather simple charac-ters. Here you have the loss of a major attribute of stories—involving the audience in the inner lives of fully rounded human beings—but it enables an intricately plotted and ingeniously in-ventive story to be told with all the advantages that cinematic storytelling has to offer.

None of these choices is "wrong," but each of them is wrong for some stories and for the intentions of some authors. The same sto-ryteller may opt for a different configuration for different stories, based on the needs of the stories themselves and his own goals. Simple doesn't mean simplistic or schematic or childish. It means that what something appears to be, it actually is; it means that screen time doesn't have to be devoted to showing something from a variety of angles for us to glean its true nature. *Schindler's List* is quite a simple story—a man tries to hide Jews from the Nazis. The Jews are really Jews, the Nazis are really Nazis. The dangers come from foreseeable directions, but that doesn't make them less dan-gerous or less suspenseful. The story elements are simple; we can understand the danger involved in protecting Jews from Nazis in the heart of German territory in World War II. Not much screen time has to be devoted to creating our understanding and fostering our participation in this aspect of the story. In other words, it's simple. The story is just as real and compelling as a complex one would be, but it's low maintenance instead of high maintenance—a modest amount of screen time needs to be devoted to setting up and maintaining the core of the story. If you don't think of simple as a value judgment, you'll have much less trouble finding the path that is best for your story and your intentions.

Citizen Kane is justly famous for the complexity of its main character, some of the supporting characters, and, perhaps most of all, for the mode in which the story is told. A nearly unseen investigator searches for clues to the meaning of a famous man's last word, and we hear from a variety of "witnesses," whose versions of that man's life we then see. There are great flourishes of cinematic style, and great latitude is taken with time. We have complex characters and complex storytelling. But the underlying story is quite simple: a boy is given a fortune, but at the expense of his family life; he spends his life, his energies, and his fortune trying to replace that love in a variety of different ways. We don't fully put it all together until the end, but the events in the lives of the various characters aren't filled with huge deceptions and major, unanticipated twists and turns. The story is relatively simple, but it is far from simplistic.

Star Wars is noted for the simplicity of its characters. There are no inner demons to summon up from these characters, no ambivalences to sort through. This simplicity allows for two things: a complex story that involves a sizable cast spread all across the universe and a particular mode of complex storytelling. While there aren't major jumps in chronology, there are other elements that require the screen time that has been made available by the simplicity of the characters. There are huge production numbers—battles, in this instance. Any story that incorporates several large production numbers necessarily comes under the category of complexly told. The "telling" of the battle takes considerable screen time to set up, elaborate on as the battle unfolds, and then finish off. Here the complexity is put into the event, but what is underlying the event is simple—the good guys versus the bad guys, with all of life at stake. The complexity is in the telling, not what role it plays in the story.

Action Time

It might seem strange that war stories, sports stories, musicals, dance stories, and special-effects stories all come under the heading "complexly told." While there may or may not be huge shifts in time or perspective or the use of flashbacks or dreams, these kinds of stories all use large-scale production numbers as part of the telling of the story. The time and focus have to come from somewhere for this kind of complexity in the storytelling. It takes screen time to line up the *Titanic* with the iceberg, or to let us know about the men inside those football uniforms and what it means when something happens in the game, or to understand the logistics of a battle in a meaningful way. This is complex because you have to devote considerable screen time and ingenuity to keeping the audience caring about the right things at the right time. If you know going in that you will have huge battles, big dance numbers, a sinking ship, or a championship game, you have already decided on one of your areas of complexity. Now you are left to choose between simple characters and a simple story line.

When the world of a story is completely different from our world—it is futuristic, fantastic, utopian, or dystopian, it's set in prehistory or a part of the world with which the audience is unfamiliar—this also becomes complexity in the telling of the story. A lot of screen time will have to be devoted to revealing the rules and dangers and social structure of this new and strange world. So again, you must opt for either a simple story with complex characters or simple characters in a complex story in this new world. However, just because a story is set in the future or past doesn't automatically make this an issue of complexity. The future or past could be sufficiently like our present that only a normal amount of screen time has to be devoted to revealing and dramatizing the world. If the world of the story is truly unique and unfamiliar to the audience, then that aspect alone will demand considerable screen time in the telling of the story.

In both cases—where the world is the source of the complexity in the storytelling or when major production numbers bring that complexity—you need to find ways in which this complexity can still move the story and the storytelling forward. It's a mistake to have the story stop while you have a ballet of bullets flying or a ballet of people flying or a ballet of technical wizardry of explosions, future worlds, or strange creatures. These things can all be great additions to a story, as long as they aren't stealing screen time for no other purpose than their own existence. We can delight in an invented creature—and marvel at the geniuses who made us believe in it—but if it stops the story cold while we're admiring their handiwork, then a major misstep has been made.

Whatever the source of complexity in the telling of a story, it must support the goals of the storyteller. We can't just set aside all concerns about the characters, their futures, and the events unfolding in the story while we admire wondrous special effects or an inventively created world. At best, this tactic will create short-lived awe in the audience. The first time we see a man believably fly or a dinosaur or a cartoon character interact with a live human being, that alone might be enough. We'll all marvel and wonder how they did that. But two minutes later in the film, we'll be bored if that effect is the only thing being offered. Those magical and fantastic feats had better connect with, support, and further the story and the lives of the characters or the audience will be bored.

The history of cinema itself is proof of this. When nickelodeons first showed movement with flipping photographs, just the novelty alone was enough to gather an audience. The same occurred when film replaced the flipping of the photos, but it didn't take long before stories had to be added to continue the popularity of moving pictures. When sound was added, for a short while it was enough for the audience simply to be able to hear the talking and singing being presented. Every advance of technical ability has created a short-lived flurry of interest for the magic it created. And every time, the need to return to stories as the core attraction, with the technical feats in support, has been rapid. Each of these technical advances—as well as imaginatively created fantastical worlds and wonderfully staged spectacle and set pieces—brings something to the table. But the bedrock foundation upon which to build and sustain an audience is: tell them a good story and the audience is yours to keep; neglect the story in favor of other fun "goodies" and the audience is yours to lose.

Spectacle provides an interesting variation on this dynamic. Audiences the world over and throughout history have enjoyed spectacle—fabulous, fantastic, over-the-top or overpowering spectacles that produce "aaaahs" and nudges to one's neighbors and mutters of "how'd they do that?" Spectacle has sometimes become intertwined with storytelling, since the ancient Greeks or before. Spectacle can be separated from storytelling—like the pomp and circumstance of the opening ceremony of the Olympics, the launching of a gigantic aircraft carrier, a three-ring circus, or a fireworks show. In these instances and many more, it's easy to see that spectacle can be its own reason for existence. This is pure entertainment; there is no other agenda than diverting the attention of an audience. Spectacle is a kind of celebration of life, even when it is death-based, like a bullfight or gladiators doing battle. We are thrilled, disgusted, or horrified, but we are kept riveted by the magnitude of the display or the danger inherent in it or even the death—real or faked—that it presents.

There have been many successful spectacular films, from biblical epics to gladiator epics to *Titanic* to films like *Jurassic Park* that use special effects to create spectacle. But in addition to sending a film's budget skyrocketing, spectacle can also be a big stealer of screen time. The same caveats apply to spectacle as to other forms of action that can distract and detract from the story: be careful how long you stay away, and be mindful of how the audience returns to the story. Because spectacle is engrossing all on its own, it can be tempting to overuse it, diminishing the screen time available to the story. Worse still, it can be so distracting, especially when it is really good spectacle, that it can make the audience forget the story and their concerns about the characters.

Amount of Story and Screen Time

With rare exceptions, like *High Noon* and *Run Lola Run*, films generally depict more time in the lives of the characters than they take to unfold; the real time shown is longer than the screen time used to show it. Some films, like *Toto the Hero*, even dramatize an entire life from birth to death or beyond. But the time in the life of the characters is not the only—or most accurate—measure of a story. If there is a single issue, as in *Toto the Hero*, that spans a great many years but essentially remains unchanged throughout, then the amount of story that those decades cover is not too great for a single, normal-length film to dramatize. It's the size of the issues at stake and the complexity of the characters' reactions and reasons for involvement that more accurately measure "how much" story there is to tell. If there are a number of important characters grappling with a variety of important and conflicting issues, and if they all have inner lives with complicated relationships to those issues and to the other characters, and if the events of the story take place either over a long period of time or on a broad canvas or in a complex world—then maybe the story itself is very large. It is possible for a story to be too big to dramatize effectively in a normal-length or even an epic-scale film. In such instances, some form of simplification, trimming, or modifying is probably necessary so that the resulting story is able to be true to the spirit of the original idea, even if it doesn't contain all the events, issues, characters, and complexities of the original.

What's wrong with a story that is "too big" for the amount of screen time available to tell it? As we've discussed at length, real drama depends on moments, on the audience connecting with the characters while being fully informed about them—their wants, needs, weaknesses, and so on. If you have too much ground to cover in the telling of the story—too many events, too many characters, too many complicated inner lives, too many simultaneous issues—then the only way to cover all that material is through dialogue. Characters can tell what they want and need and what their weaknesses are. They can tell what they did before and what is important to them. They can tell about events you don't have time to dramatize on screen. You can easily and cheaply have an army of a hundred thousand soldiers in period costumes storming an enormous fantasy castle defended by wizards, dragons, and a legion of amazons—as long as you just tell it in dialogue. But that is not dramatic. It isn't compelling; it isn't involving; it doesn't make the audience participate and care and worry and hope and fear. Dialogue used this way is simply an expedient way to deliver a lot of information. But the information isn't trustworthy or dramatic. And if the events sound exciting in the telling, the audience will wish they could have seen them and participated in them, rather than just be told about them second-hand.

The other alternative to trying to cover a lot of ground can be even worse. You could try to race through everything—even showing the storming of the fantasy castle for half a minute—but this will just diminish every single moment in the story to a shallow and dramaless depiction. You need time to set up an event and the characters involved in it; you need time for the event to unfold; and we need time to digest what has happened and what impact it has on the characters and the future of the story we care about. If you are racing through events, then the first parts to go will be the preparation and aftermath. You'll have characters we don't fully understand racing around to take care of the events in the story and then hurrying off to the next events, without them or us having a moment to ponder what difference it makes. You might hit all the bases, but no one in the audience will care one way or the other. Every moment that is the difference between the audience being involved and not involved will necessarily have been cut so there will be time to run from event to event.

So you have to find some parity between how much story you have to tell and how much time you have to tell it. If you have too little story, then it will seem that you are forever stretching things beyond what is really necessary for the audience to know and care about—meaning we will be bored. If you have too much story, then you will be missing the time needed to create the audience's involvement and trustworthy knowledge of the characters, the world, the issues, and the events. Either way, the imbalance can be fatal to the drama.

Let's explore the potential sources of imbalance. You could have too many characters, too many issues, too many events; you could be spread over too big a part of the world; one issue could be too big for the time allowed. On the other side, any of these could also be too small to warrant the amount of screen time you anticipate devoting to them. There might be a "cast of thousands," but

that means extras. As we've discussed, the primary cast is probably around six characters. Seven might be all right, eight is probably pushing your luck, nine is definitely getting you into hot water,
twenty is beyond hope. But two can be enough as long as there are
other important elements involved to help flesh out the story.

There could be too many issues: you could want to include
everything that you've ever cared about in one story. A story can't
be about equality between the sexes and abortion and racism and
religion and the degradation of modern society and the problems
of love in a time of war and coming of age too soon. Something
has to go. In this example, a lot has to go. There can be one primary issue, and secondarily we can see how it and the characters
reflect onto one or two, perhaps even three, other related side issues. But just as too many characters start stealing screen time
from each other and diminishing the impact of any one of them,
too many issues will cause the exact same problem. You won't get
any power whatsoever if there are a dozen issues dealt with in
one story. It will be perfectly clear to any audience that the storyteller wasn't able to focus his thoughts.

It's also possible for a single issue to be too big if the amount
of screen time is limited. Making a ten-minute version of *Macbeth*
or *Medea* is going to end in ruin. Making a half-hour story exploring the full range of changing dynamics between the races during
school integration in the American South in the 1950s could only
be a valiant but flawed effort. Even a feature can't possibly cover
everything about a single massive issue. The problems in Northern Ireland or the Middle East, the full spectrum of approaches to
religion or abortion or sexual orientation—none of these could
be completely and without bias dramatized in a single feature-
length film. Aspects of any of these issues can clearly be dealt
with; a particular angle on one of these issues can be handled.
But the worthy goal of giving the full background to "the troubles" in Northern Ireland and full dramatic play to characters
from all approaches to the conflict will surely end in failure. One
viewpoint from the long list of potential viewpoints will garner
much more power and drama than an attempt at comprehensive
coverage, which inevitably must be spread too thin.

Though equal treatment of all human beings is a worthy—
and elusive—goal, to treat characters equally is the shortcut to
destroying drama. All characters are not created equal and
shouldn't be treated as such. If all the characters have the same
amount of inner life depicted and all of them have character arcs
and all of them have delineated backstories and all of them receive time for preparation and aftermath from all of the big moments of their lives, then the drama will fall apart. Again, it's a
matter of available time and audience focus. We can't equally
care about the main character, his brother, his best friend, his
boss, his mother, his girlfriend, and the guy he just hit with his
car. Even if that is the entire primary cast, some of them have to
be given less time, less focus, and less complexity to their inner
lives. If everyone is equal, nothing will be made more important
to the audience. If we feel equally about the main character and
the best friend—and know their inner lives in exactly the same
depth—then how are we to choose our priorities when they come
into conflict over the girlfriend? This doesn't mean you have to
have no inner life, no backstory, and no character arc for these
other primary characters. It just means that their coverage in all
of these areas should probably be proportional to their overall
importance in the story. The protagonist gets the most focus, the
next most important character—the antagonist or the love interest, perhaps—gets the next most attention, and screen time, and
so on down the list.

Another way a story can become too big is by having too
many events. The same principles apply: you need time to dramatize events effectively, and if you have too many for the allowed
time, then something will have to be cut. Preparation or aftermath or the event itself is raced through without sufficient focus
and impact. A world that is too big can lead to similar problems.
Every new aspect of the world in the story needs its own introduction and exposition. Without it, the new location or aspect of
the world simply becomes a location without meaning or impact
to the audience or the story; it becomes relegated to a position of
simply housing the action instead of being a part of it, influencing
the characters and events and audience. If there are too many

locations competing for precious screen time, then, once again, something will have to be dropped or skipped.

So how do you find out if your story is too big or too small for the time available? And what can you do about it? Let's start with too small because it's often less of a problem, though in the end it can be just as detrimental as too big. If your story is about two people in a single room with only a modestly pressing issue between them, there might not be enough material from which to build a feature-length story. If everything feels perfect to you except the disparity between the amount of story and the amount of screen time, perhaps you need to tell a shorter story. Short films can be marvelous venues for little epiphanies in everyday life, for smaller-scale stories in terms of the emotions and pathos they engender both in the characters and in the audience.

But if your goal is a feature-length story, then chances are that all the groundwork necessary hasn't been done yet. More can be found inside the characters or their conflicts or their issues. Perhaps only one aspect of the components making up the story is "big," is just slightly beyond the range of normal, everyday life. Wonderful stories can be told about ordinary people with just one aspect of their life or world being extraordinary. It might be their passion or obsession that is slightly oversized; it might be the dilemma that is thrust at them; or it might be some aspect of the world in which they live. Go through your story material systematically and determine what aspect has this outsized quality. If none of them has it, there's your problem. If there is one and you still feel your story is "too small," then focus your attention on adding some power to that aspect. You don't have to import a family of tigers or killer bugs; just find the somewhat extraordinary aspect of your story and make it a bit more extraordinary. Push toward discomfort—it's not what you want to do in life, but it's the way you have to push your characters and their world in storytelling. Once it's got you squeamish, it probably is enough to make the audience squeamish too. You may have solved your problem.

If all the groundwork has been done thoroughly and you still are worried that your story is too small for a feature, start to explore what aspect of what you have is the biggest element. Not biggest in the sense of what takes the most screen time, but biggest in proportion to the everyday lives of the audience. If you are introducing us to a part of the real world we've never seen before or an imaginary world or a character with a passion or a character with absolutely no passion whatsoever or an average person suddenly thrust into the spotlight or up against a tiger or killer bugs—then this probably will be the source of "bigness." It will almost certainly be part of the collision that helps create your story—a clash of cultures or fish out of water or Joe Average against the big conglomerate. If everything else is smallish, then this one anomalous area is where to concentrate your efforts. One of the best sources of all for the bigness could be the inner life of the character. Walter Mitty is the perfect example of this kind of character. Ordinary in every way in his real life and faced with no real dilemmas or nasty conglomerates or killer bugs, Walter creates his own world of fantasy with himself at the center. The source of the bigness is inside the character, the richness of his invented life.

Having too little story can also stem from creating obstacles for your characters that are too easily overcome, or from creating too few obstacles at all. Beginning screenwriters often make every step easy for their characters and then realize their second act is only a few pages long. Imagine the story is about a bank robber and the whole third act will be the robbery itself; what goes in the second act? To a beginner, it might be easy to get the getaway car, find a guy who can blow off the safe's door, get the blueprints of the bank, and dig the tunnel. At every turn, this novice has undermined his own story by making the obstacles too small and too easily overcome. By placing bigger and harder and nearly impossible obstacles in the way of the character's quest, the experienced screenwriter creates a story that will test the mettle of the character and give the audience the experience it seeks. The story will fill its time out dramatically and effectively. What if the explosives guy hates our central character and refuses to work with him? What if the blueprints of the bank were destroyed in a fire ten years ago and no copy exists? What if the tunnel runs directly into a foundation that supports a high-rise building over the bank—cut through it and the building falls down on you before you get the money out? By making the actual doing of the quest into significantly difficult tasks, the drama is heightened, the characters are tested and explored—both their inner and outer lives—and the story achieves the needed bigness to fill its screen time dramatically.

Most of the time, misgivings about a story being too small are overcome simply by doing more work on the characters, on their passions, wants, and conflicts, and on the obstacles they face. But too much story often is the result of doing a great deal of work on the story, the characters, conflicts, world, and obstacles. You fall in love with all of your inventions and discoveries and can't bring yourself to "kill your darlings." Every invention stays and the story material grows. Learning to prioritize and focus will prevent cramming too much story into too small an amount of screen time.

Just as it's true that not all characters are created equal, not all plot elements or story twists and turns are created equal. Some are better than others, some are more crucial than others, and some are simply more fun or scary or intense or entertaining than others. It is far better to cut out the weaker elements and allow the good ones all the screen time they need than it is to force them all into a smaller amount of time. The latter course may save all of your darlings, but it will kill the overall story by undermining even your best parts, the crucial and resonating parts that could make the story come alive. So you must learn to prioritize and pick only the best of your material. It's far better to have more than you need and be able to pick and choose, looking for the very best, than it is to have barely enough.

At this point, before you have outlined your story, it is not a good idea to throw out much of your invention and inventiveness. You don't yet know what will be the most important parts, what will turn out to be the most fun, scary, intense, or entertaining. But you can begin to tell when you are going too far afield in your mind doodling. If we go back to our story about Lindbergh, we're unlikely to have half an hour of screen time to devote to the Wright brothers and the history of aviation. We might want intimations of how recently the airplane had been invented when

Lindbergh took off across the Atlantic. We might need to know just a bit of what it is that keeps an airplane in the sky. But we aren't going to need to explore the Wright brothers' bicycle shop, the wind currents at Kitty Hawk, or the rivalry over which brother got to ride in their plane for that historic first flight. If you find yourself inventing story material that takes you far away from the core of your story, now is a good time to return to home base.

Just as you need to spend your screen time wisely, you need to spend your writing and inventing time wisely. Focus your efforts where they are most likely to be useful. You can't and shouldn't know the exact boundaries of what you must explore of your characters, your story's world, and your own interests and intentions. But you should be able to tell when you are far off the map. That other territory, however interesting it might be, should be left for another story at another time. A beginning writer often gets in trouble in the area of research. Some writers hate research and never get their facts straight, but other writers can get lost in research, following a track through the Internet, the encyclopedia, or an entire library, delving not only into why wine is grown in particular places but how wine is made, what plants are related to grapes, how wine is made in various cultures, the history and mythology of wine and drinking, and on and on. This is a great way to avoid writing. Almost worse than the waste of time and focus on the story to be told, the resulting accumulation of facts and anecdotes can destroy the story once the researcher finally gets back to being the writer. Some wonderful material can be unearthed with this kind of excessive research, but if those tidbits are so tantalizing that they encourage the writer to skew the story toward them—rather than where the characters and their wants and needs demand—then the research is actually destroying the story for which it was undertaken.

Try to keep your eyes on the prize even while you wander around in your own imagination and the research you must absolutely do. Don't completely stop yourself from exploring, but come up for air once in a while and try to recognize when you are far off track from the core material of your story—the lives of the characters, the world of the story, the nature of the conflicts and quest and wants and arcs, and all the other things we have discussed. Don't make more problems for yourself by creating far too much story material with which you are in love and that you can't bear to cut. It will only prolong the process and undermine the final product.

Real Time versus Screen Time versus Time Frame

This preoutlining stage is also a good time to make certain you have a clear grasp on the three kinds of time dealt with in *The Tools of Screenwriting.* I won't repeat what was covered there, but rather I will expand on how these three issues affect you as you approach the outline of your story, which you will soon begin discussing. Let's start with screen time, because it's the easiest. Most feature films are between 90 and 120 minutes. It's extremely difficult to find a market for a 60-minute film, and a film story that significantly exceeds two hours had better have some epic qualities to justify its epic length—and not just the epic ego of the storyteller. A story doesn't have to be set in biblical times or involve gladiators, togas, and sandals or endless expanses of snow in order to be an epic. But it will need some form of "bigness" that dwarfs even the bigness required of a regular-length feature film. The size of the issue, the depth of the passions, the canvas on which the story takes place, the uniqueness or richness of the world it is set in—all of these can be reasons for epic-scale productions. You don't want to write an epic-length romantic comedy or an epic-length family drama. Doing so means taking more screen time than the story needs and almost guaranteeing that it will not be produced or it will be significantly rewritten—probably by others.

In all likelihood you are aiming for a story that will unfold in 90 to 120 minutes. A favorite length among producers and exhibitors seems to be about 100 minutes. That's about 100 pages of screenplay. It may seem daunting right now to write 100 pages, but you're more likely to find it difficult to hold your screenplay to 100 pages. Don't get into the dangerous game of counting pages and requiring of yourself that you manage to accomplish this part or that part of your story by such and such a page. Few things will strangle the life out of your work more efficiently than running a time clock on yourself, especially in the first draft. But just as you can tell when your research or your mind-doodling has taken you far out of the realm of your story, you should be able to hazard some kind of guess about how much screen time various important segments of your story will require.

Let's say your story is about a Vietnam vet returning home wounded, to a wife who has been protesting the war. The heart of the story is their relationship, but it's crucial that we know what he was doing in Vietnam and what she was doing at home protesting. If you are going to tell a personal story about their relationship, you can't give the detail of battle scenes found in *Platoon* and the detail of the home-front protesting of *Coming Home* and still have time for the relationship that is supposed to be the core of the story. You have to start envisioning some small part of Vietnam to give us his experience and some small part of the war protests to give us her experience. Neither can be fully and endlessly dramatized or you will find yourself with screen time problems from the outset.

The time frame of a story—how long it takes in the lives of the characters and, most importantly, a deadline of some kind looming on the distant horizon—also needs to be estimated. Are you talking about one day or months or years in a character's life from the beginning of the story until the end? You might not be able to say it's exactly two days, for instance, but that frame can be known at this point. The time frame can be part of the very design of the story—*48 Hours* and *The Lost Weekend* come to mind. A great many films have a built-in time frame—*Three Days of the Condor, Seven Days in May, High Noon,* and so on. But don't fret if you don't have one built in. You may never have a time frame in the sense of a ticking clock, but you must always have some idea of the approximate amount of time in the lives of the characters you will have to cover in your 100 pages.

If the story is about Madame Curie, the time frame might be years as she experiments with radium. If it's about Lindbergh, it might be months, including the preparation for the flight, the flight itself, and the aftermath. But maybe your story is not so much about Lindbergh's flight as it is about what compels some-one to take on a daredevil stunt. This story might start with him as a farm boy seeing his first airplane and end years later with him climbing into the *Spirit of St. Louis* to begin the flight. Or your story could be about someone who is caught up in an ex-traordinary event, trapped in a building by a fire or earthquake. The entire span of the film could be less than a day.

One question about time frame to consider is if there will be more than one actor needed for the role. Lindbergh at ten and Lindbergh at twenty-seven can't be played by the same actor. But Madame Curie at twenty-seven and Madame Curie at thirty-seven can be played by the same actress. This is an important question not because you are trying to cast the film, but because there is an essential change in the nature of a character between ten and twenty-seven, but less so between twenty-seven and thirty-seven. When this change in character is coupled with a change in actor for the part, your screenplay will need to reintroduce the charac-ter at each age. *Toto the Hero* provides a worthy example. This film goes from the birth until after the death of the protagonist and includes his alter ego for good measure. There are the baby, the young boy, the young man, and the old man plus the alter ego. In total, four actors play the five roles; the young man and alter ego are played by the same actor. When this story shifts from the perspective of the ten-year-old boy to the thirty-year-old man, the character needs to be reintroduced. This new introduction doesn't have to start from scratch, but it's important to make clear to the audience what has and has not changed in the life of the character during those ellipsed years. The same holds true for the jump from the young man to the old man; it must be made clear that the old man retains essentially the same attributes as the young man as far as the story is concerned. It can't be assumed that the same human being is the same character when large blocks of time are ellipsed; this has to be proven to the audience. So you should know going into the outline stage if you are envi-sioning a story with your character at ten, thirty, and eighty or whether it will be just a week or month in the person's life.

The rule of thumb should be to include the minimum amount

of the character's life possible to tell the story effectively. Excess time is the enemy of drama because it allows the possibility of alternative solutions to arise. This diminishes the urgency of any decisions the characters are forced to face, which undermines the drama. Often there is no avoiding a long period of time in the characters' lives as the time frame of the story, but wherever possible, try to trim it to the absolute minimum.

Real time—the actual time it takes to do real things—is much less of a consideration at this stage in the development of a story than it is when it comes time to start writing the pages. Real time functions in the scenes, not in the overall scheme of devising a story and how to tell it. But it can't hurt to do an inventory of your envisioned story events to see if there are any that might be particularly demanding of real time. If your character has to run a four-minute mile in the third act and you have to dramatize every lap around the track, it's likely to take close to four minutes of screen time. Look at the third act of *Rocky*, in which an entire fifteen-round prizefight is depicted. It isn't precisely real time from beginning to end—though it often feels like it—but enough of the punches and bursts of blood, sweat, and tears are in real time that this hour in the lives of the characters is given nearly half an hour of screen time. If you know going in that you have a chariot race or the Gettysburg Address or the protracted sinking of a battleship to deliver in your story, then you can be prepared to allot this important event the real time and screen time it will require.

The Simplest Use of Time

It must be clear by now that one of the more complex—and perplexing—things one can attempt to create is a well-made screenplay. There are so many parameters, so many things that can't be known soon enough while the process is going on, so many guesses you have to make and then come back and adjust when the guesses are proven wrong. No wonder half of the advice given here and elsewhere about screenwriting is to strive for the simple solutions. Even when consciously pursuing simple solutions, there will still be so many complicated things to deal with that it will feel mind-boggling at times. If you opt to start out complex before you have even entered the arena, how can you expect to keep everything straight once you're in there doing battle and discovering all the competing, conflicting, and monumentally difficult demands of the process and the final product? Why on earth would anyone choose to make time a source of complexity? Why alter the chronology of time? After all, it's one of the few mathematically certain things we have to deal with in this entire process.

If you have a choice in the matter, stick with straightforward chronology. One of the more self-defeating decisions you could make at this stage would be to alter time for no good reason. There *are* good reasons, and each of them warrants the added work and complexity that they generate. But if your only reason to jump out of chronology or to turn it on its head is to make your story new and unique, don't do it. It won't be either new or unique, even if you manage to finish it. Chronology has already been tipped upside down, threaded through itself, been jumped through forward and backward, twisted and repeated and varied and stopped. In most cases, these variations have been done by someone working on his second or tenth or twentieth screenplay, not his first. If you can tell your story from beginning to end following the real chronology of the lives of the characters, then do it. Save your complexity for other things like the inner lives of your characters and the brilliance of your scene writing.

Why Alter Simple Chronology?

There are a number of reasons why you have to alter the flow of time in a story. The ability to control time as it's experienced by the audience is one of the strengths of cinema. But that ability is like a tank—powerful, good for its intended use, but cumbersome and difficult to maneuver at best. You don't use a tank to dig a posthole when a shovel would do. Where do you need to use this tank? At its simplest, you should only vary from normal chronology when the intended impact of the story requires it. You might have to jump back in time to discover a formative event in a person's life, the crux of that person's creation as the character in the story. You might have to jump forward in time to tie together as cause and effect two events in the character's life that could not be closer together. You might tell your story backward because knowing the end—or nearly the end—is crucial to experiencing the full importance of the events that lead up to it. You might have to play out half the story in the past and half in the present because the events that shaped the conflict of today took place long ago and yet the resolution of those events can only happen in the present. And sometimes you have an apparent lapse in the chronology of time but it is simply a mode of storytelling—the remembrance.

Flashbacks are the most common form of altering the simple chronology of the characters' lives. You take time out from the present to visit a past incident that delivers crucial information to the audience about the characters or the story. Flashbacks have the strength of happening in the here and now that gives them much greater dramatic power than a character could generate by relating the same material in dialogue. But they have the great disadvantage that they stop the forward flow of the story in the present while we go back in time. A flashback is not warranted if there is another effective dramatic means of delivering the same material to the audience available in the present tense of the story. Could a present-day remnant of the old event still exist and carry the load? Could a reenactment or a surrogate exploration of the past event do the same job and not force you to go backward in time when drama demands that you go forward in time? Could a ritual or some other means of bringing the past into the present bring out the information you need? If the answer is yes to any of these approaches, it's usually better to solve the problem without resorting to flashbacks.

But flashbacks do have their place. They are most often necessary when a significant amount of story material exists in the past, too much material to deliver dramatically through present-tense means. Flashbacks also create a wonderful form of intimacy with the characters; we are actually seeing what the person thinks. This is a departure from the usual circumstance of our seeing what a character does and says and maybe keeps secret from others. But with flashbacks—and with fantasies, dreams, and whole reminiscences—we delve into the mind of the character. This is why flashbacks need to "belong" to a character—most often the protagonist—because it is his or her memory we are dramatizing. Rick remembers Paris with Ilsa in *Casablanca*. Alvy Singer remembers, and goes back to, school and life with his family in *Annie Hall*.

A variation on the flashback is the dramatized story being told by a character. *Rashomon* and *Courage under Fire* are based on the conflicting testimony of characters to a past incident. In both cases and in others, what we see are not the memories of the protagonist. Rather we see either what the witness character remembers or, more precisely, what the protagonist envisions of the story being told to him. This is the case for two reasons. First, someone is lying—what we see depicted isn't an accurate memory, but a story. *The Usual Suspects* is entirely based on this variation on flashbacks. The other reason is that generally—though there are exceptions—it's best to avoid giving significant flashbacks to secondary characters. This is because flashbacks can cause a crisis of identification or loyalty in the audience to be inside the mind of a secondary character when our fidelity has been pledged to the protagonist. They divide our loyalty too easily. While you might need to delve into the mind of a secondary character momentarily in a story, it's a dangerous undertaking to do it without a great deal of care and preparation so the audience doesn't get confused.

When nearly the entire story takes place in the past, then there is another variation on flashbacks: the reminiscence. Usually something is left still to be decided in the present—the framing story—but most of the story is remembered or told by the protagonist. *Amadeus*, *Double Indemnity*, and *The Conformist* are all told this way. Reminiscence is an especially effective means of telling a story when there is a long time in the life of the character to deal with, because the character/narrator can bridge the gaps, change the chronology to fit the needs of the telling of the story, and so on. The reminiscence provides latitude in how time is dealt with, because the subjectivity of the character's memory allows the story to be told in a manner similar to how people think or remember, which isn't necessarily chronological.

Jumping forward in time can create an interesting, and potentially dicey, situation. *The Sixth Sense* provides a good example of its use for an express dramatic purpose. In the opening we see Malcolm shot. We jump forward to "The Next Fall" and find him waiting to meet his patient; he has apparently healed. Clearly the story would not work if that sudden leap weren't there. If we had seen any representation of those intervening months, then we would have seen him die at the scene or the hospital. But that would be giving up the big twist at the end, so it was necessary to leap forward in a way that isn't exactly like an ellipsis. How this leap differs from an ellipsis—and what makes this a tricky thing to pull off—is that it doesn't come after a newly established status quo. With a normal ellipsis, a character establishes a new status quo—for instance, a young woman gets accepted into medical school—then we cut out the time during which that status quo doesn't change—we jump forward to her graduation from medical school. The implication is that nothing basically has changed in her situation as it pertains to the story during those years we skipped. In *The Sixth Sense*, Malcolm has just been shot in the stomach and we jump forward in time. The neat trick here is in getting us to accept this leap forward when the new status quo of his injury has not been established. The implication, and this is how the story builds up its big surprise ending, is that nothing did change in those intervening months. He must have recovered, we surmise. Once we are past that leap, we have been set up for the surprise ending. But if we don't make that leap—and there are reasons we would resist—then we would not buy into the entire story.

There is another way in which a story can jump forward at the end, after the main story is completed. This is known as a coda, and it's a simple device meant to give us a brief glimpse into the future, after the story has ended. It could be a wedding or the birth of a child or the main character's old age or her eventual completion of a project begun in the story. It is detached from the main body of the story and generally is quite short. A similarly detached—and therefore potentially "out-of-time" segment—is the pretitle sequence. This can be a good place to put a singular event that is disconnected from the main story in time but is crucial to our understanding of the character. Rather than place a flashback in the body of the story, this pretitle sequence can enable us to dramatize one past event or time period, then jump ahead to the time in the characters' lives in which the story will actually unfold. This isn't the only use for a pretitle sequence, but it can be an effective way to smooth over a single lapse in the chronology of a story. *Terms of Endearment* has a marvelous pretitle sequence. Emma is a baby in her crib and Aurora worries that she is so quiet, something must be wrong. She jostles the baby until she cries and, satisfied that Emma is safe but now unhappy, Aurora walks away, leaving the baby crying. In a nutshell, the writer has introduced us to the mother-daughter relationship at the core of the story, far in the past, disconnected in time from the story that unfolds when Emma is an adult and has a family of her own.

Sometimes a story is built around the comparison and contrast between two time periods or by a conflict beginning in one time period and resolved in a later one. *Heat and Dust, Frequency,* and *Lone Star* all deal with variations on this circumstance. In order for both halves of the story to resonate fully, they must be dramatized, so it's necessary to cut the story into two parts that then must be assembled in some kind of order. *Heat and Dust* uses a diary from one period being read by the protagonist of the later period. *Frequency* uses supernatural radio communication across the time barrier. And *Lone Star* uses the locations to weave together two stories in different time periods that took place in the same spaces. Each of these is a device to enable the telling of the story across a time span. And in each case, the bedrock design of the story demands this schism based on time. Without the ability, which cinema allows, to cross time nearly at will, none of these stories could have been told.

Time and the Lives of the Characters

The pivotal moments in the life of a character don't necessarily coincide with the pivotal moments in the telling of the story about that character. It is entirely possible to create a story in which the underlying structure of the told story doesn't follow the dictates of the life. You might shift chronology to fit your purposes, or you might emphasize only a particular portion of a life and not the same aspects the person himself pursued. Let's look at *Citizen Kane*, in which both time and emphasis are changed by the story-telling. In his "life," Kane inherited a lot of money, was sent away by his mother to be raised by an attorney, and tried his hand at running a newspaper, at politics, and at managing his wife's music career. On a conscious level, he wasn't trying to regain the love and home he lost that the word "Rosebud" comes to represent in the story. He was trying to find fulfillment from all of the opportunities given to him. But the various witnesses who tell the story of Kane overlap in time, don't follow a precise chronology, and change the emphasis of the life into something manageable for a film story. We are allowed to experience the life depicted in a way that is different from the way it would have been experienced by the protagonist had he actually lived.

For Lindbergh, a real human being with one enormous achievement around which all the rest of his life was centered, everything leading up to the decision to fly solo across the Atlantic could be seen as the first act. The preparation and actual flight would be the second act, and the lifetime of accolades, notoriety, and eventual tragedy could be the third act. If he hadn't taken the flight, he never would have had the fame, notoriety, and tragedy that befell him with the kidnapping of his child. But you could choose, as was discussed earlier, to tell simply the story of what compelled him to try such a daredevil stunt. Or you might tell the story of the famous Lindbergh and start the film with the flight or even with the landing in France. The focus could be on life under a microscope—the pressures of fame and the tragedies of notoriety.

How this ability to separate the telling of the story from the real or fictional life being depicted affects us can be profound. Most films don't attempt to tell an entire life: there's far too much material, lives don't readily break down into dramatic structure, the person who is ten and then later seventy is not usually the same character because life has changed him. Our goals generally aren't supported by the entire life, whether it's real or fictional. If we revisit Napoleon and Waterloo, our goal might be focused entirely on the twenty-four hours in which he lost the battle and came to realize his grand reign was over and he was headed to exile. Or it could be focused on the preparation for the battle and his ignorance of his fate. You can choose the portion of life you want to dramatize and the order in which those events are delivered to the audience entirely based on your intentions. You aren't limited to sticking either to chronology or to the totality of a life. You can use whichever portion fits your needs and leave the rest.

All of your work so far has been about who the characters are, what they want, what you want to make out of your story, and how you want it to affect the audience. Now is the time to assess which part of the life you are creating with your characters—even real human beings—will best fulfill your intentions. You must assess how to present that part for maximum impact. If possible, you'll try for simple chronology, but from when to when? Whether your protagonist is Joan of Arc, Abe Lincoln, a fictional mountain climber, your great-grandmother who helped settle the West, or a fictional version of yourself as a ten-year-old striving against all odds to make it on the Little League team, you have a lot of latitude in choosing when to enter and when to leave this life. Even if the story is about Lincoln's assassination, you could begin the story as he enters Ford's Theatre or when he gets elected president or as he is carted out of the theater, having been shot.

The question reverts back to, what do you want? What part of yourself are you exploring or what part of the human dilemma are you exploring or what impact do you want to have on the audience? It always comes back to the same dilemma: you're trying to hit a target you can't yet fully see, but you'll never be able to see it sharply unless you aim and give it a shot. Trust your instincts, your first best guess. You may have a solid idea of your opening or your ending, or a persistent image that you can't shake will help you identify that the whole story will unfold on the last day of high school or the first year of a marriage, or you keep getting this image of your protagonist as a grizzled old man, yet you know in the story he's a football player. This unshakable moment that's been with you since you conceived of the story is a great place to start. It's nailed down in some fashion—some era, some age for the character, some special or unique attribute.

Keep in mind that you have simultaneous but not necessarily complementary desires: to tell the story in as short a time in the character's life as will encompass what the story needs, and to start the character as far removed from his finishing point as you can to give maximum room for a character arc. Also remember that you usually strive to start stories on D Day just before the invasion begins; you want just enough time to establish the protagonist's life and world before it changes and then you drive forward to the change as quickly as possible. One more thing to keep in mind during this exploration is that you could delve into the past with a flashback or some other means of altering chronology, or you could jump into the future with a coda. Just because you keep seeing the grizzled old man yet your story is about playing football doesn't mean you have to tell it all in flashback. You could simply jump forward in a coda to learn of that eventual future for him when the main story is over.

So now it's time for more hard-hat work, more mind-doodling to discover what portion of time in the life of your protagonist will best carry your story and fulfill your intentions. Try imagining your story taking place all in one day or over one incredible weekend or the last year of the person's life or the first year of the career that is at the core of the story. Try it as one amazing summer or the period it takes to build the character's house. Each of these is a suitcase of time. Close up one of these suitcases and see how much stuff you have hanging out the sides. Is it too much? Could this stuff be dealt with either through flashbacks or modern equivalents? Maybe you need a slightly larger suitcase? Do you really need a semitruck to encompass everything you need to carry for your story? If you do, then do it; don't discard crucial material. At this point, don't even discard material you suspect might be crucial. But strive to find the smallest possible container for your story material. Remember, you're going to have to carry it for quite a while, and smaller will become more attractive every day.

If it's clear that simple chronology won't work for your story, then this is a good time for similar hard-hat work in this area. In your best mind-doodling mood, try the story as a reminiscence, with a single, major flashback, with intertwining past and present stories, with a series of witnesses or dreams or flashbacks or some kind of shake-up of chronology that you feel comfortable in controlling. As always, simpler is better than complex, if you have a choice in the matter. Unless there is something in your story that demands a particular method of changing chronology, try several methods before you settle on which will be your first best guess on how to proceed. Know from the outset that this choice will most likely need future revision. For instance, it might seem like a reminiscence will work for you, but then you realize that your protagonist being alive to reminisce proves he survives the story, which undermines your tension, in which case you need to find another mode. During this trial-and-error period, you also might discover that you don't need to alter chronology nearly as much as you originally thought.

Objective Time and Subjective Time

Just as there are objective and subjective forms of drama to sort out, there are objective and subjective time experiences to be dealt with. Objective time is real time, demonstrable time, measurable time, scientific time. This is the time that most of us live in and in which most stories are played out. But time can be made subjective, and in a certain sense nearly every film lives more in subjective time than objective time. You ellipse time, you cut out the boring parts, and by doing that, you have subjectively altered the experience of time. You can have a wheat field grow in completely during a one-minute montage, or you can depict forty days and forty nights of flooding in twenty minutes of mostly real-time scenes. This is inherently subjective for the audience.

But you can also have subjective time in which we experience a character's own anomalous relationship to time. This can be slow motion or a complete stop to motion; it can be speeded-up motion; it can even be repeating an action several times in a row. In *Groundhog Day* we experience Phil Connors's relationship to time—the day continually repeats itself. In *American Beauty* we

watch flowers fall from the body of the teenage girl in slow motion with Lester while he fantasizes about her. In *Apocalypse Now*
we reel in drunken time with Captain Willard in his hotel room.
In *Run Lola Run* we experience time with Lola that is speeded up,
slowed down, and even repeated. In all of these instances and
many more, we are being made to experience time as the character or characters do. This is above and beyond the subjectivity of
ellipsed time.

Most films have minimal subjectively experienced time, but
it's worth considering if subjective time is potentially an element
in the telling of your story. If it's merely a matter of some slow
motion to extend a bond with a character, like Lester in *American
Beauty*, it won't fundamentally change your story. But if experiencing time—and life—with the character as subjectively as we
do with Lola is part of your idea of your story, then now is a good
time to explore how that will work for you.

Basic
Dramatic
Structure

WHAT IS DRAMA?

At last we are about to discuss the building of a typical story, a "normal" story. So why start with a question that we've been answering for all these pages? The reason to discuss drama again—from a different angle—is that a lot of what has been laid out so far can start to feel like a set of rules. We are about to enter into a description of a story as a typical entity, which could also start to feel like rules or even a recipe. But just as what is typical of being human isn't the only way to be human, we must remember that just because something is normal or typical or average or fits someone's preconceived idea of the way to tell a story doesn't mean it's the only way. There is no single paradigm that covers all the potential ways to tell stories. There isn't a single "best way." The best way is the way that fits the story's needs and the storyteller's intentions most completely. Each story should be a prototype. It should be conceived and devised and revised into something that stems from the wants of the author, the wants of the characters, the theme, the shortcomings of the author and the shortcomings of his characters, and even the everyday problems that occur in the life of the author during the creation of the story and find their way into the day-to-day writing of the script. Each of these things plays a role in how a story unfolds in the creation process.

What you are ultimately after when you become a storyteller is a way of engaging an audience, giving them an experience of your invention that you control for a particular purpose or end. If you make a "normal" story or break all the rules to achieve that end, it's fine. If the story does in fact engage the audience, then it will give them some kind of experience. Whether or not that experience is the one the storyteller intends is largely up to the skill—the craft and the art—of the storyteller himself. Individuals within an audience might resist a story for personal reasons, but if a cumulative audience fails to connect with a story, the problem isn't personal to every individual in the audience; it is a failure of the storyteller to control the creation of the experience in the audience. When an audience laughs at a film in places that are meant to be serious, when an audience doesn't laugh at the intended funny parts, when an audience takes itself out of the action and collectively thinks about going to buy candy or getting its money back—in all of these cases the storyteller has lost control of the experience he is giving.

First a storyteller sets out to engage the audience, lure them into caring about his characters and believing in the world of his story. Only after he has engaged the audience can he begin to have a chance to create a particular and specific experience within them. He wants them to laugh when he means them to, fear when he makes them, feel hopeful, sad, teary, anxious, delirious, all as he controls it. And he does all this so that at the end, they will have had an actual experience—both emotional and intellectual, in some proportion—that was his intention from the very beginning. This ultimately is the purpose behind drama, the reason for its existence.

So then, what is drama? It is a means to the creation of an intended experience in an audience. Drama encompasses everything from comedy through tragedy; it covers the wildest farce and the most horrific depictions of murder, mayhem, or genocide; it can scare us, alarm us, make us think or not think; it can make us fear our neighbors or love our neighbors or understand our neighbors; it can be as forgettable as a dream or as overbearing as a nightmare. When you envision how to build your story, what you most have to keep in mind and abide by is the intended experience and how to achieve it—how to engage the audience, make them care, make them think and feel, and then release them from your creation. So long as you build the story from the

intended impact, you will find a means, a structure for your creation, that will be organic. If you start with an idea of the structure of the creation—and impact be damned, how it affects the
audience is none of your concern—then you have lost control before you've even begun. You might end up with an artfully designed whatsit, but the question will remain, what is this whatsit?
What is its purpose and use either to the audience or the storyteller?

Are there purposes or intentions that cannot be fulfilled
through drama? Clearly there are, or the world's problems would
have been solved by now. But even within the realm of what many
people think is the purpose of drama and storytelling, there are
intentions that cannot be fulfilled. Chief among these is teaching.
Most of us have been asked the question "What's the moral of the
story?" or "What does this story teach us?" Many beginning writers think in terms of "what I want to say." If you've got a solution
to world peace or widespread starvation, don't waste your genius
on writing a story. Go directly to the heart of the problem through
politics or an organization or religion or some other means of
tackling life's ills. A story is not a means of teaching the world the
error of its ways. A story is a means of holding a mirror up to
those errors, and it is a mode of exploring those errors. Teaching
isn't part of the equation. Trying to teach through a story is the
shortest route to killing your drama and thus undermining your
ability to hold the mirror or explore the issue. Teach them overtly
and you lose your audience.

This doesn't mean writers can have nothing to say. It just
means that what you have to say is in the form of questions,
dilemmas, and obstacles to wants; it isn't in the form of solutions
and answers and preaching the revelations about life you have
learned in your years on earth. What you have to say is evidenced
by the way you poke and prod your characters, the questions you
plant in the minds of the audience, the wrestling your characters
do with the events of their lives, and how that grappling provokes
some kind of corresponding battle within the audience while the
story is unfolding and, perhaps, after it is done. You don't and
can't teach solutions; you can only explore dilemmas, preferably
from a variety of angles. The end result is that the audience,

which cares about the characters enmeshed in those dilemmas, comes to grips in some fashion with the same problems and issues. In the end, the audience may "teach" itself, by forming some opinion or viewing something from a new and different direction. The story hasn't taught; it has enabled learning. There's a huge difference.

THE THREE ACTS

There's more than one way to look at the three acts of a story. An old saying from vaudeville days is "Tell them what you're going to do, then do it, then tell them what you've done." It sounds repetitive, but it is a perfectly effective and valid way of looking at certain stories. Another approach holds that in the first act you tie a knot, in the second act you tighten that knot, and in the third you untie it again. And another view says that the first act is inspiration, the second act is craft, and the third act is philosophy. It can also be said simply that a story must have a beginning, a middle, and an end. And in the terms we've used most often here, the first act is engaging an audience, the second act is elaborating on and extending that engagement, and the third act is releasing them from that engagement.

There are always iconoclasts who will insist that a drama can have only two acts, or they have heard of the four-act, the five-act, and even the seven-act structure. Certainly the material of a story can be divided up in any of these ways. You can shut off the projector halfway through a film and force everyone to go out and buy more candy and popcorn. You could put cards between segments of the film declaring "ACT I," "ACT II," and so on, going up to four or five or seven, if you want. None of these methods of dividing up the material—whether they are made overt to the audience or kept hidden and are known only to the storytellers— negates the fact that a story must have three parts, three acts. These other methods of dividing the material into segments can be valid ways of dealing with a story, but at the same time the story must, by definition, still adhere to a three-act underpinning. Remember the basic dramatic circumstance? *Somebody wants something badly and is having difficulty getting it*. The beginning of a story—Act I, the engagement of the audience, the "tell them what you're going to do" part—is *somebody wants something*. The middle of a story—Act II, the elaborating on the engagement, the "do it" part—is *wanting something badly and having difficulty getting it*. And the end of the story—Act III, the releasing of the engagement, the "tell them what you've done" part—is what happens as a result of the first two parts. Without any one of these three parts, the resulting story will die. They are like the brain, heart, and lungs—without them the animal dies. You can call them other things or count their parts in a variety of ways, but in the end it still comes down to the fact that each of these three things must be there and functioning in order for a story to work. Let's see how each part works.

The Beginning: Engaging the Audience

Though the audience has generally volunteered for the job of engaging themselves in a story—most stories are not told to captive audiences—that position as volunteers doesn't mean they are automatically engaged in the story. They have made themselves available to become engaged, but are not yet involved. Nor are they informed. In order to become engaged in a story, the audience must have some answers to basic questions—who, where, when, under what conditions. When we first are introduced into a story, we are like journalists. We want to know who these people are, what they are doing, what world this takes place in, in what time period this happens. We need to find our common ground with the characters and the world. We want to know, relative to ourselves, when this story takes place—today, yesterday, a long time ago, far in the future, in a parallel universe today. How does the world of the story compare to the one in which I live?

This desire for information has to do with our ability to connect. If we can't connect, then we can't care, and therefore the film experience will be diminished or will come to an abrupt end. We don't have to connect on every level and see the story as being about "us," but we must find at least some smidgen of common ground, some tiny area where we can understand something within a story, in order to connect. The connection isn't based on everything being familiar, but one element at least must resonate within the audience and its world experience or it will be kept at a distance and relegated to a position as witness, not as emotional and intellectual participant. If all things about a story are exotic, foreign, and unfamiliar except one tiny element that gives the audience its connection, that is enough.

"A long time ago in a galaxy far far away" takes us to a world we haven't seen, a time we haven't known, and objects that don't inhabit our real world. Yet it seems that any audience is capable of connecting with *Star Wars*. This is not simply because most of the primary cast are played by human beings. They could all be robots or it could be animated or, as in *Babe* and *Chicken Run,* the characters we are made to care about are the animals, even though there are human beings in the story. The characters we meet and spend time with in these stories have relationships with each other that we recognize, and therefore we find our means of connecting. The mobsters of *The Godfather* don't live the way most of the audience lives—neither in the realm of killing enemies nor in the realm of having an elaborate code of honor and ritualized behavior. Yet we are capable of connecting with and caring about people whose actions we may deplore. The Mob leader is proud of his son, worries about his daughter, has personal vanities—in other words, we discover human traits we recognize, and this gives us our connection. This can't be done without information.

A connection alone isn't enough to sustain audience interest and attention. We also want to become interested in the future of at least one character. This is where developing a protagonist and his want come into play. *Somebody wants something.* By virtue of wanting something, a character is revealing intentions about the future, and we are encouraged to look forward in time, to anticipate. Once a story has connected with the audience on some plane and made them anticipate the future of at least one character based on that character's want, then the first act is over. The beginning has ended. We are connected, caring at least to some slight degree and anticipating what may or may not happen.

The Middle: Elaborating and Extending the Engagement

We can care just a little bit about a character and be only mildly interested in his or her future, and that will be enough to get us through the first act. But the middle of the story has to make everything more important to us or we won't have much of an experience. Neither our emotions nor our brains will be significantly challenged if we remain only slightly closer than complete indifference. We probably need to learn and care more about the character we are mildly interested in, the character probably needs to want his "something" much more passionately, and the obstacles that we knew were "probably out there" must now become real, distinct, and difficult to surmount. At the same time as the achievement of the want becomes harder, the audience's connection to the character or characters deepens. Both the character and the audience must be pushed past the point of no return, the point at which they could walk away, no harm done. Then both the characters and the audience must be challenged and "put through the wringer" in whatever way is appropriate to the story.

This section, generally the largest section of a story—in which the audience and character connection becomes stronger and the character's conflicts worse, thereby involving the audience on a deeper and more intense level—is the second act, the middle of the story. If the first act told them what the story was going to do by declaring the want, the intention, then this section is doing it. If doing it is easy, then the story will be boring, without much conflict. So out of the frying pan and into the fire, then into the broiler and finally into the oven, is the basic method of achieving a viable and compelling second act. Whatever "it" was declared in the first act becomes increasingly difficult to achieve. At the same time, the character's want must also be strengthened or his passion extended, along with our connection to it. When the character crawls out of the frying pan and lands in the fire, we need to be with him. If he crawls out of a perfectly comfortable setting and intentionally puts himself in the fire for reasons we don't know or can't fathom, we probably end our connection, we won't make the leap with him. We quit identifying with him, or these seemingly strange actions make our connection to him more tenuous. Either way, the audience pays the price by having a lesser experience.

So the first goal of the second act, the middle section, returns to the audience's connection to the protagonist and possibly other characters in the story. This connection has to be made "permanent"; we have to want to be with him when he's required to enter the burning building, face the villain, or come to grips with his own inner demon. This means the second act will contain more basic information about the character and his relationship to the world of the story. It means we must achieve greater understanding of the character. We don't have to agree with his goals, worldview, or efforts, but we must understand how he comes by them. We must be encouraged in our hopes about the character's future and have our fears strengthened in equal measure. The second act fluctuates between hope and fear continually. There is a main tension, a primary hope-versus-fear circumstance, which becomes increasingly intense and focused throughout the second act.

At the same time, our connections to and understanding of other characters can be elaborated on in the second act. We may discover the antagonist to be a complex and far-from-evil person. We might discover a fatal flaw in the best friend or a terrible blind spot the mother. A love affair may begin or end. In other words, the story is filled with life and complexity, gray areas, and not just black and white areas. There might be full-fledged subplots or just asides, but either way, the story must become fleshed out and whole in this middle section. More happens than the simple demands of the plot. Life happens in spite of other plans. Now that we are hooked into the story—by the end of the first act, we are connected and hoping and fearing about the character's want—we will tolerate and even crave more tangential or seemingly tangential material. The story can delve more into the backstory, into the broader reaches of the world, into a wider array of characters. And all the while, the audience can still stay focused on the central problem, the main tension that concerns the protagonist and his primary want.

Just as the first act has a moment in time that signals its completion—when we know *somebody wants something*—the second act has a similar moment. When *wanting something badly and having difficulty getting it* is finished, the second act is over. Those difficulties have increased in intensity, the passion to have the want has been extended and tested, and the character has gone as far as he or she can, given the limitations of the character and the world of the story, to achieve the want. The main tension has been completed, but this doesn't mean the story is over by any means. It means the quest for the original want has been completed in some fashion—success, failure, or transformation of that original want. What happens as a result of the character's having attempted to achieve his want is what's left for the third act.

The End: Releasing the Engagement

"What's left": that sounds too small an amount of material from which to build a whole act of a story. Isn't the story over if the character has completed the want? Not by any means. Whether it's James Bond in *Dr. No* or it's Will Kane in *High Noon*, the want is not begging the resolution of the story. Bond wants to find out why another agent was killed and what's going on in the Caribbean. Once he knows, he wants to stop Dr. No, but that's the third act; that want to stop the villain comes from having completed the original want—to find out what was behind those strange events. Will Kane's original want in *High Noon* isn't to beat the gang coming to kill him, it's to get help from the townspeople. When he fails at that, he has to face the gang on his own; that's the result of the second act. By taking on a want and its quest in whatever way she does it, a protagonist necessarily upsets the status quo of her life. She does different things, marshals her resources in different ways and toward different goals, and impacts on those around her differently because of this increasingly passionate pursuit of an increasingly difficult goal. This quest changes the character's position in her world or the character herself or the world itself. Even the want can have grown or fostered a new want. The third act is the collision of this possibly altered character with the possibly altered world or the pursuit of the transformed or new want that was the outgrowth of the second-act want.

At the same time that the third act deals with the results of the previous two acts, it must also aim toward severing the tie so carefully cultivated between the audience and the story. This is more complicated than simply stopping the story. Stopping at the wrong moment or without having taken care of the audience's involvement can destroy the whole experience the rest of the story has created. Remember, one of the primary reasons every culture has created stories throughout history is that they are finite, they end, they complete themselves, unlike most of daily life. There are times in our lives when we can anticipate an ending—we know the trip is almost over or one's lover has to leave for the war or school or work halfway across the country or the world. But much if not most of life goes on and on and rarely gives us satisfying moments of completion. Even when it does, we may be so wrapped up in our joy at the wedding or grief at the funeral that we don't exactly "enjoy" it. So the value of stories stems, at least in part, from the fact that they end in a way that humans crave— not always happily, but fully.

A full and complete ending doesn't mean the hero has to get the girl, the ranch, the respect of the people in town, *and* the bag of gold. He can have lost or failed on all those accounts and it can still be a satisfying ending; we can be released from caring about his future even if that future isn't set and predictable. When we signed on for the story, we agreed to care about the character and to fret about his quest or want. We even went along when that original want led us to another predicament—can Will Kane face the gang of killers without the help of the town? By the end of the story, this ferocious loyalty and connection must be put to rest. If it isn't, we feel cheated when the film is over. Until our connection is definitively ended, we will want more to be made of that hard-won connection; if the story doesn't deliver it, we will rebel and the whole experience might be destroyed.

The connection should end first and then the remnants of the story should end; this will feel satisfying. We want to stay connected until the main issues are resolved. We want to find out "what happens." But then we want to regain our aesthetic distance, to sever the connection while we still have the characters around. It's as if we need to say good-bye. We can retain curiosity about the character's future, we can continue to appreciate the connection we had with the character, but we have been made to quit worrying about the future. When our hope versus fear about the immediate future of the character has been ended, then the connection will be severed; we will be released from the engagement that began in the first act. This is accomplished through the same means as making the connection in the first place—the character's wants and actions. If the character ceases wanting—by his own choice, by completing the want or failing to complete it—and acts on having ended the want, then we will cease our participation on his behalf.

The Writer's Relationship to the Acts

The audience isn't the only part of the equation. The author also has a unique and complex connection with the discovery, creation, and refinement of the three acts of the story he is telling. In a nutshell, for the writer of a story the three acts are: inspiration, craft, and philosophy. Each of these three aspects of story creation influences all three acts, but each dominates one act over the others.

What the first act evidences most is the original inspiration for the story—the somebody and the want or the circumstances that lead to a want. When a writer becomes obsessed with an image, a character, a circumstance, a world, or some other aspect of the final story, that first inspiration usually finds most of its expression in the beginning of the story. Usually that inspiration entails a character and either the want or the world of the story; sometimes, when you're lucky, all three. None of these is fully fleshed out at this stage, but something keeps coming to mind that helps you arrive at the early work of exploration, the mind-doodling from which you will eventually create the story.

Where stories come from, what inspires them, what triggers them to come alive, seems like a mystical bit of voodoo. A writer conjures a story up out of the blue, from nothing. In reality, while inspiration is a wonderful and at times troubling thing, it isn't beyond the realm of comprehension. Triggers for possible stories teem all around us, not unlike viruses or spores. You see an incident, overhear a bit of conversation, or have a lady on the bus tell you about her life or her brother or her dog. Whether you are susceptible to these viruses and spores—these little triggers that could incite an entire story—depends partly on sensitivity and partly on training. The story on the bus could be a bother to one traveler and the origins of a great story to another. Both hear it in the same detail, but one rider is open to the story, available to be inspired, and capable of recognizing useful elements or intriguing aspects of the otherwise seemingly mundane commuter's lament, the overly talkative neighbor.

The writer is ultimately dependent on the muse—inspiration—for some aspect of starting the process of creating a story. Each writer must become capable of seducing his own muse, listening to it, being aware when it is delivering good stuff, and—perhaps most important of all—remembering those inspired moments that all too easily evaporate like a dream. How many fantastic ideas for stories have you been given or had pop into your head that are now long gone? Probably enough to keep you busy for the rest of your career, if you only had them readily available.

The second act is dominated by craftsmanship, the bulk of the material dealt with in this book. Once inspiration does its job—it gives you part of a character, part of a world, part of a want, a fuzzy image or two—then the craftsman must take over. You must go through the paces outlined at length in earlier sections here, digging deeper, finding out the rest of the story, the characters, the wants and circumstances, and what's really on our mind. Most of this work comes into play in the second act. You have deepened your characters, refined their wants, created and heightened the obstacles, elevated the passions, and surrounded the protagonist with characters and a world that help reveal all that this character can carry in the story. This isn't accidental, and it doesn't depend on inspiration. It depends on knowing how stories are built, how they unfold, how they impact an audience, and how you want to impact the audience. Of course, craft can become art in the right hands, remain craft in lesser hands, or become hack work in the hands of a cynical or shallow worker. But the same tenets apply in any case, used with whatever level of mastery the storyteller can muster.

Perhaps the most surprising of the three elements used in creating the acts is philosophy. Some of you are saying, "I'm a storyteller, not a philosopher." And others are saying, "Didn't you just say that stories can't—or shouldn't try to—teach?" The latter is true and the former might be true, but that doesn't stop you from resolving your story in a way that reflects your view of the world. You may not be a philosopher, but you do have a philosophy of some kind. It could be shallow, stupid, perverse, or even nonsensical, but you must have some kind of feeling about how the world works and how your story should end. The old "Is the glass half full or half empty?" question is part of every ending, though life is more complicated than that question. The glass could be stolen, broken, deceptive, filled with poison, half full of holy water, or leaking slowly. Each of these responses betrays a worldview—a philosophy—behind it. When you choose a resolution for your story, you have revealed your philosophy, at least as it pertains to this story, circumstance, and issue. Maybe your philosophy is simply that a story has to have a happy ending in order to sell and get made. That's an abdication of your role as a storyteller, but even there you have revealed some aspect of your worldview.

Clearly, there are elements of inspiration and craft in the third act and elements of philosophy in the first and second and so on throughout a story. But each section is dominated by one aspect over the others. How you start a story "comes to you," how you develop it comes from your training and your skill, and how you end it comes from within you. This is another way of looking at the three acts as they emerge from the character of the writer.

SEQUENCES

Most people who spend time working with stories have become accustomed to the three-act divisions, but not many are equally familiar with the concept and usage of sequences. Sequences were invented with the advent of feature films, but they weren't fully understood or explained until my friend and mentor, Frank Daniel, started to analyze storytelling in cinema. Once you come to understand sequences, you will discover that this is one of the best tools you can master as a screenwriter.

How could the sequences have been invented, yet not been understood for so long? If so many people have worked without understanding sequences, then why can't I? Why bother to master them at all? You use gravity all day every day and you don't have to understand it in order to use it. But if you want to create something predicated on gravity, you're generally better off understanding it. You will have a better chance of success in utilizing this power if you understand it than if you don't. Since the time of Isaac Newton, we have had a good idea of what gravity is and how it works, yet knowing it hasn't harmed our ability to stay on the ground. The more pertinent question isn't why learn about it, but why be willfully ignorant of something as basic, bedrock, and useful as gravity?

Sequences are nearly as primal as gravity in the world of film storytelling. Once motion was created on film, it attracted an audience, but the novelty of mere motion wore off and motion pictures soon needed stories to continue to attract an audience.

These stories quickly grew from a few minutes long to a hour or hour and a half or even two hours. But a reel of film could only hold about ten or twelve minutes of film. Before automatic switching from one projector to another and long before huge platens to hold an entire film were invented, reels of film had to be switched by hand by the projectionist. This was an inexact science, and so it was decided that a fade-out at the end of one reel and a fade-in at the start of the next reel was the most effective way of keeping the film-viewing experience relatively seamless. At this point the sequence was invented, but it was simply called the reel. In fact, many editors and the directors with whom they worked began to think about and discuss their stories in terms of reel one, reel two, "we have a problem in reel five." The organism of a sequence was already alive, but it wasn't really understood for what it was until Frank Daniel formulated it, named it a sequence, and helped us gain greater control over it from the initiating stage of the script, rather than solely in the postproduction stage of editing.

Just like the chapters of a book, sequences build on each other and, together, create the whole. We no longer have to fade out and fade in, we have even surpassed automatic switching from projector to projector and can project a film in one continuous stream of film, yet the underlying sense of chapters—segments, reels—has remained with us. Writers who have never heard of nor thought about sequences create them within their screenplays. Audiences who have never thought about dramatic structure in any way react to sequences and feel the absence when there is a problem in the sequences of a story. Because they offer so many advantages in our working methods and in the organization of story material, as well as our own thought processes in the development phase of screenwriting, sequences are the screenwriter's best friend.

So what is a sequence? Is it just a chapter, just ten or twelve minutes of a story? What's so special about that? A sequence is actually a story in and of itself. It is a self-contained portion of the overall story with its own tension, its own beginning, middle, and end. A sequence "belongs" to a character—someone who wants something badly and has difficulty getting it within this shorter time frame. A sequence dovetails with the sequence before it and the one after it to form the seamless dream that is our ultimate goal as screen storytellers. Sequences—now that we don't have the time limitation of reels of film—tend to be between ten and fifteen minutes long. And the proportions of their beginning, middle, and end are more flexible than those of the three acts of a typical feature-length story.

From Acts to Sequences

Do sequences work within the three-act structure, or do they supplant it? In fact, these two means of dividing up and focusing story material mesh and support each other. In the roughest approximation, the first and third acts of a film are each about one-quarter of the story material and screen time, while the second act is about half. Within this framework, sequences form subdivisions of each of these acts. In the classical or "normal" structure of a story, there would be two sequences in the first act, four sequences in the second act, and two sequences in the third act. When wrestling with writing a feature screenplay, you face the formidable task of trying to shape and control nearly two hours of story material. Fortunately, with the act structure, you don't have to face the full length of a script as a single entity; acts allow you to break up that massive amount of material into something more manageable. But even one act is a daunting amount of material to try to shape all at one time; the second act alone can be nearly an hour in a normal-length feature. Because the sequences are subdivisions of these acts, they cut down to significantly more manageable size the amount of material one has to command at any given moment—10 to 15 minutes, not 30 minutes, 60 minutes, or 120 minutes. So in practice, sequences don't alter the proportions of the three-act structure at all; they simply divide it further, allowing a smaller increment than an entire act to be dealt with as one entity. This is one of the primary advantages of sequences.

Because a sequence has its own beginning, middle, and end, those subdivisions of the sequence typically come down to three or four or five minutes each. In this way, you keep chopping the building of the story down to workable size. You create segments that are designed to fit together into one seamless dream. During the creation process these segments can be formed, shaped, and refined individually, like the parts that will be assembled into a chair. It's only a chair once it's assembled, but while building it, you can form the legs, the back, the seat, the armrests, and the hidden substructure as separate elements. The same holds true for the building of a story. Once you've designed the parts so that they will all go together to become one story, you can work on them—think about them, envision them in detail, then shape and refine them—as individual pieces.

The advantage of sequences doesn't stop with your use of them; they are equally useful to the audience. Perhaps this is best seen in a quest-type story, a search for some variation on the Holy Grail. If the only tension you establish is about finding the Grail itself, then you are necessarily going to play one note over and over—find that Grail! But the reality of a quest isn't like that. First you have to find the map, then the person who can interpret the map, then the place that will become the starting point, then the landmarks along the way. Finally we arrive at the location of the Grail, but of course there's a dragon guarding it. So the dragon must be defeated and then the Grail itself must be withdrawn from the perilous niche in the side of a cliff where it has perched for millennia. Underneath the whole story is the quest for the Grail, but at any given time, our attention—and tension— is riveted on finding the map or the starting point or the destination point. Each of these is a sequence, a story of its own. We set out to find the map, the beginning of the sequence. Then we discover where it might be and who stands in our way of getting there, and we have to fight through to the place where the map is supposed to be—the middle of the sequence. Then we break in to find that the map is there, but it is unreadable—the end of the sequence, with a twist. Now we have a whole new quest, to find the person who can read the map—which will be the next sequence. Out of the frying pan and into the fire.

Sequences create short-term tensions for the audience to become involved in. Instead of just one tension to get us through from beginning to end of the whole story, you have a whole series of them. You can create many more variations in intensity of audience involvement by orchestrating all these short-term tensions. The audience's experience of the story is greatly enhanced by the skillful use of sequences and their tensions. And because sequences "belong" to characters, just as stories "belong" to their protagonists, you also have the ability to strengthen audience identification with more than one character without upsetting the balance of having a clear-cut protagonist for the overall story. There usually is at least one sequence that belongs to another character—the antagonist, the love interest, the best friend. For this short period of time, the focus of our attention will be on the want of another important character and its pursuit by that character. Usually the tension of these sequences focuses on the relationship between the secondary character and the protagonist. The want we follow isn't that of the protagonist, but what we are following is the love interest's effort to reveal her attraction to the protagonist or the antagonist's struggle to find a weakness in the protagonist. In this way, the sequence can give us greater connection with a secondary character and at the same time elaborate on the plight of or obstacles to the protagonist.

When a film takes on epic proportions—meaning length as well as scope of story and themes—the sequence breakdown can become significantly altered from the eight sequences in three acts outlined above. In many epics, there are really two stories either interwoven or played out one after the other. *The Godfather* is made up of two interwoven stories, Vito's and Michael's. *Lawrence of Arabia* is made up of two stories played one after the other, each with a different version of the same man as its protagonist. If an epic is really two stories put into one, then each story has its own three acts and, most likely, around eight sequences. But in a singular story of epic proportions—and production value and scale—there could simply be more sequences subdividing the three acts of the overall story. Some of the sequences themselves may become expanded beyond the ten- to fifteen-minute realm. This can happen in an epic that involves large set pieces—production numbers like battles, dances, or other major uses of spectacle. But an epic likely will have more than eight sequences simply because the canvas on which the story plays out is bigger, which means more screen time to fill, more events in more characters' lives. You may have several sequences belonging to other characters within the overall setup of a single protagonist carrying us through the story.

There are reasons besides epic scale that could alter the number of sequences in a film, not the least of which is what the storyteller finds most interesting. *North by Northwest* provides a fine example. Perhaps the most famous sequence in all of cinema is the crop duster sequence, which is about ten minutes long. In plot terms, the only essential ingredients to this sequence are that Thornhill discovers he has been set up to be killed by Eve Kendall and that he escapes that fate. In any other film this might have played out with him waiting at a phone booth to meet Kaplan, a car careening by, and men shooting at him. It could have been one scene of a minute or so. But Alfred Hitchcock and Ernest Lehman wanted to explore the creation of a sense of danger in a seemingly safe place at a safe time—an empty corn field in the middle of the day. Their interest expanded what could have been a scene into a sequence. And this expansion created a fifth sequence in the second act of the film. It isn't a problem; it's just a variation from the "norm."

The Elements of a Sequence

Because a sequence is a self-contained story with a tension of its own, it resembles a larger story, with many of the same hallmarks, needs, and limitations. But there are differences and variations.

Just like any other story, you have to ask whose story it is. But for the sake of clarity, let's stick to "Whose sequence is it?" Most sequences necessarily belong to the protagonist, because it is her primary want that propels the overall story. The subdivisions of that larger story still need to feed into the main want, so most of the sequences will be propelled by the protagonist in pursuit of some aspect of her larger goal. In the Holy Grail story, finding the map is a crucial first part of finding the Grail, so it's probably best to make the map-finding sequence belong to the protagonist who is after the Grail. But she is probably not on this quest alone, and there probably is someone else of great significance who is part of the quest—the love interest or best friend or parental figure. Perhaps the sequence that is about finding someone who can interpret the map could belong to this character. The reason to give the want of a sequence—its ownership—to another character is to allow greater depth to that character and to elaborate on the relationship between the protagonist and this secondary character. For instance, let's imagine the most important secondary character is the love interest, a warrior who initially disapproves of the woman seeking the Grail; he is a reluctant and resistant follower. Perhaps the acquisition of the map has convinced him the protagonist is worthy of the quest, but you have yet to create his love for and undying loyalty to her, which will be tested when they face the dragon. By putting the potential map reader—let's make him a blind old seer—in the warrior's home village, you can put him at the center of the sequence. The sequence tension belongs to the warrior, and along the way he falls in love with the protagonist and reveals his background and the source of his many battle scars; he becomes a more fully developed character. But his want in the sequence is in furtherance of the protagonist's want, not for any need of his own. So the sequence doesn't detract from the protagonist; it just broadens our perspective on her quest.

As you can see, by deciding whose sequence it is, you dive into other aspects of creating a story—what does he want, why is it difficult to get or achieve? In other words, what is the tension of the sequence? As with any other tension, it's best to phrase it as a question and to use the name of the "owner" of the sequence. "Will the warrior be able to find the seer and convince him to read the map for the Grail seeker?" As with the story requirements we have dealt with before, there needs to be some difficulty in achieving the want. If it's just a matter of taking the A train to the seer's house, it won't be enough of a sequence. It won't reveal much of the warrior or his growing relationship with the protagonist, and it will be boring. But here is one of our first variations from larger stories. Most sequences revolve around a single significant event, as opposed to the overall story, which contains a number of significant events. The event at the core of a sequence may be at the beginning of the sequence, which then is about dealing with the results and aftermath of that event. Or the event could be the center of the sequence, which then is structured to give us a buildup to the event, the event itself, and then its aftermath. Or the event could be near the end of the sequence, and the sequence elaborates the buildup to the event.

To stay with the Grail story, let's imagine the seer lives on an island surrounded by alligators. The event of the sequence might be meeting the seer. First there is the obstacle of finding the lake, then getting past the alligators, which entails making amends with the warrior's brother in order to get a boat. This is all first-section preparation and the major onus is on the warrior. Then we get onto the island and it is up to the warrior to get us inside the seer's hut so we can meet him and reveal to him the map and the group's needs. Here the warrior has to delve into even more of his past, this time with the seer, as well as his present when he introduces the protagonist and her quest. This would be the middle section. And then there is the reading of the map, the discovery that there are ever greater dangers ahead, and predictions of death and uncertainty about success; the reading and predicting could be part of uniting the warrior with the protagonist. This is the end part of the sequence.

Not every sequence will have a huge event like a wedding, a death, or a pot of gold. What's more important is that there is a clear-cut tension within every sequence. But also keep in mind that the significant events in your story need proper placement so they have the greatest possible impact. Using their placement within a sequence enables you to give them all the importance they deserve within your overall story. The focus of a sequence can be getting the maximum impact out of an event that is crucial to the overall story. What is important about the event? Is it the buildup to it, the event itself, or the aftermath or result of the event? Depending on the answer to that question, you know where within the sequence it's most effective to place the event. A wedding is a simple example. The importance for your story might be whether the wedding will even take place because of jitters between the couple. Here the wedding would probably be at the end, and the bulk of the sequence would be used to elaborate on the uncertainty of the wedding. Or perhaps the wedding itself is a spectacle or is uniquely dramatic and you want to expend our screen time on it, with some preparation and some aftermath but giving your sharpest focus to the event itself. In this case, the wedding would be in the middle of the sequence. And how many times have you seen weddings in films that actually begin with the couple leaving the church and the rice being thrown? If the wedding isn't the real issue of the sequence but is still the event that gives the sequence its shape, then the event is at the beginning and our attention is focused most on the aftermath and the results of the wedding.

Another way in which sequences resemble larger stories, but with variation, comes in the area of resolution. A story has a beginning, middle, and end, and so does a sequence. But the end of a sequence can't be a complete resolution and sever our ties with the story and the characters. If it does, our story will stop and we'll have to start up all over again. It might be worthwhile rereading the section "Tension from First to Last," especially as it deals with incomplete resolutions. With sequences there are two basic approaches to resolving them without the story coming to a standstill. A sequence can have a partial resolution, or the resolution of a sequence creates the dilemma of the next sequence. We could arrive at the destination of the sequence, the goal has been fulfilled, yet the Grail is nowhere to be seen. It's a partial resolution because the overriding issue isn't resolved when the smaller issue—getting to the location—is resolved. Or we could find the map, which resolves the sequence, but the map isn't readable. So the resolution of the sequence creates the next sequence's dilemma. Out of the frying pan and into the fire.

Perhaps the greatest variation on story building that sequences require is the ability to dovetail with the sequences before and after them. They must be built as part of the whole, even if they can also be dealt with as self-contained entities. As you can see from the incompleteness of some resolutions, often this dovetailing is quite easy and seamless. Some problem left over from the incomplete resolution helps create the next sequence or its dilemma, which will then shape and propel the next sequence. But there are many circumstances where you have to invent the fire beneath the frying pan so that when that sequence is resolved by escaping the pan, there is a new dilemma and a new obstacle to face. It might appear simple and logical, even inevitable, to the audience of the film, but it was craftsmanship that enabled the storyteller to arrive at that fire as the dovetailing of the new sequence with the previous one.

Seamless dovetailing isn't always an incomplete resolution that automatically creates a new problem. Again, in the section "Tension from First to Last," we dealt with overlapping tensions. We can become involved in—care about, hope and fear about—a number of issues for the protagonist as well as all the other characters. We harbor tensions about the futures of these characters, their issues, dilemmas, wants, and so on. While these various tensions are simultaneously in our psyches, one will take center stage for a period of time, perhaps become the focusing element of a sequence. When that sequence is over, one of those other overlapping tensions could take center stage, providing the next sequence with its focal point. In this way, you don't have to start from scratch at the beginning of a new sequence—the tension has been there for some time—and you have the means of making the sequence dovetail with the previous one. This is an effective way of hiding the stitches.

You might plant ahead of time the conflict that will rise to the level of a sequence tension in the next sequence. You could just as easily create the tension of the next sequence from scratch, but in order to smooth over the seam between the sequences, you pull some information forward to make the tension predate the shift from one sequence to the next. This hides the stitches and makes the whole story seem more organic. For instance, you could wait to reveal the dragon guarding the Grail in the sequence after our crew arrives at the location. But to smooth over the seam between sequences, you might want to bring some of that conflict forward, so that we anticipate and feel hope and fear about having to face the dragon. Maybe we meet a one-legged man along the way who tells of his ferocious battle with a dragon that cost him his leg—but not necessarily the same dragon guarding the

Grail. During this exchange, we learn our warrior once froze when facing a dragon and has a deathly fear he will do it again. We're creating a means of dovetailing the sequences and planting a weakness in our warrior to make his eventual triumph over the dragon all the more unpredictable.

Another means of helping sequences to dovetail comes from one of the earlier definitions of the three acts: tell them what you're going to do, then do it, then tell them what you've done. One way of looking at the second act is as a series of obstacles in the path of the protagonist and his want. If you tell the audience the obstacles in advance, they will not seem to come out of the blue as we reach them. Clearly this technique won't work with every story, and it runs the risk of making the story predictable. But many fantastic films do indeed have a scene in which all the future obstacles or wants are delineated, and the storytellers not only get away with it, but succeed in part because of having done this "giveaway" as part of weaving the sequences into one whole. From bank heists to save-the-world-from-the-asteroid to staging the world's worst Broadway play, there are many superb examples of telling us in advance what needs to be done or overcome. The tension comes not from knowing what must be done but from the difficulty in accomplishing it. Once we know the series of obstacles to be faced, that knowledge helps bridge the gap from one sequence—or obstacle—to the next, and dovetailing is achieved.

A variation on seeing the second act as a series of obstacles is seeing it as a series of potential solutions, usually in escalating order of difficulty. Again, you can have a scene in which those potential solutions are spelled out in advance. So long as the potential solutions aren't easy to accomplish, there will be plenty of tension to spare. This is just a larger-scale variation on the difference between suspense and surprise. It isn't a problem—it doesn't diminish suspense—for us to know in advance that we have a cliff ahead of us or a potential savior, just as long as overcoming the cliff or enlisting the help of the savior is sufficiently difficult. In fact, just like the difference between surprise and suspense, it's usually better to have the suspense and, very often, you get to have the surprise as well. Just because we know there is a cliff doesn't mean we'll know how high it is, how awful the gusts of wind are that blow across it, or the fact that poisonous spiders live on the cliffside.

The focusing that sequences enable in the telling of a story is not just about the plot and tensions or even solely about the depth of characters. The sequence structure of storytelling is also an ingenious way for the author to organize her own material for maximum impact and efficiency. As you gather all the hard-hat material dealt with in earlier chapters, you have things from all over the lives of the characters and all over the map of the world. It can be a daunting prospect to figure out what information goes where and how to organize our own thoughts about it all. As you are building your sequences and devising their tensions and events that help to give them shape, you discover you have repositories for different kinds of information you have gathered. In a larger sense, the wedding sequence is about love, and so you start to find all the elements of many of the characters' relationships to love and coalesce them into this one section. The dragon-fighting sequence is about courage, so all the information you have dredged up that fits that element can start to go there. Certainly you must take bits and pieces to plant elsewhere, to pay off later and so on, but if you know that most of this or that kind of material will go together, you have a great starting point for building the substructure of your story.

This also lends much greater narrative efficiency to the overall story. If the subject matter of the sequence is already established, it takes less screen time to bring in the secondary character's relationship to love or courage than it would if you had to create the subject anew in a variety of places throughout the story. It's as if a sequence can have a theme of its own that the audience picks up on subliminally. This theme, explored from the perspective of the protagonist, antagonist, and secondary characters, will resonate more distinctly and with greater power if those various perspectives are brought together than if they are spread over the course of the story.

Another significant factor in the usage of sequences is their ability to focus the audience's involvement in shorter increments, meaning that we can have more ups and downs, more emotional shifts in the course of a story. As we've discussed, tension is the principal means of focusing the audience's emotional connection with a story. You make them hope and fear, you stoke the fires of those two conflicting feelings, and, in the process, the audience experiences an intensified connection with the characters and the story. This is focusing their experience, but don't mistake focusing to mean that other thoughts and feelings in the audience are excluded. Just because we are concerned with finding the seer to read the map or with the upcoming battle with the dragon doesn't mean no other material in the story can be dealt with. On the contrary, having a clearly defined and "present" tension—meaning that it is visceral and manifested in some fashion—enables you to take the time and latitude to explore other issues and not worry that the audience will get lost or distracted. They will know that the cliff is there or the dragon is nearby, so you can take time out for the warrior and the protagonist to kiss and declare their love and stroll through a field of wildflowers adjacent to the scorched earth surrounding the dragon's lair. You can take this "time out" to follow other tracks precisely because your sequence tension is clear.

In fact, once a sequence tension is clearly defined and you set the character in pursuit of the short-term want, this enables you to spend considerable portions of your screen time on all manner of other issues, characters, tensions, and even asides. Without the sequence tension, all these secondary issues would diminish each other in vying for precedence over the others in the minds of the audience. But once the audience knows the principal problem or goal or obstacle or potential solution that is giving the sequence its shape, we have our short-term priorities straight. Once those priorities are in place, we don't fret about taking a bit of time for other issues, because we are secure in the knowledge of "where we're going" and confident the sequence tension will still be our primary focus. As you've seen with several other seeming limitations that beginning screenwriters rebel against, having a clearly defined sequence tension is liberating rather than limiting. It's the very thing that allows you to take your time with other issues, characters, conflicts, and periods of pure entertainment. Without the tension, these same elements will confuse and confound the audience, who are looking for the next thing to worry about.

Special Needs of the First Sequence

First sequences are different from other sequences. They can't have their tension created by the previous sequence, and they can't have any overlapping tensions to bring into greater play. Also, first sequences are saddled with the need for more exposition than any other sequence. On top of that, the story hasn't begun yet and the audience is its most susceptible to being distracted or resistant to the story. Thus the need for a viable tension to the first sequence is even greater than for later sequences, yet the creation of the first-sequence tension is by far the most difficult. So how do you create the first-sequence tension?

A common mistake is attempting to jump right into the story material—the search for the Grail or the attempt to destroy Dr. No's empire. This often results in disaster for the story. In almost all cases, it's a better strategy simply to start out with the characters and the world. But where can the sequence tension come from in this instance? The most common solution is to find the tension, the short-term want or goal or obstacle, in the life of the protagonist. There are also instances where the world of the story is so new and unique and crucial to the eventual story that the first sequence can really be about establishing that world and the conflicts inherent in it. Once your protagonist is dropped into the world, we see the collision coming even while we are getting to know the character. But most of the time, it is the life of the protagonist that gives you that first-sequence tension.

Remember "life is what happens when you're busy making other plans"? This is a good time to put that knowledge of your character's other plans to use. Your protagonist should be in active pursuit of his or her own life, most often with no knowledge of the upcoming events—the collision—that will create the story. Not only is this an organic tension, because it springs from within the character of your protagonist, but it is a helpful tool in introducing the inner life of your protagonist and the nature of the life he or she lives. This first sequence is most often about the undisturbed status quo of the character; the collision creating the story has yet to occur. But that status quo should generally not be inactive. There should be *active* pursuit; showing the protagonist striving to do or be or find or have or accomplish something of importance to him is not a static state of being. So you must look to all that hard-hat research you did on your protagonist to find a conflict that will enable you to explore his inner life, reveal his present, undisturbed life and the world in which he lives.

Most people want something most of the time, so finding *a* tension isn't that difficult. Finding the *right* tension can be a bit trickier. Ideally we want to look for something that goes to the core of that part of the protagonist that the story will explore. A fine example is the opening of *Rocky*, in which he is being evicted from his locker at the gym. The entire story is about Rocky's sense of self-worth; he wants to deserve to be in the ring with the world heavyweight champion. The conflict over his locker goes to the heart of his sense of worthiness—he is being told he doesn't even deserve a permanent locker in a run-down neighborhood gym. The story material hasn't begun—the champion hasn't offered him a title fight—but already the story is exploring Rocky's exist-ing feelings of self-worth. *Schindler's List* provides an equally ef-fective first-sequence tension about Schindler's effort to sell pots and pans to the Nazi brass. It goes to the core aspect of the man's life that will be explored and tested in the film, without yet deal-ing with the nature of the story to come. Is this civilian brazen and persuasive enough to take on a formidable group of Nazi of-ficers and succeed in selling them what we suspect might be a pig in a poke? The story of protecting Jews from the Nazis hasn't be-gun, but the life, personality, and temperament of the main char-acter are being revealed prior to the establishment of the main conflict.

How can you find your own first-sequence tension? Look to what your story is "really about." It's not about the plot; the plot is the vehicle for delivering the real material, but what is that real ma-terial? It might be worth rereading the section on "Theme." Is there a way to explore the character's undisturbed relationship to the theme or issue of the story before the collision begins? What are the events of his normal life, the aspirations, frustrations, and daily hassles that might be elevated to the scale of a genuine ten-sion? What is unique or interesting about this character that could be challenged in a revealing way? What part of the character is going to be most directly challenged? Is there a way to involve this aspect of the character in a conflict that is part of his daily, undisturbed status quo? These questions can also be approached from the other end of the story. Remember that you usually strive to start your character far removed from where he or she ends up for maximum character arc. If you have a clearer idea of the ending than you do of the beginning, first explore what is the opposite of the ending in terms of the nature of the character, his inner life or where he resides on the scale of your theme. Is there something in finding that starting aspect of the character that triggers a conflict or tension, that could reveal who the character is before the main conflicts of the story have begun?

Remember that the tension should be about the character's current life, his status quo, not about his backstory. If you make the tension about the status quo, it's an effective way of establishing that status quo and the baseline for comparison to the character at the other end of the story. The same goes for the exposition you deliver early in the story; it should be about the status quo, not about the backstory. Give only enough exposition at this point for us to understand the conflict and tension of the sequence, not all the exposition we'll need for the full film.

Pretitle Sequences and Codas

One of the problems with discussing stories and drama comes from the inexactness of the language and conflicting uses of some terms from one person to another. The pretitle sequence is a well-known tool in storytelling, one dealt with earlier in this book. This out-of-time and disconnected episode is called a "sequence" in general parlance in the film community—and so is a series of scenes, irrespective of whether they hold together as a sequence as the word is used here. But a pretitle sequence should rarely actually be a sequence as we define it. If there is enough material to become a full sequence, it would rarely go before the titles. That would put the titles about ten to fifteen minutes into the film, which is a potentially very disruptive place to put them. It's quite legitimate to leave the main titles for the end of the film, but it would be a bad idea in most stories to interrupt our connection with the story fifteen minutes in and give us the main credits. Even a James Bond film, which ritually has a pretitle sequence that is a ministory all its own, doesn't push us more than about five minutes into the screen time. Here it is done for a good reason. The creation of the next case for Bond generally requires a lot of rather dull exposition and demonstration of some gadgetry relieved by humor. But these films are expressly for an action-oriented audience, and they need a good little teaser of excitement in order to help the audience over the boring establishment of the latest megalomaniacal villain and Bond's task of stopping him.

So we won't endeavor to change the widely accepted terminology for a pretitle sequence. Rather, just make sure you realize it doesn't mean a full sequence as described here. The same is true for codas, the disconnected bit of story at the end of some films. This too would not be a full sequence's worth of material. Generally codas are even shorter than pretitle sequences, usually weighing in at a minute or two at most.

CRUCIAL MOMENTS

Not all moments in a story are created equal. There are several moments in a screenplay that tower above all others. These are the moments without which the story would not work at all. Imagine *The Godfather* without the moment when Don Vito is shot or when Michael kills the men responsible. Imagine *Saving Private Ryan* without the moment Ryan is found. Imagine *Blade Runner* without the moment when Deckard discovers Rachael is also a replicant, one of those he is supposed to kill. Imagine *Chinatown* without "She's my sister, she's my daughter." Imagine *Some Like It Hot* without the moment when Jerry and Joe first present themselves as women. These moments and several more in each story are absolutely crucial to the telling of the story. There are also crucial moments in the lives of the characters, but they are not necessarily the same moments. While it is an important moment in Evelyn's life when she reveals to Gittes that her sister is her daughter, it was the rape/seduction by her father that was infinitely more crucial in the creation of her character. You must sort through the crucial moments and determine which of them are crucial to the telling of the story and which are crucial merely to the characters. Then you must pick places within the overall structure of the story to place those critical moments for maximum exposure and power. When the moment is equally crucial to the storytelling and to the life of the protagonist, you must strive to make those two powerful events coincide.

Crucial Moments in the Main
Character's Life

Clearly there will be more crucial moments in a character's life than in the story told from that life. The person usually has decades of life, and many things from birth to death are crucial, including marriages, births of children, job and career changes, aspirations and failures. For your purposes, most of those moments won't be important other than how they impact the inner life of the character. Although you won't be dealing with those moments in the telling of the story, you can't forget them. In fact, there are four kinds of crucial moments that you need to explore with your protagonist: moments that occur within the story at hand; moments within the backstory; moments of decision; and moments of change within the character. Some moments will obviously qualify in more than one category.

The most important crucial moments in the protagonist's life are the ones that will be within the time frame of the actual story. These should include both moments of decision and moments of change in the character or moments that push toward change, whether the change comes about or not. Sometimes these moments either won't resonate or can't be found without first identifying similar or motivational moments in the character's backstory. Let's say a key moment within your story comes when your protagonist decides to quit his job and punch his boss in the nose. This is a moment of decision, a moment of change, and it occurs within the telling of your story. How you arrive at that moment and discover the trigger that sets him off might be most easily found by the hard-hat work of exploring the last time he punched someone in the nose or he was punched in the nose or he desperately wanted to punch someone but was stopped or stopped himself. If that moment leads you back to his father or an authority figure—like his boss, within the story—then it's all the better. You have found a handle on that scene within the story from the similar crucial moment in the backstory. Sometimes this background information will find its way into the script, but that isn't as important as the fact that you have found the key to making the character's crucial moment in the story play believably because the impulse has been with him for much of his life.

Something monumental in a character's life occurring within the time frame of the story doesn't automatically confer on it crucial moment status. The marriage of the protagonist in one story will be everything, the most crucial element in the entire story. But in another story, it's possible to imagine that the marriage—or the birth of a child or a major car accident—might be just another event, not one of critical importance to the story. If the story doesn't play out in the married life of the character, then the marriage won't achieve that degree of importance. Oskar Schindler has a wife, upon whom he cheats with distressing regularity and casualness, yet most of the audience would be hard pressed to remember her name. Even so, his marrying her—and his cheating on her—must have reached some level of importance in the man's life. Yet it achieves no importance for us. On the other hand, his relationship with Stern is the stuff of crucial scenes, for the simple reason that this is the core material of the story, not Schindler's marriage. In *The War of the Roses* it is nearly the opposite situation. While the family has a lot of money and both Oliver and Barbara have significant careers, this is barely a concern of the story. What's important is the marriage, and all the crucial moments we follow in the telling of that story have to do with that core relationship.

Crucial Moments in the Telling of the Story

A good exercise to do with your research into the life and story of your protagonist is to identify the moments that are so critical they cannot be cut out without destroying the whole story. There will probably be about half a dozen moments that rise to this level of importance, though at this juncture it might not be possible to know. Clearly it would be better to have too many on your list than not enough. Let's revisit our Holy Grail quest. What moments must we have in order to tell the story? When our protagonist first hears of the Grail or learns of its supposed existence would be one. When she decides to go after it herself for some purpose is another. When she successfully locates the map would qualify because it refines and focuses her quest. When she leads her team to the specified location on the map is definitely another. When she first sees or touches the Grail and discovers it is indeed real must qualify as a critical moment. And what happens to her and the Grail as a result of her quest and finding it must surely be one. We don't have to have her love affair with the warrior, her relationships with the others on the quest, or the inner life of the dragon in order to tell this story. Each of the actual crucial moments is tied to the protagonist directly and, ideally, elicits a visceral reaction from the audience as well.

For the most part in this schematic, these moments seem entirely plot oriented and have little to do with the nature of her character, nor do they seem to generate much of an emotional response—yet. An unfortunate choice would be to rush into the script from this bare-bones outline. Unless there is something special in the potential existence of the Grail for our protagonist, the whole quest will be shallow and nearly meaningless to the audience. Unless her decision to go after it is from within the character and is heartfelt, we won't have much connection with her along the path of the quest. In fact, each of these critical moments on her journey should ideally coincide with, stem from, illuminate, or cross-pollinate with something crucial within her life. If the two things can be made into one moment, all the better. When her decision to seek the Grail stems from something deep inside her that we know and care about and we come to see the decision as the extension of that inner life or as an expression of it, then we have a wonderfully powerful moment. There are times when the two sides—the plot and character sides—can't be made to coincide precisely. But it's a worthy goal, and you still must explore those plot-oriented crucial moments while keeping an eye on the possibilities of tying them inextricably with your character's crucial moments.

First let's explore the typical crucial moments in a story.

The *point of attack* is the first revelation of the material that will eventually create the main story. Imagine the main story is a thunderstorm and the undisturbed status quo of the protagonist is quiet life on the farm. The point of attack would be the moment when we first hear thunder in the distance. We don't yet know the storm will reach our protagonist, nor do we know how severe the storm will be, but we do know there is a storm in the world of the story and it isn't far away. In our Grail story, this moment would be when our protagonist first hears about the Grail or learns that it might truly exist. She has yet to decide to go after it and we don't yet know that it is in fact real, but the material out of which the story will be built has first been revealed to us and to her. Generally you should strive to separate the point of attack from the end of the first act, so that the material of the story has "been around for a while" and we have grown accustomed to its presence. This is a form of hiding the stitches, making it seem as if the story is growing naturally from within itself. In *Shakespeare in Love*, the point of attack is when we discover that Viola has every word of Will's play memorized. We don't yet know that this "storm" will enter Will's life, but we know that this important woman is in love with the work of the playwright. In *Midnight Run*, the point of attack comes when the bail bondsman tells Jack about Duke, who embezzled money from the Mob. In *Body Heat*, the point of attack is when Ned first meets Matty and makes a pass at her. In *The Piano*, the point of attack comes when Ada's new husband, Alisdair, leaves the piano on the beach, to her distress. In each case, there is an indication of potential future trouble, but no guarantee of it. It is not inevitable that the character and the world will collide, but we now know that there is something in the world with which he or she may well collide, though in what way, we can't predict.

The *main tension* is the tension that is established at the end of the first act, carries throughout the second act, and is a critical moment in the telling of the story. The main tension, culmination, and resolution were all dealt with in *The Tools of Screenwriting*, but some of the information warrants repeating here. Unlike sequence tensions, which get resolved within the short term of the sequence, the main tension carries over several sequences and unifies the entire second act. It does not beg the eventual resolution of the story; rather it gives focus and drive to the second act. For instance, with our Grail seeker, the end of the first act is her decision to seek the Holy Grail, and this establishes the main tension, "Will she be able to find the Holy Grail?" This tension continues while she is assembling a team to travel with her, finding the map, traveling through hardships and turmoil, and finally arriving at the actual location of the Grail. Those shorter tensions all fall underneath the main tension's umbrella. It would be a misstep to try to make the main tension encompass everything all the way to the resolution. For example, if the main tension were, "Will she be able to hold the Holy Grail and use its magic power for her expressed need?" then the remainder of the story would become cloudy and ill-shaped. The quest of the second act is about *finding* the Grail, the third act is about managing to hold it and use it. Without this seemingly subtle distinction between giving a tension to the second act and begging the resolution, you will find it very difficult to give the crucial moments you have just discovered their proper placement of amplified importance. This is similar to trying to start out immediately with story material; it's jumping ahead of where you should be and, in the process, missing or bungling the parts you are trying to jump over.

For instance, in *Shakespeare in Love*, the main tension is not about Will being able to sustain his love for Viola, it's about the creation of his play about love. "Will Shakespeare be able to write the play *Romeo and Ethel, the Pirate's Daughter*?" would be an accurate main tension. In the process of trying to write the play, he casts a worthy Romeo and falls in love with Viola and eventually discovers these two muses are in fact one person, one muse, who enables him to write his play. He falls in love with Viola and this leads to all manner of complications, as does a woman playing a man—or anyone in the theater of that age—but all of this comes under the umbrella of the main tension about writing the play. In *The Silence of the Lambs*, the main tension is something like, "Will Starling be able to use Lecter's help to find Buffalo Bill?" It is not about stopping Bill in time or saving his latest captive; those are for the third act. The second act is about her increasingly desperate search for a serial killer on the loose and, most particularly, her use of a serial killer in prison as her primary tool of detective work. When Lecter escapes and she no longer has her best source of help, she has to work on her own and the tension switches to saving the captive and capturing Buffalo Bill.

The *midpoint* or *first culmination of the second act* is the second most important moment in the second act and generally is a turning point in the story. It is another of our critical storytelling moments. In the Grail story, it would be the moment when the map is read and the final destination is known. We know the Grail exists and we know where it is supposed to be, where the journey will have to take us now. The getting there has to be difficult, so there is still plenty to do, but the quest has become much more specific and refined. The chore has narrowed, but it is still far from complete. There may be moments to come in the second act that are more exciting, but in terms of building the story, this is a crucial moment because of what it does to the main tension. The midpoint makes the main tension much tighter and more specific. It's no longer a generalized "Will she find the Grail?" but a specific, "Will she be able to get to this exact place where the Grail is?"

In *The Silence of the Lambs*, the midpoint comes when Starling enters into a formal deal with Lecter, a transfer for him in exchange for his answering her specific questions. The midpoint refines and narrows the main tension and is a significant event which changes the path of the story. In *Shakespeare in Love*, the midpoint comes when it seems that Will loses his writing muse—Viola announces her plans to marry Lord Wessex. He began writing the play with twin muses, and now it seems that he has lost one, maybe both. But he has experienced the love the play is about, and his relationships with Viola and Thomas, her alter ego, are not over; they are just made much more difficult. The possible directions of the second act are significantly narrowed by the midpoint, and this leads to rising tension and greater audience participation.

The *culmination* is the completion of the main tension, comes at the end of the second act, and is another crucial storytelling moment. Like sequence tensions, the main tension should have a partial resolution or at least help create the tension that will carry us through to the end of the story. At its simplest, this culmination answers the question posed by the main tension. Will she find the place where the Holy Grail has been hidden? Yes. She arrives at the place and she has succeeded in a very difficult journey, but the ordeal isn't over yet. Being there and having the Grail are far from the same thing; there are still the dragon and the cliff to face. In *Shakespeare in Love,* does Will manage to write the play? Yes, he has the play written and it is wonderful, but Thomas is unmasked as a woman, the theater is closed, and Viola marries Wessex. So the performance of the play is still very much up in the air, as is the love between Will and Viola. In *The Silence of the Lambs,* will Starling find the killer with Lecter's help? The answer is no, he escapes before she has fulfilled her task. But she isn't done yet; she continues on her own, now seemingly hampered by the absence of her uncertain but crucial ally.

In the third act, usually close to the middle, there is a major *twist* that is a crucial moment. A twist comes about when we have been made to expect one thing, but that thing is turned around or inside out or upside down in some fashion. Twists can occur within scenes and sequences, but *the* twist of a story should occur in the third act in order to make the end of the story less predictable and the third act less linear. The twist is a last surprise you have kept in store to make life more difficult for your protagonist and more tense for the audience. In the Grail story, the twist would come after the dragon is slain by the warrior, who has been mortally wounded in the battle. We spot the Grail in all its glory perched on the side of a cliff above a bottomless chasm, and our protagonist—whose paralyzing fear of heights has long been established—is the only one left who could climb down to it. The map showed us the dragon, perhaps, and it might even have shown us the Grail in a niche in a cliff wall, but we didn't know that it was such a high wall, nor did we know the protagonist herself would have to climb it. It would probably be best that they brought a rope in preparation, but it was incinerated in the battle with the dragon. This way you don't make your characters look foolish or ill-prepared by forgetting to bring a rope—which *decreases* our sympathy for them. Rather, it makes them unfortunate for having their careful preparations destroyed in a ferocious battle—which *increases* our sympathy for them.

In *Shakespeare in Love* the twist is that Will plays Romeo and Viola plays Juliet in order for the play to be performed. This is after they have been sanctioned for having a woman act in the theater. Now they are doing so blatantly and in front of a large audience, including Viola's new husband. This unexpected turn of events—and the seemingly endless march across London of the villainous Tilney and his soldiers, who are coming to stop the play—provide new tension from a logical but unplanned direction. In *The Silence of the Lambs,* the twist comes when the FBI believe they have found Buffalo Bill and leave Starling alone at the house that turns out to be Bill's actual location. She has been prepared for the face-off with plenty of well-armed backup so she doesn't look foolish. But instead of the first plan with FBI backup, she is left on her own and there is no time to waste if she is to save the latest victim of the killer. It's do or die, and both alternatives seem completely possible.

The *resolution* comes very near the end of the story, tells us what happens as a result of all that went on before, and severs our ties with the future of the protagonist. Unlike the incomplete resolutions that most other tensions have had, this one is complete. The final resolution stops the story and stops the audience's involvement. Subplots, which we'll discuss next, also have complete resolutions, but these resolutions have to be made so they don't detract from the main story line and its resolution. In the Holy Grail story, the resolution comes when our protagonist has finally gotten the Grail into her hands and completed whatever task she had set out to use the Grail for—or failed because the Grail didn't have the power she thought it did. It could be, as it is in *The Wizard of Oz*, that the magic had been in her all along and the Grail merely makes her aware of it. Or it could be, as in *Raiders of the Lost Ark,* that the magic powers of the Grail are completely different from what the seekers have thought. But however the Grail is used or not used, however it affects the protagonist or fails to affect her, there is nothing left to be done. She has found the thing she was after, held it as she had hoped to do, and tried to extract her underlying goal—in *The Wizard of Oz* it is to get home, in *Raiders of the Lost Ark* it is to have a controllable power of cosmic dimensions or to keep that power from being used.

Whatever direction the resolution takes, there is no seeking left to do, no want left to yearn for. The protagonist is done with whatever part of his life we have been exploring. There might be the same desire still inside of the character—to get home, to hide a source of power, to use the Grail to bring peace to the world—but this particular quest, this effort, this protracted and dramatized pursuit of that want is over and the next has not yet begun to materialize. So we have a sense of completion, of ending our connection with the future of the character. We can have this feeling even when we know that the character will dream up another quest within minutes. We aren't yet hooked into that one; we haven't been made to care about the next minute more than the last. If we have, the story has taken a misstep. It has foiled its own resolution. But you can still point forward without destroying the sense of resolution.

In *The Silence of the Lambs,* Starling stops Buffalo Bill and saves his latest victim in time. Then we have a coda about Lecter on the loose and we know full well that this even more vicious serial killer will continue his cannibalistic ways. At first, this would seem to be undermining the resolution of the story, but in fact, it's merely an aside, a taste of the future. We aren't made to hope that Starling will catch him before he starts killing or fear that Lecter will turn his attentions to her. We aren't encouraged to start all over again. That would be a major mistake; that would destroy the effectiveness of the resolution or make it seem incomplete. Making the final resolution, *the* resolution, feel incomplete goes directly against the reason we enjoy stories—because they end. We are made to care, we have our emotions wrung from us, and then we are released from our involvement.

In *Shakespeare in Love* we have a similar pointer to the future without any destruction of the resolution of the story. It is determined that Viola will be with Wessex and travel to the Colonies while Will must stay in London. This is the resolution. The writing of *Romeo and Juliet* is complete and all the parts of Will's life that were affected by the writing of the play are completed: his love affair with Viola, his position in the theater, his position as a writer-for-hire, even the attention of the Queen. Yet we are brought into the idea for his next play and his use of Viola as his muse-in-absentia for that play. We aren't made to hope and fear about it, we aren't made to worry about Will's future, but we are encouraged to look at it from the satisfied position of resolution. We have been freed from minute-to-minute caring while at the same time allowed to believe that life will go on for the characters. We can go home and fondly recall our involvement in the lives of the characters and know their lives will go on and have hardships, but we are no longer actively concerned.

SUBPLOTS

Weaving subplots in with the main story line is a major part of organizing material into the final structure of a screenplay, so now is a good time to have a clear understanding of what subplots are and how they function within a story. The first question is logically, do we need subplots? Clearly we've gone this far discussing stories with only an occasional mention of subplots, so maybe we can dispense with them. After all, we have lots of material on our main character, his story and all the wants and obstacles and conflicts. The crucial moments of the story don't require subplots; they necessarily are about the protagonist and the main story line. Why complicate our lives with having to devise more stories to stuff inside what already looks like an overflowing package? There are very good reasons why the overwhelming majority of films have at least one—and often as many as three or four—subplots.

So what is a subplot? A subplot is a story with a beginning, middle, and end; it has its own tension and culmination and resolution; and it is a story that belongs to a secondary character. Nearly everything that we have dealt with concerning the protagonist and developing the story from within his character and his wants and strengths and weaknesses applies to subplots and their "central characters." The antagonist or best friend or love interest might be the focus of a subplot, meaning the tension of the subplot stems from the want of that secondary character, not from the protagonist of the overall story. Each of your significant secondary characters potentially carries a subplot, but there is no automatic guarantee that they all will. Subplots should not distract from or diminish the main story. They shouldn't take us off to a different world so completely that we lose our primary focus, which must remain on the protagonist's story. So the subplot must somehow be subordinate to the main story, thematically related, within the same world as the main story, and play out under the overall structure of the protagonist's story. No wonder we ask whether we can dispense with subplots altogether.

The Role of Subplots

Even a cursory cost-benefit analysis of subplots reveals a significant cost in terms of thinking, planning, organizing, weaving the subplot story into the main story, the potential for distraction or diminishment of the main story, and overall difficulty in conception and follow-through. So a subplot needs a substantial benefit to offset this cost. As usual, the benefit is to be found in the experience the whole story, including subplots, gives to the audience. With no subplots, a protagonist's story—no matter how compelling and difficult it is for the character and the audience—will usually feel one-sided and lacking in context. We are getting only one experience of this character's problem or dilemma or want. No one else in the story rises to a significant enough level of importance for us to get involved in his or her life and wants. The story seems to take on a tunnel vision. There might be wonderful and exciting things happening in that tunnel, but we will subliminally start to wonder if there is a world outside of the tunnel, outside of this singular pursuit and want. Subplots satisfy this need to surround the story with a broader world, with characters of depth, with other views of the same want or dilemma. We have a vastly broader experience in a story that contains a subplot or two than we would in the same protagonist's story without these second-level stories against which to measure and compare and reflect. This benefit far outweighs the cost of creating and managing subplots.

Just as a good protagonist needs and deserves a worthy antagonist—and an antagonist's subplot may well fulfill the function of creating worthiness—a protagonist also needs and deserves others around him who rise to the level of "life." A character with a subplot is more likely to come alive than one whose life we don't enter and in which we never become involved. As has been discussed at length, our becoming involved in a story stems from our having interest in the character and then our being made privy to the wants and hopes and fears of the character. When we go through this same process with a few secondary characters, they become fleshed out, our experience of the story and its world is broadened, and we have explored "worthy" characters around our protagonist.

By spending time with and becoming involved in the lives of the secondary characters—forming hopes and fears about their futures in addition to the main character's future—the story plays a broader spectrum of "notes." No matter how much you vary the obstacles and potential solutions in the course of the second act, in a story with no subplots there could come a time where it seems as if you've been harping relentlessly on only slightly varied aspects of the same want, been playing the same note too many times in a row. Subplots give you a chance to vary the notes and change the tune without throwing out the primary melody—the protagonist's journey. You can give the main story a rest for a scene or two and turn your concerns to a secondary story before you come back to the main story in full force. This kind of "breather" actually will enable the audience to give a greater emotional commitment to the main story.

The ability of the subplot to take us away from the main story, yet continue to be connected to it, particularly comes into play in the second act, where we are following the main tension for roughly half the entire film. We can get bits and pieces of the love story subplot along the way, then take a break altogether for a number of scenes when a subplot takes over and the main story is put on the back burner to simmer for a while. Refreshed from the change of scenery we got from the subplot, we can come back to the main story recharged, our emotions renewed, and we are ready for more with our protagonist.

BASIC DRAMATIC STRUCTURE

Subplot Characters

Which characters from your group around the main character
warrant subplots? Do you have to give a story to each of them?
How many subplots is too many? How do you find the wants for
the subplots? How do you keep from creating an unnecessary
subplot around a character whom you need in the story?

Perhaps the best starting point for these questions is to look
at a relatively simple story, one that is practically a two-person
story. *Misery* has Paul Sheldon imprisoned by his "number-one
fan." The main story is Sheldon's and has to do with his efforts
to escape his increasingly dangerous entrapment. But Annie
Wilkes has a major subplot, which revolves around the creation
of the new *Misery* novel to bring the fictional character back to
life. There is also a second subplot: Buster, the sheriff who looks
for the writer who went missing in a blizzard in his county, has
a subplot story. But the sheriff's wife, who has nearly as much
screen time as her husband, doesn't have a subplot. Let's explore
these three secondary characters and their relationship to creating subplots. Perhaps the first thing you'll notice about Annie's
subplot is that, though the want of her story belongs to her, it directly involves the protagonist. She wants something directly
from him. This is a hallmark of a well-built subplot. Though the
subplot tension belongs to a secondary character, it still involves
the protagonist in some way. The tension is about the relationship of the secondary character to the main character. The same
is true of the sheriff's story—he wants to find the protagonist, so
his tension is also about the main character. But the sheriff's
wife wants nothing from the protagonist or about the protagonist. Her only concern seems to be about the sheriff himself,
and we are not made sufficiently curious about where that is going to create a story. We aren't given a sense of uncertainty
about the future between them.

This question is the key to whether or not a character has a
subplot: Is there uncertainty about that character's future created for us and made important to us? If there is, then you're
well on the way to creating a subplot from that character. Then

the other element must come into play: What does the character want from or through or with or in spite of his relationship with the protagonist? If what the character wants is utterly tangential to the protagonist and his story, then the subplot will have an uneasy place in the story and might become detrimental to the whole. If the sheriff wants to write a book—and it's not about the missing author in his district—and spends his time alone with his own typewriter, we will rightly wonder what his story is doing inside Paul Sheldon's story. It won't be made out of the same material as the main story. If Annie spends all of her time and energy on her collection of figurines and pays no attention to her captive and those figurines have no influence on her relationship to the writer or her conduct of her kidnapping, then again, we'll wonder why such material is in this story.

So first look to the characters with whom you have surrounded your protagonist and determine if you have already created some uncertainty about their future. Probably you will have done so with some and not with others. With the ones about whom there is some uncertainty, you must determine what they want that is creating that uncertainty. If what they want has nothing whatsoever to do with the protagonist or the main story or their relationship to the protagonist, then those characters may not be useful and might even have to be diminished or adjusted. If a secondary character wants something from or about the protagonist and we have some interest in the character and some uncertainty about the future as a result of that want, then there is a subplot in place, ready to be woven into the overall story. If any of those elements is weak, then it needs bolstering to generate the right level of interest, uncertainty, and relationship to the protagonist.

There could be a circumstance when the second most important character in your whole story doesn't seem to have a subplot. This is generally a problem and one that should be solved early in the story-building process. The problem may stem from trying to put too many aspects of the story on the shoulders of the protagonist. There is a tendency to put both the main want on the protagonist as well as the want of—for instance—the love story subplot. This will necessarily divide the audience's loyalties, because there will come a time when the main story comes into conflict with the subplot. If both wants are carried by the protagonist, then we will be uncertain of which way our loyalties can best be tied to the protagonist. It's a far better strategy to give the love story subplot to the love interest—make the want driving that subplot hers, not the protagonist's. This doesn't mean you can only have a subplot in which the love interest wants love from the protagonist; the want driving the love subplot could be her attempts to hold him at bay or to match him up with her sister only to fall in love with him herself.

The Annie subplot in *Misery*, while obviously not a love subplot, could easily have been misdirected onto the story's protagonist. He could have come up with the idea of writing a book just for his captor and convinced her to give him a chance to do it "for her" as a strategy in his overall effort to escape his prison. But then Annie would have no real want of her own, and Sheldon's efforts to use the writing of the book for his own ends would become fuzzy. It is a far better strategy to give the want that propels this story line—the book written throughout the film—to Annie so that it can deepen our understanding of the character; we can see her own strategies and peek through windows into her inner life. We will feel no divided loyalty when the effort to escape comes into direct conflict with the desire to have the book written.

Truly important characters—such as the second character in an essentially two-character story—generally need subplots of their own. If there is no story for this character to pursue, it usually means we are being kept outside the character. But there are instances where you might not want to explore the inner life, for instance, of the antagonist. For example, in *The Terminator*, a three-person story, we have Sarah's story about survival, the main story. We also have Kyle's story, which is the love story. Then we have the Terminator himself; he does not have a subplot story even though he is the title character and has every bit as much screen time as Kyle. Looking at how and why this is done helps us to understand how best to use our subplot efforts to support and strengthen the protagonist's story. Kyle wants to save Sarah, but a large part of why is that he has been in love with her for many years, from the stories told him by his friend, Sarah's not-yet-conceived son. Kyle carries the want that creates the love story—and ironically conceives the son, his friend. We have interest in Kyle, we are given his backstory, we are made uncertain about his future and his interest in Sarah—it is a complete and fully fleshed-out subplot. Even though the Terminator wants something from Sarah—he wants to kill her—that want is simply wrapped up in the main story line. Without his wanting to kill Sarah, there would be no main story. He doesn't have an inner life, and we aren't encouraged to have any feelings about his future other than as they impact Sarah.

The two characters are dealt with in opposite ways and elicit opposite results. We delve into Kyle and his life and hopes and dreams extensively, particularly as they involve Sarah and her unborn son. This familiarity with his inner life fosters our interest and uncertainty about his future. Add his want to that and we have a subplot. We don't delve into the Terminator at all as an individual. We aren't made interested or curious or uncertain about his personal future—we are kept distant from his inner life—and even though he has a strong want, there is no subplot from the character. If a subplot had been created for the Terminator—he had an inner life and wants and doubts—it would have fostered some level of sympathy in the audience. In this story, a sympathetic or understandable antagonist would have been less compelling than a killing machine that seemingly couldn't be stopped. Similarly, we are not made privy to the inner life of the shark in *Jaws* for exactly the same reason—it wouldn't be in the best interest of the story to create the understanding that would stem from a full subplot.

When there are a number of characters around the protagonist, the choices of which ones have subplots and which don't can be difficult. If one character is decidedly more important than the others, he's a likely subplot character. But there may well be characters in the world of the story who are important, even crucial, yet don't warrant subplots of their own. Instead, they might be supporters in other characters' subplots. *Shakespeare in Love*, with its large cast, is worth exploring. The main story is Will's and concerns the writing of the play. The principal subplot is Viola's and is the love story. There is a fine subplot with Fennyman, the moneylender, who falls in love with the theater. Lord Wessex has a small subplot concerning his bet with Will about a play depicting love, but his primary function is as the other side of the love triangle in Viola's subplot. And Burbage has a subplot about the future of theaters in London, which intersects with Will. First Burbage wants a play from Will and eventually he offers his theater for a performance of his play. But Henslowe, the theater owner, who enjoys more screen time than either Burbage or Wessex, does not have a subplot, even though it is his feet that are held over a fire in the very opening of the story. He helps personify Will's desire to write the play; he functions both as a sounding board and as a conscience for what it is that Will wants. Viola's nurse, who enjoys considerable screen time, also is not given a subplot. Just like Henslowe in the main story, she is there as an assistant to the carrying of the love story, helping to reveal Viola's inner life.

So significant secondary characters can have their own subplots, even if they are small ones, or they can function as reflective characters in support of someone else's story. Either function earns their inclusion in the story. How you choose which characters go in which category comes down partly to what is already in the story and partly to finding wants that help to support and flesh out the main story—thematically, emotionally, even factually. You shouldn't feel obligated to give subplots to every single significant character. The better strategy is to explore which of your secondary characters can best carry stories that tie back in to the main story, the protagonist and the theme of the story, and which secondary characters best function solely as reflections of larger stories—the main story or a primary subplot. As we've seen with Lord Wessex in *Shakespeare in Love*, a character can do both.

How many subplots can we have? If one is the usual minimum, what's the usual maximum and why? Two or three subplots are quite common; even having four subplots isn't too distracting from the main story. But if you try to stretch much past that in a normal-scale film, the subplots will start to steal time from each other. Worse still, too many subplots could distract from the main story and your ability to flesh out characters, conflicts, and obstacles. Screen time and the audience's ability to focus are the determining—and limiting—factors. You want the subplots to be in support of the protagonist and his story, not detracting or distracting from them. If you push the limits and create five subplots or six, meaning a total of six or seven stories in the screenplay, you may well have pushed into the realm of an ensemble story and out of the realm of a story with a clearly defined central character. As long as you know this and can control it, there is nothing wrong with telling an ensemble story. The problem is when it's done without knowing it or without the finesse to pull it off.

Beginning, Middle, and End

For the sake of clarity, let's not call the three parts of a subplot three acts. That could be confusing. However, a subplot does have three parts; it has a beginning, middle, and end, just like the overall story and sequences. Anytime a tension is created, there will be three parts—creating the tension, elaborating on it, and ending it. So a subplot, as a tension-based organism, has three parts. But there is more latitude in how these are dealt with in subplots than in either sequences or the overall story. The proportions of screen time given to each part can vary greatly, and the three parts can be placed nearly anywhere within the larger story.

Because subplots are generally focused on some aspect of the relationship between the subplot character and the protagonist or his story, elements of the creation of the subplot tension could already be in play in the main story. The material of the main story could clearly be affecting both the protagonist and the subplot character. For instance, they are together in a sinking ship. The major difference between the two stories would be in approach to that material, because of the strengths, weaknesses, blind spots, obsessions, and all the other signs of inner life of the subplot character. This different approach creates a want for

the subplot character that is different from the want of the protagonist. In such a circumstance, the first part of the subplot
story might be quite short. It could contain only what is needed
to reveal the different approach the subplot character has to the
same story circumstances. A larger portion of the subplot's screen
time could then be devoted to the second part—how he differs in
approach to the same circumstances—or to the third part—the
result for the subplot character, which is different from the protagonist's resolution.

But the middle of the subplot might be far less than half of the
total subplot screen time, or the third part might be dispropor-
tionately small or large. Because, as we'll discover, subplots float
inside of the larger narrative, how much time is apportioned to
the three necessary parts is much less critical. The proportion of
the parts will barely be noticed by the audience, because the parts
are usually separated by other story material. Whichever part
gives us the greatest understanding of the character and his relationship to the protagonist and main story is the part that should
be given the most emphasis. The sheriff in *Misery* is a fine example. Once Sheldon's car is found and Buster thinks the circumstances are odd, the first part is over; it's quite brief. At the other
end, once he arrives at Annie's house, he has found the writer and
has his suspicions confirmed. Very little of Buster's screen time is
devoted to the interval between his discovery of Sheldon and his
own death, which ends his subplot. Here the major portion of the
subplot has been devoted to the middle part, the search for the
protagonist. This serves a great function in the story, because it
prolongs and encourages our hope that the writer will be rescued.
Before someone looks for him, we can't have hope for his rescue,
and once he is found, he can't be rescued by an outsider or it would
undermine the protagonist's need to complete his own story. It's in
this middle section that the meat of this subplot creates the most
effective drama.

But look at Fennyman in *Shakespeare in Love*. At first he considers theater simply a moneymaking operation; then he discovers the wonder and joy of it and falls head over heels in love with
the theater. Here the screen time has been reserved primarily for
a protracted exploration of his newfound love for what it is that

Will creates—drama on the stage. While he generally wants something from Will—the play and his role in it—Fennyman's subplot is more thematically tied to the story than driven by his direct connection to Shakespeare. His transformation from indifference to love of theater helps amplify the purpose of all the struggles Will goes through in his process of creation. The bit with the cleric who decries the theater as decadent and ends up wailing in tears of joy at the play plays like a miniversion of Fennyman's subplot, a brief reminder of his larger transformation and a thematic echo of why all these people—our primary cast—rightly care about drama.

Resolution of Subplots and Main Plot

Unlike sequences, subplots have complete resolutions of their own. Our concern for the future of the subplot character and his want must be ended definitively or the resulting vestiges could interfere with the main story. Why is it that these resolutions don't stop the forward progress of the main story? How can you get away with these complete resolutions when all the other parts must be kept going with partial resolutions and overlapping tensions? The answer comes back to the source of the want of the subplot; the subplot character's want in some way relates to the protagonist and/or his story. So even when the subplot is resolved, its completion simply reverts our attention to the ongoing story of the protagonist. As we see with Buster in *Misery,* the resolution of the subplot—the death of the would-be rescuer—actually can increase our tension in the main story. In this case, we no longer hold out any hope of there being a rescue; when that subplot is resolved, our protagonist is desperately alone with his dilemma.

Whenever possible, strive to resolve your subplots before the resolution of the main story. This is stagecraft—you don't want to steal thunder from your main story by making a lot of noise with competing resolutions. However, trying to force early resolution to subplots is worse than allowing them to end after the primary resolution. Whenever possible, you should resolve the subplots first, and each subplot resolution should be given its own moment at center stage. *Shakespeare in Love* provides several examples. Burbage's subplot, in which he discovers his true enemy is not other theater owners but the censorious Tilney, is resolved early in the third act when he offers his theater for the premiere of *Romeo and Juliet*. Fennyman's subplot is resolved when he seeks and receives Will's approval for his performance in the play. But Viola's subplot and Lord Wessex's subplot are actually resolved after the main story, and for good reason. With Wessex, the subplot is just a small externalization of the success of the play; it gives the Queen an opportunity to declare the play truthful and good. This subplot about the wager couldn't be completed until the play is performed and given the Queen's approval. Because the wager is with his rival rather than with the Queen or someone else, this last little success of Will's helps to set up the final moments of the story, in which he will fail at what we all hope for—Viola's continued love and presence in his life.

The love story, Viola's subplot, is the very last thing to be resolved. Here the reason has everything to do with the subject of the story and how the third act plays out. Imagine if the love story had been definitively resolved before the performance of *Romeo and Juliet*. Wouldn't that virtually destroy the performance of the play? The lovers have to be allowed to act out their love, if only for one performance. Delaying the resolution of this subplot until after the main story is resolved—the play is written, performed, and granted public and royal praise—allows both parts to rise to their maximum level of emotion and suspense. But doesn't this then steal the thunder from our main story's resolution? Potentially it could, but in this case, it had to be delayed in order to allow the main resolution to have its full thunder. If we knew for absolute certain that Viola was going to go off with Wessex after the play, then the very subject matter of the play would be undermined—and so would Will's resolution.

Most of the time, you want the main resolution last. It's the moment the audience has been waiting for—first in general terms, and then in increasingly specific terms. Once our emotions are spent on the final resolution, there usually is very little story left to tell. Once Luke proves his Jedi powers and blows up the

Death Star in *Star Wars*, there isn't much to do but give medals to everyone. Once Captain Miller finds Private Ryan and manages to extract him from a circumstance of nearly certain death—at the price of his own life—there isn't much left to do. Once Agent Starling has successfully stopped Buffalo Bill and saved his last victim, what more is there to do in *The Silence of the Lambs*? There is a coda about Lecter, but his subplot was actually resolved back when he escaped.

Once Schindler has managed to keep his group of Jews alive until the end of the war, there is one more thing to be done. Here we have Stern's subplot being completed after the main resolution, again because of the needs of the story. Stern, as representative of the saved Jews and all victims of the Nazis, can't fully thank Schindler for his success until that success is complete. It's interesting to discover that when there is a single vestigial subplot it is often the love story or concerns the protagonist's personal growth, when the main story has been about striving for success. The real love story in *Schindler's List* is Stern's story. It's about approval, acceptance, belief in Schindler's commitment. Viola's subplot is the love story in *Shakespeare in Love*, where the main story is about the creation of the play. In *Witness*, the love story is also resolved after the main story, which is about saving the boy from the killers. Yet it isn't always the love story that performs this subplot function. In *One Flew over the Cuckoo's Nest*, the resolution comes with McMurphy's death, but the resolution of Chief's subplot—his flight from the cuckoo's nest—follows McMurphy's resolution. Here we have the subplot completing the mission of the protagonist when his resolution is failure. The mechanism remains the same in all these instances. When the main story hinges on an outside accomplishment of the protagonist—whether he succeeds or fails is irrelevant—there is a greater likelihood of needing a subplot to resolve later. The reason comes back to the audience and its relationship to character. Usually we would much rather experience our last feelings about the protagonist on a personal level than on a success or outwardly defined level. If that personal level is carried by the subplot instead of the main story, this subplot is more likely to be the last resolved.

As a group, the ends of all the stories—main story and all

subplots—usually should represent a variety of resolutions. If our primary story ends in success for the protagonist, there should probably be a failure somewhere in the story, and the most likely place is in a significant subplot. The reverse is equally true. When McMurphy dies—indirectly at the hands of Nurse Ratched and the system against which he so valiantly railed—that failure is partly ameliorated by the successful escape of Chief. When Shakespeare wins as a playwright, he loses as a lover. Though Starling succeeds in stopping the serial killer and rescuing his last victim, she fails to keep another serial killer captive, and the onus of that failure is partly on her for the deal she instigated with him. While John Book successfully protects his witness from the police-killers, he isn't able to fulfill the love of the boy's mother.

When there are multiple subplots, there usually should also be some bittersweet or mixed resolutions; unless the main resolution is mixed, the subplots should be contrasted in some way. What we are looking for is a variety of experiences. Recall the notion that the third act is dominated by philosophy. If you want to tip your hand—as opposed to remaining the invisible philosopher/manipulator behind the scenes of the whole story—you could have every story resolve the same way. Everyone ends in tragedy or everyone gets his cake and eats it too. This sameness might work in a story that reaches the difficult and rarely met height of true tragedy—*Hamlet* comes to mind. But in the realm of drama, where the vast majority of screenwriting takes place in today's cinema, spreading the various story resolutions over a spectrum is generally a more effective choice. It gives the audience the chance to laugh and cry, to feel good with one character and sad with another, to balance off the main story against the smaller stories around it for a complex feeling and final relationship with the whole story.

It isn't impossible, nor is it always destructive of the final screenplay, to have an ending that is happy all the way around or sad or failure-based for everyone. The ultimate experience the story gives to the audience is simpler and more one-sided than it could have been, but this may be the intent. Certainly with a children's film, a complicated final experience often isn't the goal. But beginners often get themselves into trouble with the downer ending. Anything smacking of a happy ending, even for a subplot character, is anathema to some starting screenwriters. They have the feeling that only something heavy and downbeat can ever achieve seriousness and be worthwhile. So with this "philosophy" in mind—I want my story to be taken seriously, so everyone has to die an awful death or suffer horribly—they wreak havoc on their characters. It works in *Hamlet*, right? It does indeed work in *Hamlet*, but that play also has a tragic protagonist, one who reaches the very height of tragic hero. It also wasn't Shakespeare's first play.

The likely result of this "everyone must die" impetus is that the story will be diminished and become more simplistic than it could have been if there had been more care and discretion put into the treatment and resolution of the various interwoven stories. Generally, whether your story is a wild comedy or a true tragedy, wherever it sits on the spectrum of drama, you usually will be better served by offering a variety of resolutions from among the several stories you tell. They don't negate each other; they make the audience's emotional completion more complex.

How to Weave in Subplots

Subplots come in a variety of shapes and sizes, some with emphasis on the first part, some the second or third part. They can be contained entirely within a single sequence or span essentially the same length of the story as the main story. Some subplots begin and end within the second act and even—rarely—they can occur in their entirety in the first or third act. And most subplots resolve before the main story resolves. Most of the time, the segments of a subplot are strewn throughout the other story material for a sizable period of the story, meaning it is quite possible for the audience to lose the thread of the subplot between segments and need reminding or renewal. This makes the management and organization of subplots a difficult task, one that can't be done independently of building the main story from beginning to end. First the overall shape of the screenplay must be created through the main character's story, but the existence and shape of the subplots should also be dealt with before much of the meat is hung on the skeleton of the story.

Here arises another chicken-and-egg dilemma: How can you know for sure what your subplots will be while you're still working out your main story? You can't and shouldn't expect to. It's better simply to push the main story forward to a somewhat satisfying position, stop, and look to see how this new position impacts the lives of the other characters and what they may or may not want within the context of the story. Experiment a little with the stories the secondary characters might carry and see how they could affect your main story. By trial and error, you can inch your way forward and, in the process, perhaps even discover the thematic link between your subplots and main story. Continue with this trial and error until you have a clearer idea of which characters will probably have subplots and which ones will be reflective and supportive of aspects of the protagonist or a subplot character.

As we will discover, there is even a sequence that typically is dominated by the chief subplot, and any sequence that belongs to a secondary character is focused on that character's subplot. But in the absence of a subplot reaching sequence level, there are still guideposts to look for when first attempting to weave subplots into the overall story. It is crucial to keep the secondary character true to his own wants and inner life, rather than make him conveniently serve the protagonist's goals. This means the character's through-line should be explored. The through-line is an extraction of this character's story—his wants, actions, and the events in which he participates—from the overall story. Remember, the characters don't know who the protagonist is. They all believe they are the main character; this is their life. Does the secondary character obey his own wants and pursue his own goals, or does he simply perform a function for the protagonist that goes against his own self-interest and inner drives?

By exploring the through-line of each significant character you can discover where you have forced characters to do things that aren't in their nature. This often happens because you need the character to throw himself on a grenade to save the hero, or give up his love for the girl because she must be free to love your protagonist. If these events are crucial to our story, then you have to find the inner drives of the secondary characters that propel them to these actions. When you explore the through-line of a secondary character, you should always be able to identify what inner need or want or desire or obsession or failing makes the actions of the character personally justifiable and believable. In other words, you have to hold the secondary characters to the same standards of motivation that you hold for the protagonist.

While you are assessing his through-line, you are then also exploring the subplot any secondary character might carry. These characters must be true to themselves in their actions. They must act from self-interest, however that might manifest itself, not out of obedience to the plot or the author. You must know what the secondary character wants, which is a major part of the creation of his subplot—he wants something and has difficulty getting it. A subplot character wants something from or for or in spite of the protagonist, which is what ties the subplot to the main story. By extracting the through-line, you have a chance to assure a logical progression of the events in which the subplot character participates. So in *Misery*, when Annie discovers Paul Sheldon has been roaming around the house looking for a means of escape, it's true to her want—getting the new book written—to pull out the sledgehammer and break the poor man's ankles. She is pursuing her want, following her own inner drives. When the sheriff learns Annie is buying reams of paper, he follows his own drive—to locate the missing writer—when he visits her house and snoops around.

By testing a subplot character's actions against his own wants, you are making certain the subplot makes sense from the point of view of its driving character, but you still haven't dealt with how it is woven into the fabric of the main story. Until now, most of your organizing efforts have been focused on finding smaller and smaller increments of story to build and control. But there is a limit to how small you can go in blocks of story material, and in subplots you see this limit in action. If you were to try to break a subplot into sequences, the resulting increments would be so small they could get lost and could lead to confusion. It's a better strategy to think primarily in terms of the subplot's beginning, middle, and end and to keep the character obedient to his own inner drives in intervening moments. Sometimes it might be necessary or desirable to use smaller bits and pieces of a subplot spread throughout a sequence—for instance, in establishing the subplot character's want. But generally speaking, you want to try to take the subplots in significant chunks wherever possible. Because the secondary character's wants are secondary, they are easier for the audience to forget than the protagonist's want. If you must remind the audience of a subplot character's want and story line, you don't want to have to spend too much screen time doing it. So remind them if it seems necessary, and then let a significant portion of a subplot play out in a relatively finite amount of screen time. It's a matter of narrative efficiency; you don't want to waste screen time with a lot of reminders of things we knew but lost in the hectic pace of the main story.

So when you are looking to weave your subplots together with the main story, you first determine the subplot as if it is its own self-contained story, then look for openings in which to place segments of the story in significant chunks. Since the subplot is thematically related to the main story and the characters who carry the subplots are wanting things from the protagonist, there likely will be segments of the subplots that stem from material similar to segments of the main story. The protagonist and his best friend are hanging from the side of a cliff as a blizzard is approaching. Their circumstances are similar, but who they are as people and as climbers are completely different. What they want are two different things. So you might elaborate on the protagonist's relationship to their dilemma—the main story—then do the exact same thing with the subplot character—his subplot. This affords you a good venue to contrast the two as well as to deepen our understanding of each of them as individuals.

The first place to look for logical and useful locations for subplot portions is where you have placed similar material from the main story. *Shakespeare in Love* provides a fine example. Viola carries the love story subplot while Will carries the play-writing main story. When these two become lovers it inspires Will to craft a masterful play while rehearsals go on. Since the play is a love story, his pursuit of his goal melds wonderfully with her pursuit of her goal, the love story. These two stories are interwoven throughout much of the film, but most intensely in a sequence during which Viola is drawn in two directions at once—obligation, meaning Wessex and the Queen, against true love, meaning Will and the theater. The placement of subplot story elements—Wessex courting her, her meeting with the Queen—in the midst of his story elements—the continuing evolution of the play in rehearsals—enables the two story lines to feed and spur each other. This becomes so seamless that it's difficult for the uninitiated to distinguish between main story and subplot.

Sometimes subplots are contained in their entirety within a single sequence. This will be particularly true in stories that have an episodic nature, such as road pictures. In this sort of story, you might have a new cast of characters in each episode along the road who interact with the one, two, or three people who are together on the journey. Though these episodes will likely belong to your protagonist or to one of his fellow travelers, you still might have a subplot played out completely during a single, sequence-long episode. The truck driver in *Central Station* is a fine example. All the sequences in the film belong either to Dora or Josué, but the truck driver becomes a significant player for one sequence and has a complete subplot during this limited time. He wants to help them, to be good and Christian. At first it is fairly easy and he is generous, then the boy and woman steal from his friend and he is forgiving, but when Dora begins to express interest in him, that scares him and he takes a most ungenerous and unhelpful means of escape—he slips away when they aren't looking. It's a complete story focused on his relationship with the protagonist and takes place solely in one sequence.

Perhaps the most common positioning of subplots within the overall story is having them span several sequences. Our warrior's love story with the seeker of the Holy Grail is a good example. At first he disapproves of her and her quest, which raises his interest in her, but not his love; this is in the first act. When she rises to the occasion and finds the map through wit, skill, and determination, he approves of and admires her; this perhaps is during the first sequence of the second act and is the end of the first part of the warrior's subplot. Then he manages to lead them past the alligators to his friend who can read the map, and he rises in her estimation; this is probably the second sequence of the second act. Now they are both interested, so the third sequence of the second act may well be the warrior's sequence and be primarily about the love subplot. By the end of this sequence, they are in love. He will do anything for her and her quest. This is the bulk of the subplot, but there is still more to happen. Will they be able to stay together? When they get to the Grail's location and find the dragon, it's the culmination of the main story—they find the Grail. This last sequence of the second act has probably contained very little of the subplot. But now comes the true test—the warrior must face the dragon to protect his love and her quest, but we know this once froze him in the past. It could be that he dies in the battle with the dragon and the final resolution of the love subplot comes in his dying declaration or their death-bed marriage by the priest we have conveniently brought on this journey. Once the subplot is resolved, then we're back to the main story until the end. The subplot has been spread out through all three acts and has one sequence nearly all its own, and its resolution comes before the main story is resolved.

THE CLASSICAL SCREENPLAY
STRUCTURE

What is ideal or classical in a story confers no more importance and exclusivity than having 20-20 vision. If you can, you want to have good eyesight, but if you can't, you live with it and put your efforts elsewhere. If you had to make a choice between 20-20 vision and normal blood pressure, "ideal" vision would lose out. When creating a story, these are the kinds of decisions you have to make. You should know the ideals, the norms and averages— what is classical—but at the same time, you must remain aware that "classical" isn't a mold for creating a perfect story. Somewhere there will be variations from the ideal, and it may well be that the variations are the source of what is most interesting in the story.

So you must study the classical screenplay structure, but you shouldn't pursue it as if it's a recipe. It's not wise to aspire to make every single part of one's story "ideal" as if that confers value or is a measure of quality. Instead, you should look at classical structure as something of a guide, not unlike the guidelines for ideal weights or cholesterol levels. These are not commandments and the people who made them are not gods. But "the prevailing wisdom" included in guidelines should not be totally ignored or flaunted, either. The key is in balancing all the considerations and conflicting needs in order to make wise, informed decisions. Know the classical story structure inside and out, but don't become a slave to it.

How did we get classical structure anyway? Didn't Hollywood

force some kind of formula on all of us? Much as you might want to idealize or vilify Hollywood, either as a place or as a sensibility, Hollywood isn't to blame—if blame is warranted for classical screenplay structure. The roots lie in ancient Greece and Aristotle, while the trunk grows through France and England in the nineteenth and early twentieth centuries. Remember, cinema as a storytelling vehicle was invented near the beginning of the twentieth century, and most of the early writers for this new art form came from the theater of that time. While these pioneers searched for an effective means of using this new system of delivering a story to an audience, they naturally fell back on what they knew about storytelling and drama from the theater. Aristotle was the acknowledged pinnacle of dramatic theory, and his ideas found their way into film storytelling just as surely as they influenced European and world theater and literature before it.

Many recognizable remnants of Aristotle can be found in this and all books on film storytelling. Among them are the assertions that drama (tragedy in the *Poetics,* but a close enough approximation for this analysis) produces a catharsis between pity (read hope) and fear; that drama uses elements of dance, melody (including timing and being time-based), and spectacle; that drama should be brief and direct (meaning intense); and that concentration (more intensity) brings power to the work. Aristotle also suggested that both the action (pursuit of a want) and protagonist should be singular; actions should have beginnings and ends; and events should follow one another in apparently necessary sequence. These basic principles found their way into most European drama from the sixteenth century on.

In the early nineteenth century the "well-made play" came into lasting popularity. Many plays of today still adhere to many or most of its basic tenets: the use of secrets; the creation and major use of suspense; early exposition of backstory; precisely timed entrances and exits; planting and withholding information; extreme highs and lows for the protagonist in his quest; a logical and believable resolution growing out of the story rather than superimposed on the story and characters; and some kind of moral judgment, reflective of the audience's moral standards, implied in the resolution.

Major early proponents of the well-made play were Eugène

Labiche, Victorien Sardou, Alexandre Dumas *fils*, and Georges Feydeau. After more than half a century of popularity, these plays and playwrights were attacked in France by Émile Zola, who proposed his theory of naturalism, and in England by George Bernard Shaw. Ironically, both Zola and Shaw made liberal use of many aspects of the well-made play in their own works, while in Norway, Henrik Ibsen, the father of realism, incorporated much of the well-made play stagecraft into his many works. The turn of the nineteenth to the twentieth century saw the theater infused with many vigorous and sometimes competing ideas: pure entertainment, often found in the well-made plays of the day; naturalism, which demanded intelligible motives behind human actions, from both social and personal causes; and realism, with its emphasis on believable and recognizable human behavior.

Out of this cauldron, the beginning of film storytelling was born. As you can see, the underpinnings of what we discuss here a century later still adhere to those sometimes warring notions. Early cinema fused singular protagonists and intensity from Aristotle with suspense and timing and morality from the well-made play, which it then bonded with motivated actions from naturalism and recognizable behavior from realism. All of these elements were developed over time and were extended when sound was added to the visual dynamism of film. This sense of how to tell a story in film spread throughout the world's national cinemas. It stuck for the simple reason that it worked extremely well.

From this birth in European theater, the underlying mode of telling a story in film was brought to America with the import of European writers, directors, and producers who were largely responsible for inventing and developing what came to be known as Hollywood. So if you need to lay blame or credit, place it there; if you feel confined and constricted by the idea that there even is an ideal, a classical cinematic storytelling form, blame Shaw and Ibsen and Zola and Labiche and Aristotle. Or, more appropriately, thank them. What they did was lay the groundwork for and help invent what were essentially the "norms" against which you can measure your stories to see how you are doing. These norms aren't laws or commandments, and they aren't there to be copied precisely. Nor should you force yourself into compliance with an abstract classical ideal. But this classical ideal can be a barometer of the "health" of your stories. The classical screenplay story structure is a warning device. It can help you discover when you are severely off course, and it can stand as an example of ideals to follow in your own unique ways.

What is this fabled classical structure you have now vowed not to use as a set of commandments? How does it work with all that we've discussed? How could all those great Old World playwrights have given us something that works with sequences when, in fact, sequences weren't invented until feature film stories were first being told? Remember, the playwrights at the cusp of the nineteenth and twentieth centuries provided the setting from which the early screenwriters sprang and the theories of drama from which they picked and chose, but they were not the inventors of this new form. Just as picture editing and the addition of sound took time to invent, so too did the mode of story structure we now consider classical. Some of the invention of the eight-reel feature was through trial and error, and a lot of it was from gut instinct that stemmed from the inventors' theatrical background. With the articulation by Frank Daniel of sequences as a distinct element in the creation of story structure came a major leap forward in understanding the interplay of the chapters of a film and the form that had been created and honed by trial and error and instinct. It is this weaving of sequences with acts and the ebb and flow of tensions, subplots, obstacles, and crucial moments that we will be exploring below, sequence by sequence, in the classical paradigm of two sequences in Act I, four in Act II, and two in Act III.

Main Character's Undisturbed Status Quo

The first sequence, as mentioned earlier, has its own set of problems stemming in part from the fact that the story hasn't begun yet, in part from the greater need for exposition at the outset of the story and the vulnerability of the audience to distraction from or resistance to involvement in the story. Nonetheless, a story has to start somewhere, and in the classical scheme, it starts with the life of the protagonist prior to the collision that will create the eventual story. We discover the main character in active pursuit of his own life, his undisturbed (precollision) status quo. The tension of this first sequence, the toughest to find and usually the weakest of the sequence tensions, should be about the life of the protagonist. It may well be about the "other plans" with which life (the collision and story) will interfere. This sequence should answer some basic "journalistic" questions for the audience: who, where, when, under what conditions? We don't necessarily meet the entire cast, but we do meet and get to know the protagonist and at least a few of the people who will contribute to his future and to the story. Of particular importance is identifying the protagonist as the true main character, more important than the other characters we meet from the beginning. We discover in what time period the story takes place and in what part of the world, real or imagined. We should also get our first indication of what version of the world the story will inhabit—the Napoleonic Wars of beautiful people in beautiful costumes with cannons and death in the distance, or the Napoleonic Wars of gruesome death, blood, and men-as-cannon-fodder.

One of the most crucial aspects of the first sequence is establishing the style of the story to be told, the mode of storytelling, and the worldview we are entering. While you might strive eventually to build contrasts between Napoléon at a grand ball and his men dying in the fields, this first sequence should give us some indication of the form of "realism" we can expect in our future. The opening minutes of the film should also give us an idea of how the story will be told in terms of our relationships with the characters. Can we see what any characters think, their memories or fantasies or dreams? Must we be with the protagonist in every single scene, or can we go where he does not? What is our relationship in this story to the flow of time? Will we have flashbacks or jumps forward? Will time be scrambled up or flow chronologically?

Whatever mode you will eventually need to use in all of these stylistic elements should be first planted in this opening sequence. When we start to watch a film, we will accept nearly anything presented as we become adjusted to this new story. Over the course of the first sequence we come to accept whatever we have been given as the "rules of the game" and expect them to continue for the rest of this story. If Peter Pan flies in the beginning of the story, we have no trouble with the other kids learning to fly later. But if we are an hour into an otherwise realistic story and someone learns to fly, we'll rebel and become estranged from the story. So this first sequence is the place to lure the audience into accepting whatever mode of storytelling you will need to use throughout the story. Even if you don't actually need to have a flashback, see a character's fantasy, or have him fly in the first sequence, you should incorporate that special element here as a way of giving yourself permission—inclusion in the rules of this particular story—for later use.

The same is true of tone. If you are making a comedy based on realistic underpinnings, you'd better make the audience laugh early. If not, they might not laugh at all, because they had been led to believe this story was not a comedy; we need early permission to laugh at the tragedies and foibles of the characters. How we are meant to take the story needs to be established early— romance, fable, comedy, gritty realism, nihilism, horror. In fact, any unique stylistic element—editing technique, use of time or sound or camera or point of view, supernatural elements or hyper-real elements—should be "planted" in the beginning of the story, in this first sequence. You don't have to give away all your secrets or spoil your surprises, but you should let the audience know some portion of the entire world you are drawing them into or they might refuse to follow when the crucial moment arrives. This jam-packed first sequence is the best opportunity to assure that the audience will follow where the story leads.

The first sequence often ends with the point of attack, which was dealt with earlier. By the middle of the first act we should have our first intimation of what will eventually create the collision that makes the story happen. So from a dead stop, popcorn-and-candy-eating people must be galvanized into an audience that has some idea of the style and tone of the story, knows approximately where and when it takes place, has identified a protagonist and learned something of his life and "other plans," and has even gotten the first hint of the coming upset to that status quo. It's not surprising that many beginners write monstrous first sequences. It's also understandable that the tension of this sequence can be hard to find and focus. Nevertheless, these are the needs of your first and very important sequence.

Creating the Dilemma

The second sequence creates the central dilemma of the story; this is where the collision occurs, and it ends with the establishment of the main tension. The focus of this sequence is usually considerably narrower than that of the first sequence, because you are now zeroing in on establishing the protagonist's want and main pursuit within the story. But it isn't simply a matter of racing hell-bent from the point of attack to the collision. The main tension of a story depends on the audience having three kinds of information: whose story this is, what that character wants, and some inkling of why that might be difficult to achieve within the world of this story. Often these three things are not in that order, but usually we will have identified the protagonist within the first sequence. So either you need to elaborate more on the world and potential conflicts or obstacles first, or you need to focus on the creation of the want within the protagonist. Both methods work perfectly well. In *Saving Private Ryan* we have ample demonstration of why any mission in the world of this story will be fraught with obstacles and conflicts, and then Captain Miller is given and accepts the assignment. In *One Flew over the Cuckoo's Nest* we quickly learn that McMurphy wants to leverage the psychiatric ward to his advantage, but before the main tension can fully begin, we have to learn why that might be difficult to do and, in this case, identify the antagonist.

It may be surprising to learn that this second sequence can sometimes belong to a character other than the protagonist. This can't work, of course, without firmly establishing the protagonist in the first sequence, but once that is done, you may well focus on the want of another character who carries with him the collision that will create the protagonist's story. In *Central Station*, the overall story is Dora's, but the second sequence begins with the point of attack, when the boy's mother is killed by a truck and the sequence belongs to the boy, Josué. He pursues his want—to find help—which is what creates the collision of Dora becoming involved in his life. As we've discussed, the main tension doesn't have to be overwhelmingly compelling from the first second, but it must be a tension. We must know there is the potential for difficulty in achieving the want the character has chosen to pursue. That information can come through another character—the antagonist may well own this sequence—as long as we see the potential for difficulty in the future of the protagonist once he chooses to pursue his want.

Because stories are about change within the protagonist, not just about the lives of the characters and the events involved in their pursuits of goals, the changeable part of the protagonist's life must also be developed within the first act. In all likelihood, that development is here in the second sequence, because there is some kind of relationship between the main dilemma facing the protagonist—the main tension—and the part of the character that will be tested and urged toward change. These are not disconnected elements; the main tension should directly play into the part of the character that must or might change. If the story is about a coward finding courage, then the story must deliver danger and opportunities for courage, some attempts that fail, and finally at least one that succeeds. If the story is about a change from being a hermit to being involved with others, then pressures involved in the main tension and its pursuit must eventually push for human interaction. Who the protagonist is in the first act is generally different from who he is in the third act, and it is the second act—the main tension and its pursuit—that is the vehicle of this change. Here you must plant the position of the protagonist from which he will change or from which he will strongly be pushed to change, even if, in the end, he does not succeed.

So the chores of the second sequence are: possibly to start with the point of attack if it wasn't in the first sequence; to create the circumstances that lead to the collision; to give us sufficient reason to believe there are potential conflicts and obstacles to the protagonist's course of action; to establish the position of the protagonist on the spectrum of his existence that will be changed or urged toward change; and, most importantly, to establish the main tension that will carry us throughout the second act. As part of establishing the main tension, the sequence must also prepare us for the protagonist's decision at the core of the main tension and give it enough emphasis that we realize we are at a turning point in this person's life.

Though this sequence doesn't have the breadth of demands that the first sequence must bear, other elements come into play during the creation of the critical elements listed above. You will continue to be introducing important characters, fleshing out the world of the story, and elaborating on the life of the protagonist. If there is a clearly defined outside antagonist, this character—or perhaps just the results of his actions—should probably be introduced here if we have not yet met him. Or perhaps you should clarify for the audience that the antagonist is a pretend friend, even if the protagonist doesn't know it. This can be crucial in the establishment of the main tension—the war between the two sides, which we understand even if the protagonist does not.

Elaborating on the Dilemma and the World of the Story

The third sequence, the beginning of the second act, comes after the audience has been hooked into the story. The protagonist has made a decision, we have reason to anticipate difficulties ahead for him, and we have taken some interest in him and his quest. Because the audience is hooked—it cares and anticipates—it will tolerate a slowdown, making this a good time to give more expositional information and to elaborate on things only briefly touched on in the first act. You may need to give more information on just how difficult the achievement of the want could become. You may need to provide more information on the nature of your protagonist and, in particular, his weaknesses and blind spots as they affect his quest. And you may have additional important characters to introduce.

Though you may now feel secure that our audience has enlisted to care about this story and your protagonist—they are indeed involved—you can't dispense with tension. So this sequence may house considerably more exposition and give us more information about obstacles and conflicts to come, but you still must establish and use tension for this sequence. This is where we first are in the frying pan with the main character; this is the first attempt to solve the dilemma or eliminate an obstacle or reach a possible solution. This sequence should contain the least arduous of your successive obstacles or the least difficult of your potential solutions because the second act should have ascending action, increasing difficulty from sequence to sequence.

This is the sequence in which your protagonist tries to deny the reality of his dilemma or tries to enlist someone else to solve it for him or tries to run away from it. This is also the sequence in which the protagonist should be locked into the story, if he has not already been locked in. Often the very nature of the decision creating the main tension locks the character into the story— Lindbergh takes off in the *Spirit of St. Louis* in his attempt to fly across the Atlantic. But sometimes the protagonist could still walk away, no harm done. If so, then you must find a way to lock the door. You don't want a prolonged circumstance where the character could simply change his mind about the decision and forget the whole enterprise. That will undercut the tension, which should be unswervingly rising. If he isn't locked in, we will subliminally begin to wonder why he doesn't just quit when things start to get really difficult. It's usually easy to identify stories that don't take care of this issue; everyone around the hero keeps asking, why are you doing this? The storytellers have felt the need to reinforce the protagonist's commitment by having him answer that question. It's far better simply to answer it once and for all in a major way. The most likely place to do that is within this sequence. Once he jumps out of that frying pan and into the fire, there's no going back; he's locked in and so are we.

First Potential Breakthrough

After the first attempt to deal with the major dilemma by the protagonist—whether that is simply gathering information, denying there is a problem, or asking someone else to fix it—the protagonist must make a more concerted effort. This is the nature of the fourth sequence. Generally this sequence belongs to the protagonist and includes some kind of breakthrough or direct approach to the issue. In *Shakespeare in Love*, Will is fervently writing the play and feverishly loving Viola. In *Central Station*, Dora has spent most of her money to buy tickets for them to the town in which the father is supposed to live, and they are directly (for a time) traveling toward that destination. Lindbergh has probably thrown off his early jitters from the near-crash at takeoff with his heavy load of fuel and is now hitting his stride, navigating by the stars, switching fuel tanks, enjoying the freedom.

So this sequence is dominated by the drive of the main character and the main tension; it is firmly focused on the protagonist and his quest. You already may be reaping some payoffs from earlier plants about the difficulty of the pursuit, or obstacles once warned of are now appearing on the horizon. Though other characters and their subplots may be afoot here, the major focus remains with your central character. You probably are not introducing new characters at this time; they would have been introduced in the third sequence, early in Act II, not here in the middle. This is also the first time in the story when you create sharply contrasting highs and lows for the protagonist's quest. You have established and extended both hope and fear, but now you are pushing those extremes closer together in time and farther apart in their extremes. In *The Terminator*, Sarah is taken in by the police and guarded by dozens of cops; our hope is encouraged. Then the Terminator breaks into the stationhouse and kills seemingly all of the Los Angeles Police Department; our fear is given a huge jolt. In *Central Station*, the sequence starts out hopeful—they are on the bus heading to the destination, what can go wrong? Then they both get drunk, and their conflict with each other comes out. She tries to ditch the boy, sending him the rest of the way alone—and our fear is pushed ahead. The highs and lows not only become stronger, but they are now closer, gaining strength from the immediacy of the contrast.

This fourth sequence ends with the midpoint, the halfway point in the second act and the pivotal center of the story. This first culmination of the second act has been dealt with earlier, but here we see it is the outgrowth of the first concerted effort by the protagonist to do or get or achieve his want. The midpoint sharpens the focus of the main tension, largely through the elimination of some alternative solutions or some obstacles. The search is more focused by the time the midpoint occurs or as a result of the midpoint event. In either case, this first culmination comes about because the protagonist has aggressively faced the dilemma and wrestled with it. Lindbergh has flown through the night and is now nodding off to sleep. Midpoint may be when he nearly crashes into the sea while asleep, only to save himself at the last second with a frantic maneuver. Viola declares to Will that she intends to marry Wessex, and Shakespeare seems to lose the muse who has made it possible for him to write the play so far. Dora ditches the boy after leaving him money, only to find he can't be ditched, though they still lose the money. Sarah can no longer turn to the Los Angeles police to save her from the Terminator; she must rely on her seemingly crazy rescuer from the future. In all of these cases, the main tension becomes refined and focused in large part because the protagonist has made his or her first serious attempt to solve the problem.

Main Subplot and Main Character

After the intensity of the midpoint, there is a tendency for a story to suffer what is known as second-act sag. This is a sense of letdown we experience after a major emotional event. Our hero has made a concerted effort and it has not had the result he and we had hoped. He might have succeeded in what he was trying to do, but that merely turned the dilemma upside down. Or he might have failed and the failure has made the predicament even worse. Either way, we have just come from a major high or low contrasting moment—the midpoint—and there is a tendency to sink, lose energy, or lose focus. The best way to overcome second-act sag is to let the major subplot take over for a while. We haven't yet had any truly significant change or first culmination in that second most important story, so it can arrive energized, hopeful or fearful, and very tense.

Lindbergh's publicist or wife can now take center stage for a while. Dora and Josué can get a ride from the truck driver, steal food from his friend, and turn their attentions to personal goals such as love. Sarah and Kyle take time out of their flight from the Terminator to fall in love and create the baby at the center of the struggle. Viola has declared her intention to marry Wessex and now our attentions are drawn to a wager over the depiction of love in a play, the rivalry with Burbage, and the untimely death of Christopher Marlowe. Here, because Viola's subplot has been so interwoven with the main story in the previous sequences, the lesser subplots are all brought together to form a distraction or lift up from the second-act sag.

This sequence does not absolutely have to belong to a secondary character, but there is a stronger likelihood here than in any other single sequence of a subplot taking center stage. However it is done, whether focusing on a single significant subplot or a number of smaller ones, you strive to distract the audience at this point from the main pursuit of the protagonist. This is a variation on preparation by contrast; you force the audience's mind to grapple with other issues for a time so that you can come back to the main issue renewed and revived, ready for a full frontal assault.

Greatest Exertion

The most major assault the protagonist is capable of mounting toward his original goal is the job of this sixth sequence, the last sequence in the second act. Like the fourth sequence, this one almost always belongs to the protagonist because it is so purely focused on the main tension, which must end by the finish of the sequence. The audience is refreshed from its breather of delving into other issues and is now ready for the emotional commitment that this last and biggest and most difficult attempt requires. If there's a cliff to climb or a sumo wrestler to pin to the mat, this is the sequence in which that most difficult obstacle is faced. Lindbergh is running low on fuel, flying through fog, has no idea where he is, and can't keep his eyes open. The challenge to his will has become its most intense. Sarah has the Terminator right on her tail with an arsenal in his hands and nothing between her and this killing machine except a mere, fallible human from the future, who then is wounded and needs her protection. Dora spends her last valuable, her watch, to get her and Josué a ride to the town his father supposedly lives in—only to find out that he's not there any longer. Will finishes writing his play, but his theater is closed, Viola marries Wessex, and the boy who is supposed to play Juliet goes through a voice change.

Many things that have been brewing in the main story begin to coalesce, making the attainment of the main tension goal seem nearly impossible. Not only does your hero finally have to get in the ring with the sumo wrestler, but he has an injured hand, is temporarily blind in one eye, and is distracted by the fact that his lover seems to be sitting on the lap of a fat-cat promoter at ringside. After getting out of the frying pan and escaping the fire, then clambering out of the broiler only to find himself inside the oven, the hero no longer seems to have any options and he has been burned and used up his water and the air supply is running out. At this point, everything is about that original goal, which is now refined and honed and sharpened into some kind of crisis situation.

When that final point is reached—there are only two possible ways to go, do or die—you are at the culmination of the story. There is an answer to the main tension question: success, failure, or transformation of the dilemma. Either Lindbergh gives up and lets the plane crash into the sea or he soars higher above the fog in his last, fuel-expensive effort to spot land. Either Sarah takes up her own defense or she, and eventually all life on earth, will die. Either Dora and Josué bond into a united team or both will languish forever. Either Will can mount his play against all the odds or he is finished as a playwright in Elizabethan England. In each case, a decision is made that is manifested by an accomplishment or action: Lindbergh spots land and knows where he is; Sarah takes over defending herself and Kyle; Dora and Josué finally become partners; Will decides to perform the play no matter what—even the marriage of his lover/muse can't stop him. The question of the main tension is answered and with that answer comes a new question, a new difficulty: What will happen as a result of this character making this decision in this circumstance with these known weaknesses and inabilities and obstacles? This new question drives us into the third act.

Let's also remember another charge of the second act of the story—the character arc, the change in our protagonist. Normally, this arc is completed by the end of the second act—ideally the culmination itself is the first step, or the first visible sign, into being the new, changed manifestation of the character. Sarah isn't looking for someone to save her from the Terminator; she is trying to do that herself for the first time. Will is confident he can complete his play, with or without his muse. Lindbergh has completed the most impossible portion of his journey, but he has yet to arrive at his destination. Dora and Josué have formed a loving bond; she is transformed from the woman who didn't want to take him on and who tried to ditch him. We have quit trying to escape the stove and have turned around to attack the gas supply. It's a first, tentative step in a new direction that signals a life change in the protagonist.

False Resolution

The seventh sequence, the first sequence in the third act, is often called the false resolution. The story seems to have a straightforward direction as a result of the culmination and the decision that came about at the end of the second act. By ascending, Lindbergh spots land; he can now simply drop down and land the plane in the first open field he spots. Dora and Josué are now partners, a little family, and they invent a way of making money that is a perfect union of their skills and sensibilities. Will and Viola play Romeo and Juliet and pour their hearts and souls and all their love into the performance. Sarah manages to get the Terminator's fuel truck to crash, which seems to burn up the killing machine. Once we've failed to get out of the oven and decided to turn around to attack the gas supply in the stove that is cooking us alive, it seems all we have to do is find the gas knob and turn it.

In other words, the easiest or most direct solution, given the contents of the story, is the first solution to explore and elaborate on in this seventh sequence. If this first, easiest solution works, then the third act is short, linear, and predictable. That's why this is so often a false resolution. While we are heading to this seemingly easy solution, we learn the parameters of the real solution—that this machine won't die, that landing in Scotland won't solve Lindbergh's problem of flying from New York to Paris, that performing true and enduring love onstage won't overcome the individual and social pressures on the lovers. We explore what will really be needed to resolve the whole story while pursuing a potential solution that is either doomed to failure or a success with unexpected consequences.

This is why the twist, which we discussed earlier, is such a crucial part of the third act and usually comes at the end of this sequence. Without the twist, we can clearly see the final resolution of the story from the end of the second act; it's too easy and too predictable. It's far better to head your characters toward that first solution only to have the effort fail, either directly or indirectly. The twist also is part of the buildup to testing the character arc that has usually been achieved by the end of the second act. Your character is no longer striving to escape from the stove that has been cooking him alive and has decided to face the dilemma, to fight. This is a change in the character. Sarah no longer is looking for someone else to save her and has taken on battling the Terminator herself. This is a change in the character. Once that change occurs, it must be tested; was it simply an anomaly, a momentary shift, and the character will revert back just as soon as she can, or is it a real and permanent change in the character? By aiming the character at a first, relatively easy test of that change, you get her in motion, showing her determination to shut off that gas valve, to crash the Terminator's fuel truck and burn him up. It seems as if the character has proven her change is real, but all she has shown yet is that she is resolute in her desire to be changed. Now you drop the twist on her—that the Terminator is not stopped by having its flesh burned off and is as determined as ever to kill her; the gas knob breaks off in your protagonist's hands, creating a jet of fire in her face. You have put the character in motion on the new road, the one defined by the change in the character, but it isn't a simple and straight road. There is a bigger and tougher challenge ahead, the big test, the final exam—the last sequence.

At the same time, you are resolving most or all of the subplots in this sequence, in advance of the main resolution. These secondary story lines can be resolved in this sequence or even earlier. By resolving the subplots now, the deck is cleared for a total focus on the protagonist and his final dilemma, his final test.

Final Test of Character and True Resolution

The eighth and last sequence leads to the true resolution of the story and ends the audience's involvement with the lives and futures of the characters. It is also where whatever change has come about in the protagonist is given its greatest test. This sequence must belong to the protagonist. To give the tension of this sequence to another character would be to diminish the protagonist and steal his story from him, or at least some of its power. As we've discussed, for better or worse, the main character must solve his own problem; he can't be rescued by someone else. It might be that his dilemma is holding off the enemy until the cavalry arrives, in which case it can seem he is being rescued; but in fact, his job was to hold the fort and he put all his energies into that goal. He succeeded or failed on his own merits at the task laid out for him.

Because we have just come off the twist to the story, the easy solution has failed or transformed into something else, the protagonist is suddenly faced with a new dilemma with no time and limited resources. Most of her preparations had gone into getting that gas knob turned or getting the Terminator to burn up. Now, wounded, tired, without resources or help or time to think, she is at an even greater do-or-die moment. *The* do or die moment. Your protagonist has to think on her feet if she has any hope to succeed. This is the final resolution of the story, and this last sequence is the buildup to that resolution, the resolution itself, and its aftermath. If there are any vestigial subplots, they should be resolved before the main story, if at all possible. Payoffs to earlier plants come one after the other now, and, more than anything, we face this final test with a changed but uncertain character who proves with every action that the change inside her is real.

In *Central Station,* Dora and Josué have succeeded in finding the boy's brothers, but have not identified the boy to them. Their newly created loyalty to each other has not allowed them to chance splitting up. The twist came when Josué lied about his name and Dora backed him up. Now they find out details of the parents' relationship, what the brothers are like, and what life is like for them. Finally Dora decides to do what is best for the boy, though it breaks her heart—leave him with his family. This is the toughest test for a character who began being selfish and superior, but who has fallen in love, perhaps for the first time. Can she do this most selfless thing? That is her final exam. We have the buildup to the decision, the decision as manifested by leaving in the morning wearing the new dress—a gift from Josué—and then later writing him a letter on the bus.

In *The Terminator,* the twist has been that the machine still won't die even after burning up. In order to defeat it, which is now of paramount importance to Sarah, she has to use herself as bait and use a machine to kill the machine.

In *Shakespeare in Love,* the third act varies considerably from the classical paradigm we've been discussing. The twist has been having Viola play the Juliet role just after marrying Wessex and shortly after playing a man in the theater, which caused the theater to be closed. This twist is protracted throughout the performance of the play and played for all its irony and power. But in essence, this is also the resolution of Will's story, his tension about the play. All that is left is the verdict, which is not in his hands. Has the play he poured himself into fulfilled its promise? Has it depicted genuine love and pathos? The Queen declares the play a success and forces Wessex to pay off on the bet, quickly dispatching the main story's resolution in favor of the subplot story. Viola's story—will she stay or go, and how will it affect Will and herself?—is given the final moments of the film, even though this is the main subplot being resolved at length after the main story has ended.

In our battle-of-the-appliance story, our protagonist has taken on the gas jet, and all life in the stove is at stake. By thinking fast and devising a wrench from the blisteringly hot handle remnants, she manages to shut off the gas and relieve this little world of its feverish global warming. And Lindbergh? The twist must be that he chooses to fly past a perfectly fine and safe field somewhere in Scotland and fly ahead—on nothing but fumes—toward his intended destination, Paris. Now that the fumes in the first tank are exhausted and the second is going quickly, he finds Paris fogged in and has difficulty locating the air strip, yet the city below denies him any safe or reasonable landing spot. But he is beyond doubting himself and his plane. Sputtering and looking ready to drop like a rock at any moment, the plane—with Lindy in wide-awake control—drops from the sky. Lindbergh finds the landing strip and sets the *Spirit of St. Louis* down for his glory and a permanent place in history.

In each of these stories, there must be some aftermath to this most crucial moment, the one that resolves the whole story. But that aftermath doesn't have to be protracted, and when it is over, there is nothing left to be done. The character has ceased actively wanting something that we are engaged in, and we are allowed our consciousness and emotions back to take with us out of the theater. Whether the aftermath plays in the same time period— Dora writes a letter to Josué from the bus that takes her away from him and his world—or we need a coda—Lindbergh is given a parade down the Champs Élysées—this last aftermath, the saying good-bye at the end of the film, is usually only a minute or two after the final resolution. We have spent our emotions and exhausted our intellects; now it's time to separate from the characters and their world. We know Lindbergh has much life left to live, Shakespeare has many plays yet to write, Dora has a new life to create for herself, Sarah heads to Mexico to arm the world against future machines, and our appliance-captive hasn't even seen the dishwasher yet—but those potential futures are not of crucial interest to us. We are allowed to separate, safe in the knowledge that life will continue on.

Typical Placements and Proportions

In this classical screenplay structure there are also classical proportions. We can't all enjoy the same proportions as classical Greek sculptures, but those classical figures are interesting and worth knowing. But the same caveats apply to proportions as to the classical structure as a whole: don't take it as a set of commandments, but merely as a guide against which to measure and perhaps adjust when the proportions of your story go far out of sight.

As we've discussed, the first and third acts are typically about one-quarter of the story material each, and the second act is about half of it. Sequences tend to be about twelve to fifteen minutes long. By this simple arithmetic, then, the first act should be twenty-four to thirty pages, the second act forty-eight to sixty pages, and the third act twenty-four to thirty pages. If the intended film is meant to be about one hundred minutes long, then it would be twenty-five pages for the first act, fifty for the second, and twenty-five for the third. But obsessing on page counts is putting your energies in the wrong place. At the same time, if your first act is fifty pages long and you are not writing an epic but a normal-length film, this rough guide will give you a warning that you have a dangerous imbalance. These basic proportions can be used as a yardstick to help you discover the gross problems, but they can't be used as a ruler to fine-tune down to exact page lengths. There is nothing that exact in the proportions.

In fact, even this rough rule of thumb of one-quarter, one-half, one-quarter isn't completely accurate. Typically, the first act is slightly longer than the third act. The first act has to build up everything from a dead stop, and it needs screen time to get us hooked. Conversely, the third act has the advantage of all that came before it. The scenes tend to be shorter and more intense, the payoffs take less screen time than the plants, the story has been focused and honed to a fine point, and this all takes less time. But there are hundreds of exceptions that are perfectly acceptable and workable ways of telling stories. So just use the proportions as an approximation, not a demand to cut out a page and five-eighths from your first act. Take as long as you need to complete the needs of the first act, but don't be inefficient; don't take more time than you absolutely must to get us hooked.

The same is true for the typical or classical placements of pivotal moments. Strive to have the point of attack in the middle of the first act and the major twist in the middle of the third act, but there is nothing sacred in these placements. In a classically told story, the creation of the main tension, the decision of the protagonist and the beginning of the quest or journey or pursuit of the goal, all coincide in one huge, important moment. Likewise with the culmination—you want to have the first tentative completion of the character arc, the completion of the main tension quest or journey, and the creation of the third act dilemma all coincide. But these are ideals and can't always be accomplished. There are times where it would actually diminish the impact of the story to force classical placements on the characters, on the events, and on ourselves as the writers. Know them and use them as a measure or guide, but not as a commandment. You may have a much stronger story if you listen to your own drummer and march out of step with the rest of the hordes around you than if you perfectly obey the drummer's classical cadence.

Relationships of Midpoint, Culmination, and Resolution

See *The Tools of Screenwriting* for a detailed discussion of the relationships among these three crucial moments in the telling of any story. But here let's touch on the classical relationships. A story needs highs and lows; the audience's hopes must be encouraged, and also its fears. A story with a happy—high, hopeful—resolution needs to have a significant low moment for that ending to feel earned, justified, and unpredictable. The inverse is equally true. If there is an unhappy—low, fearful—resolution, then there needs to have been a significant high point for this ending to have its full emotional resonance as well as being unpredictable. As we've seen with sequences, you can have some successful and some unsuccessful resolutions, but these intervening resolutions by themselves aren't big enough to balance against the final resolution. There are two crucial moments in a story that potentially could deliver the opposite result from the final resolution with sufficient power and impact to give the needed balance—the midpoint and the culmination. It isn't necessary that they both be the opposite of the resolution, but one or the other must be the opposite or else you will go into the third act with your resolution being predictable.

If your protagonist is a boxer and he wins a fight at the midpoint and another at the culmination, it will be the audience's expectation that he'll win in the end. If you use that expectation to your advantage and have him lose at the end, then your outcome will be unpredictable. If he wins all three, the final win will feel unearned and unsatisfying to the audience. But you don't need both to be the opposite. Let's look at a boxing film *Rocky*. Our protagonist loses the fight in the resolution, but he has no other boxing match in the film to offset that loss. He does, however, have that memorable moment that signifies the end of his training and his preparedness for this fight—the triumphant ascent of the stairs and dancing around like a champion. This is the film's culmination. It functions in the same way as winning a fight would; it gives him that winning moment, that opposite sensibility from the ending loss. Even that ending loss is a successful completion of his objective—to deserve to be in the ring with the champion.

Central Station provides a fine example. At the midpoint, Dora tries to ditch the boy and only succeeds in losing all their money and stranding herself, with the boy attached, in a difficult spot. At the culmination, she frantically searches for him, fearful she has lost him, and finally they come together, now bonded into a unit. In one crucial moment she loses, in the other she wins, so we go into the ending not knowing how it will resolve. This is a perfect setup for the bittersweet ending that is delivered. She does the right thing, fulfills the transformation in her character and acts out of love, but by doing so loses the boy she has come to love.

In *The Terminator,* the midpoint comes when the Terminator kills the L.A. police and Sarah escapes with Kyle. The culmination comes when she turns around to defend herself for the first time, and this results in what seems like a triumph—the Terminator is caught in a gas truck explosion. She loses one, then she wins one, and now she has to go one-on-one with the killing machine, making the final resolution less predictable.

In our Lindbergh story, the midpoint comes when he nearly crashes into the sea by falling asleep. The culmination comes when he rises above the clouds to spy land. He wins one and loses the other, leaving the final resolution up in the air since we know his fuel is already nearly gone.

Where Does "Climax" Fit In?

You don't have to spend too long around the discussion of stories before the word *climax* comes into play. But what is the climax and how does it fit into the classical structure we've just outlined? Of all the confusing terminology used with stories, this word is perhaps the most difficult, because it implies intensity, which is fine, but it also seems to imply excitement in many people's minds. It also usually implies ending everything with a huge bang. This is perhaps a crossover from the word's sexual meaning. The climax of a series of events is its completion, so in this sense it should mean the resolution of the story. And this is the closest it comes to finding a parallel meaning in the parlance used here. But as we've seen, that resolution doesn't need bells and whistles and car chases to be satisfying, though it can, of course, employ them.

The resolution of *Central Station* has Dora leaving Josué with his brothers and going off to discover her new life. This is exciting in a totally subjective way, but there is nothing to the uninitiated that could possibly resemble the usual definition of climax. This film is not going out with a bang. Earlier, the film has an escape from murderers and a frantic chase through a crowd of pilgrims, both far more "climactic" than its final resolution. Even in an action-packed story such as *The Terminator,* the resolution of

Sarah crushing the Terminator in a machine press is far less objectively exciting than the explosion of the gas truck or the battle in the police station or the escape in the disco. Yet these two very different films both have satisfying resolutions. Their resolutions are the ends of the series of events the story tells, and they sever our ties with the futures of the characters. To force these resolutions to be more objectively exciting and explosive moments—in addition to completing the story and ending our involvement—would actually diminish them. Resolutions of that sort would lose the power of intimacy.

Of course many stories do resolve with big, exciting scenes. All James Bond films end with the villain's empire being demolished by all the pyrotechnics available at the time. Saving the earth from meteors or aliens or the town from marauders can all come to such resolutions. Even a romantic comedy can conceivably save its most exciting moments for the ending. In *The Full Monty*, they leave the "full Monty" for last. But this kind of ending represents only a portion of all well-told stories. This is why the word *climax* is not used here. Using *climax* instead of *resolution* creates an expectation that all stories have to end with explosions and physical excitement. Some stories end this way and have satisfying resolutions. Many stories don't end that way and have equally satisfying resolutions.

Beyond Classical Dramatic Structure

THE SINGLE UNBREAKABLE
RULE OF DRAMA

At last we're getting to the fun stuff: breaking the rules! That's where all the artists and iconoclasts function, isn't it? If I hear one more rule, I'm going to choke. All I really want to do is be outrageous, thumb my nose at society and all who came before me, and prove to them I'm more worthy, talented, and hip than they could ever possibly hope to be. And I want them to give me lots of money to do it, flock to my movies in droves, and idolize me for inventing new ways of telling stories that have never been tried before.

You've come to the right part of the book, because here we will explore how to break the rules, why you might want to do that, what price you will have to pay—within story terms, anyway—for breaking different kinds of rules, and just how much of an iconoclast you really are. But first, there is one more rule. Only one. In fact, it is the only rule that can't be broken. So you probably want to break this rule first, but be warned. Break this rule and your career as a screenwriter will end quickly, if it ever gets off the ground in the first place.

In a nutshell, the one unbreakable rule of screenwriting is: *You can't be boring too long.*

What happens if your story is boring too long? You lose your audience. Either physically they leave the theater or emotionally or intellectually they separate from your story. They are bored and their minds wander; they quit caring about your story and what your characters are doing and wanting within it. Just as the

true opposite of love is not hate but indifference, the true opposite of involvement in a story is boredom, not hating the story. If
your audience hates what you are doing in your story, it means
they care enough to hate it. If they are bored, they are indifferent
to it, uninvolved, unconcerned. They don't care if your protagonist runs into the burning building or gets shot or gets the girl or
the pot of gold. If they don't care, if they are bored and indifferent, then you have no chance of influencing them, no chance of
giving them an experience. You have blown the opportunity they
presented you when they bought a ticket and sat down in the theater. They gave themselves to you and your world, willing to be
made to care, to become involved, to have the experience you
were offering them, but you bored them into distraction and they
left, one way or the other.

It's their loss, right? If they're too stupid or impatient to stick
with it, then they don't deserve the benefit of your story, right?
As we've discussed, if one or a few members of an audience defect
while the others remain involved, it is their individual problem.
In all likelihood, their defection stems from their own baggage.
But if an audience defects en masse, it is solely the fault of the
storytellers. An entire audience cannot be at fault. If they weren't
engaged in the story or if the story had and then lost their engagement, that reflects major problems with the story and its
telling. Being boring too long stifles that engagement and, thus, is
something that must be remedied.

What is a storyteller without an audience? He is a person wasting his time, energy, and, if filmmaking is involved, somebody's
money. Whoever put up the money for one story with no audience
is unlikely to make the same mistake again—ergo, the end of one's
storytelling career. But isn't there some value in telling a story,
even if no one else experiences it? I have expressed myself, even if
no one listened, right? You might have expressed yourself, but you
didn't communicate. To communicate means to be understood; it
doesn't mean to make a statement. If a statement is made and not
understood, no communication has taken place. It may well come
as a shock, but storytelling isn't about the storyteller. It isn't even
about the characters. It's about the audience. Storytelling is about
giving the audience some kind of experience. This is the essence of

communication, of being understood. This is the primary transaction of a story—a storyteller invents characters and events and tensions and resolutions to create an impact on the audience. If that transaction does not take place, if nothing is communicated, then the story is a complete failure. If the audience is bored too long, this crucial transaction, the creation of an experience in the audience, can never happen. So you must be able to communicate with an audience to be a storyteller; this is why there is one unbreakable rule. Everything else can be manipulated, turned upside down, inside out, or ignored—all with some consequence, of course, but it can be done.

But how long is too long? It isn't a problem to bore the audience a little bit; if what has been happening in the story has been engaging, we'll tolerate a bit of boredom. One minute of boredom is probably fine. Five minutes might be pushing your luck, but, depending on what has already happened or what we anticipate is yet to come, we could even tolerate five consecutive minutes of boredom. Ten minutes? That's definitely pushing the limit. An entire act? The theater will be nearly empty before it ends.

How can you tell if you're being boring at all, much less for one or five or ten minutes? What is boring in a story, anyway? This might be a good time to reread the section "Tension from First to Last." Screen time without tension tends to be boring screen time. Tension about the future of characters whose actions we don't understand tends to be boring screen time. Tension with an utterly predictable ending tends to be boring screen time. Uncertainty about the future of characters we understand tends to be exciting screen time. So long as your desire to break the rules doesn't undermine our ability to identify with and care about and understand some of your characters some of the time and at least one of your characters most of the time, and so long as your desire to break the rules doesn't leach away the many levels and instances of tension, you don't have to worry about being boring too long.

A little bit of boredom used artfully can be an effective tool. It's a form of preparation by contrast. Two of the grand masters of exciting films, Alfred Hitchcock and Steven Spielberg, both use boring scenes—usually expositional scenes that could have been done more invisibly—as a means of retardation, making the audience wait for the "good stuff" to come, and as a preparation by contrast. In *North by Northwest*, there's a protracted "clipboard" scene, the introduction of the professor, in which we learn there is no George Kaplan and that Roger Thornhill will be left to fend for himself. Hitchcock had the decided advantage of knowing that the audience knew they were in a Hitchcock film. In other words, he knew we knew there were thrills and chills to come. We have already had a harrowing escape in a car and a murder in the UN to get our blood pumping shortly before the boring expositional scene, and we have the crop duster and Mount Rushmore scenes to come. In *Raiders of the Lost Ark* there's an equally protracted "chalkboard" scene in which Indiana Jones explains the upcoming quest and the Ark itself. Here too, Spielberg knows we know we're in one of his films, and he has already delivered the thrilling opening sequence in the Amazon jungle. Neither of these scenes is weak because the storytellers were incapable of making them more exciting, more tension-based or humor-based. They are purposely made to be dull to lull us into a complacency that affords a greater contrast with the excitement to come.

In the right hands, even boredom can become an effective tool of storytelling. In lesser hands, it becomes boredom, plain and simple. You are not obligated, however, to be thrilling, harrowing, exciting, and excruciatingly tense every minute of a story. In fact, that would be boring. Even an audience of twelve-year-old boys— the target audience for many action films—would soon thin ranks with a film that was truly nonstop explosions and flying bullets. As we discussed earlier, audience excitement stems more from involvement than pyrotechnics. If we don't care about, or even know, the characters dodging bullets and explosions, then we will eventually grow bored with the exciting-looking razzmatazz.

ANYTHING BUT CLASSICAL
SCREENPLAY STRUCTURE

Okay, you promise not to be boring too long, but you're still champing at the bit, ready to break all the rules. You don't want to do anything that remotely resembles the classical screenplay structure because that's been done before and you want to do something new, unique, unprecedented, something no one has ever thought or dared to do before. You're a rebel, you have a cause, you're an artist, a rule-breaker, an iconoclast. You know there are new things under the sun and you're going to prove it. Let's start demolishing rules.

Being Different

The urge to be different, to stand out from the crowd, is a powerful impulse. It also isn't a drive that should be stifled, either by rules or timidity. Rather, it can be a fantastic impetus to work and create and get things done. But strangely enough, being unique requires more discipline, not less, than blending in with the crowd. Standing out isn't a promiscuous state of being, a jumble of knee-jerk rebellion and ego and unfocused ambition. This confused and ill-considered state of being is anything but different; it's alarmingly common. And it leads no one to worthwhile creations. Instead, it is a state one has to escape from, grow out of, or overcome in order to become truly different, unique, and self-defined. In other words, it's a lot harder and a lot more work to be different and unique. But it can be worth all the extra effort.

What is different? Fresh and new? Unique? Are these all ways of saying, "Break all the rules and let the chips fall where they may"? That, in fact, is the promiscuous state of being alluded to above. It fails to take into account the need to communicate, the need to give an experience and, most especially, the need to create an experience of the storyteller's choice and intention. If you happen to have a few million dollars you want to spend—you won't get it from someone else—go ahead and do exactly that. Make your revolutionary new film that breaks all the rules and doesn't care about the audience or the experience it gives the audience. Nothing is easier than breaking every single rule; you don't have to know anything. Once your film is done, you won't even be alone watching it. It's always possible to fool a few people into thinking nearly anything is artful, meaningful, and profound. "I don't understand it, so it must be art," is a painfully common and shallow response in our modern society. So you'll find a few fools, but you will have fooled yourself the most. How awful to wake up days or years later, millions of dollars poorer, and realize that it was all delusion. Art does not stem from ignorance. Rebellion and new forms are not made by unfocused and uninformed people.

Pick your favorite rebels—Salvador Dali, Luis Buñuel, Che Guevara, Joan of Arc, William S. Burroughs—and look for their common thread. Each of them was totally focused, completely enmeshed in a single direction to explore and excavate, and each was utterly disciplined in some fashion, though it might not appear so to the untrained eye. This is the key. The appearance of making it up as you go along is just that, an appearance; it is not possible to achieve such grace with no forethought, no plan, no inner drive or inner demon propelling you in a focused direction. Each of these rebels picked his battles, zeroed in on one direction to break the rules, and used the rules to his advantage in all other areas. This is why we know them. There are many others who tried to make it up as they went along with no plan or inner focusing drive, but we have no idea who they were because their efforts were wasted. It's not possible to wage any kind of battle on all fronts at the same time. Pick your battles and put everything you have into them. Let the other fronts be more "conventional." This isn't capitulating; it's being effective, it's giving drive to your true battle.

Breaking the Form

The first area almost all would-be rebels zero in on is the form of telling a story: you want to put all your scenes on cards, toss the cards to the wind, and then pick them up and write the story in the order you picked the cards up. Sorry, it's been done; it isn't revolutionary. Nor will it actually work. A perfectly effective story could appear to have that arbitrary scrambling of scenes and events, but if it's effective, it isn't arbitrary. Don't be fooled just because at first viewing a film seems to be haphazard.

There are many ways the form of a story can be altered. Every essay in this book that deals with form has implicit information about various ways that particular aspect of form can be dealt with in a story. Because all those rules can be broken, some effectively told story has resulted from breaking each of those form-based rules. The trouble for would-be rebels is that the rules have all been broken before. You want to tell your story in reverse chronology? It's been done. You want to tell your story without a central character, but a whole gang of characters? It's been done. You want to tell a story about someone who wants nothing? It's been done. You want to tell a story about someone who achieves his goals easily? It's been done. You want to tell a story that is completely subjective and only takes place in the mind of the protagonist? It's been done. You want to tell a story in which your protagonist is dead in the opening scene? It's been done. You want to tell a story that forces us to identify with and care about a despicable killer of babies and cute animals? It's been done.

In fact, most story form variations were accomplished a couple thousand years ago. The remaining few, which depended on the unique strengths of cinema for playing with time and place and juxtaposing elements, were experimented with early in the invention of screen storytelling. Most of these variations have been played with repeatedly since their first appearance in the last 2,000 or 100 years. We find ourselves in a situation described by the T-shirt slogan Karla Jackson wears in *Texasville*, the sequel to *The Last Picture Show*: YOU CAN'T BE FIRST, BUT YOU COULD BE NEXT. If your desire to be different depends on being the first to try any variation on how a story is told, you're doomed to failure and frustration.

But don't give up hope. There are still good reasons to break the rules, still infinite possibilities for you to stand apart, separate, distinct, and unique. You just can't do it through inventing a new form of storytelling. Even if you manage to find some lapse in the oeuvre of rule-breaking and race out to smash that unbroken rule to smithereens, that won't necessarily grant you entrance to the pantheon. There needs to be a reason behind the breaking of the rules; any particular rule-breaking should be done only because it is the best means of accomplishing a specific goal. Form follows function: what target are you aiming for that you can't hit in any other way than by breaking this fabled as-yet-unbroken rule? If the only target is the rule itself, then your story will be a shallow exercise indeed. Remember, storytelling is about the impact on the audience that you intend to create. How you create that impact is secondary to the intended impact; the mode of telling the story is in service of your intention. As we've discussed from the beginning, how you build your characters, the world of the story, and the story itself should all be in support of the intended impact you wish to have on the audience. If it takes breaking rules to get that impact, fine—go for it. Don't simply break the rules and then discover what impact that might have on the audience. This goes right back to the core of promiscuous rebellion— no focus, no plan, no intention. And in the end, no story worth our time.

But you still might want to break rules, even though they've been broken before by accomplished and celebrated storytellers. You can still stand out as different and new and fresh and unique. Nobody was ever you before; nobody had your exact intentions and nobody ever invented characters exactly the way you do. It doesn't get any fresher than that. Form an intention that is your own, that springs from you and your unique perspective, develop characters who can carry that intention and place them in a world that can pose opposition to those characters, and then break whatever rules stand in your way in the telling of that story. Break only those rules that actually stand in your way. Generally speaking, the fewer broken rules the better—in each story. In another story you can break other rules. The rule-breaking itself never will be new and unique. But the combination of storyteller, character, world, and the form of storytelling put in service of them—that can be utterly without precedent. Do this and you will find your place to stand out from the rest. Breaking rules simply because you now know them and you can break them will only give you broken rules, not a better or fresher story. Yes, rules are made to be broken; but there should be a good reason to do it, one that is in support of your own goals. If that's the case, break away.

Storyteller Intentions and Priorities

We've discussed what your intentions are, what kind of experience you want to give to your audience. But we've discussed it in terms of discovering your protagonist and the world of your story and the theme that resonates for you. How do a storyteller's intentions affect rule-breaking? Or, more precisely, how do the kinds of goals that stories can promote alter or influence classical screenplay structure? There are three basic categories of intended impacts we can strive for: an emotional connection with the audience, an intellectual challenge to the audience, and spectacle to impress the audience. There are combinations of any two or all three, with one or the other category dominating. None of these intended impacts is exclusive of genre. In other words, we can make a comedy that is intellectually challenging or a thriller that is emotionally engaging or a romance that relies heavily on spectacle. Each of these kinds of intentions can function within nearly any genre.

But different intended impacts imply different sets of rules that may be more effectively broken than others. For example, if your primary intention is for an emotional connection between the audience and the story being told, it's unlikely that you will want to do anything that will diminish the audience's identification with the protagonist. This is, after all, the primary source of what emotional influence you have on your audience. You probably won't have multiple protagonists in an ensemble story, because that will divide the audience's loyalties and decrease their emotional connection to each of the competing protagonists of the interwoven stories. However, you might need to break the rules in ways that make the audience's connection with the protagonist stronger. Maybe they see his thoughts and dreams and memories. Maybe they experience time in the same way he does. Maybe you have to create another sequence in the first act just to carry all the fascinating inner-life material you have created for him. Maybe you'll need to push the point of attack far forward in the story in order to have enough character time with your protagonist after the story material has started to be revealed. Maybe you'll want your protagonist to lose at midpoint, lose at the culmination, and lose at the end, with the false resolution looking like a surefire win, because this will jolt our emotional impact higher.

If your primary intention is for an intellectual challenge to the audience, ratcheting up the emotions to a fever pitch might be a mistake, might detract from the intellectual construct you have so carefully built. Here you may need to change the form of the storytelling in service of that intellectual challenge. Maybe we need to experience the events in reverse chronology. Maybe just one element must be taken out and coated with ideas, like breading on a pork chop, so that your audience has to work extra hard to see what is inside. Maybe you'll need to make it seem as if you scattered your scenes to the wind and put them together in an arbitrary order. You will need a carefully orchestrated substructure, built to be invisible, made to seem random while being anything but random. You will be building a puzzle for your audience to wrestle with and try to solve while the story is going on.

If your primary intention is the achievement of spectacle, it might be counterproductive to put too much emphasis on intellectual puzzles or games, because spectacle requires clarity. A fireworks display in the fog isn't much of a show. Here you might need to alter the proportions of your story—by acts or sequences—in order to provide sufficient screen time for the spectacle moments, the dances, battles, songs, fireworks, and even production design or breathtaking locations. You might need to trim back on the amount of story you tell because you have huge set pieces to orchestrate. Or you might need to streamline your cast or the complexity of some of your characters to allow for the grandeur of your sets or real locations to be explored.

As is often the case, you might have two or all three of these basic intentions commingling and competing, and you must negotiate balances among their various needs and limitations. You need to know what's most important so that your efforts, and the rules you forsake, are in support of your central goal, not fighting against it. If you want our emotional connection to the protagonist, don't make us wade through lots of puzzles to get to him. If you want to provoke your audience to thought and contemplation, don't stifle our ability to do that by blocking our way with wondrous distractions. If you want to put us into a state of awe and wonder, don't filter it through the eyes of someone else; let us experience it for ourselves. What's wonderful about film storytelling is that you can have all of these things working in concert in the same film.

You still need to decide which basic goal dominates and strive to accentuate it above the others—by breaking rules in support of only that goal, for instance. At different times within a story you can still put us in a state of awe or puzzlement or intense emotional connection. But to be effective, for the two secondary, though still important, goals, it's best to stick to the rules pretty closely. For example, let's say intellectual challenge and spectacle are secondary and emotional connection is primary. In that case, you may want to pull out all the stops to beef up our connection to the protagonist and break rules in order to support that goal. But in the other two areas, it would be a good idea to play it straight, play by the rules as much as possible. This strategy enables each element to have its moment at center stage and to be communicated effectively to the audience. At the same time, it allows the highest-priority goal to be given a brighter spotlight, a bigger pedestal, a more sharply drawn or uniquely envisioned mode of coming across to the audience.

Let's look at a few examples. In *Saving Private Ryan* we have elements of two intentions in evidence, but it seems clear that the primary intention is one of emotional connection. There is ample spectacle, particularly in the opening sequence, which is considerably out of proportion to the rest of the film in order to allow time for the spectacle to be shown off. The telling of the story is quite straightforward; no games are being played with the mode of storytelling and there isn't a huge intellectual challenge being made. We know who the good guys and bad guys are, we know what we want to happen all along, and any ideas we had about World War II before coming into the theater are not being challenged or dispelled. It is with Captain Miller and, secondarily, with his men that we are given the bulk of the time and emphasis. We are being put into their shoes and made to experience the terror and the minor relief moments of such a mission.

But in *Raiders of the Lost Ark*, from the same director and set in the same time period, we see different priorities. Here the primary goal is spectacle—elaborate set pieces that dominate all other things around them. Again, there is no emphasis on intellectual challenge, and the time given to emotional connection is secondary to the time and emphasis given to spectacle. In a third war film, *Dr. Strangelove*, the priority is with the intellectual challenge. We are also shown spectacle, which is the second priority, and the characters—delightful and chilling as they are—are given third priority. Their inner lives and our connection to them are not of great interest in this film. Yet another film from that same director, *A Clockwork Orange*, which also is dominated by intellectual challenge, has as its second priority the characters, and spectacle is relegated to third priority. A third Stanley Kubrick film, *Spartacus*, has very little intellectual challenge. Its first priority is spectacle, with the emotional connection to the characters a close second.

Clearly, not all these films significantly break rules in order to reorient their priorities, but it should be clear that there is no inherent value judgment involved in one choice over another. To say that a film isn't putting emphasis on an intellectual challenge doesn't imply that it is mindless or simplistic. It just means that this aspect of the story is straightforward; the story doesn't present contradictions and doubts that need to be wrestled with, and it doesn't play with the mode of telling the story. It might be worth rereading the sections "Time and Complexity" and "Action Time." Equally accomplished and worthy films from the top filmmakers can have different priorities, depending on the three basic elements of emotion, intellect, and spectacle, because the stories and the intentions of the storytellers are different from one story to the next.

If we get away from war and drama, do the same relationships of storyteller's goals apply? Let's look at *Some Like It Hot*. There is no intellectual challenge in evidence, but a high priority is placed on the characters and our emotional connection. If we weren't connected, it wouldn't be nearly as funny. There is a secondary emphasis put on spectacle with big production numbers and set pieces sprinkled throughout the film. In *Being John Malkovich*, there is the greatest priority placed on the intellectual challenge. The quirkiness of this world and worldview—the ideas in this story—are the hallmarks of the film. Here too we find elements of spectacle in the way we experience the story events, the production design and perspectives, and there is an almost equal emphasis on character. But in *Brazil*, while spectacle is the first priority, the emotional connection to our protagonist is a strong second, with little emphasis being given to intellectual challenge.

In order to know where to exercise your freedom most effectively, where to play fast and loose with the rules, you have to know where your priorities lie. This is true whether you need to break any rules or not; you need to know where your precious screen time and your hard-hat work need to be oriented. Once you have an idea—which is all you can hope to have at this juncture—then you can start to explore the potential need to break rules. Even if it looks unlikely that you will need to break any rules, you still know where to put your heavy artillery, where to pull out all the stops and get the most from your story—and put the most into it.

THE LIMITS OF CLASSICAL, THE
BEGINNINGS OF REVOLUTIONARY

There's no sense in reinventing the wheel, so let's see what we can learn from some of the past experiments with breaking rules. Maybe this way we can avoid making some of the initial mistakes and use the things that were discovered to our own advantage. It smacks of following rules, following someone else's rule-breaking, but we've already determined that there are no new ways to break rules; there are only new characters and the storytellers behind them.

So where does classical end and revolutionary begin? It's probably disappointing to some, but the classical structure we've discussed is amazingly flexible and resilient. Because it grows out of the protagonist and his want and pursuit of that want, there immediately is a sense of subjectivity to the structure; it isn't a form into which a story must be forced. Rather, structure is a mode of organizing material, both for one's own thoughts and skills and for the audience's experience of the material. Structure is a means of giving the greatest emphasis to the most important aspects of the story and the experience the audience is having. This isn't a terribly constricting set of organizing principles. But there are limits to its flexibility.

Are All "Revolutionary"
Films Revolutionary?

Having come this far in exploring story-building issues, you are probably beginning to suspect that some of the more revolutionary rule-battering films you have favored might not be as radical a departure from "all those old guys and Hollywood" as you'd once thought. In different times and places, the favored rebels have included Luis Buñuel, Jean-Luc Godard, Federico Fellini, Quentin Tarantino, David Lynch, Todd Solondz, Paul Thomas Anderson, and Lars von Trier. What we will do here is not an exhaustive or scholarly exploration of storytelling rebellion and revolution. Rather, we will peek into some of the ways that the limits of storytelling have been tested and discover just how consistently revolutionary some filmmakers have been, while others have made notable attempts more sporadically.

Luis Buñuel is a good place to start. Nearly everyone who desperately wants to break the rules will cite *Un Chien andalou*, which Buñuel made with Salvador Dali in 1929. One of the pinnacles of surrealism, *Un Chien andalou*, was a short film, a dream or nightmare, with no story or rational explanation. It was probably as experimental as any film ever made, and it obeyed no rules—that was its whole point. Since it was first released it has been copied continuously in dream and nightmare sequences within films the world over. It creates a powerful visceral reaction in audiences from the images shown—including the slitting of an eye with a razor and ants crawling from a hole in a hand. Throughout the rest of his long career, Buñuel continued to experiment with film, though from early on he showed signs of gravitating much more toward story and storytelling than he did in his first short film. Of his better-known works, some used ensemble stories—interwoven stories—such as *The Discreet Charm of the Bourgeoisie* and *The Exterminating Angel*. But in one of his most noted films, *The Diary of a Chambermaid*, he told a straightforward story about a protagonist—in an admittedly strange world—but the story was told with all the norms of classical structure. So even Buñuel, the paragon of surrealism, would occasionally go to the straight and narrow of classical story structure when it suited the needs of his narrative.

Jean-Luc Godard rocketed to international recognition with his first feature, *Breathless*, which was a straightforward story of a young man running from the police. But the casually amoral actions of the characters and a unique editing style gave a good impression of being revolutionary and galvanized young filmmakers and critics. Godard had long been a film critic and theorist, and this first attempt at a dramatic feature effectively stuck with the rules while appearing to be "different." Godard has never made another film to match the renown of his first effort, though his *Pierrot le fou*, which was nearly a remake of the first—at least in star and basics of story—kept him in the spotlight. Many of his large body of subsequent films were experiments in narrative style or complete abandonments of story, though he would periodically return to storytelling conventions, such as in *Godard's Passion*, which was a reworking of *Fellini's 8 1/2*. Godard's work also became extremely political, and he subordinated all other aspects of cinema and storytelling to his political theses, which tended to work more effectively in his many documentaries than in his narratives.

The works of Lars von Trier and the Dogme '95 group are an interesting experiment in cinema and storytelling. A group of European filmmakers gathered to make a manifesto, a challenge to themselves and the world to veer directly away from high-gloss "Hollywood"-style films and production. Rebels in their own cabal, it would seem. Among the limitations they put on themselves and their films were: there should be no artificial lighting; the camera should be handheld; no filters should be used; there should be no special effects and no gunplay. While this amounts to a revolution in how these films look, the irony for would-be rebels is that it drove the adherents of Dogme '95 ever deeper into the need for a well-crafted screenplay. Without glamorous images or special effects to distract the audience from any weakness in story or character, these films have had to succeed or fail on the quality of the stories they tell and the acting presented in them. The best known among these films, von Trier's *Breaking the Waves*, *Italian for Beginners*, and *Festen*, have all worked from strong, classically structured screenplays. So it would seem that, even though there is a revolution in this approach, the revolution is not in the form of the narrative but in the presentation of the images and some limitation on subject matter.

David Lynch, an iconoclast who is very popular among the rebellious youth of the film world, was in fact a student of Frank

Daniel's and learned all of the classical structures of film story-telling. His first film, *Eraserhead*, while eerie, disquieting, and uniquely strange, falls within the realm of a classically told story. His best-known later works, *Blue Velvet*, *Wild at Heart*, and *Lost Highway*, expanded his experimentation with cinema, which has mostly been centered on the area of identifiable character mo-tivations. The actual building of his stories tends to be fairly traditional, though the images, subject matter, and character mo-tivations often stray far from the norm. One of his most recent films, *The Straight Story*, couldn't be straighter; it's classical right up and down the line. So again, what we discover is that the vari-ations from the classical have been in service of his intentions. When he has needed to break the rules, particularly in the realm of character development, he hasn't hesitated. But it's always been in direct support of the experience he was intending to give the audience, however straight or disquieting that might be.

In fact, what we discover with other rebellious-seeming story-tellers, like Todd Solondz, is that it is primarily in the subject matter and the images and moments they choose to deliver that this rebellion manifests itself. In the telling of the story in *Wel-come to the Dollhouse*, Solondz uses straightforward narrative techniques. In *Happiness*, he tells three interwoven stories, each with its own protagonist. Paul Thomas Anderson tends to make ensemble stories, much like Robert Altman, and is differentiated from Altman more in subject matter and sensibility than in story-telling structures.

Is there anything we can conclude from a brief exploration of a few widely admired rebels, writer-directors, and their careers? There are true rule-breakers, but none of them does so in a con-sistent way from film to film. Instead, they break the rules they need to and, when the story requires a classical structure like David Lynch's *Straight Story* or Luis Buñuel's *Diary of a Chamber-maid*, they head right for the most traditional techniques that will work. The most common variation on the classical one-protagonist story is the telling of interwoven stories in an ensem-ble picture of two, three, or more stories making up the whole. We can conclude that many films that outwardly seem to be full of rebellion and iconoclasm are, in fact, traditionally told stories about rebellious and iconoclastic characters, or they use subject matter and imagery for shock value, but within a traditional story structure. Another thing we will discover is that some of the unique experiments in film storytelling have been done by some of the most famous of the "traditionalists." In other words, just because it looks like rebellion doesn't mean a film is breaking all the rules, and just because it comes from someone who often tells classically built stories doesn't mean that this traditionalist isn't pushing the boundaries of film storytelling.

Mainstream Experiments in Storytelling

While it shouldn't shock most people who know something about film to learn that Orson Welles was an experimenter in narrative techniques, even some initiates might be surprised to think of Alfred Hitchcock as a rebel, a rule breaker and boundary extender. Isn't he the man who made the most Hollywood of Hollywood movies? The man who made blockbusters before the term was even minted? He had Cary Grant and Grace Kelly and James Stewart in his films, what kind of rebel is that? A very canny thinker about what makes a story work and what can be done in film to affect the audience—that's the kind of rule breaker he was. Hitchcock, who started out as an art director in the silent era and became a screenwriter and then director before moving from England to America for much of his career, was always fascinated with how far he could push the audience—in identifying with killers, for instance—and in how stories worked in general. He made *Lifeboat,* in which a cast of nine was literally "in the same boat." He made *Rope,* in which he shot the film in long, continuous takes. He made *Rear Window,* in which the protagonist was confined to a wheelchair and had to depend on others to take action for him. He made *Psycho,* in which the woman we believe is the main character is killed partway through the story and we are made to identify with her killer. In *Torn Curtain* he experimented with how long an audience could continue to identify with a handsome, sympathetic hero while he is committing a murder that takes up a great deal of screen time. In *Frenzy* he lured us into identifying with a serial killer and actually hoping for his success, even after he has just murdered the most sympathetic character in the film. By playing with the mode of telling a story and by testing the limits of an audience's tolerance for nasty behavior by characters we sometimes identify with against our will, Hitchcock is nearly without parallel as an experimenter with the use of cinematic storytelling.

But he was hardly alone among mainstream filmmakers to experiment with what might work in telling a film story. In *High Noon*, Fred Zinnemann, director of such films as *The Member of the Wedding, From Here to Eternity, The Old Man and the Sea, A Man for All Seasons*, and *Julia*, worked together with Carl Foreman, the screenwriter of such films as *Young Man with a Horn, The Men, Cyrano de Bergerac, A Hatful of Rain, The Guns of Navarone*, and *Mackenna's Gold*. In *High Noon* they told a story that takes place in nearly real time—about an hour and a half in the lives of the characters in about an hour and a half of screen time. In *Lady in the Lake*, actor Robert Montgomery directed from a script adapted from a Raymond Chandler novel. Montgomery also plays the lead, Philip Marlowe, through whose eyes we see the entire film. This film shows its lead character to us only when he is looking in a mirror and has all the other characters addressing the camera as if it is Marlowe.

In *Rashomon*, Akira Kurosawa, the writer-director of such films as *The Seven Samurai, Yojimbo, Dersu Uzala, Kagemusha*, and *Ran*, experimented with the unity of a film story by exploring four conflicting versions of a single event. This film was analyzed in *The Tools of Screenwriting* and has been remade in various guises—as a western in *The Outrage* and as a war story in *Courage under Fire*. Of course, Orson Welles's *Citizen Kane* was a watershed film for its revolutionary mode of storytelling. It too is analyzed in *The Tools of Screenwriting*. More recently, John Sayles, the writer-director of such films as *Eight Men Out, Matewan, Passion Fish*, and *The Brother from Another Planet*, experimented in *Lone Star* with telling interwoven stories set in the same locations but forty years apart. Robert Altman, the director or writer-director of such films as *McCabe and Mrs. Miller, Brewster*

McCloud, M*A*S*H, The Player, Cookie's Fortune, and *Dr. T and the Women,* has continually worked in the realm of ensemble stories, including *Nashville, Short Cuts,* and *Prêt à Porter.* Finally Lawrence Kasdan, writer-director of such films as *Body Heat, Silverado, The Accidental Tourist,* and *Wyatt Earp* and writer of such films as *Raiders of the Lost Ark* and *The Empire Strikes Back,* experimented with ensemble stories in *The Big Chill* and *Grand Canyon.*

Much as you might want to believe that pushing the boundaries of film storytelling is the sport of "angry young men," the truth is that the limits of cinema have been tested as often by "wizened old men,"—in reality, vibrant film storytellers in their prime. Though you might want to believe that the rebels show their mettle in their first films, such experimentation—with some notable exceptions—has been later in their careers. After they have mastered "the rules," these storytellers have worked at breaking them in thoughtful and provocative ways, and only when it's been in service of the story being told.

A Few Lessons from Past Experiments

What can we glean from past experiments, both successful and unsuccessful? Are there general lessons to be extracted from what has come before us so that we might avoid stepping on land mines others have already identified? Let's look at the kinds of rules being tested and broken, starting with the basic dramatic circumstance: somebody wants something badly and is having difficulty getting it. Breaking any of the particulars of this statement constitutes breaking the rules. If you don't have a "somebody," if you don't have a central character, then you're clearly in nonclassical territory. As we've already seen, this is the most common rule to break. Ensemble films or films that have interwoven stories such as *Nashville, Short Cuts, Diner, Pulp Fiction, The Big Chill,* and *Magnolia* have been made since early in the development of feature-length cinema. This form denies the most basic tenet of the classical screenplay structure—the protagonist. But ironically, it breaks the rules and at the same time obeys them. Any ensemble story is really a group of stories. Each story has its own protagonist; its beginning, middle, and end; its own tension and obstacles and so on. In other words, each story goes right back to obeying "the rules," while the overall story remains outside of them.

What is different and difficult in this kind of storytelling is how the stories are made to coalesce into one longer unit, the film. It's possible for the stories to play out in their entirety, one after the other, as in *Lawrence of Arabia,* or nearly in their entirety as in *The Bridge on the River Kwai.* Or two stories can be more intimately interwoven, as in *The Godfather.* Three stories can play out more or less in major chunks of material, then wind back around themselves, as in *Pulp Fiction.* Or they can be interwoven from the very outset, as in *Diner, Nashville,* and *Magnolia.* Each of these is a valid mode of taking self-contained stories that have a thematic link and blending the edges so they cohere into one whole. In dramaturgical terms, they are still individual stories that utilize the basic dramatic circumstance in a classical way.

So this form of storytelling breaks the traditional rule of unity, which is usually focused on a single character, the protagonist. In place of the unity of the protagonist's pursuit of a goal, an ensemble story must find another form of unity. In *Rashomon* and *Courage under Fire,* the unity is time; one moment in time is revisited with several different characters, each from his own perspective. In *Lone Star,* the unity is one of place; the father's story and the son's story both play out in the same locations forty years apart. In a way, the two stories in *The Bridge on the River Kwai* also are given unity by place as well as theme. Colonel Nicholson's story is about building the bridge—the place—and Major Shears's story is about destroying the same exact place. And in some ensemble stories, like *Diner* and *Nashville,* the unity is thematic as evoked by a place—the eatery or the city. Each story finds its unity from a state of being or state of mind in which the various characters find themselves and through which they work.

What about breaking the "wants something badly" part of the basic dramatic circumstance? This is a much different animal. It implies you have a protagonist, so you have the source of your unity and the start of your story. But without a want, without a goal, what does the character do? As you recall from several earlier sections, not wanting something is still wanting something; wanting to maintain the status quo is still wanting something; not wanting to take action is wanting something; wanting to disappear or die or be killed or be vaporized into oblivion by aliens are all still wanting something. So in order to break this rule, you would need a character who wants something passive—to be left alone, for instance—in an indifferent universe, a world that doesn't want to bother him. To explore this circumstance, you need to include the rest of the paradigm: "wants something badly and has difficulty getting it." If you have a character who wants a passive thing and there is no outside action against his achieving it—nothing is making his solitude difficult—then you are breaking the rules. But can you also still tell a story this way?

Stories such as this are often called "slice of life" stories because there is nothing driving them forward. Rather, they are illustrations of a moment in time or a state of being or a way of life. These can be beautiful and poetic or raucous and assaulting—whatever view of the world the storyteller wishes to convey. But once the characters in this sort of story start to act, to aspire to something or want something, it's no longer a slice of life; it's becoming a regular story. The problem with slice of life is that it's very difficult to sustain for the length of a feature. In most circumstances, this sort of story will break the only unbreakable rule—it's boring for too long. If nobody does anything and there's no conflict, what are we going to watch for ninety or a hundred minutes? What's going to keep our attention after the beauty or the assault of the slice of life wears off? This sort of story is so difficult to sustain that it's hard to come up with an example of a feature film that does it. Even films that often are referred to as slice of life, like *Enchanted April,* actually have stories with characters pursuing goals and facing conflicts. And the films of Eric Rohmer, famed for their strong and witty dialogue and relative lack of dynamic action—*My Night at Maud's, Claire's Knee,* and *Chloé in the Afternoon,* among many—all still have characters in pursuit of objectives and facing obstacles. Quietly or sedately pursued goals are still pursued goals.

Another way in which the basic dramatic circumstance can be broken is when a protagonist wants something and does nothing to attempt to get it. He wants it, but not badly enough to face the obstacles in his way. If the character can't compel himself to make an effort, why would the audience want to participate? Again, it can seem as if a character doesn't want something badly enough to do anything about it, but then the world of the story, or someone in it, pushes hard enough and we discover the action inside the passive character. *Chloé in the Afternoon* is a perfect example: Frédéric is a married man who dreams of affairs with other women but has no intention of doing anything about those dreams until Chloé decides to seduce him. Now he has a problem and has to make a decision and a story is created—from a want, a collision, obstacles; something is at stake, all the necessary elements are there. If the world had not interfered in his private reveries, there would have been no way to build a story out of this character. Characters can dither and change their mind, they can want but not dare act, they can act without understanding their own want, but a character who wants but doesn't act in a world that wants nothing from him is not a character you can build a story around.

Outside of the realm of the basic dramatic circumstance, there have been other rules broken. For instance, David Lynch is famed for his quirky, sometimes surreal, often difficult-to-understand, and always intriguing films. But are the rules he's breaking structural, do they have to do with how he builds his stories? Or do they have more to do with how we are made to participate in them? Is this still breaking the rules? He always has a protagonist who wants something that is difficult to get and that he actively pursues. So in that sense, Lynch breaks no rules. Still, we don't always understand the characters, we can't always fathom cause and effect, and the flow from one moment in time to another can be strange, bizarre, or nonintuitive. So where this rule-breaking is taking place is not in the bedrock structure of the stories, which often are classical all the way, but instead in how we connect to the characters and perceive the scenes and moments in the story. Lynch's method amounts to a form of subjectivity, in which we are sometimes given an experience analogous or identical to the protagonist's experience. Rule-breaking within a classical structure can be a very effective mode of communication and rebellion.

The idea of putting the audience inside the experience of the character is a frequently used diversion from the norm. At its extreme, as in *Lady in the Lake*, this tactic may become off-putting because it can feel so artificial. We're not accustomed to characters speaking to the camera, as if we are a participant in the story. This is a breach of the dreamlike state discussed at the beginning as an ideal—we experience a dream both as an outsider and as a participant, much as we normally experience a film. But other films have put us inside the character without making the rest of the characters see the camera as the character. *Jacob's Ladder* and *Memento* both take on a surreal subjectivity—the same experience the protagonists are going through in the stories is given directly to the audience. A powerful bond forms between the audience and the character and, so long as the storytellers are willing to make compromises in other parts of the story, this approach can be effective.

One of the major lessons here is just how often rule-shattering is a matter of subject, sensibility, and the kinds of images and moments chosen to present what is otherwise a classically told story. *Natural Born Killers* and its precursor, *Badlands*, are perfect examples to explore. Each is about a couple of lovers who become killers and go on the run. Both were considered sensational when they were released; they were both hailed as revolutionary and decried as revolting. Both stories have relatively straightforward narrative lines—clearly defined protagonists who want something difficult to get in a hostile and antagonistic world. The subject matter and the way it is treated raised the level of attention more than the mode of storytelling. In *Natural Born Killers* there are levels of subjectivity that *Badlands* didn't utilize. We are sometimes placed into the surreal world and worldview of the lovers, even experiencing a game show version of their meeting and first murder together. There is rule-breaking in service of the storytellers' intentions to pillory the scandal-obsessed media and to give us the experience of the wild ride Mickey and Mallory are on. But compared to the cries of outrage, the rule-breaking is fairly straightforward.

But there is another entire mode of rule-breaking—or perhaps rule-bending would be more appropriate—worth exploring here. Once again, Hitchcock offers us fine examples. In *North by Northwest,* the point of attack is just five minutes into the story. We have barely gotten to meet Roger Thornhill before he is mistaken for a spy and kidnapped. This is pushing a pivotal moment far ahead of its classical placement. But it's done in service of the story. We are thrown into the deep end of the pool with our protagonist; we don't know what's going on or much of how this happened to him. He is put into his dilemma—being mistaken for a spy—before we know the full world he lives in or who he is. We catch up with his life and status quo after his first brush with death and narrow escape from his kidnappers. Later in the film the crop duster sequence bulks up the second act with a fifth full sequence, but for good reasons and with a dramatic result. In both places, the classical form of the story is stretched or broken in order to create a particular effect or circumstance. Meanwhile, the rest of the story follows the classical mode.

Many films have stretched the sequences and acts in ways that served their stories while technically breaking the rules. *The Crying Game* has a first act that's nearly half the story. In a sense, it has two stories grafted together, but the entire first story is also part of the first act of the second story. *Melvin and Howard* has a similarly long first act, for similar reasons. *Chinatown* has an inordinately long second act leading to a very brief third act. Here the proportions are skewed to sustain the mystery about Evelyn and the girl as long as possible, to keep Gittes in the state of confusion the title represents. *Saving Private Ryan* has a particularly long first act in order to give us the D Day invasion and put us into the full context of all that is yet to come. *The Deer Hunter* also has a protracted first act—again, almost its own self-contained story, which also provides the first act of the larger story. As you can see, the proportions of acts and even the placement of the crucial moments in the overall structure can be manipulated and broken in the service of the story.

The last major area of rule-breaking is in the order of events. A number of films deliver events out of chronological order, either repeatedly or even with a single instance. These films range from *Casablanca* to *The Godfather: Part II,* from *The Usual Suspects* to *Amadeus,* from *The Terminator* to *Double Indemnity*. It's a valid question whether departing from chronology even technically breaks the rules or simply uses the classical system to its greatest advantage.

Telling a story out of chronological order does create another issue for the storyteller to wrestle with: is there a difference in structure—act breaks and sequences—between the lives of the characters as lived (chronological order) and the story as told (the order presented in the story)? If the out-of-chronology material is a matter of a single flashback or two, it probably is backstory and technically simply part of the first act; the exposition has been dramatized in this circumstance. But if, as is the case with *Amadeus, The Conformist, Double Indemnity,* and many other stories, the past material is the real story, the bulk of the material, then the structuring of the story must be taken from the past. There must be a means of incorporating the "present" of the story into the overall structure. Often stories told by someone or remembered by someone have as their framing story either the third act or the last sequence of the whole story; it's just split up, with a portion being at the very beginning of the telling of the story. But then there are stories like *The Godfather: Part II* and *Lone Star* in which past story and present story are of nearly equal weight and screen time. In this case, when structuring the stories, you must build the acts and sequences of each story separately and then find a means of logically weaving them together into a whole that also has its own structural underpinnings. This whole won't have an act structure that is different or above the two nearly equal stories, but rather one that encompasses them. In *Lone Star* it's quite clear, because the son is trying to solve the mystery behind the father's story from forty years earlier. So the tension of the son's story incorporates the father's story to make the whole seamlessly told.

One last note stemming from the works of acknowledged rebels and experimenters from the mainstream: when any aspect of the telling of a story is put in service of an outside element—a philosophical or political stance or the desire to break a rule for no other reason than to break it—it almost inevitably leads to the weakest work from that storyteller. The most successful films these filmmakers have created—not successful in the box office sense, but in terms of being powerful, memorable, effective, and affective, and representing their creators at their best—have been the ones in which the story remained primary. The rule-breaking, politics, and philosophy all found their appropriate places in support of the story, not the other way around.

Storytelling Myths, Legends, and Lies

Sometimes it's easy to forget when one is a member of a film audience that nothing is real, that everything is being constructed, orchestrated, and manipulated for maximum impact upon us. In this environment, it shouldn't be surprising that myths, legends, and beliefs persist about how films themselves actually are made.

Perhaps the most enduring of these myths is that a film can be made up on the set, that it can be all improvised on the spot by a true artist. Writer-director Mike Leigh is famous for improvisation with his actors in such films as *Life Is Sweet, Naked,* and *Secrets and Lies,* and Christopher Guest has had considerable success with a similar approach in such films as *Waiting for Guffman* and *Best in Show.* In both cases, the directors start with a detailed outline, cast well, and go into rehearsals, during which they flesh out the script with improvisation among the actors. This is not unlike the way Shakespeare supposedly wrote plays, but it is a far cry from making it up as you go along. The structure of the story and the characters are already in place. The scenes that will tell the story have already been determined. What is being invented in rehearsal is the ownership of the characters by the actors. Judging by the quality of performance, this can be quite an effective approach. In both cases cited, the writer-directors take the developments of the improvisation and make final decisions—with their writer's hats on—about what from the wealth of ideas generated in improvisation works best.

This myth may have begun with Fellini. If it didn't start with him, he definitely threw fuel on the fire with his films about directors who seem to make it up on the spur of the moment. One of the ironies is that Fellini did no such thing himself. His films, as personal and idiosyncratic as they were, mostly adhered to classical forms and were scripted in advance. *Fellini's 8 1/2* is quite classically built at its base, but to all outward appearances, it's as rule-breaking as they get.

Of course stories are made up at some time—that's what this book is about, making up stories. Of course some or a lot of rewriting can take place during production, though it is a less than perfect circumstance. And of course actors do occasionally make up their lines, or scenes are altered in the course of shooting. This is the norm. It allows actors to possess their characters, to speak from within the person they play. It allows for happy accidents that, one hopes, can improve upon the script, which was usually written by someone alone—or these days, a whole series of someones, each working alone. The realities of production and the limitations that arise can prompt last-minute changes. The ideas the director comes up with when doing a walk-through of a scene can add exactly the right touch to a scene that was written with no actors, sets, or any other particulars available.

But none of this is making up the story on the set. This is polishing a creation, elaborating on it, perhaps fixing a blemish that had escaped earlier notice, giving room for inspiration from all of the collaborators who join in the creation of a feature film. But prior to this last-minute change, a script was written and rewritten and probably rewritten again. The director may have done his own polish of the script and, even if he didn't, he still spent months envisioning each scene, each moment, the visuals he wanted, the nature of the characters he was seeking during casting, the ways in which he would hide or reveal information as called for in the script, and his own notes on it. All of this has happened—along with incredible numbers of man-hours of creative work and input by production staff of all capacities—before either the actors or the director could even have a chance to "make it up on the set." That last-second change is but a small proportion of the whole. The whole—the story, the characters, the world, the wants and obstacles, all of it—had to be built in the script and preproduction stages.

Many beginners believe that screenwriting isn't really film-making. By believing that it can all be made up on the set, one diminishes the necessity of a script. It might be necessary in the process of raising the financing for the film you want to make—you have to show the money people something—but writing a screenplay really has nothing to do with filmmaking. Composing the music has nothing to do with a symphony; the musicians just make it up in the orchestra pit. Writing the play has nothing to do with the performance; the actors just make it up onstage. Creating the designs and drawings for a skyscraper has nothing to do with the building; the construction workers just make it up on the site. Perhaps none of these is identical to the circumstances involved in a film's production, but the point is clear. There is plenty of input to be garnered in the making of a film, but the actual making of a film begins in the mind of the screenwriter and on the pages he or she creates. Without that work, there is no spine, no core, on which all the collaborators can hang their input, no matter how inspired it might be. With luck and hard work, all the collaborators improve upon what was dreamt up by someone alone. But the only one building from scratch is the writer. Film-making starts there.

Another strange myth—actually two opposing myths—surrounds familiarity. Beginning screenwriters often subscribe to the notion that different is always good and familiar is always bad. On the other side of the process, there are producers and marketing people who feel the opposite—familiar is sellable, different is unsellable. There's the old joke about the production executive who reads a great and unique script and says, "We can't make this film. It's never been done before." The first myth encourages writers to break the rules for the simple reason that it seems an expedient way to be "different." The second myth leads to production companies rejecting films like *Star Wars* and *Platoon*, among many others, because they seem to be too different from what has recently been made. The first myth is about the storyteller wanting to stand out from the crowd himself, rather than his script. The second myth is about the film being easily pigeonholed for quick sales. Both myths equally misjudge the audience and what the audience actually cherishes about films and stories.

We don't go to films either because they are different or because they are familiar; we go to them in spite of the fact that they are different or familiar. If we're told by a friend that a film is unlike anything we've ever seen, but the story's really good, we'll go see it. If we're told a film is the 10,348th version of *Romeo and Juliet*, but it's really good, we'll go see it. Different or familiar is not a qualitative judgment; neither label confers a need-to-see or need-to-avoid on the film for the audience as a whole. We'll rush out to see yet another "rogue cop whose partner is killed so he turns in his badge and takes on the underworld alone" if it seems as if the characters are interesting and the setting is intriguing and the story is well told. We'll rush out to see *Shakespeare in Love*, which is, after all, yet another version of *Romeo and Juliet*, because it is so well done; we like the characters so much, we can't guess ahead to the resolution, it milks our hopes and fears, it engages us. In other words, we go for the experience. We listen to an orchestra play Beethoven not because it's new or because it's familiar; we go because the experience of this orchestra playing this piece is one we want to have.

Different or familiar is an attribute, but one that does not determine if a story will find an audience. Some portion of an audience might be conservative and refuse to go see any film they don't already know inside out; they go to sequels and James Bond films. Some portion of an audience will only see films that purport to be utterly new and unique. The vast majority of the audience in between these two extremes want to see a good film, whatever it takes to make that. If it's different, convince me it's good and I'll go. If it's familiar, convince me it's good and I'll go. Maybe I'll go to a double feature of *Being John Malkovich* and *Shakespeare in Love*. If it engages me, gives me a great experience—emotional, intellectual, spectacular, or some combination—and resolves itself satisfactorily, then where's the line, I want to see it.

So don't believe everything you hear: one revolutionary film might really be a paint-by-numbers story; that script everyone says was written in four days or sixteen hours is someone engaging in personal mythmaking; the whole film they made up on the set is either not worth your time or only some small portion of it was made up on the set; you don't have to know anything about filmmaking to be a screenwriter, it's not filmmaking, after all—and you don't need to know about music to compose it; your story is too familiar or too different to find an audience. This is advice that doesn't deal with the real issue: is it a good story? If someone tells you your script is too good to be made, say they're half right; then find someone else to listen to.

HOW TO SHAKE UP CLASSICAL
STRUCTURE—AND WHY

Given how difficult you now know it is just to make a conventional, classically told story work well, why would you want to choose to venture into seemingly uncharted territory and throw out any aspect of that safety net, the classical form? As you've seen, it isn't really uncharted territory. But as you'll also discover, once you start breaking rules, it can be difficult to get back to what's left of the safety net. Yet there simply are stories and authors' intentions that can't be fulfilled by the classical story structure.

For some stories and some storytellers' goals, the worst idea is to try to make the story work in a completely conventional way. That could be the kiss of death. What is the best way to tell a story? There is no single paradigm. Even the classical form we've discussed at length doesn't require a single mode of storytelling, any more than the structure of a symphony requires that you write music like Brahms and not like Beethoven. There's still room in the canon for Charles Ives, John Cage, and Philip Glass. The same goes for breakers of storytelling rules; not only is there room for them, but there are times when their approach is the only effective one.

Why Some Stories Can't Be
Classically Told

The two most common reasons to breach the classical form derive from the number of protagonists or stories to be told together and the way time in the lives of the characters is covered in the story. In both cases, the antecedents are in the realm of fiction more than the realm of theater. A play has a much more difficult time spanning years and decades in the lives of its characters. A few plays, like *Same Time, Next Year,* build the ellipses of time into the structure of the story, but this play uses the same hotel room, with minor changes, from year to year. If you plan to change time period and location repeatedly, the theater is at a disadvantage simply for logistical reasons, the changing of sets. In a film, you don't face this same limitation; it's quite simple to leap over time, and, once you're leaping, there is no limit to how much time you can span or even in what chronological order you place your scenes. As in *Toto the Hero,* a single ninety-minute film can span from before birth to after death and even have the order significantly scrambled. A novel shares this same ability to leap over time, to bring time back on itself, or to come and go through time as the story carries us, without any fidelity to chronology.

A collection of short stories by the same author is the literary precedent for an ensemble film with interwoven stories, each with its own protagonist. *Short Cuts* is literally an ensemble film woven from short stories by the same fiction author. So these two most common reasons for stretching to and beyond the limits of the classical screenplay structure enable a film storyteller to achieve what a fiction writer is capable of doing. As is the case with almost everything else in storytelling, it just takes some doing, some planning and preparation, and some sacrifice in other areas to make it work. Let's explore both reasons:

If you have the entire span of a protagonist's life to cover in a couple of hours, you clearly need time ellipsis, sometimes decades at a time. As we've discussed, ellipsing time is best done when a new status quo is established and before that status quo is broken by the next change in the character's life. If you have to ellipse repeatedly—there isn't simply one jump from the character at twenty to the character at seventy—then the story might feel staccato, always stopping and starting. One effective mode of overcoming this sense of choppiness is to have a narrator, a storyteller or a character remembering, which smoothes over these ellipses. This smoothing comes in different forms. The on-screen storyteller or narrator or person remembering can help us across the bridges of time simply by telling us, "It was fifteen years before I heard from her again" and so on. But the smoothing is more than just a verbal assist; we have the continuity of our relationship with the character who is telling the story. In *Amadeus,* we have Salieri as a very old man telling the story of his relationship with Mozart, which spanned decades. Once he is telling the story, the author is not obliged to adhere to chronology. Our relationship to the old Salieri carries across leaps in time, from first seeing Mozart to first meeting him to first working with him to last working with him. We jump over time, but we maintain a continuing relationship and this is what smoothes over the repeated jumps.

In *Forrest Gump* the hero tells strangers on park benches about his many disparate and seemingly unconnected adventures. This film is almost a combination of short stories, one after the other, with leaps in time and place carried for us by our relationship to the on-screen storyteller. Other films might have the opposite problem with time—for example, when one moment is explored from different points of view, as in *Rashomon* and *Courage under Fire.* Or when time runs backward, as in *Betrayal,* or backward and forward, as in *Memento.* Or when time loops back on itself, as in *Pulp Fiction.* Each of these stories has its purpose, which could have been restricted or completely destroyed by a conventional use of chronological time.

When a group of short stories is attempted in film—whether they come from a book, mythology, the various reactions to a disaster, or simply an author wanting to explore a theme from a variety of angles—then you have another purpose that the classical form cannot fulfill. As we've seen, an ensemble story is really a group of stories woven together into one whole. This kind of story breaks the one-protagonist rule on the large scale, but obeys it within the individual stories. Weaving several short stories together into a single whole is one means of giving a variety of points of view to a single issue or theme or circumstance. Disaster films fall into this category; each of the story lines followed gives us a different perspective on dealing with the unifying element of the disaster itself. Here there is no significant ellipsing of

time, but we go from story to story and follow how different individuals or groups deal with the impact of the disaster. These sorts
of stories have a kinship with films like *Rashomon* and *Courage
under Fire,* because they deal with varying viewpoints on a single
event or circumstance, but the latter two add the perspective of
hindsight and memory, whereas a disaster film plays out in the
time of the disaster itself.

Sometimes the reason for a break with the classical is simply the size of the canvas the story is being painted on. As we've
discussed, an epic often has several more sequences than a regular-
length film, maybe even twice as many. It often has two protagonists, either on screen simultaneously or coming one after the
other. And they might make use of various perspectives in the way
a disaster film often does, rather than having two protagonists or
one who carries us throughout the whole. As always, the reason for
varying from classical comes back to the intention: What goal is
this story trying to reach? If you want to show the fall of the Rus-
sian czar and the rise of the Bolsheviks and the impact of both
events on the peasants as well as the aristocrats, then you are creating an epic. You probably are offering several different perspectives as their own self-contained stories, all unified by the moment
in history. If you wanted to cover the same events in history, but
from the perspective only of the czarina or of Lenin or of a footman
for the czar's carriage, then this canvas would be smaller and there
would be less need to depart from classical form.

The need to break form often arises from a particular point of
view or interwoven points of view that you wish to capture within
a story. Whether those differing perspectives are played out simultaneously, one after the other or all in retrospect, you are en-
abling the comparison and contrast of different lives faced with
similar or related dilemmas. This might be done on a huge canvas, like the birth of a Communist state in 1917 or a single incident in a forest in Japan. Scale can impact the story, but the real
difference comes when the storyteller wants to follow more than
one person through the same or similar events or the results of a
single event. When this is the case, some latitude with the classical form will have to be taken to accomplish that goal.

The goal of a story could be to get at the "truth" of a person or an event or a situation as opposed to the "facts" of it. With one story, we could get the facts of Joan of Arc's life and death; we could see her as a political and religious tool or emblem, but not delve into her inner life and joys and torments. With another story, the outward facts of her life and battles could be of relatively little consequence, the real goal being to give the audience the experience as she perceived it, as well as how she was seen by her followers and her enemies. In the former, she could be presented as a conventional heroine in a classically told story. But in the latter, something "extra" outside of the classical must be added. This isn't to say that you can't and don't delve into characters' inner lives in a classically told story; that is a major goal for most stories. But to get at the "truth" as it existed inside of Joan of Arc—visitations by God and visions and emotions—another level of subjectivity needs to be established.

So sometimes the goal is a special level of intimacy with a protagonist. *The Messenger: The Story of Joan of Arc, Trainspotting, Jacob's Ladder, Taxi Driver,* and *Brazil* all share this kind of goal. The experience of the protagonist and our relationship to it are placed at a much higher level of importance than the outward "facts" of the story. In order to put the audience in the shoes of the protagonist, you must bend or break a few rules.

If you want to create an intellectual construct, a neat little puzzle to tantalize and frustrate the audience—a four-dimensional crossword puzzle—then a classical story might not readily support that goal. For instance, *The Usual Suspects* could not be told in simple chronology. It depends on having a storyteller—"Verbal" Kint—weaving a yarn. It is a very cleverly and neatly resolved game, and to put it into normal chronology would have killed it. Would *Groundhog Day* be a story if it weren't playing with time as the crucial element in its intellectual construct? And what about *Memento*—it would be a fifteen-minute, not especially interesting story if it were played out in chronology. The whole reason for some stories to be told demands that considerable liberty be taken with the storytelling form.

The Physics of Drama

I went into screenwriting to get away from science, and now you're telling me I have to know physics? We got through vectors, didn't we? This one is even simpler. One of the laws of physics is that for every action there is an equal and opposite reaction. For instance, when you shoot a gun, the gun recoils. The bullet is being pushed in one direction and it pushes back against that gun in the opposite direction with the same exact amount of force. All that kickback into the gun and the hand of the shooter is equal to the power put into the bullet. Let's spare ourselves too much thought about that and instead focus on the principle *For every action there is an equal and opposite reaction.* What does that have to do with film and screenwriting and storytelling and what I really want to do, which is break all the rules? Perhaps if we adapt it a little further, it will make sense: *For every exception to the classical structure, there is a price to pay equal to the degree of exception.*

Think of the classical screenplay structure as stasis, as the state of being that is poised and unchanged. The classical form has evolved into a well-balanced, flexible, and stable organism. Every time you poke that organism somewhere, there must be a reaction to that invasion or change or broken rule, which is proportional to the degree you poke it. As the sign in the china shop says, "You break it, you pay for it." But the price you pay in your stories can't be put on your credit cards or taken out of your soul after death; you have to pay within the story. As long as you know what you're paying for and what you're getting in return, you are in control of the story-building process. When you are in control of what you are doing and the prices you are paying, the variations you take from the classical form can be weighed against your personal priorities for the story. If it's worth it to you and works within the context of the story, there isn't any rule that you can't break—except being boring too long. That gives you a lot of latitude.

Is there a way to determine in advance what trade-offs will need to be made and which of those are justified? You can arm yourself with the knowledge of where to look for the equal and opposite reaction you are generating every time you make an exception or break a rule. Once you know where to look, then you can decide what is worth the price and what is not. But before you look to see how much something is going to cost, check to make sure you want it. Will it be useful, or will it just be an overpriced adornment that obscures the simple beauty of your story?

How to Stir the Pot

There seems to be no way to avoid this question, which comes up again and again at nearly every stage of the process: What do you want your story to be? What kind of reaction do you want to generate? What do you want to explore? What's on your mind? What target are you trying to hit? The simplest questions are often the hardest questions. It isn't enough to say simply, "I want to be entertaining." Entertaining in what way? To whom, with what behind it, for what purpose? Let's imagine for a second that instead of storytelling, we were talking about fishing. "I just want to go fishing." Is this sportfishing, catching a marlin in deep water and spending hours with it on the line, wrestling with it, tiring it out, outsmarting it, and outlasting it? Or is this sitting in the back of a rowboat, miles from civilization, not a care in the world, not a mechanical sound—just me, my gear, the water, and some worms? Who cares if I actually catch a fish? I just want to be. Or is this fishing on a river, fly casting, achieving some Zen-like state of oneness with the line and fly? Or is this commercial fishing to make a living, dragging nets through schools of fish? Or is this some ill-conceived quest to make an overnight killing by dropping dynamite into the water and scooping up all the fish I've just killed—the future and the ecology be damned? Or is this survival fishing because I'm lost in the wilderness with nothing to eat or stranded at sea in a lifeboat? Or am I like Captain Ahab or Chief Brody, out to catch one particular fish of all those in the sea? There are a lot of ways to go fishing.

There are even more ways to tell stories—and to "be entertaining"—and reasons for doing so. None of them is without some underlying purpose. Without knowing that purpose, there is no way to know what substructure will best support your creation, what rules to obey or bend or break to reach your goal. Is your goal character based, action based, theme based, world based, other-world based, sociology based, psychology based, religion based? Or is your intended impact primarily to make the audience become scared or sad or melancholy or to make them laugh or think or to be grateful for their lives as they are or disturbed by their own complacency? Do you want to tell an intensely personal story, or paint on a huge canvas? Do you want to delve inside the head of your protagonist, into his despair or rapture, or do you want to stay outside a comic fool and laugh at his inane exploits?

What you must find is the one most important aspect in the telling of your story. What is the fixed point in the universe around which everything else can swirl and find its place? What is your highest priority, the thing without which you would never bother to tell this story? Once you find that, you have the stick to stir your own pot of ingredients—the characters, wants, actions, themes, emotions, thoughts, and images in addition to your own goals, desires, hopes, and aspirations for the story. No matter what you put in or take out, that stirring stick must remain. Often the stick is the character—Vito Corleone, Oskar Schindler, Randle McMurphy, Jake La Motta. Sometimes it's revealed by the title— *Star Wars, Alien, Terminator, The Princess Bride, The Great Escape.* Sometimes it's the theme (and title)—*Happiness, Chinatown, Apocalypse Now, The Best Years of Our Lives.* Sometimes it's even the intended impact—*Scream, It's a Wonderful Life, Singin' in the Rain, Deliverance.* The storyteller knows what is most important in his own story and to himself. This is what will be used to shape everything else, and it is your tool for mixing up the meal you're cooking for our audience.

Now that you know this fixed point, this central ingredient for yourself, you're halfway to having the pot fully stirred. How does this central thing come up against all the other things you want to belong in your story—not just the characters and wants and obstacles and resolutions, the plot side, but also the theme and tone and style, the parts of yourself you will dredge up and the impact you hope to have on the audience, every single thing you can imagine even attempting to include in your story? You know the stirring stick will remain; you're less certain about everything else.

As you stir, some things—actually, a lot of things you start with—will get thrown out of the pot. You're making *Singin' in the Rain*, Jake La Motta has to go. You're writing *The Princess Bride*, the masked killer from *Scream* won't fit. Some things in the pot will mesh perfectly with your stirring stick. Other things won't readily fall out of the pot or adhere to the stick in a perfect match. These are the elements that might lead you to bend or break rules. What you're doing is establishing a hierarchy of priorities— what things are "keepers," which ones should you throw back for another time, another story, and which do you want to continue to consider?

Imagine you were striving to work out *One Flew over the Cuckoo's Nest* from scratch. Your stirring stick is Randle McMurphy, and Nurse Ratched fits perfectly with it as the villain. You want a love story somewhere in this deep, dark story, yet it's an all-male psychiatric ward. That circumstance can't change without changing the dynamic between your protagonist and your antagonist, and that relationship is more important than your desire to have a love story. But you have Billy Bibbit, who can carry the love story. His love and admiration for McMurphy, coupled with his own inner struggles with sex and "Mother"—Nurse Ratched—can be made to function as the love story. All you've needed is a little bending. But you also want to deliver what the great title has promised, someone escaping the nuthouse, and there needs to be something that brings this story back up at the end a little bit, even though it is a tragedy. To his core, Mc-Murphy is a tragic character, and, as you now know, that can't change. But you have Chief. McMurphy fails in his battle with the system and Nurse Ratched—he is a true tragic hero—and he pays for it with his brain, but not his life. It could end there, in abject failure. But you want a slight up curve at the end, so you create a circumstance where Chief kills what's left of McMurphy and escapes from the hospital, now presumably as a wanted murderer. Killing your charismatic protagonist and having the killer escape are an "up" ending? There have to be some rules broken in there—more than a few.

So by stirring around—weighing your highest priority against all your other wants and ingredients—you can start to identify which elements can fit with the classical form, where you have to bend a bit to make things work, and where you have to break a rule or two in service of the whole enterprise. Now you know where to concentrate your efforts—on building Chief as a character who can pull off this last major event and on breaking whatever rules stand in the way of that one pressing need. By stirring around in the pot of your ideas and conflicting wants for your story and the experience it gives, you identify what can work without alteration, what must be tailored a bit, and where you have to venture away from the classical in order to achieve your goals. You don't want to spend too much time—screen time and your own precious work time—unnecessarily scrambling to make broken rules work when the classical route could have done the same job more easily. You won't know if the priorities you've established here can still all be made to work. That's a balancing act, almost a high-wire act, to be done after you know a bit more about the value of these prioritized elements and the cost of making them work.

Cost-Benefit Analyses with Rule-Breaking

How can you determine what price you have to pay for the things you want to mess around with? How can you tell if the price is too high? How do you run a cost-benefit analysis for a story? From physics to accounting, can't we get away from all those classes we avoided taking? We're not in a laboratory or balancing anyone's books. Since you've read this far, you can probably already guess the two most likely places you have to pay for rule-breaking: screen time and audience connection.

Your most precious commodity, screen time, must be spent wisely if you hope to have your story do all it is capable of doing. This is where many of your trade-offs will be made. Is it worth the screen time to make this or that happen? A perfect example is the crop duster sequence from *North by Northwest*, which we discussed earlier. The story events—Thornhill survives the setup at the hands of Eve Kendall and realizes she betrayed him—could have been completed in a minute or two rather than the ten minutes of the crop duster sequence. Was it worth the extra screen time? In this instance it was. But the decision won't always be that simple.

Let's say you want to expand a screen event beyond its normal proportion. Ask yourself, how much screen time can I afford to devote to this expanded version? The interlocking factors in that decision are complex, and the question can only be answered by you. How many characters are also vying for screen time? How many action sequences or production numbers or songs or uses of spectacle are also using screen time? How complex is your story and the way you are delivering it? How deeply are you delving into your characters, and how many are getting "the full treatment"? In other words, do you have any stockpile of screen time available to draw from? On the other side of the question, what are you getting for this expenditure of your most cherished resource? Will it really be another crop duster sequence, still riveting forty years later? Or will it be a long aside, an indulgence you're taking that won't convince the audience to follow, that they will tire of before you've used up the time you devote to it?

Sometimes asking such questions of yourself will lead to a clear and simple answer—it's worth the cost or it's not. But often you'll be stymied by the dilemma: you think the extended section will be worthwhile in the story, but too little screen time is available. Then prioritizing begins. Can you do it justice in a shortened version, or must it take so many minutes of screen time? Is there another place you can tighten and buy yourself the time for your tour de force crop-duster sequence? Is your limited time better spent on this extended element, or on the inner life of the best friend? Or can you just make your film longer and have it both ways? Certainly making your film longer seems like the easy solution; you can have your cake and eat it too. Maybe that will work. But how long was it before? What kind of story is it? Will you really find someone who wants to produce a four-hour romantic comedy? If someone produces it, can an audience be lured into sitting through a four-hour romantic comedy? How much will you have to spend on photocopies of a 240-page script to distribute to all the people it will take to get your foot in the door? Okay, you've decided four hours is too long.

The point is, you can't simply keep adding screen time ad infinitum or the whole script will be blown out of proportion to the story being told. Whatever your limit is, you'll still end up pushing against it, trying to cram more and more in. Which of those minutes are worthy indulgences that earn their keep, and which are wasted minutes, propelled by ego over the needs of the story and the tolerance of the audience? Lengthening the script isn't free; writing a longer story is also paying a price. Producing those extra minutes generates real production expenses and, if flagrant, might cause a potential producer to refuse a project.

The audience also has its own limits for how long it wants to devote to you and your story. For an epic length of sitting in the theater seat, they expect an epic story. If you're telling an epic story, you'll still run into trouble by adding time, because you need more story in an epic, not just more screen time. If you tell a normal amount of story in an epic length, you'll be breaking the one unbreakable rule—somewhere you must be boring for quite some time. So you have to hold yourself to a rational, proportional length or pay the price.

Not all exceptions that require screen time are about extending a scene into a sequence or adding a huge production number. In fact, most aren't. Sometimes you simply need to spend screen time in a lot of smaller increments, to smooth over and explain to the audience the games you are playing with the story and storytelling. If you are playing around with the order of time or the point of view of the story or have multiple interwoven stories, there will be screen time spent making these things work. This won't be time that is pushing the story forward or driving our understanding of the characters deeper or making our connection stronger. It will be time spent sustaining our connection; in some stories it can take a lot of time keeping the audience from getting lost. In this case, the telling of the story has become high maintenance, and time spent maintaining is time not spent moving forward. It's possible that this is the very best use of time, but it should be subjected to the same cost-benefit analysis: Is what you're getting for this time in the maintenance shop worth the loss of forward motion (story, character, connection)? Is there a way you can get the same thing—sustaining the audience connection—without having to spend as much time maintaining? How much maintenance time can you afford, given the complexity of your story, the number and depth of your characters, and the demands of other aspects of the telling of your story?

Balancing screen time against exceptions, broken rules, and other demands is relatively straightforward compared to assessing the cost one pays with the audience for taking the same kinds of liberties. At least time is measurable, so you can reason with yourself—I'll pay a minute for this but I won't pay two minutes. And time can be seen—your page count rises when you have to spend time justifying things or making certain the audience has kept up with the changes and exceptions and multiple directions. But how can you assess the audience's response to liberties you intend to take? The best you can hope for is a reasoned, considered judgment, a good guess. Half the essays in this book deal directly with how various aspects of storytelling can be expected to affect the audience. Usually these essays are striving to reveal a goal or an ideal. So by inference, you should be able to see what a failure or partial completion of one of those goals could begin to cost you with the audience.

For instance, let's say you're going to tell an ensemble story, with five clear and distinct stories interwoven from the outset. This could be *Diner* or *Nashville* or, with more stories still, *Magnolia*. By having not one but multiple protagonists, you already know that you will be dispersing the audience's loyalties among these characters. Not only will we have divided loyalties—we can't possibly care about five different characters in exactly the same measure and way—but also you will have shorter stories and less time in each to delve deeply into your characters. So in an ensemble story the price in terms of individual character-to-audience connection is quite high. Each protagonist is only getting, at best, about twenty or twenty-five minutes of screen time at center stage to engage us in his story; you can't expect that short story to create as much depth of connection as a longer one. On a per-protagonist basis, you lose some strength of connection, some degree of tension and elaboration in your connection, and some power to the resolution of the weaker story. It's possible that the cumulative impact when all five stories are added together reaches the same power the film would have generated with just a single protagonist. But given that these are five short stories that can't delve into their characters as deeply or elaborate on their dilemmas as fully, the emotional connection as a whole will likely be less.

Is it worth it? That depends on your goals and priorities. At first glance, the cost of an ensemble story seems to be a lot to pay. But if your principal goal is an exploration of a state of being—like *Diner*—or your top priority is a sociological exploration—like *Magnolia*—then individual connection is not as important as immersion in the totality of the issue being explored from a variety of different angles. In the end, an ensemble film can't be as emotionally compelling as a single protagonist film, for all the reasons cited. But it can achieve its goal for its author, because the storyteller chose to pay the price in one area to create the gain in another, higher-priority area.

What if you want to throw the audience into the same maelstrom your protagonist is living through? You want to pull out all the stops of subjectivity. This could be *Trainspotting* or *Memento* or *Jacob's Ladder*. In each of these, all or a significant portion of the film is played out with the audience so inside the head of a single protagonist that we come away with an experience much like his. We see what the protagonist thinks and remembers or doesn't remember. We experience his paranoia and panic and moments of elation. We are as intimate as possible with this character, so you're not paying any price in audience connection. Maybe there's no price to be paid. You wish.

Here the price comes in the world of the story: what is real, what is not, what is just the imagination of the protagonist, and what, if anything, is real memory? And what is real action in the present? What is true and what is false? This level of subjectivity is akin to solipsism, the theory that the only reality is the self, that everything else is just imagination, not reality. If conveying this is your goal, then dive into it. Give us an experience that is the same as or closely analogous to the protagonist's experience. We don't know if this experience is real, or whether it is just Walter Mitty sitting alone in his room having a vivid fantasy. Perhaps that doesn't matter to us, in which case the storyteller has made some correct choices. But if it matters to the audience what is real and what is not, then some adjustments had better be made or the target of the storyteller will be unreachable. If everything we are watching is a fantasy and none of the exertion of the characters amounts to anything or creates change in the world or the lives of the characters, then we are likely to care considerably less than if something real is at stake, even in a fantasy story.

Maybe you want to tell two stories in the same locations but in two different time periods, so you can compare and contrast the lives of the characters and the decisions they make, the dilemmas they face, the mores of their respective places in history. This could be *Lone Star* or *Heat and Dust* or *The Godfather: Part II*. You are cutting your screen time for the two protagonists in half, not in fifths. So you have a good chance at creating deep and well-rounded characters—there is enough time. You can create compelling stories because there is also enough time for that. And if you streamline elsewhere, for instance cut to the bone the number of subplots in both stories, then perhaps you can get away without paying too high a price. You are starting to think in an informed way—limiting where and how many and how often your breaks are with the classical form, cutting back in one place to allow room for an expansion somewhere else. Even so, you can't get off scot-free. You still have two protagonists vying for primacy in the audience's loyalties. This might not be a problem; it might even be the point, and it very well could be worth it. But let's make the decision by asking questions. Do you want the audience to engage with one character more than the other? Does one carry the other's story in addition to his own, as the modern character in *Lone Star* carries his father's story? The same is true for the modern character in *Heat and Dust*, who carries her grandmother's story.

The Godfather: Part II has an epic story and an epic scale, so each protagonist gets a full feature film to dominate. Just as in the earlier *Godfather*, the sequel depicts two different men, father and son, each with the same position in the same Mafia family. In the earlier film, there is the transfer of power from one man to the other; in the second, there is a comparison of establishing a Mafia family in America and the attempts to grow with the times to sustain an already established family. Once the two stories are woven together, must one still dominate the other? It seems built into the time differential. We know one story is in the past—and in the case of Vito Corleone, we already know his future accomplishments and fate—while the other is in the "present." Even if we don't know the fate of the past story, as in *Lone Star* and *Heat and Dust*, it has been determined, whereas we have the feeling that the story of the more modern character is yet to be determined. As a result, the more contemporary story almost certainly dominates in a story that is split between two protagonists of almost equal weight. In a story like *Amadeus*, however, where the bulk of the story is in the past and there is only a small framing story in the "present," the past will dominate. So if it is important that the older story dominate the present one, the proportions might need to be skewed to accomplish that. As always, there's a way to get there. It just needs to be consciously made to work—and paid for.

Using the Rules to Break the Rules

Nearly every page you've read so far has some clue about how you can bend or break rules, or what it will cost you to do so. When we've discussed the importance of establishing or sustaining the main tension, by inference you should be able to see where the cost would lie if you chose to use a weak main tension or forgo one altogether. When we've discussed the proportions of the acts or the number of sequences in the acts or the events that help to give the sequences their shape, you can discern just how big the price might be to alter or abandon any of the classical structures considered in each essay. The essays on time, on character, on action and dialogue and rising action, and the sections on the various crucial moments in the lives of the characters and in the classical telling of a story all contain hints about what to expect if you should choose to ignore, invert, or subvert the ideas of the section. But this is not a book about upending the classical; there is no revolution to foment here—just the idea that it is sometimes better to break a rule or two in service of a more important cause than to be utterly obedient and miss the mark by a mile in your story.

In life the end doesn't always justify the means, but in telling a story it most certainly does—not in the content of the story, but in the means of telling it. If something gets you where you want to go and, along the way, it brutalizes a fictitious character of your own making, where exactly is the harm? If it brutalizes the audience, that's another matter. So you are all Agent 007; you all have a license to kill. And you should use it. Kill and maim, torment and harass your characters into action, thereby revealing themselves and, in the process, revealing what is on your mind. You have the same license with the strictures and structures of cinematic storytelling. You have the right—and sometimes the obligation—to render the means of your storytelling unrecognizable. Sometimes the worst idea is obeying all the rules. More often, breaking all the rules is the worst idea. But in the great middle ground between absolute obedience and total abandonment of the classical underpinnings of story, there is ample territory for anyone to tell just about any story intended to give just about any impact to the audience.

But how do you start? You feel like you have more information about the price you'll pay for breaches than about the benefits to be won from making them. How do you know when you've pushed the story—and yourself—enough? The sad truth is, you do have more information about the cost than the benefit. It's like laws on civil disobedience—what you hope to gain by flaunting them with sit-ins or peaceful protests is inherently subjective, but the laws being broken and the subsequent punishment are crystal clear. When is it worth it? It depends on your cause, your commitment to your cause, the gain you realistically hope to garner from the civil disobedience, and from how far you go in railing against the powers that be. But the wonderful thing about putting your civil disobedience into a story instead of into the streets is that you don't face jail time or impending war. You have just as much chance of influencing the ideas and feelings of others as you would in the middle of a noisy protest. Actually, you have a greater chance because you have dramatized what's on your mind and seduced the audience into buying into some or all of it. *That* is revolutionary.

Sometimes you know from conception that you will have to break rules. You have two protagonists' stories interwoven, let's say. First, it's a good idea to explore if one can be made the protagonist and the other the major subplot character. The first effort at any storytelling impasse should always be to try to stick to the classical and see if you can make it work for your needs. It's simply easier and, most of the time, incredibly effective. The classical structure as we've come to understand it is not a cookie-cutter maze with stone walls that cannot be breached. There's an amazing amount of flex to be found. Bend rules first; break only when you must. But you've stirred the pot and discovered you can't make one the protagonist and the other a subplot character; the whole idea of the story is the interplay of these two similar but divergent stories. Once the pot stirring has helped you settle your need to break a rule and helped you prioritize your other elements, you have the basics in hand to begin the balancing act— what this is going to cost you and where that toll will be extracted.

Since there are two stories, maybe you can get away with a slightly longer screenplay; that can buy you a little extra time. But maybe you'd better also look at what you're doing for subplots (you'll still need at least a couple, by the way). Maybe the entire Battle of the Bulge and that Busby Berkeley number can't both stay in your story. Maybe you can streamline your backstory and not get into so much detail about the first time one of your protagonists rode a bicycle. In fact, maybe you can just put both of them in a foxhole at the Battle of the Bulge and dispense with how they met, went through training camp together, fell in love with and got jilted by the same girl at the fantastic Busby Berkeley USO dance, and finally forgave each other the night they shipped out.

This is some of the toughest hard-hat work you'll do. You're weighing valuable element against valuable element; you're coming face to face with the realities of storytelling, which, among other things, means that you can't tell everything you ever thought about in one story. Trust yourself to write more stories. By stirring the pot, you focused on what the story is really about and what your priorities are. This story isn't about the first bicycle, but both men being jilted by the same girl on the eve of shipping off to war has to stay—because she is part of what will remain on their minds and in their friendship throughout the battle to come, and you concluded this story is about friendship in a time a war. But maybe the huge production number at the dance isn't necessary; maybe each of them tapping the other on the shoulder to step in, only to have her tire of this competition and go off with someone else, will do just as well. What you're striving to do here is weigh each element for its usefulness at building the real material for the story.

It should be clear why it's not a good idea to break rules at a wholesale pace. Each one of them will require some kind of trade-off, which means some prioritizing among things you already want to include. The working approach should be something like this: first try to solve the problem or reach the intention you set for yourself within the classical form; if that isn't possible, try bending the form to your needs; if that fails, identify the least radical or all-encompassing way of breaking the classical form that will allow you to go where you want to go; prioritize among all the other aspects of your story to help "pay" for this breakage; and finally return to the classical in all aspects that you still can.

This last point is an important one that is often overlooked. Once you have had to abandon the classical form, sometimes you feel that you're now making everything up as you go along. You're acting like Mickey and Mallory in *Natural Born Killers*—you killed one time, so you might as well kill some more and more and more. This rationale cannot lead to good things. Just because you've had to murder one rule to get your story to work doesn't mean you have to go on a seven-state killing spree until you are gunned down yourself. You can do this in the content of your story, sure, but in the means of telling it, it's not a good idea. What will be shot dead is your script, your story, and your hope of getting it in front of an audience. As we've explored, the best rule-breaking films pick their rules to break very carefully and obey all the others that they can.

It can be tricky getting back on track once you decide to become a renegade. In order to tell the story of your heroin-addicted protagonist, you have to make the audience experience the highs of the drug and the lows of it. You have to drive them inside his head and actually have them climb down the filthiest toilet in the world with him to get his lost narcotics. *Trainspotting* does this and more. But it also has clearly defined acts and sequences and tensions. It has subplots and backstory; it has a point of attack, a midpoint, a culmination, and a satisfying resolution. We have been given the sensation of being thrown into the deep end of the pool—and in some ways, it's true—but that illusion is superbly supported by a classical substructure that allows the exceptions to stand out and do their job more effectively. The story holds together despite the rule-breaking so that it still engages the audience, elaborates on that engagement, and releases them from it. You still have to do that job, after all.

In many films, the subject matter and its treatment are what is most rebellious and revolutionary. We're now accustomed to stories about killers, addicts, Nazis, predators of all kinds, and an array of depravities, so it can be difficult to shock and repel the audience. Still, you can use your rage against the system or the machine or the powers that be or the complacency of society to tell your tale and break the rules along the way. Don't underestimate rage as a fine motivation to write. It might not seem logical, but rage can be a fine starting point for a comedy—and a conventional one at that. Nothing is more revolutionary or nose-thumbing than making a large audience laugh at power or complacency. Look at *Wag the Dog, The Producers, Fargo, Modern Times, Brazil,* and *Clerks.* They all have social or political undertones, which strengthen their connection with the audience because they grew from the feelings of their storytellers. Comedy is the most rebellious of enterprises. Can you imagine a repressive regime anywhere in the world, at any time in history, that indulged in a sense of humor? Comedy is usually the first thing to be stamped out because of its power of subversion.

By knowing what your priorities are for your story, knowing the hierarchy of the subsequent elements, identifying which few rules you may need to break while using the rules of the classical form, and utilizing all the means of communicating with your audience, you can find ways to balance out the conflicting needs you are pursuing. You want to break some rules. You want to obey as many rules as you can. You want to give extra time to your tour de force moments and extra focus to the inner lives of your characters. You want to fill your story to the brim with everything that is important to you and that fleshes out the experience for the audience. You want to make it all flow with logic in a seamless dream that is tense, exhilarating, harrowing, funny, nerve-wracking, and satisfying. And you want to do it in the shortest possible amount of time that will fit the story and world and characters you have in mind.

Clarity and Obscurity

While all those wants and needs compete with each other and sometimes feel as if they are at war with each other, the mode of storytelling you finally settle on must not be in conflict with itself. A basic requirement of storytelling is some degree of clarity and accessibility for the audience. If the audience can't get into the story because of how you've chosen to tell it or they can't understand what is going on for significant periods of time, then you will have broken the only unbreakable rule. Being too obscure or too foggy is a shortcut to being boring. This is why you strive to adhere to the classical form wherever you can. So many of the potential kinks in the system have been worked out in the classical screenplay structure that it helps overcome the easy traps of obscurity and inaccessibility. You have to remind yourself that this is all being done for the audience, not in spite of them. If they aren't along for the ride, it doesn't matter what else you have prepared for them; they won't experience it.

But clarity does not mean being unsubtle, obvious. You don't have to spoon-feed a predigested story to the audience for them to stay with you. You can be as subtle as the circumstances allow and still attain the quality of being understood. At times you can be subtle to the point of being obscure, but only if you make up for it elsewhere—yet another one of the many trade-offs you have to negotiate with yourself. But too much obscurity, too much subtlety, leads to confusion. Instead of delivering the variation on storytelling that you'd been aiming for, you deliver a muddle. This wastes your opportunity to influence the audience and to give them an experience of your intentional creation.

There is a world of difference between temporary disorientation and complete confusion. Disorientation can be an effective tool to soften up the audience for a later surprise, for example, or to pique their curiosity about what's to come. But prolonged disorientation leads the audience into thinking in the past tense, missing what's going on in the present, and not being concerned about what is about to happen—all of which is crushing to any potential dramatic tension you have tried to establish. Yet it is precisely in this area—striving to break the rules and be subtle at the same time—that you run the greatest risk of getting yourself into a muddle. If you don't lean back on the classical forms wherever possible, if you don't value carrying the audience forward into the story more than you value the ego-driven desire to be perceived as subtle, then you will lose the audience and, with it, your reason for telling the story.

To be a cinematic Che Guevara, you'd better pick your battles carefully and otherwise play by the rules. The classical underpinnings are never more crucial than when you are attempting to break the rules in a few places. They give you a stable footing on which to build your revolutionary piece. So when you have identified where you are going to break the rules and where you are going to find the screen time to pay for it, it is also important to work through exactly how your new idea of the story will play inside the heads of the audience members. Know how to compensate for things that might take them too far out of your story. Challenge them, shock them, even repel them, but only when you have a firm enough grasp on them that you don't lose them. That grasp is most likely to stem from the classical choices you use in concert with your revolutionary ones.

For instance, *Blue Velvet* is a film worth exploring. It is widely perceived as obscure and sometimes a bit of an indulgence, but it packs a powerful punch for most audiences. As we've discussed, Lynch typically uses a classical form on which he builds his uniquely twisted and personal stories. *Blue Velvet* is no exception. At the core, a young man falls in love with a woman who is in trouble and he strives to help her. Sometimes this makes life more difficult for her, and it definitely makes life more difficult for him. At the center of the film is a simple, classical love story. The very existence of this foundation, which can keep the audience oriented, grounded, and involved, is what enables the strange and often obscure elements—moments, characters, and visuals—to have their day. Without the clear foundation helping to keep the audience in the film's grasp, none of the hallmarks of the film would be able to give their full impact to the audience. If the story is just as obscure as the strangest visuals and moments in the film, then the audience becomes lost, not knowing either what to care about or what to make of the strange trappings. Lingering too long in that state of being is a sure road to boredom and losing your audience.

You also can work from the opposite direction. If the telling of your story is obscure and strange and might lead to trouble with the audience, then you need to give them the classical in another area, in the characters and the events. *This Is Spinal Tap* is a good example. One of the first mockumentaries, a narrative film masquerading as a documentary, *This Is Spinal Tap* doesn't readily lend itself to the classical form in terms of protagonist, antagonist, main tension, rising action, and all the rest of the foundation elements. Those elements are there, but they can feel obscure much of the time. But what we get from the characters is classical behavior for a rock band—from the joys of creating their music to backstage bickering to the feuding of egos and petty jealousies. Each of the band members is quite recognizable as a type, though they are fleshed out from there. So when the delivery system is unusual, what is delivered should be fairly conventional.

So the more "out there" you want to be, the more you need to build your obscure and obtuse vision on top of solid—read classical—foundations. Or you must use conventional-seeming characters and events if the telling of the story is off-putting. You want to give the audience your unique take on the world and characters and story, not confusion. Something has to keep the audience involved.

Writing
and
Work
Strategies

BEFORE THE FIRST DRAFT

We've discussed strategies for how to shake up your stories, your characters, and the audience. We've explored what it will cost you in time and connection to the audience, as well as your potential for affecting them. But nothing is more important than keeping the audience in their seats, involved in the story and the lives of the characters; without this, all your other efforts are for naught. The danger of losing the audience grows in proportion to the liberties you take shaking up the forms they have intuitively come to expect. So you must make certain that you keep them, even as you challenge them.

What Keeps the Audience in Their Seats

You know you can't be boring for too long, and, ideally, you want to be far from boring; you want your stories to be exciting, riveting, can't-take-your-eyes-away thrilling. What would be the point of aspiring to create a story that is halfway engrossing to the audience? Why limit yourself at the goal-setting stage? There are many things that can go wrong between the onset of your storytelling and the final film screened to an audience—and many things can be improved upon by the creative input of all those who are downstream of you, as well. Now is a good time to reassess what elements weigh most heavily in your potential success. Let's take our storytellers' hard hats off and put on those nice little soft caps the audience wears. Let's think like them; let's analyze what you have in mind to tell as a story and the mode of telling it you have devised and see how it plays for the audience— before you put in the arduous work of creating the first draft and the many rewrites to follow.

The first question to ask yourself is, "Would I want to go see this film?" Do you want to tell a story that you would go see if someone else made it? Have you ever paid to see a film that is like the one you plan to write? It's amazing how lost you can get in the throes of devising and developing. It's possible to get carried away with notions of what you *should* be writing—how a "serious artist" works and what a "serious artist" writes about—and forget that you are the best judge of your own market. If you like films and you go to films and you don't trash every single film you ever see but occasionally mutter to yourself, "I wish I'd written that," then your film-viewing tastes likely are shared by many other people. If you truthfully would pay to see the film you intend to write, then others likely would as well.

What if your honest answer is no? Don't start your first draft and hope it will get better as you write. The first draft can be fun and thrilling, but there is also a serious component of "coming down to earth" about your story, facing the reality of the distance between your vision of your story and your ability to make it come about. If you add to that already difficult circumstance the fact that you're not even sure that the finished product would at-tract you to the theater, you have a recipe for an abandoned script. You need to go into the first draft with faith and hope that what you are writing will be great. You have to fall in love with your story, if you aren't already, and believe that it will be won-derful. This feeling can get you through the first draft and past those moments where it isn't feeling quite as perfect and won-drous as your first idea of it had been. A first draft is never fantas-tic, even in the most experienced hands. It is written so that it can be improved; it has to exist first, then it can be refined and shaped closer and closer to your dream of it, your ideal version of the story. If you are not in love with your story and looking forward to seeing it as a film, then that road of revision and improvement could become impossibly long.

So perhaps you have to go back and find the elements that are missing or half-formed or clouded over, which are the difference between so-so and gotta-see. The answers are in the work you've already done; there must have been a time you were in love with the story. You must have been filled with hope and enthusiasm or you wouldn't have gotten this far. Think as if you're a member of the audience and find the things that will make them want to see it, to become engaged in your world and characters and story. This will lead you back to what engaged you in the first place.

Consider the Audience's Position

Once you have that handle—the thing that would make you want to see your own film if someone else made it—then you know the spine of your connection to the audience. We've discussed that connection in every possible way, but you need just one more re- minder that the audience is made of individuals who have some kinship with you. They are there for the same reason you would be there. Tantalize their curiosity, play with their emotions, se- duce them as you'd like to be seduced into a story. Make them ex- cited to be in the audience of your film. Promise them a story that will give them what they came for and then give it to them. Don't promise one thing and deliver another.

Doesn't this sort of thinking—creating an excited and satisfied audience—lead to pandering to the lowest common denominator, just giving the audience what it wants? In fact, what does giving the audience what it wants mean? Does it mean that "feel good" movies and syrupy sweet endings are all you can aspire to if you want an excited and satisfied audience? Can you measure what an audience wants in any other way besides gross sales? Again, use yourself as the measure; put yourself in the audience of the film you are about to write. Do you want only a feel-good, syrupy sweet story, or do you want something more? You *are* your audi- ence. Do you see only films that gross hundreds of millions of dol- lars or do you see a wider variety than that? Even films with high grosses aren't necessarily feel-good and syrupy sweet. *Titanic* ends with the ship sinking, most people we know dying, and the survivor still longing for her lost love seventy years later. *Pearl Harbor* ends with the naval base demolished and a horrible war beginning. *Saving Private Ryan* ends with the protagonist dying. The *Godfather* films each end with their characters further enmeshed in crime and corruption. *American Beauty* ends with its protagonist dead and most of the other characters either guilty or looking guilty of his murder. *Braveheart* ends with the death and defeat of the protagonist. These are popular films, films that gave the audience what they apparently wanted, yet none of them offered a sweet and nice and pat ending.

When you're in the audience of a film, don't you want a little respect for your sophistication and for your contribution—your involvement and continued thinking and analyzing and guessing? Don't you want to work a bit? Or a whole lot? Don't you want to understand and "get it" and feel a resolution when it's all over? Giving the audience what they want involves giving them an experience, not candy and Pollyanna smiles. This isn't pandering; pandering is condescending to your audience, predigesting the story because you think they are too stupid and lazy to do it themselves, giving them only the most simplistic characters and formulaic conflicts and pat resolutions. Making the audience work, making them think and feel and be involved and done-in when the story is over, is not pandering. Chances are, that experience is what you want as a member of an audience. If you like any films that have ever found an audience and you succeed at making one you would like to experience, then your film will also find an audience.

So giving the audience what they really want is challenging them, making life difficult for them, making them work and think and feel, focusing their worry and anxiety and bringing all that to a satisfying—not necessarily happy—resolution. Challenge the audience, but don't make it impossible for them to participate or understand. As you did at the outset—before you had a story fleshed out in your head, before you had ideas of your acts and sequences, crucial moments, conflicts, and resolutions—you should revisit one of your favorite film-going experiences, one of those seamless dreams that made you fall in love with the idea of being a film storyteller. Could you understand what was going on? Could you understand the characters and the conflicts, the wants and hopes and fears? Did you know why the protagonist ran into the burning building? Could you follow the flow of the story and time and the inner workings of the minds of the characters, whether you saw those workings or not? Could you follow the plot and anticipate what might happen without being able to predict exactly what would happen? It's a safe wager that you did. Do the same for your audience and you'll create someone else's seamless dream experience and make them fall in love with film storytelling.

Play all the games you want with the story and with the characters and with the audience, challenge the hell out of us and make us work harder than we're used to, and we'll love you for it—as long as we understand most of the time, aren't bored much of the time, are only disoriented or confused or ahead of the story some small portion of the time. Make us think about difficult things and make us feel awe at wondrous things, marvel us with your imagined world and the reality of your characters, and we'll follow you anywhere. But don't cheat us. We'll drop you like a scorpion the moment we figure out you're cheating.

Cheating? We haven't talked about cheating. There's a good reason—you shouldn't do it, and this book is about things you should do and how to make those things work. Cheating is when you set up the rules of your world, the way your story is told, the nature and mores of the world and the characters—and then you stealthily don't obey your own rules. There's no reason to cheat, because you can set up any rules you'll need for later in the story. But that doesn't stop people from trying to do it. Sometimes it's just ignorance. More often it stems from not trusting yourself, fearing that if you show the rules of the world and story you are telling, the audience will be able to predict future events. Sometimes it comes from a misguided joke or adding a last little twist in a story. But if you pull the rug out from under the audience, we tend not to be very forgiving.

The classic cheat is that "it was all a dream" but we aren't let in on it until the last second. Here the storyteller is thumbing his nose at the audience, saying, "Fooled you." We invested ourselves in the characters and the story, we experienced real emotions and thought real thoughts, and now you laugh at us and tell us it wasn't even real for the characters. As we've discussed, there are ways of making this *almost* be the case and having the audience love it. But if you haven't made it possible for us to figure it out— you've given us the rules and then disregarded them—we'll feel cheated. A cheated audience will not experience a satisfying resolution.

THE FIRST DRAFT

Don't expect to use each exploration undertaken here in the order presented and have a draft at the end. This isn't a screenwrite-by-numbers book. There isn't an assignment to fulfill with each section and then, poof, there's your first draft. Many sections suggest hard-hat work and explorations, delineations and decisions about what you want, what you value, what you can most effectively use, and what might have to be left for later consideration. This is essential work in preparing for writing your first draft, which means that much of your hardest work has been done before you write your first page of script. If you have been wrestling with your own wants and those of your characters, if you have been striving to make your constellation of characters a tight and effective group to carry your story, if you have been making decisions about the many facets of storytelling discussed here, then you have most of the elements of your first-draft game plan at hand. Now you must assemble them into usable form—two outlines. These outlines will be your safety net for the high-wire act of writing the first draft. You need to outline your story in two phases, for two different purposes. Both of these outlines will make the writing of your first draft simpler, faster, easier, and more likely to end in a happy result—a script you like, want to continue to work on, and which reflects a significant portion of your hopes and aspirations for it.

The Sequence Breakdown

In the sections about the classical screenplay structure, we discussed sequences and their progression through a story. Now it is time to create this progression of sequences for your own story. As we've discussed, in the absence of some overriding reason to build your story another way, start by attempting to make it work in the classical form. That means you need to find the eight or so sequences as segments of story material and begin to shape each of those to have its own beginning, middle, and end. It means that you need to find and clearly define all the crucial moments: the point of attack, the main tension, the midpoint, the culmination, the twist, and the resolution. It also means you need to make some decisions about your subplots and the constellation of characters who will have elements of their inner life depicted in the story. But before all of this, you must begin with the three acts of your story. The dividing points of your story's acts might already be clear in your mind: they are the establishment of the main tension and the culmination. If you know those two points, you know your act breaks.

If you know your act breaks in theory but not in concrete moments of decision and accomplishment, then it's time for the hard hat. Nail down what decision your protagonist makes that carries him and us through the bulk of the story, the pursuit he attempts, the goal he sets—the second act. Will our protagonist be able to find the Holy Grail? Will John Book be able to hide his witness from the police who want to kill him? Will Sarah Connor be able to get someone to stop the Terminator from trying to kill her? Will the sheriff in *High Noon* be able to enlist the town citizens to help in his upcoming battle? Once the main tension is clear and phrased in a question, jump over all your second-act material and find the moment that answers that question, the culmination. Remember, at its simplest, the answer is yes or no. Yes, our protagonist finds the Holy Grail. No, John Book can't keep his witness hidden from the police. No, Sarah can't get someone else to stop the Terminator. No, the sheriff can't get the town to join in the upcoming battle. Now you have your act breaks and the overall shape of your story.

The next moment to find is your resolution, and this is often one of your easiest decisions; it's quite common to have a clear idea of where and how you want to end your story, even when all the material leading up to that end is still indistinct. Remember, this choice is often a reflection of your personal philosophy, but put into the life of the character. Once you have a clear resolution—both in factual terms for the character and in emotional terms for the audience—it is time to wrestle with the generally harder placement, the beginning. Keep in mind, it should be as far removed from the ending as possible within the context of your story to allow for maximum character arc.

Now, using the earlier sections as a guide, find the other crucial moments: in the first act, find your point of attack; in your second act, find your midpoint; in your third act, find your twist. The story is already taking shape. It would be possible to tell the story just from knowing these elements: a discontented nonbeliever lives an unfulfilled life (the beginning); she is our seeker who hears about the Holy Grail (point of attack); she decides to try to find it (main tension); she discovers its distant location on a map and knows the Grail truly exists (midpoint); she finds that actual location and the Grail itself (culmination); but she discovers that it is guarded by a dragon and hangs off the side of a cliff (twist); and finally she succeeds in reaching the Grail and holding it in her hand, to create a cosmic change in her and her world (resolution). It sounds simple, but it is clearly hard work making those decisions and discoveries. Each of these elements has been thoroughly discussed and you have doubtless begun to form solid opinions about what in your story will work as a point of attack or a midpoint and so on. Now you must bring these various decisions together into one document and balance them so they mesh together as well as support each other.

With just these crucial moments decided, you are more than halfway to determining where your sequences begin and end. Now it is time to sort through all the story material you have been amassing. If you have a chronologically told story, this is an easier process than with a scrambled chronology, but in either case, you have doubtless been making some decisions about what material belongs together. At least one sequence will belong to another character, perhaps more; at least one will probably be focused on a subplot, and so on. The story material about the undisturbed status quo goes together, the material about the creation of the want goes together, the first major attempt to solve the problem belongs together, the last attempt leading to success or failure of the main tension belongs together, the false-resolution material goes together, and the true resolution belongs together. Once you've found these combinations as they fit the overall, three-act shape of your story, you have the lumps of clay from which you will sculpt your sequences.

You will probably find that some lumps are bigger than others; some might barely exist. This may be a good time to revisit pertinent sections of the book for help in finding what is missing or whether or not you have assembled too many things together into one area. But it isn't critical that everything fit perfectly at this point; you're making your first attempt at assembling your many story ideas into one cohesive whole. There is a great deal of adjusting yet to come. So for now, accept most disparities in the amounts of story material unless they are clearly far off the mark. Your time is better spent in making your first attempt at melding the story material with the crucial moments you have decided upon. Don't expect a perfect fit. Rather, have faith that you can make things fit when the time comes. What you must do right now is discover whether your story material for the undisturbed status quo could possibly lead toward the point of attack and so on throughout the story.

Do this now, in short form and in rough approximations, to save yourself time and anguish later on. There is a lot of trial and error involved, many false starts will occur, and you will occasionally have to settle for having faith that you can make parts fit together later. This is normal and to be expected. Remember, every screenplay is a prototype; you're inventing something brand-new, from scratch. It can't be easy. It won't be easy with your twentieth screenplay, either, but it can be done. The key to keep in mind is that you are looking for threads inside story material. For instance, with the Holy Grail story, we start with a discontented nonbeliever. If her discontent is economic, it will feel disconnected from the direction the story is going. If it's religious,

if she hates the church or she hates God for some perceived failure and this leads to her discontent and her disbelief, the thread
of the story exists in her life that we discover in the early story
material. It's possible to see how this person could be attracted to
tales of the Holy Grail and eventually decide to pursue it.

Once you have gone through all of your story material and
found how the pieces might approximately fit together with your
crucial moments, you have only one more step to the completion
of your sequence breakdown, which will become the single most
important aid you have created for yourself in the writing of your
first draft. You have divided your material into approximately
eight lumps of shapeless but related story material. These lumps
are now punctuated by your well-designed crucial moments. Now
look at each of these lumps as if it were a story itself, find its beginning, middle, and end, find its tension, find which character it
belongs to. All of your attention and focus can now be put on this
smaller increment of story—ten to fifteen minutes of screen time,
the sequence. Whose sequence is it, what does he want, why is it
difficult to get, what are the obstacles or the potential solutions to
the problem of this sequence? Is there a crucial event around
which this sequence will be built? Where in the sequence would it
be best to place that event?

It should feel like a relief to think about such "small" issues
that take place on a small canvas, compared to the more cosmic
thinking you have had to do for the overall story. You now have
one character in pursuit of one short-term goal with finite obstacles in his path. Revisit the sections on each of the sequences and
what they typically contain. This paradigm might not hold true
throughout your story, but it's a good starting point to discover
how to build each of your sequences in a progression that makes
sense and has dramatic impact. With work and some trial and error, you will start to see the pattern that is your story, your progression from sequence to sequence.

Strive to write down each sequence in a schematic way. It can
be helpful to give a title to each sequence as a way of focusing on
the subject of the sequence. The Wedding. Whiskey and Horses.
The Car Crash. Rehab Turns Deadly. The Sister-in-Law. Titles can
help you find the cohesion that each sequence needs. After the

title, write the sequence tension as a question about the future: "Will Roger get to his own wedding on time?" If there is a clear event in the sequence—and don't panic if there isn't yet—write down the event and perhaps some idea of its placement in the sequence. Finally, strive to divide the lump of story material you have into its three parts—beginning, middle, and end. Because you have your sequence tension, this should not be difficult. Don't overthink exactly how you write down for yourself the various elements within those divisions of the sequence. Instead, work to get the divisions into logical places: Roger is happily getting into his tuxedo when disaster strikes and his house floods, but he still wants to get to the wedding—end of first part; fighting his way through the flood, the car that washed away, the ruined tuxedo, hitchhiking, borrowing a cell phone and discovering it has bad reception, the race through the cow pasture, and the stink as he arrives outside the church—end of second section; he races into the crowded church looking a mess, offending one and all and with a cow trailing behind, exchanges tuxedos with the best man, and says "I do"—end of sequence. What exactly will make all of it work, you don't need to worry about just yet. That will come.

What is important at this stage is that you have now envisioned your entire story from beginning to end, and you have written all of it down into a sequence breakdown or sequence outline. This outline is probably only two or three pages long, but it will be your best guide from now through the completion of the first draft. All of the most important decisions you've made are in it; guideposts for where you are in your story are contained in it; the most important tensions you will create are in it; even the beginnings, middles, and ends of your sequences are included. Those three pages are your work assignments, the breakdown of your chore of writing the first draft. On any given day of writing, you can see where you are and trust that the pages you are creating today fit into the overall plan and contribute to the overall progression of the story.

But what do you do with all the thousands of other things you've thought about to include in your script? Don't put them into the sequence breakdown, because that will make the document less accessible to you during your writing and, as a result, considerably less helpful to you. Instead, keep notes, files, Post-its, whatever helps you keep track of all those wonderful ideas that have occurred to you throughout the development process. These are what you might already have sorted through to amass your lumps of story material for your sequences. There is also another outline that will help you contain and organize all those ideas, half ideas, and wishes for your story.

The Step Outline

The second outline you need to create before starting to write your first draft is called a step outline. This is an extension of the sequence breakdown and can only be written after the former is complete and solid. The step outline is a list of the scenes that will need to be written to fulfill the chores you have set for yourself with the sequence breakdown. As you can see, you are moving incrementally closer to scene writing and the actual creation of the first draft. It would be possible to start writing scenes after the completion of the sequence breakdown, but it's a far better tactic to spend another day or two giving yourself a gift for which you will be grateful once you start writing scenes. The step outline is your last chance to draw a detailed road map of your journey while you still have a panoramic view. Once you start writing pages, you are in the midst of a tempestuous world of your own devising, and it can be difficult to regain perspective.

Now that you have your sequences broken down into their component parts and you have identified your tensions and your crucial moments, the last job before writing scenes is envisioning them one at a time. Where exactly does the scene take place, when exactly does the scene take place, who exactly is there, what exactly do they want, why exactly is it difficult to get, what exactly happens by the end of the scene? These are the questions you are attempting to answer now, before you write the moment-by-moment scene itself. This outline is an overview of each scene, in the most schematic way.

Many beginners tend to write step outlines with as many words as a finished screenplay; this is wasting precious time and making the outline less useful than if it were truly an outline. Instead, write the scene heading—including interior or exterior, location, and time of day—then as briefly as possible give yourself an overview of the scene to be written. For example: "EXT. COW PASTURE, DAY, Roger decides to cut across to get to the church faster, but gets chased by a herd of cows, Daisy in particular, who breaks down the fence to follow him as he escapes, shredded and muddy." When you write the scene, you will add more detail, including the cow pies he steps in, the incident with the bull, Daisy's runaway affection for him, their dance at the fence in his attempt to ditch her, and her decision to keep right on going despite the barbed wire. But in three lines you have already given yourself a plan for where the scene takes place, whose scene it is, what he wants, why it might be difficult, what his obstacles might be, and what happens. You've only spent minutes on the scene and then gone to the next and the next, until the sequence is done and you continue into the next one. In a day or two you will have given yourself hints about and plans for all the scenes you need to write.

You will also have done a great deal more than communicate with your future self, the one who will be writing your first-draft scenes. You will have envisioned the entire flow of the story. You can read this outline, which shouldn't be more than eight to twelve pages, and see where you might already have built in some problems for yourself. If thirty scenes in a row are interiors, you can spot it now and remedy the problem. If one sequence has sixty scenes, that means each is about fifteen seconds long and you have a problem to remedy. If scene after scene seems talky and static, you know before you've written them that it would be a good idea to revise that section. It's so much easier to throw out a scene you spent two minutes envisioning and replace it with a new, more dynamic one that you also spend only a few minutes creating. The step outline allows you to scan your intended scenes, sequence by sequence, to see where you might have problems, to discover that you've forgotten your protagonist or her love interest for far too long, or that you have gone off on a tangent that will ultimately have to be discarded. Get rid of it now, before you spend a day or two writing that tangent. The pressure you will put on yourself to keep some or all of that tangential material will be much greater once it is written. Save yourself that hardship now. Keep yourself on track by giving yourself a scene-by-scene plan and revising it to focus on your story, what's truly important to you, your characters, and the audience.

But if you don't know what scenes will tell your story, sequence by sequence, then how can you envision them now? It won't be any easier to envision them later, so now is still the time to do it. The transition from thinking in the larger sense about your characters and your story to imagining the details, moment by moment, is difficult to make. It is one thing to have the idea that Oskar Schindler must be introduced as bold and audacious; it's another altogether to envision the scene where he approaches a group of Nazi officers with plans to sell them pots and pans. This is where all your hard work on your characters and their lives and the world of the story will start to pay off. You know your story revolves in its own way around the making of mundane kitchenware for the Nazis; maybe something around food would be a good idea. Nazis are the danger in this story, and a bold, audacious man must be willing to face danger. The protagonist is one who will be called upon to fool many people for a prolonged period of time, so that is an aspect of his personality worthy of including in his introduction. In your character exploration, you have concluded that charm and affability will be the primary tools he uses in keeping the Nazis from suspecting his real intentions and actions. Food, Nazis, fooling people with charm for a period of time—these are the elements for which you want to find a vehicle, a scene or two that will display them succinctly, dramatically, and effectively.

Your extensive story development work has doubtless already given you clues. Many scenes are logical within the lives of the characters and the goals they have set for themselves. The hapless groom is getting married and has to dress in his tuxedo. His biggest conflict seems to be learning to tie the blasted bow tie. Then he must merely grab the ring, get in his car, and go to his wedding. But you want conflict. You want to make life as difficult as possible for your characters. You must dredge up within yourself all the cruelty you can muster. Be kind to your characters and destroy your story. Be heartless and ingenious in the ways you torture your characters and we will love you for it. Think in terms of what can go wrong, what can be made difficult. What would you hate to have happen to you? That's what you need to do to your character.

Don't let yourself get bogged down. Don't spend hours wrestling with each scene. The idea here is to get into a flow with your material and to move forward quickly. You are sketching in charcoal on the canvas you will paint with oils; you don't need the details of the face or the folds of the robe as it plays in the light. You need the shape of the scene, the general placement of the face, the robe, and the source of light. While you sketch each scene briefly, if no good conflict comes, if no scene of selling pots and pans to Nazis presents itself to you, put down a half-formed idea for the scene and move on. Perhaps a scene later on will spur you to the right idea for this one, or, if all else fails, you still have a chance when you're writing the scene to envision wonderfully torturous things to do to your characters.

Writing the First Draft

With the completed sequence breakdown and the full step out- line, you now have a safety net for the writing of the first draft. Neither is a set of commandments, neither is cast in stone, nei- ther stops you from continuing to have imagination or from de- vising even better moments, scenes, and interactions once your characters are walking and talking and interacting. But you have a plan that will work, it will get you to the end of your draft and reflects your best envisioning of the telling of the story. It will pro- pel you right past the Page 70 Syndrome; it will help you push through the doubts and frustrations that are inevitable; and it will give your future self the springboard from which to create scenes that might surprise you. If something wonderful begins to hap- pen during your scene writing, a synergy you could never have envisioned while in the outlining phase, you are free to take it and run with it. The safety net isn't there to constrict you; it's there to catch you if you fall. If that synergy takes you somewhere far afield, the sequence breakdown and outline give you the means of finding your way back to your story without having to start over, to throw out days or weeks of work. This safety net keeps you from getting hopelessly lost, yet allows you the latitude of enjoying new discoveries and unexpected vistas along the way. Take the guidance of your outlines, but don't make yourself a slave to them.

Because you have done so much work developing your story, you have structured it completely, you have all the major tensions devised, and you have envisioned the story down to the scene-by-scene level, it should not take you months to write your first draft. Your total focus each day now can be placed solely on the individual scenes: the moments in the lives of the characters, the visuals you present to the audience, the atmosphere, setting, world, costumes, whatever is important to give us the experience of your story. Depending in part upon how good you are at getting out of your own way, you should be able to write your first draft in a matter of weeks, not months. Put all your second-guessing aside. Shelve all your doubts; you have a good plan, a safety net, clear ideas, and high hopes. Use those to your benefit. Write your draft as fast as you can without being careless or haphazard. Don't look back, don't punish yourself because your scenes aren't perfect, don't waste your energy on wondering if this will really be as good as you hope it will be. It won't be yet, but it can be eventually. What's important at this stage is that the draft comes into existence.

One of the ironies of writing is that, within reason, the faster you write, the better you write. If it takes you a day to get a page, that page will reflect dithering, questioning, revising, doubting, and uncertainty with every word. You have been editor as well as writer. Instead of focusing solely on the job at hand—this individual scene for which you already have a plan—you have brought in another facet of yourself that is stifling your creative work. The editor in you can be very creative as well, but only when there is something to edit. The full script must exist first, then be edited, revised, evaluated for quality and effectiveness. The writing of your first draft should be done with all those thoughts not only out of your mind, but out of the room entirely. Just write as best you can, accepting the notion that you will come back to your script later with another thought process in mind. First, make it exist in one continuous burst of creative energy. It won't be perfect, but it will exist, and it will have been written during a short enough period of time that you still like the script rather than resent it or feel disappointment in it. If you did edit as you went along, it would take far longer, you would doubtless tire of your story, and your script still wouldn't be perfect. So accept imperfection before you begin and then write as fast as you reasonably can.

AFTER THE FIRST DRAFT

No matter how you slave over your first draft or how inspired you are as you write it, you will still need to rewrite. Embrace this idea; rewriting is an opportunity to close the gap between your hopes for your story and the reality of what you have been able to create. If you've written relatively quickly and have not tired of your story, you will find that you have all the energy and hope needed to continue the process through the next draft.

Clarifying Your Theme

The writing of a first draft is a process of continual discovery. You discover the realities of your characters, the richness of the world of your story, and the true nature of the conflicts you set in motion. You discover where you did enough preparatory work and where you need to do more exploration. You also discover what is really on your mind, what your story is really about. The light comedy you thought you were writing became darker and more meaningful than you expected. The tragedy you thought you were writing became fun and funny. These are not necessarily failings. No matter how much preparation you have done, you can't know entirely what the creative corners of your mind have in store for you until you let them loose on the page. It can be both wonderful and terrifying to realize that you have been in much less conscious control than you thought you were. There have been forces at work that you didn't realize, and you have the proof in your hands. Embrace this creative input from an unexpected source. In truth, you were never fully in conscious control; your conscious mind was merely gathering material from every available source, including all that mind-doodling you did, all those character explorations. Much of that material has been dredged up from unknown or forgotten parts of your mind. Be thankful for that input and listen to it.

Along with what has really been on your mind, the other most important discovery you can make from the writing of your first draft is your theme. You had a theme in mind when you developed your story, but now that you have a draft, you need to discover if it is still there or if perhaps another theme is in its place. The theme is likely part of what was really on your mind, and it found its way into your story while you were busy writing scenes. Reread your draft with one thing in mind: what is the common thread of the main story and all the subplots? This will be the theme that you have actually been exploring from a variety of angles. It's unlikely there will already be a perfect and clear thread among your main and subplot stories. Before beginning your rewrite, find ways to strengthen your theme, to make your stories coalesce around a single thread. Whether it is the theme you thought you were writing about or not is less important than having your interlocking stories be varied explorations of some aspect of the human dilemma. That is the theme that was really on your mind. Embrace it, focus your stories around it, and then delve into your rewrite to assure that the theme you have discovered comes through clearly.

Sometimes the theme is actually clearer in the subplots than it is in your protagonist's story. A disconnect between protagonist and theme is a common trait of first drafts. Your secondary characters also can often be in sharper focus and have stronger personalities than your protagonist. Your central character wanders through the story and never takes on a hard edge, never achieves the clarity that was so easy to give to a secondary character. This stems in part from there being so many demands on the protagonist and in part from your own closeness to the character. You've been reluctant to be hard enough on her, to make her wrong and fallible, pigheaded, blind, and downright obsessed. In other words, you have inadvertently rounded off all her edges, softened her from the clear character you thought you had. At the same time, her connection to the theme has been buffed away. Both should be brought into focus—and back to center stage—before you start a rewrite.

If there is a unifying thread to the subplots and not in the main story—and there isn't a powerful and clear theme at play there—then see if this theme works with your protagonist. Can this thread also be woven through the protagonist's life? Will it focus and sharpen that character's life, or turn her into someone who no longer fits with the overall story? If the change is that bedrock, then clearly the theme will not work. By trial and error, always using the draft you now have as the first and best source for directions to pursue, try unifying themes until you have located the best and most effective common ground for your script. The solution is quite possibly already in the material; you simply haven't recognized it yet for what it is. Once you discover your true theme, you need to bring it out more, making certain that it is clear that each of the characters is wrestling with or avoiding this aspect of the human dilemma.

Once you have that theme, you have a much better chance of also clarifying the bland protagonist you've discovered you created rather than the dynamic one you started out to build. Whatever the theme is, the protagonist carries it in a bigger way than any of the other characters. That means she has farther to go on that road, is more "wrong" or misguided, has more to learn or overcome, is more resistant to change. If the theme wasn't clear as you were writing the first draft—and it rarely is—it's little wonder the character became less distinct than you had hoped. Now, armed with a clear theme, you can search through your draft for all the areas where you rounded edges, softened corners, pulled back from making the character truly clear, strong, and dynamic.

To a lesser extent, you need to do the same with the other core members of your constellation of characters. Clarify how they relate to the theme, both in approach to it and in the resolution of their individual stories if they carry a subplot. This will sharpen these characters and make them come more alive on the page of your second draft. Those members of your core constellation who don't have subplots but are there as support or reflections for the protagonist and other characters, still should be exercising their roles in the story in relationship to the theme. The best friend who supports one side of a conflicted protagonist should be pulling and pushing in a thematically related way, not in a way that is tangential to the theme. Similarly, your conflicts and obstacles might need sharpening to test the very areas of the characters most in need of exploring—those areas related to the theme.

Rewriting

Rewriting is faster than writing the first draft, and in some ways the results are even more substantial. In truth, the difference between the story's not existing on the page and its existing as a first draft is enormous. But the ways that a rewrite improves the story—focusing the characters, conflicts, wants, obstacles, high moments and low—can be just as exciting as that first rush of creation. Some beginning writers hate rewriting: I already wrote it, and I'm tired of the story. If you complete the first draft before you're tired of the story, you are already ahead of the game. If you realize that you can truly improve your story and make it much more like what you hoped it would be, you have the motivation you need to get another draft written. In the time it would have taken you to write a draft you hated and never wanted to touch again—by outlining less and editing at the same time as you wrote—you could write two or three drafts and have a script you love that reflects much of what you hoped it would become.

Rewriting is not going back to square one and starting over completely, but neither is it a matter of merely correcting spelling and grammar. Now that the full script exists, subject it to the same questions that helped you form your story and plan for it in the first place. Check all your crucial moments, your short-term tensions, the interplay of your characters, the subplots, and the world of the story. You will likely have fallen short of the mark in a number of places. These are likely to be the very same places about which you feel discomfort with your first draft. The nagging problems most often result from basic lapses: a character doesn't pursue his goal or doesn't have a goal; the obstacle is too easily overcome or there is no obstacle; a subplot has nothing to do with the relationship between the protagonist and the subplot character; somebody isn't wanting something badly enough and isn't having enough difficulty getting it. Once you identify the basic lapses, the solutions become easier to find.

Sometimes a first draft reveals greater problems than mere lapses from the dramatic progression of a story. Perhaps a conceptual problem has been laid bare by the writing of the first draft. The rule-breaking you so wanted to engage in has misfired, or the rule-obeying you forced upon yourself has so hamstrung your story that it truly isn't working. Don't throw your story away in disgust and start inventing a new one. While this is a larger dilemma to wrestle with than a few sequence tensions that are vague, it doesn't mean the story is not worth continuing to pursue. It just means you have to go back farther in the process to the bedrock issues of what you want your story to be and how you envision making it work. If it is clearly not working as first written, you have eliminated one potential solution and can narrow your focus to other, more productive ones.

Let's say you tried to write *Memento,* but in a classical screenplay structure. All of the beats of the man's story are there, but it doesn't work for the audience, because making the story linear destroys the essential ingredient of that film. We are not given the same experience of disorientation the protagonist suffers. We have been kept at a distance from his experience, and that has undermined the telling of the story. You still have done all your work on your characters and you have written some wonderful scenes and the conflicts and world are solid; it's the organization of the material that is at fault. Reorganize, accepting the fact that you will have to diverge from the classical structure, but don't throw away all that wonderful material simply because your first attempt at a very difficult story didn't work. The same will be equally true if you played the rebel and broke every rule you could find and now have a story that doesn't hold together. Keep the things of value, keep the broken rules that help you, but accept the fact you may have to tell your story in a more conventional way than you had originally thought.

Make a new plan for yourself. Now that you have a draft done, step back and regain that panoramic view, recapture your perspective. It might be helpful to write a new sequence breakdown as part of that exploration. You will find the process faster and much easier than the first effort. You are filled up with the story, you know the characters so much better than you did before, you know the world, the wants, the obstacles, and your own goals for the script with much greater intimacy than you did when first devising your outlines. You may only need to rewrite your sequence breakdown or step outline for a problem area, rather than for the whole story.

Know Your Long Suit and Short Suit

Some writers are great with story, some with character, some with scenes, some with dialogue; some are better at pitching stories than they are at writing them. Every writer has some corresponding weakness. One might be great with story, but weak at scene writing, and so on. When studying screenwriting and working toward a career in it, it's always a good idea to put more effort into your weak suit, the thing you don't do as well, in hopes of developing it to catch up with your strong suit. This is good advice and something each of us should strive to do, even after we quit studying, even after we've sold scripts and had work produced.

However, for the purpose of this discussion, the issue is not the writer's long and short suits, but the story's. What is the greatest asset your story has? What is its greatest weakness? The same basic advice applies here: put some of your energy into the parts of your story that are weakest. In the creation process, do everything in your power to beef up your weak spots, to improve the things that are pulling your creation down, the things that aren't adding as fully as other aspects. It might be the plot or your protagonist or antagonist or the sense of inevitability or predictability of your story. There are many things that can go wrong or be less than optimal. These things will take up a disproportionate amount of your time—and probably already have. They might continue to plague you through several rewrites before you find the solution.

But there's a twist on the "work on your short suit" advice. The audience is wondering whether your film is the one to see, if the experience you are offering is distinctive. No matter how much you have improved the weakest part of your story, it is unlikely to be the aspect of your film that most attracts an audience. If you can't attract an audience, you have no chance of influencing them and giving them an experience. You have to lure them into the seats before you can keep them there. Chances are, what will lure them in is your strong suit. Therefore, you want to give a good platform to your strongest suit, your best element. Give it plenty of emphasis—not to the point of boring us to death with it, but enough that it has the best chance to attract an audience.

If a story has an abundance of something that we as an audience value, then we are likely to forgive a multitude of other sins and shortcomings. Judge from your own experience as an audience member. Have you ever enjoyed a film that was less than perfect? You must have, or you have enjoyed very few films. Maybe a film made you laugh a lot, but the plot was a bit thin or weak. Or a film was incredibly tense and exciting and intriguing, but in the end, there were a few questions about the logic that cropped up as you went home. Maybe there was a character you couldn't spend enough time with, someone you wanted to know—or felt you already knew—and love, but the story didn't quite do enough with the character. You might have found yourself musing over how you would have done it better. The truth is that it was incredibly difficult to get the characters and world and story and every other aspect of the film to work as well as they did; a few lapses are forgivable precisely because a few lapses are almost inevitable.

You don't want to accept lapses and shortcomings while there is still time to improve them. But keep in mind that your long suit—your best and most attractive element—can buy you a measure of forgiveness from the audience. It won't buy you unconditional forgiveness, but it will grant you a sizable amount of latitude. Don't take this latitude to the bank or count on it while you're working; keep trying to improve your weaker elements and deliver your best stuff with all the power and emphasis and cinematic strength that you can muster. But be sure to shine all the light you can on your strongest element, the aspect of your script or story most likely to attract an audience.

Dramatic Instincts

Dramatic instincts are gut reactions that help you discover when there is something wrong that needs your attention. Like so many things we call instincts, they aren't instinctual at all. Dramatic instincts are the result of extensive training and thinking, all on a conscious level, that has then been "pushed to the back of your brain" as if it's been forgotten. It's like muscle memory for an athlete or finger memory for a musician. After doing the same chore again and again, in every possible combination, the athlete or the musician doesn't think about what he's doing with his hands or body; he lets them take care of themselves. In fact, nothing can make him flub faster than thinking about each action as he is doing it. This can lead to a vicious cycle of overthinking every minute action, which leads to more errors.

So how do you get dramatic instincts? How do you know it and not have to think about it? The same way athletes and musicians get their instincts, their muscle memory. You do the chores over and over and over, from every possible angle, until you know what each of them really means and is about and, most importantly, what it feels like when something works and when it doesn't. Then you have to drop the conscious side of the analyzing exercise while retaining the subliminal message of when things feel right or wrong. Achieve that and you'll have your dramatic instinct, well earned and hard fought; it's nothing instinctual. Once you start to acquire dramatic instincts, they can be your warning signals, and only when they go off should you kick into the conscious mode. After the gut feeling helps you find a problem area, bring your "forgotten" training to the front of your brain to help identify the exact problems and find solutions.

In order to get to that point, you have to do much more analyzing than your own scripts will allow. The more stories in which
you immerse yourself, the more story problems you ferret out,
the more time you spend doing hard-hat work on all kinds of stories, the faster you will train your gut instincts. The more analyzing of other stories you do—films you see, professionals' and
friends' screenplays you read—the more you'll start intuitively
getting your own stories closer to right on the first try. Repeat the
work on a conscious level until the self-consciousness fades away,
leaving only the training and the gut reactions and the intuition
and the muscle memory.

A FINAL NOTE

As you start to develop your gut feelings, your dramatic instincts, and you're on your third or fourth draft or working on a rewrite of another project or critiquing a friend's script, the essays contained here can also be a good reference to help clarify problems or a place to search for solutions. Each story is unique and will present you with a different collection of strengths and weaknesses, problems, exceptions, and conundrums. You won't find all the answers to every conceivable difficulty, but the material here should arm you with the requisite bedrock knowledge and a growing dramatic instinct. Those, in turn, can help you reason through the newest impossible question or balancing act between cost and benefit. In this sense, the final goal is for you to invent your own style, your own gut feeling, your own instinct. That is, after all, what underlies all great stories.

INDEX

INDEX

ABOUT THE AUTHOR

DAVID HOWARD is an international screenwriter, script doctor, and script consultant. He is the founding director of the Graduate Screenwriting Program at the University of Southern California's renowned School of Cinema-Television, and he travels widely as a lecturer and teacher, in addition to consulting extensively for television networks and film production companies. He has written or cowritten numerous theatrical films, television episodes, and television films in America and Europe. His theatrical film *My Friend Joe* has won five Best Picture prizes at international film festivals; included among its dozen awards worldwide are Best Children's Film at Berlin and an audience prize at Edinburgh. He has also written or cowritten projects that have won such awards as the Humanitas Prize, the Cable/ACE Award, and the Emmy Award. His most recent film is *Sea of Dreams*, which he cowrote and coproduced. He has a feature film currently in production in Germany and an animated feature in production in Puerto Rico.

He has worked professionally with Academy Award winners Diane Keaton, Joel Grey, and Hans de Weers, nominees Seymour Cassel and Veljko Bulajic, and Golden Globe and Emmy winner Sonia Braga, among many others.

His students have gone on to write and/or direct a wide range of films: in America they include *Air Force One, Chicken Run, The Hand that Rocks the Cradle, Sweet Home Alabama, While You Were Sleeping, Natural Born Killers, Mob Queen, End of Days, Permanent Midnight, Hush, Behind Enemy Lines, The Hollow Man, Bread and Roses,* and a great many more; in Europe they include such award-winning films as *Crazy, It's a Jungle Out There, Carla's Song, Mates, Just One Night, My Name Is Joe, 23, The Pharmacist, One of My Oldest Friends,* and the Academy Award-nominated German film *Beyond Silence.* In addition, his students have written for or become staff writers and even head writers on such television series as *Coach, ER, Murphy Brown, Home Improvement, The Cosby Show, Wings, Roseanne, What About Joan, NYPD Blue,* and *The X-Files.*

His first book, *The Tools of Screenwriting* (St. Martin's Press, 1993), which has been translated into five languages, is required reading in many of the world's top film schools and screenwriting programs. He lives in Los Angeles with his wife, Vicki, and daughter, Jessa.